The Enduring Legacy

AMERICAN ENCOUNTERS/GLOBAL INTERACTIONS

A series edited by Gilbert M. Joseph and Emily S. Rosenberg

This series aims to stimulate critical perspectives and fresh interpretive frameworks for scholarship on the history of the imposing global presence of the United States. Its primary concerns include the deployment and contestation of power, the construction and deconstruction of cultural and political borders, the fluid meanings of intercultural encounters, and the complex interplay between the global and the local. American Encounters seeks to strengthen dialogue and collaboration between historians of U.S. international relations and area studies specialists.

The series encourages scholarship based on multiarchival historical research. At the same time, it supports a recognition of the representational character of all stories about the past and promotes critical inquiry into issues of subjectivity and narrative. In the process, American Encounters strives to understand the context in which meanings related to nations, cultures, and political economy are continually produced, challenged, and reshaped.

The Enduring Legacy

OIL, CULTURE, AND SOCIETY
IN VENEZUELA

MIGUEL TINKER SALAS

Duke University Press

Durham and London

2009

Designed by Heather Hensley

Typeset in Adobe Caslon by Achorn International, Inc.

Library of Congress Cataloging-in-Publication Data
appear on the last printed page of this book.

Contents

Preface

Despite its profound importance in Venezuelan society, the rich tapestry of social and cultural relations engendered by the oil industry has not been the subject of significant scholarly attention. Existing scholarship on Venezuelan oil tends to be divided between studies that take a traditional approach to production and economics and nationalistic studies, both of which largely ignore the lived experiences of employees and workers.[1] The literature typically fails to show how the evolution of the foreign-controlled enterprises reshaped the lives of those employed by them and how oil influenced the social and political environment. The handful of works that do mention life in the oilfields range from romanticized celebrations of the "best days of our lives" to condemnations of the experience as the agent of a new "colonizing" order. Also common are portrayals of the oil industry as "agents of modernization" that introduced advanced western social practices to a backward population.[2] None of these approaches adequately captures the complexity of the residential compounds where workers lived or the lasting impact of the oil industry on the nation. In a country in which the majority of the population was rural and depended on agriculture for subsistence, oil production fundamentally altered the sociocultural landscape.

As in other parts of Latin America, the economic activities of foreign enterprises often produced unexpected social, cultural, and racial outcomes. The construction of the Panama Canal in the early decades of the twentieth century spurred the migration of thousands of Afro-Caribbean people to the isthmus.[3] The expansion of copper mines in Sonora, Mexico, stimulated significant national and international migration to the area.[4] The labor policies of the United Fruit Company in Cuba, Costa Rica, and Honduras produced similar results.[5] In each instance laborers found that corporate and political interests sought to expand the labor pool, reduce wages, and exploit racial and social distinctions. In Venezuela the oil industry attracted Chinese, West Indians, and Mexicans, and their presence was also manipulated by political and economic interests. In particular, the arrival of West Indians of African descent from Trinidad alarmed élites and the middle class, for whom a discussion of Black immigrants embodied racist concerns about Venezuela's own population of African heritage.

With few exceptions, traditional scholarship has also ignored the contentious racial climate that initially framed labor relations in the oil fields. The subtext for this omission is a nationalist agenda that highlights the racist views of foreigners while pretending that Venezuela is racially unified. While it is true that the presence of whites from the United States, where segregation was in effect, intensified the distinction between foreigners and locals, élites and the middle class held equally insidious views toward indigenous people, Afro-Venezuelan immigrants, and Afro–West Indian immigrants.[6] The development of Venezuela's oil industry provides an opportunity to assess the overlapping contradictions that Afro-Caribbean immigration generated in this formerly agrarian nation where matters of race had been mostly dictated by élite interests.

The ways in which the class expectations engendered by the industry shaped the views of various social classes, and the pivotal role of the oil companies in the political process, have also received insufficient attention. Instead most studies have focused on Venezuela's struggle against foreign companies for control of its subsoil, or the institutional and corporate structures involved in petroleum production. Most of these accounts provide a general chronology or broad overview of these complex and contradictory developments.[7] In addition, the oil companies influenced the literature by funding and originating publications that were sympathetic to their views.[8] Other accounts focus almost exclusively on the significant labor strikes that occurred in 1925 and 1936, defining the labor movement in terms of its political impact at the expense of accounts of workers' lives. Past union and political leaders, social democrats, and communists such as Valmore Rodríguez,

Jesús Prieto Soto, and Rodolfo Quintero have written very divergent accounts of their activities.[9] Quintero remains among the few scholars who have attempted to address the social consequences of oil production.[10] For the most part, Venezuelan labor histories have emphasized the struggles of workers against the regime of Juan Vicente Gómez, the political parties that vied for control of the movement, and the democratic period that began in the 1960s.[11]

On this subject, work by scholars in the United States has proved no more revealing. During the 1960s and 1970s their study of Venezuelan history and politics in the United States followed a well-worn path, reflecting the traditional themes that framed their historiography of Latin America. Not viewed as one of the "important" countries, Venezuela was studied with much the same methods applied earlier to Mexico, Argentina, and Brazil, countries that were of strategic geopolitical importance to the United States and therefore dominated the study of the region. Consequently, despite the importance of oil during this period, historians focused on traditional topics such as the figure of the caudillo, the military, the nature of Venezuelan relations with Washington, and the role of slavery.[12] The political, cultural, and social concerns of the United States became the lens through which Venezuela (like most of Latin America) was studied. The examination of slavery and race, as John Lombardi acknowledged in a speech to the Venezuelan National Academy of History in 2000, "rested on the hope that the Latin American experience, properly understood, could clarify a United States economic, social, and political dilemma."[13] Venezuela and Latin America in general offered a way to understand and assess developments in the United States.

The literature of the 1980s produced two important generalist works, one by Lombardi and the other by Judith Ewell; as the first overviews of Venezuelan history since the work of Edwin Lieuwen and the Venezuelan Guillermo Morón in 1961, these filled an important lacuna.[14] During this same decade, regional and micro-studies assumed new importance in the field of Latin American history, and Venezuela was no exception.[15] In addition, social history and new interdisciplinary methodologies found expression in the study of colonial Venezuela and the assessment of land tenure systems, social relations, and coffee production.[16] Brian McBeth provided a comprehensive examination of oil policy during the Gómez era, and

Stephen Rabe wrote on the conditions that eventually compelled Venezuela to help found the Organization of Petroleum Exporting Countries (OPEC), and on Venezuelan relations with Washington at the height of the cold war.[17] Edwin Lieuwen had written a study of Venezuelan oil in 1954 that was essentially an institutional and political history of the industry.[18] Steve Ellner and Charles Berquist expanded the field, adding meaningful insights into the labor movement, political parties, and new social actors.[19]

The 1990s and the early years of the following decade witnessed a somewhat varied approach to the study of Venezuela in the English language, and the topics covered expanded somewhat. Terry Lynn Karl provided a comprehensive examination of why repeated petro-booms failed to spur long-term development in Venezuela.[20] Fernando Coronil broke ground by assessing the role of nature in capitalist production and analyzing the evolution of the all-encompassing and seemingly all-powerful Venezuelan petro-state.[21] Douglas Yarrington produced an excellent account of land tenure, coffee production, and social and political relations in the state of Lara. Arlene Díaz employed legal and social history to examine the often-neglected role of women in the independence process and throughout the nineteenth century.[22] Charles Briggs and Clara Mantini-Briggs analyzed the cholera epidemic that devastated the indigenous Warao who inhabited the Delta region on the eve of the much-heralded Apertura Petrolera ("oil opening") of the early 1990s.[23] In the same manner that Castro's and the Sandinistas' revolutions generated concern for Cuba and Nicaragua, the election of Hugo Chávez has dramatically increased interest in the study of Venezuela.

As indicated earlier, this book explores a number of issues that traditional scholarship on Venezuelan oil has overlooked. Chapter 1 provides a survey of western Venezuela before the advent of the oil industry. Too often those writing on oil fail to capture the character of the social and economic interaction that predated the industry. Studies generally portray the areas in which oil developed as social and economic backwaters that were transformed overnight by the arrival of the industry. This approach is also applied to the early Venezuelan governments that dealt with the oil companies, in particular the regime of Juan Vicente Gómez. This perspective,

according to Coronil, is rooted in efforts by democratic parties to portray Gómez as an inept country bumpkin and thus to highlight their own role in transforming the country.[24] Seldom questioned, the association between oil, modernity, and democracy has been firmly embedded in the national mind.[25] Thus the discourse on the oil industry invariably divides its history into periods before (largely backward) and after (mostly modern and democratic). Moreover, accounts of the oil industry consistently privilege corporate leaders, technocrats, and foreigners, who are assumed to be the purveyors of modernity. These portrayals repeatedly marginalize workers, women, the indigenous, and people of color, who emerge as important participants. Chapter 1 depicts the complex social and economic activities in which people engaged, paralleling patterns of development present throughout Latin America at the time.

Chapter 2 assesses the initial efforts by foreign companies to uncover oil deposits in Venezuela. It traces the evolution of the industry from the exploration of the tar lakes at Guanaco in the first decade of the twentieth century to the discovery of the promising field at Mene Grande in 1914, and the changes initiated by this first wave of oil production, including the establishment of residential enclaves for laborers. Chapter 3 describes the process that led to the discovery of the gusher at La Rosa in 1922 and the migratory stream that developed between oil-producing regions and their local communities. It examines the dramatic changes that oil produced in the environment, the people, and the communities dotting the Maracaibo lakeshore and analyzes the companies' first steps toward organizing production and controlling and refashioning their new labor force.

Chapter 4 analyzes the dramatic social and racial hierarchy that developed in the oil fields. Beyond Venezuelans, oil attracted a patchwork of immigrants from the United States, the nearby Caribbean, Mexico, and as far away as China. The appearance of a diverse transnational labor force created fertile ground for racial conflict, and company and government policy exacerbated these conditions. The reaction by Venezuelan intellectual and political leaders to the presence of Afro-Antillean immigrants reflected deep-seated prejudices toward people of color. These attitudes brought Venezuela's racial practices and prejudices into stark relief and clashed with the prevailing myth that miscegenation, or café con leche (coffee and milk), as it is known in the country, had produced a racial democracy.

Chapter 5 explores life behind the fences of the camp for senior staff from the United States, focusing on the dynamics of gender. It documents how the oil industry shifted from a male-dominated enterprise to a settled and mostly professional one that now included entire families. Within the fences that enclosed the camps, expatriates from areas as disparate as Texas, Massachusetts, and California attempted to recreate their homeland in the tropical Venezuelan countryside. Though expatriates and their families selectively adopted some culinary customs and a few local practices, residential camp life retained the fundamental features that characterize white society in the United States. Portrayed as the traditional purveyors of cultural norms, expatriate women played a fundamental role in reproducing the lifestyle of their homeland. Gradually, through daily interaction within the hierarchical setting of the oil camps, foreign practices became normalized and used as a reference point for denoting social class status among Venezuelans and foreigners.

Chapter 6 examines the role of the oil companies in promoting class aspirations and inspiring a model of citizenship that connected the interests of the industry with those of larger society. The result was the evolution of social and political practices that influenced the nature of public participation in civic society. Camp life for Venezuelans involved more than merely adapting to a new urban landscape. The use of ordered space sought to reorient previous patterns of behavior to suit a corporate model and a new social and political order. It generated a new sensibility and a structured lifestyle that would produce predictable non-disruptive social and political outcomes. The new practices affected both men and women among several generations of Venezuelans to whom the industry offered access to a middle-class life. The benefits derived from participation in the oil industry created divided loyalties—to the oil company and to social class—against which the nation-state was forced to compete. For those employed in the industry, their privileged status was tied to the well-being of the oil company, irrespective of whether it was foreign or had been nationalized.

Chapter 7 analyzes how the oil companies created a complex web of power relations that allowed them to influence the political process in Venezuela. Considering the importance that oil had assumed in the international economy, its central role in any power's ability to wage war, and the millions of dollars invested in the country, neither the companies nor the

United States could afford to be passive observers. Rather, their objective became maintaining the unique position that foreign companies played in the extraction, refining, and export of Venezuela's rich oil resources. They considered preservation of their role in the Venezuelan economy paramount because they had promoted their experience in the country as a model for the oil-producing nations of the Middle East.

The book analyzes the rise of the oil industry and the multiple ways in which a foreign-dominated enterprise intersected with emerging class interests to fashion a distinctive view of citizenship and the nation among groups employed by the industry. It joins a growing body of scholarship that is critically reexamining the social and cultural dimensions of extractive industries throughout Latin America and elsewhere in the Third World.[26] It breaks with the tradition of examining political economy and culture as distinct components and instead evaluates the cultural and political dimensions of economic practices.[27] The intersection between power and culture is evident in the emergence of a "modern" structured lifestyle that was premised upon everyday practices and embedded loyalties that fostered civic life in the oil industry and its residential camps. The basic argument of this book is that the oil industry in Venezuela did not function as an isolated outpost of the export economy. Rather, the industry broadly influenced the formation of social and political values evident among oil workers, intellectuals, and members of the middle class. The industry's residential complexes were a social laboratory where companies promoted labor practices, notions of citizenship, and an accompanying worldview that favored their continued operation in Venezuela. Although the control of oil by foreign interests inspired nationalist sentiments, they were muted by the country's dependence on oil and the lifestyle and benefits that it generated . The oil industry and the cultural and social agenda that it promoted offer an important setting for the study of how the industry altered the lives of Venezuelans and foreigners, and how it influenced the social, political, and cultural values of important segments of society.

At crucial junctures during the course of this work I have received encouragement from colleagues, students, family, and friends, and financial assistance from public and private institutions. From my earliest days in graduate school, Ramón Eduardo Ruiz provided unfailing support and an important model. Michael Monteon always encouraged me to follow my interest and write on Venezuela. I have also benefited from the insights and encouragement of many colleagues and friends in the United States, Venezuela, and Mexico, in particular Allen Wells, Daniel Mato, Carlos Sanchez Silva, Ismael Valencia, Manuel Santillana, Yolanda Salas, Adolfo Gilly, Kimberly Welch, Mark Overmyer Velázquez, Jan Rus, Ron Chilcote, and several others. My colleagues at *Latin American Perspectives* have provided an intellectually challenging environment in which to exchange ideas. In the Department of History and Latin American Studies my colleagues Sidney Lemelle, Susana Chávez Silverman, and Victor Silverman encouraged my work, read chapters as they evolved, and made suggestions. Sidney Lemelle generously made time to read the entire manuscript more than once. At Arizona State University I am indebted to Steven Koppe for his meticulous efforts in locating sources on the diplomatic history of the United States. As the work evolved, several students at Pomona College assisted me in research efforts. I would like to acknowledge my former students Peter Kuhns, José Julio Melgoza, Elizabeth Dorr, Jane Cho, Maria Luz García, and Ariana Klitzner for their assistance. In addition, I thank Barbara Metzger and Fred Kameny for their editorial advice. At Duke University Press the guidance and patience of Valerie Millholland helped bring this project to fruition. Financial support from the National Endowment for the Humanities, the Pomona College Research Committee, the Graves Fellowship, and the Howard Foundation allowed me the independence to research, reflect, and write this book. For their support I am extremely grateful.

In Venezuela the distinguished historian Ramón J. Velazquez provided early advice and opened many doors. The late José Giacopini Zárraga, a key figure in the oil industry, shared ideas and made important suggestions. At the Universidad de los Andes (ULA) Ali López provided constructive insights, and at the University of Zulia (LUZ) Germán Cardozo Galué shared his perspective of western Venezuela. Also at LUZ, Alicia Pineda offered ideas about sources. At the Universidad Andres Bello (UAB) Tomas Straka exchanged views on the impact of oil on culture and society. Over the years I have benefited from the work of Steve Ellner at the Universidad de Oriente (UDO), whose publications on Venezuelan politics and society provided critical insights.

This work would not have been possible without the support and assistance of archivists and librarians in Venezuela, the United States, and Britain. In Caracas, Guillermo Moreno and the staff of the Archivo Histórico de Miraflores facilitated my work. At the former Biblioteca de Lagoven, María Elena Dalessandro and the library staff gave me complete access to the facility. In Mérida, Egla Charmell, the former director of the Tulio Febres Cordero library and archive, not only provided assistance with the collection but also read chapters. In Maracaibo, at the Archivo Histórico del Estado de Zulia, Dilian Ferer and Ivan Salazar shared their knowledge of the collection and the region's history. Hudilu Rodríguez Sangroni also helped locate materials. At the Academia Nacional de Historia in Caracas, Zoila Chacón facilitated my work. The staff at the Biblioteca Nacional in Caracas, the National Archives in Maryland, and the Public Record Office in London were extremely helpful in locating documents.

I am most appreciative of the former employees of Creole and Shell in Venezuela and the United States who shared their accounts and insights of life in the oil camps. In particular I am grateful to José Omar Colmenares and his group of retired friends, who willingly spent countless hours recounting their lives in the camps. In the United States I am especially indebted to the members of the Creole Annuitants Association and their families, who freely shared their experiences. In particular, the family of Clinton and Joan Lieffers provided access to their personal materials.

I am grateful to the estate of Adolf Dehn for permission to use the image of his painting on the cover and in particular to Andrew Lowe for his assistance.

Throughout this project my immediate and extended family allowed me to stay in their homes, nourished my body and soul, and offered counsel and criticism. The social conscience and boundless energy of Luisa Amelia, my nonagenarian mother, continue to inspire. María Eva Valle, my partner in life, offered insightful comments and suggestions throughout this project. I am most indebted to our daughters Rosa Elena and Ana Luisa for the countless hours that I robbed from our family to complete this work. For their patience and love I am most grateful.

The conclusions discussed in this book are based on years of archival research in Venezuela, the United States, and England. Besides being an academic project, the work had a personal component, since I was raised and socialized in Venezuela's oil camps, especially Caripito in eastern Venezuela, where I was born. My father, an expatriate from California, and my mother, a Venezuelan from the Andean state of Mérida, both worked in the oil industry. My father labored as a steam engineer, an all-encompassing category that took him from the Caripito refinery to pipeline crews and eventually to the San Juan River docks, where he helped to outfit vessels. As a single woman, my mother was employed by Creole Petroleum Corporation as a laboratory technician in the Caripito hospital. She and my father met at the company mess hall for single employees and married a short time later. Like most oil families we moved often, from Caripito, to Adaro on the Paraguana peninsula, to Brazil and back. Eventually, facing a host of stereotypes, from both North Americans and Venezuelans, and seeking to avoid the social demands of camp life, my parents moved to the nearby community of Los Mangos, from which my mother faithfully drove me every day into the camp so that I could attend school. I learned English and Spanish simultaneously but grew up largely among my Venezuelan neighbors and family members. A host of relatives and family friends also worked in the oil industry. This history places a unique burden on my work; it provided me unequaled access to private collections, and even corporate archives, but it also created a series of expectations that I will never be able to fulfill. Some would prefer that I had limited myself to describing the "good old days" in the camps rather than address the myriad contradictions that framed life in these unique residential enclaves. Instead, my goal is to provide a balanced account of life in the oil industry and how this experience influenced and continues to shape the lives of generations of Venezuelans and foreigners, ensuring oil's enduring legacy.

Oil, Culture, and Society

Mass mobilizations for and against the government, a failed military coup in April 2002, a lockout and strike engineered by oil company managers and opposition forces in December 2002, sporadic acts of violence in 2004 to promote instability, and an unsuccessful presidential recall—all these have exposed profound divisions within Venezuelan society. The presence of deep-seated political and social fissures challenges the view of Venezuela as a "model democracy" able to avoid the crippling instability and divisions that have beset other Latin American nations.[1] And the class, political, and even racial polarization that has surfaced since the election of President Hugo Chávez Frías can be traced in part to very different visions of the nation and society that evolved from protracted experience with the oil industry.[2]

The oil industry remains the central component of the Venezuelan economy and has been a decisive factor in the evolution of social and class structures since its development in the early twentieth century. Venezuelan élites and middle classes expected that oil would transform the country on many levels, introducing modern technology, fomenting economic development, breaking the stranglehold of the old landed élite, encouraging new democratic political forces, stimulating the growth of the middle class, and creating an efficient workforce.[3] The actions of the foreign oil companies that operated in Venezuela played out on a vast stage. They reorganized physical space, determined national policy, transformed the lives of employees, and in the end influenced the perspective of generations of Venezuelans. Oil, to cite the historian and former communist leader Juan Bautista Fuenmayor, is the "key that permits us to decipher the political enigma of Venezuelan politics in the last seventy years."[4] More to the point, Domingo Alberto Rangel argues that "no event in Venezuela can be separated from oil. . . . It is the fundamental force that shapes national life. All aspects of the Venezuelan economy are the legitimate or bastard children of that substance that irrevocably stained our history."[5] Thus oil is fundamental to any understanding of the military regimes of the early twentieth century, the period of the Trienio (1945–48), and the subsequent system of "pacted democracy" after 1959, as well as the government of the radical president Hugo Chávez since 1999.

AGENT OF MODERNIZATION

As the new source of revenue for the nation, the oil companies exercised a tremendous influence over both local and national affairs. The beginnings of the oil industry coincided with efforts by the military strongman Juan Vicente Gómez (1908–35) to consolidate control over a fractured polity and a nation in which local and regional cultural expression predominated. To accomplish this task, Gómez sought to reduce the power of regional élites and limit landed and commercial interests while asserting the authority of the national government. The international oil companies provided Gómez with the political legitimacy and economic resources needed to consolidate power; for their support they were generously rewarded.[6] During the Gómez era the foreign oil industry and the Venezuelan state became inextricable.

Attentive to the exercise of power and to foreign investments, however, the government did little in the area of social investment.[7] With a relatively weak state apparatus offering few if any services to its population, the foreign oil companies found themselves fulfilling many of the traditional functions associated with the local, state, and even national government. Investments in infrastructure including roads, sanitation, water, and electrical works as well as social investments in schools, sports, churches, and health facilities proved essential to initiating and maintaining company operations. This investment was part of the strategy of "progressive industrialism," which in the long run helped the companies co-opt the opposition and avert disruption from labor militancy, community protests, and expressions of nationalism. Moreover, since their activities were typically framed in the language of modernization, the foreign oil companies usually enjoyed the support of the state, and more importantly of a rising middle class that hoped to benefit from the presence of the industry. Some elements of society, as Fernando Coronil points out, conflated nationalism with the "pursuit of economic development and collective prosperity."[8] Thus it was not surprising for the minister of development Juan Pablo Pérez Alfonzo to assert in 1947 that foreign investment in the oil industry was largely "irrelevant; what is important is that they function in the country with a Venezuelan labor force and that is why we consider them as Venezuelan enterprises."[9] Accepted by those in power as "Venezuelan enterprises," the foreign oil companies gradually evolved their own separate power structure that created alternative sets of loyalties among their employees and other sectors of society.

THE VENEZUELAN OIL INDUSTRY

The Venezuelan oil industry, and by extension the social relations that it engendered, can be divided into several phases. The first began in 1914 at Mene Grande and lasted until the Great Depression, initiating the first of many cycles of growth and contraction of the industry and the dislocation of thousands of workers, both Venezuelan and foreign.[10] The second, consolidation phase extended from the Depression through the Second World War and was characterized by the oligopolization of the industry by three major foreign oil producers. The advent of the war introduced a new urgency to the restructuring of the Venezuelan oil industry under way since the mid-1930s. The third, or institutionalized phase, beginning in the 1950s, witnessed the rise of normalized relations between government, foreign companies, labor, and Venezuelan society.[11]

Three enterprises—the Creole Petroleum Corporation (a subsidiary of Standard Oil Company of New Jersey), the Royal Dutch Shell Oil Company, and Mene Grande (a subsidiary of Gulf Oil)—emerged as the leading producers. The labor movement, active since the late 1920s, became an important political force and demanded a greater voice. The nationwide oil strike of 1936 exemplified the emerging power of the nascent labor movement. A decade later, in 1946, the oil unions signed their first formal contract with the companies, inaugurating a new era in labor-management relations. Venezuelan labor remained bitterly divided, however, between the communist factions and the Social Democrats represented by Acción Democrática

(AD). The roughneck from the United States and the Venezuelan day laborer, or obrero, who characterized the expansion phase of the industry slowly gave way to university-trained engineers and career company employees. During the consolidation phase the number of Venezuelan workers in the industry increased, and many acquired administrative positions in the companies. Despite the rhetoric of meritocracy, for most Venezuelans employment was increasingly contingent on an extended network of family relations and personal contacts within the industry.

After the Second World War oil production acquired a certain "normalcy." Exploration continued and well production increased, but the chaos and exhilaration of the early years no longer permeated operations. This institutionalized period was marked by a settled and established industry, including formal relations between the large oil companies, national and state governments, labor organizations, the church, and civil society. By the 1960s upwards of 25 percent of the Venezuelan population lived in or near an oil camp.[12] Camp life became more routinized and hierarchically stratified. For both expatriates from the United States and Venezuelans, status in the company determined one's social networks and living arrangements. Thus the oil camps included separate living areas—senior and junior staff residences and the more modest campo obrero (workers' camp). Distinctions were also evident even among the senior employees, and not all expatriates had the same privileges. Differences in housing and status notwithstanding, a pervasive corporate culture permeated labor relations and social arrangements.

The residential communities, or campos petroleros, that the foreign oil companies fashioned to house their local and foreign employees became the most important stage for the profound economic, social, and cultural changes that Venezuelans experienced after the discovery of oil. At the economic level the companies controlled employment and provided housing, while at the social and cultural level they organized recreational activities and oversaw the education of employees and their families. The creation of these Venezuelan residential enclaves involved an unparalleled degree of social engineering. The oil camp thus embodied a multidimensional process of social adaptation and acculturation that ranged from the uses of private and public space to the encouragement of preferred cultural norms and social practices.[13] Characterized by a symmetrical urban schema and efficient administration, these communities represented a modern economic and social order. In contrast, lacking even basic services, most rural Venezuelan communities were the antithesis of this new modernity. Employees of the oil industry found themselves in a unique position. As the highest-paid workers and professionals in Venezuelan society, they were important models for the nation, a situation that the foreign companies repeatedly used to their advantage. If the industry was an instrument of modernity, its employees were expected to "model" modernity for other Venezuelans. The oil camp, and its seemingly ordered society, were a tool of socialization as well as control of the workers and their families. In this male-dominated industry, the family became the framework for crafting new social values and organizing civic society and everyday life. While traditional studies minimize their role, women were a key component of the oil industries' broader socialization project at work, in the camps, and in society at large.

Those employed by the foreign oil companies and many in the middle class developed a vision of a modern Venezuelan nation rooted in the social and political values promoted by the industry. Under these conditions, the industry in general and the oil camp in particular were sites of social engineering and cultural hegemony.[14] Gradually the values promulgated in the industry influenced the ever-evolving "common sense" beliefs of important segments of the population. Many directly employed or indirectly benefiting from the oil industry subsequently assumed key positions in Venezuelan society, government, commerce, and industry. Their views reflected a series of self-sustaining myths about the oil industry and its importance to the nation and society. Paramount among these was the notion that for Venezuela the oil industry was the means to achieve modernity in all its forms. For those employed by the industry, these new modern traditions accentuated certain traits and behavior patterns—discipline, efficiency, work ethic, meritocracy, and in some cases even bilingualism—that helped define the "collective consciousness" of the oil industry and distinguished those working in it from the rest of society.[15] For them the interests of the industry increasingly become synonymous with the interests of the nation, a conflation that had its roots in the Gómez era. Their outlook celebrated Venezuela's newfound importance in the international economy, which in turn necessitated close relations with the economic system of the United States. The perspective of oil industry interests evolved over time, adjusting to new social conditions and relations of power. Oil, to paraphrase the famed essayist Arturo Uslar Pietri, not only determined the character of the Venezuelan economy but also created a false image of the nation, a national consensus premised on the illusion of prosperity.[16] The portrayal of a prosperous oil economy transforming the nation obscured the fact that a significant portion of the Venezuelan population existed on the margins of the oil economy.

BLACK GOLD

After nearly a decade of exploration, a gusher at the Barroso no. 2 well near the town of La Rosa on the eastern shore of Lake Maracaibo on 14 December 1922 captured the attention of the nation and the world. Soon dozens of foreign companies acquired vast tracts of territory in the hope of striking it rich, and by 1928 Venezuela became the world's leading oil exporter.[17] Oil ended Venezuela's relative anonymity in the eyes of world powers, making it a linchpin of an ever-expanding international oil industry and a new consideration in global policymaking.[18] Venezuela's oil production became a major factor in policy making in Washington before the Second World War.

The initial stage of oil production in Venezuela proved chaotic, socially explosive, and largely uncontrolled. The establishment of the oil industry prompted the relocation of thousands of rural Venezuelans and their families to the emerging oil towns that dotted the Lake Maracaibo area, the principal site of oil production. It brought an untold number of workers from the United States and Britain to the new oil fields. Roustabouts, roughnecks, and drillers from Texas, Louisiana, and Oklahoma, some with previous experience in Mexico's oil fields, constituted the initial wave of expatriates.[19] Despite their status as private citizens, most Venezuelans viewed employees from the United States as de facto representatives of their government, who sought special status and in many cases were afforded it. The industry also attracted a significant number of West Indians, Chinese, and some veteran oil workers from Mexico.

The much-heralded arrival of the oil industry, typically framed as the harbinger of a new modern era, proved rather disappointing for the local people whose communities stood in the way of "progress." The presence of the oil companies and the waves of newcomers, not all employed in the industry, compelled the wholesale reorganization of society. These changes introduced new patterns of labor relations and forms of production, recast traditional gender expectations, inspired labor organizing and political activity, and created new patterns of consumption and fashion. It also spurred an unprecedented land grab by oil companies and regional élites that forced the dislocation of small and medium-sized local proprietors. The uncontrolled search for oil also proved damaging to the environment and the health of the people who inhabited the production sites. Wells often spewed their contents over lakes, land, and foliage. The smell of oil and leaking gas wafted over the communities, and the once pristine Lake Maracaibo, the largest body of freshwater in South America, became quickly contaminated.

Located in relatively isolated parts of Venezuela with almost no effective infrastructure or services, the local municipalities proved incapable of addressing the needs of the industry or the new population that it attracted. As they had done elsewhere in Latin America, the foreign oil companies, to initiate extractive operations, had to secure and train a reliable labor force and begin refashioning the tropical environment that lay atop the vast underground oil reserves. The newly assembled labor force quickly laid pipelines and erected drilling platforms, storage tanks, and working facilities. Initially accommodations for workers were rudimentary at best, usually consisting of tents or adobe structures for the foreigners and simple lean-tos and hammocks for the Venezuelans. The waves of migrants produced a reconfiguration of urban space and prompted new economic ventures catering to the needs of the expanding population. During their initial phase the settlements that took shape alongside the oil fields resembled a makeshift society in which each regional group and nationality sought to recreate its social norms and cultural traditions against the backdrop of an emerging corporate culture. As the labor force expanded and companies sought to exercise greater control over their employees and their lifestyle, they began to construct formal residential communities to house foreign and Venezuelan workers.

The organizational framework of the Venezuelan oil camps borrowed from the experience of the company town in the United States during the late nineteenth century and the early twentieth. Near textile mills and in remote mining regions, employers in the United States built facilities for their workers and families. The company town as an institution declined in the United States in the 1920s at almost the same time that it expanded in Venezuela.[20] While many labor unions in the United States fought against the visible symbols of corporate intrusion into their lives, including company housing, recreational clubs, and commissaries, Venezuelan oil unions ironically defended these as benefits.[21] Oil workers and their unions, for example, adamantly supported the comisariato (commissary) system that provided them with a wide array of foodstuffs at regulated prices.

Reflecting the Jim Crow policies prevailing in their own country, firms such as the United Fruit Company established racially segregated residential camps for employees from the United States working in Cuba, Guatemala, Honduras, and the Dominican Republic. A de facto camp operated by the United States government provided housing for foreigners employed in the Panama Canal Zone. Mining companies in Mexico, such as those at Cananea, Sonora, also maintained separate residences for foreign and local workers. In the neighboring island of Trinidad, on the edges of the Bermudez tar lake, the Pitch Lake Company built separate quarters for its employees.[22]

In Venezuela the new residential enclaves brought populations from throughout the country face to face for the first time. Not since the wars of independence had Venezuela witnessed such a dramatic movement of people within its borders. The results of this discourse could not always be predicted. Groups as distinct as the Andinos (Andeans) and the Orientales (Easterners) began a process of mutual recognition. Encounters between these groups of Venezuelans created the conditions for negotiating regional differences. Exchanges about contrasting lived experiences initiated discussions on what it meant to be a Venezuelan, beginning a national discourse in the oil camps and adjacent communities. Interaction between diverse groups of Venezuelans with no previous contact also exposed underlying tensions that could be exploited by local politicians. In Zulia, for example, state officials confronted by labor militancy in the late 1930s scapegoated residents of the island of Margarita and ordered their expulsion from the state.

The early industry was characterized by tangled and discordant class and racial antagonisms, and as a result there has been a tendency for the study of oil workers to focus on labor struggles. Yet the complex process of socialization that oil workers, their families, and Venezuelan society underwent has attracted scant attention. This book breaks from the traditional approach to the study of the Venezuelan oil industry and addresses other, often more complex, forms in which workers and the middle class were integrated into a national project centered on oil production. Moreover, it contrasts the experiences of Venezuelans to those of foreigners in the industry, who were an essential economic and social component of this broader process. At different stages foreigners, whether from the West Indies or from the United States, were the "other" against which sectors of Venezuelan society evaluated their own situation. This perspective does not negate the role of class struggles, but rather highlights the dramatic social and political changes that the oil industry promoted after the 1930s.

The internal social dynamics of the oil industry and its residential camps helped to frame the power relationships between the foreign companies and the evolving nation-state. The acculturation process experienced in the camps deeply influenced politics, models of citizenship, and socialization among broad segments of the population. Notions of citizenship that developed in the camps rested on a vision of the nation framed not only by systems of inclusion but also by exclusion, since these forces coexisted side by side and were regularly being redefined and renegotiated.[23] They reflected the promotion of social practices, customs, values, and normative expectations encouraged by the industry and not the nation-state. By using a sociohistorical approach, it is possible to explore the unique role occupied by the oil industry and the preeminent position that it acquired in Venezuelan society. This method of analysis also provides important insights into the nature of contemporary Venezuelan politics and society, in which competing notions of the state and the role of the oil industry remain at the heart of the political debate.

As oil became an important source of employment, attracting thousands of former agricultural laborers, the industry undermined the political and economic power of the traditional landed élite. It also restructured political relations, forcing the national government and state entities to negotiate new arrangements and incorporate new actors, especially the middle class and workers. Despite the outward support of the strongman Juan Vicente Gómez, during this chaotic boom period the oil companies confronted labor protests, disputes with local municipalities, and the increasing resentment of the traditional landed oligarchy. Faced by powerful international trusts that had the support of their respective governments, Gómez skillfully manipulated political and social discontent to improve his negotiating position and extract concessions from the oil companies.[24] For the foreign companies these vexing problems were reminiscent of conflicts earlier encountered in Mexico, which led to the nationalization of the industry in 1938. Learning from these experiences and seeking to avoid "another Mexico," after Gómez's death the larger foreign companies gradually elaborated a vision of corporate citizenship that sought to allay nationalist concerns over their role in Venezuelan society. As a strategic resource in the world economy that was central to any nation's ability to wage war, oil assumed a special position among export products. On the eve of the Second World War, oil companies and the powers they represented could not afford to let Venezuela go the way of Mexico and disrupt world oil supplies.

Over time, Venezuelan governments gradually wrested concessions from the foreign oil companies, augmenting their share of revenues but never challenging the companies' fundamental role in the economy.[25] After the Mexican nationalization, Venezuela became the only nation in Latin America that permitted large-scale production of oil by foreign companies. Seeking to portray themselves as indispensable partners in the development of the Venezuelan nation, the companies embarked on an ambitious program that went beyond paying wages and making housing arrangements to extend to shaping the social and cultural practices of their employees.[26] What began as a gradual policy of hiring and training Venezuelan engineers and professionals in the early 1930s had by the late 1940s become a formal policy of "Venezolanization," promoting Venezuelans to assume most daily operations, while still reserving key management posts for foreigners. Within this framework the foreign companies promoted the image of the model worker and the ideal public citizen who associated corporate interests with the progress of the nation. Undoubtedly this policy also sought to mitigate labor and middle class unrest, but implemented over several decades, it generated broad and far-reaching social outcomes.

The central role of oil in the Venezuelan economy had the effect of privileging the demands of the oil workers and their unions, whose struggles came to symbolize the nation's valiant struggle for equality and dignity against greedy foreign cartels.[27] The labor unions in the oil industry stood for the aspirations of all workers, since the policies adopted by the industry set the pace for the rest of the labor movement, and on occasion evoked international solidarity. Owing in part to their long legacy of militancy, by 1946 oil workers enjoyed the Venezuelan workforce's highest salaries and best benefits packages, becoming what some have called a "labor aristocracy."[28] No other collective bargaining agreement matched the enviable benefits provided for by more than one hundred clauses of the oil workers' contracts. Although they never accounted for more than a small fraction of the workforce, oil workers and their unions became the most powerful component of the Venezuelan labor movement.

Attempts by the Venezuelan middle class to acquire employment in the industry reflected its goal of displacing traditional economic and political élites and gaining new ground in society. For the small yet ambitious Venezuelan professional and managerial class, employment in the oil industry offered the opportunity to enjoy a life comparable to that of the middle class in the United States, a life that was otherwise unattainable. With employment in the oil industry increasingly dependent on family relations and other connections, the company nurtured an interlocking social network of bonds of obligation and loyalty among its employees. The values that workers and middle managers forged throughout the industry created a strong sense of group solidarity that transcended traditional class boundaries. The continued success and expansion of the industry became the guarantor of their lifestyle and privileged status.

Definitions of the middle class in Latin America remain elusive; the term is often used and seldom fully defined. The definition of middle class employed here borrows from the work of Alejandro Portes, who sought to capture the "basic cleavages of interests around which large social groups coalesce."[29] In relative terms the middle class is small, yet it enjoys a privileged social status and a disproportionately large degree of power. Portes describes the middle class as a bureaucratic and technical class that "lacks effective control over the means of production" but that nonetheless directs and controls the labor of others. Besides maintaining "the infrastructure required for economic production," the middle class is expected to perform an important political role and "guarantee the stability of the social order."[30] Within the oil industry it encompassed upper- and middle-level managers and professionals including lawyers, engineers, geologists, technicians, and doctors. As the most educated sector of society, it played an important role in the formation of public opinion and in countering ideas "opposed to the status quo."[31] As a matter of policy, the foreign oil companies focused much attention on the middle class, encouraging the expectation that through personal initiative every employee had the opportunity to join its ranks.

Dominating the economy and confronting a relatively weak state, the oil companies and their employees came to represent a separate and distinct power within Venezuela, what some have described as a state within a state. Increasingly dependent on maintaining an export-driven economic model, a generation of political leaders, intellectuals, and others incorporated elements of the foreign companies' perspective of "development" into their own discourse. In post-Gómez Venezuela, acceptance of this model by influential segments of society provided foreign corporate interests with an important political, social, and cultural shield against nationalist and leftist challenges. The nexus of oil company interests and Venezuelan discourse on development was the popular notion of *sembrar el petróleo*, or sowing oil. Dating from the 1930s and employed by the foreign oil companies, the government, and leading intellectuals, the concept embodied the idea that oil profits could be metaphorically planted, producing nonpetroleum economic growth and helping the country achieve alternative forms of development. Allowed to operate freely, the companies provided the profits that the Venezuelan state would judiciously invest to nurture modernization and growth. Sembrar el petróleo became a mildly nationalist slogan that adorned government buildings and oil company offices and was featured prominently in publications and other media. It defined the perspective of government and political leaders and intellectuals, who accepted the premise that the operations of foreign oil could be reconciled with national interests.

By the late 1950s foreign oil companies operating in Venezuela began to abandon the policy of progressive industrialism that previously characterized their relationship with Venezuelans and the state. During the early, formative period of the industry, the foreign companies had performed functions normally assumed by the state. As political conditions changed in the 1950s the oil companies began to withdraw from the social arena. Several factors drove the change in policy; the cost of maintaining older residential camps and providing services increased, while the expiration of existing oil concessions loomed ever closer. With the ouster of the dictator Marcos Pérez Jiménez in 1958, Venezuela entered a new democratic phase. Venezuelans resented the ubiquitous presence of the foreign oil companies, especially when they eclipsed the newly emerging democratic state. The new Venezuelan state increasingly assumed responsibility for social services and played a greater role in the economy. This trend continued throughout the 1960s, setting the stage for the eventual nationalization of the industry in January 1976.

After nationalization the newly formed Venezuelan oil company Petróleos de Venezuela (PDVSA) continued under the direction of its former Venezuelan managers and inherited the corporate culture of the previous foreign multinationals. Throughout the 1990s PDVSA officials attempted to insulate the enterprise from government intrusion and sought to recast the newly formed enterprise in the role of an international oil conglomerate. By attempting to shield PDVSA they repeated the economic and political practices pursued by the foreign companies, but without implementing the social agenda that had mitigated concerns about the role of an all-powerful multinational on Venezuelan economy and society.

The lockout and strike of 2002–3 against Chávez's government, in which PDVSA officials played a decisive role, again prompted discussion about whether the oil company was a power separate from the state. Some scholars advanced the notion that PDVSA and its board of directors, like the foreign managers before them, functioned largely as an independent power, restraining and at times coercing the nation-state.[32] They highlighted the way the PDVSA directors imposed their will on previous administrations and now pursued a similar course of action against Chávez's government.[33] This book argues that the proposition of a state within a state has an important cultural and social component as well, one that is framed by the profound experience of thousands of Venezuelans who participated directly and indirectly in the oil industry. The ability of the oil conglomerate and its former executives to influence politics rested not only on economic power but also on a set of cultural and social experiences that informed the lives of generations of Venezuelans employed by or associated with the oil industry. Efforts by Chávez's government to "renationalize the industry," gain control over previously negotiated heavy crude contracts, and establish a new set of relations between PDVSA, the state, and the populace did not occur in a vacuum. A historical overview of the factors that gave rise to the oil industry provides one way to understand current developments in Venezuela. With declarations that "Venezuela is now ours" and of a "new PDVSA," the discourse on the oil industry has come full circle.

CHAPTER I

A Tropical Mediterranean

Lake Maracaibo at the Turn of the Century

Rather than the prototypical colonial backwater that was often represented, Venezuela before the advent of the oil industry exhibited patterns of development commonly found throughout Latin America toward the end of the nineteenth century.[1] The notion of a backward Venezuela is rooted in the idea that the discovery of oil was synonymous with progress and modernization, an argument that has increasingly proved unsustainable not only in Venezuela but also in other oil-producing countries throughout the world.[2] An overview of Venezuelan society and politics in the regions where the industry developed, as well as the states from which workers were drawn, provides the background against which to assess this purported transformation. Too often descriptions of Venezuela commence with the rise of the oil industry and fail to provide a point of comparison from which to evaluate the changes that the industry purportedly introduced. Moreover, they assume that oil swept away all existing social, economic, and political structures. In the words of the oil industry pioneer José Antonio Giacopini Zárraga, with oil Venezuela went from a "society that had nothing to a society that had almost everything. These are two very distinct Venezuela's."[3] The Venezuela that had existed before did not disappear, however, but rather coexisted with the new reality. While touching on other regions, the focus of this chapter is western Venezuela, where Lake Maracaibo resembled a tropical Mediterranean linking the various communities around its shores and other distinct regions in a single, broad socioeconomic unit.[4] It outlines the environmental, demographic, and social conditions of the area and its principal economic activities. Though the lake provided the basis for an active export economy rooted in coffee production, there was little contact between inhabitants of the area, and local experiences continued to determine social practices and patterns of identity.

At the beginning of the twentieth century Venezuela remained an assortment of discrete regional entities, driven by a host of contradictory forces. The Spanish had imposed their political administrative structure over the country's three distinct ecosystems—the lush tropical rain forest in the south; the sweeping plains, bathed by a network of rivers; and the coastal and Andean mountain ranges, with fertile valleys and the largest freshwater lake in South America.[5] The country's limited population remained dispersed over its 912,050 square kilometers. Population density was among the lowest in Latin America, and there was little if any interaction among the regions. As the essayist Mariano Picón Salas noted, "with poor communication across its vast territory, which at that moment never surpassed two million inhabitants, each region with its climatic, racial, and dietary particularities seemed to engender its own ethnic type."[6] As late as 1936 Venezuela still only had five inhabitants per square kilometer.[7] Caracas, called the tropical Paris by Venezuelan intellectuals obsessed with European analogies, had a population that hovered near ninety thousand, making it the undisputed political and social center of the country.[8] If Caracas was the center of power, the interior was the "barbarian" hinterland, inhabited, according to one intellectual, by the Venezuelan equivalent of "Goths, Visigoths, Sweves, and Burgundians."[9] Besides Caracas, secondary cities such as Valencia, Maracay, Cumana, Mérida, San Cristóbal, and Maracaibo were important regional centers, although most people continued to live in the rural countryside.

Throughout the nineteenth century politics had been marked by intense struggles spilling over into prolonged periods of civil war that devastated the country. Conflicts resulted not only from the deep-seated divisions between conservatives and liberals unwilling to share power that were so common throughout Latin America, but also from the determination of regional élites to retain local autonomy. On many occasions, as one Venezuelan historian has noted, "local political bosses exploited these conflicts to consolidate or expand their power."[10] At no time during most of the nineteenth century, the historian Germán Cardozo Galué writes, did there emerge a "dominant class with national support, with capacity or presence to dominate the vast territory or unite and formulate . . . a [national] project."[11]

In 1899 the first of a series of Andean strongmen from the state of Táchira descended on Caracas. Cipriano Castro's rise to power signaled a break with the past caudillos who had mobilized the campesino masses to assume power.[12] From the outset the presence of his army of fewer than two thousand soldiers could not explain his hold on the capital. Rather, it reflected the turning of the tide against decades of civil war and political conflict. With only a tenuous hold on power, Castro found it necessary to negotiate with the Caracas élite and include them in his government, and this situation eventually weakened his ability to challenge the established order. Forces internal to the Andean faction that controlled power eventually led to his demise and his replacement by Juan Vicente Gómez, who ruled the country from 1908 until he died peacefully in his sleep in December 1935. Gómez, according to the historian Domingo Alberto Rangel, "became the demolisher of the old caste of caudillos and their tacit allies the intellectuals who had not adapted to the changes produced by 1908."[13]

ORIENTE, THE EAST

The states of Sucre, Monagas, and Anzoategui and the island of Nueva Esparta (Margarita), generally known as Oriente, or the East, were linked by little beyond their geographic location. With its two peninsulas resembling stretched extremities protruding into the Caribbean, Sucre had been settled early on by the Spaniards. Its ports of Cumana and Carupano, dating from the colonial period, depended on fishing and on maritime trade centered on the export of coffee and cacao. These agricultural crops flourished in the lush tropical valleys in the interior of the state. Corsicans had migrated to the region at the turn of the century and established a foothold in commerce. The lush tropical vegetation in Sucre continued into Monagas, in cool, fertile valleys such as those around Caripe. The central and southern reaches of the state included broad llanos, or plains, well suited to cattle production. Monagas also benefited from a series of river and delta systems that became trade routes. The city of Maturín took shape near the banks of the Guarapiche and engaged in overseas trade with Trinidad and other ports. In similar fashion, on the banks of the San Juan River, Caripito exported cattle and agricultural goods, mostly as contraband to the nearby British-controlled islands. The southern reaches of the state, near the banks of the mighty Orinoco, relied on cattle production and subsistence agriculture. Overland routes proved largely nonexistent, and the exchange of goods and personal travel relied on river networks and intercoastal shipping that linked the states of eastern Venezuela with Trinidad and then far-off Caracas.

On Nueva Esparta, Margariteños eked out an existence on a barren island. Visitors immediately noted its desert-like conditions. One geologist from the United States in 1912 described it as "arid, the usual tall, thin corrugated cacti and thorny bushes being evident along the coast."[14] Confronted by these conditions, the indigenous ancestors of the present-day inhabitants, the Waikéri, had visited the northern coast of Venezuela and the Antilles decades before the arrival of the Spanish. They traded salt, which was abundant in the island lagoons, as well as casaba, ritual and musical instruments, and *hoya* (a plant similar to coca) throughout the region.[15] The arrival of the Spanish and the development of an extractive pearl industry devastated the island's resources, accentuating the process of deforestation and heightening dependence on the sea. Margariteños grew increasingly reliant on seafaring that at times carried them as far away as the Gulf of Venezuela at the entrance to Lake Maracaibo and brought them into contact with their western compatriots. Their reputation as experienced sailors made them a valuable asset on board the ships that plied the waters off northern Venezuela. The Orientales were seen as "extroverts: . . . treating others without much formality, they are open to strangers, always employing popular adages, . . . rely on jokes, and speak quickly as if possessed by a certain hyperness."[16]

THE ANDES

In most of western Venezuela, life followed established traditional patterns in place since the late colonial period. Contrary to popular Venezuelan lore, however, the Andes did not generate a unified experience, much less a shared identity.[17] Differences in ethnicity, agriculture, land tenure, access to markets, and social structures produced divergent outcomes for the residents of the states of Trujillo, Mérida, and Táchira.[18] Outside a few towns—Trujillo, Mérida, and San Cristóbal—little had changed in the region for some time. Privileged during the colonial period with an adminis-trative structure, a bishopric, a university, and in the view of one historian "legions of voracious bureaucrats," the city of Mérida attempted to exercise control over the Andean region.[19] Despite differences, agricultural activity and by extension social activity in the Andes followed the cyclical rhythms imposed by nature. Settlements in the high mountain chains that enclosed the territory resembled "small islands of houses and corrals lost amidst the ferocity of regal valleys."[20] According to the historian Ramón J. Velásquez, at night, except for the flicker of a few oil lamps, darkness enveloped the area.[21] Though it remains problematic to speak of a unified Andean culture, in the popular mind isolation had produced a reserved, stoic, and distrustful Andean character popularly known as a *gocho*.[22]

The Andes experienced important changes during the later decades of the nineteenth century. Traditional landholders had leveraged existing fam-ily networks, joining forces with recent Italian immigrants and arrivals from the neighboring state of Barinas to produce coffee that they exported to German firms in Maracaibo and on to world markets.[23] The rivers of the region, the Chama, the Motatan, and the Albarregas, emptied into Lake Maracaibo, and so did most overland trails. Mule trains loaded with sacks of coffee made their way over well-worn mountain trails to the principal cities of the region and from there to the railroad that connected the An-des to Lake Maracaibo.[24] German merchants from Maracaibo frequently made the journey into the Andes and as far south as Cúcuta in Colombia to establish trade arrangements and ensure the availability of supplies.[25] Cúcuta proved critical to the region's trade; it was in a position to link the merchants of the Magdalena River and Lake Maracaibo.[26] Besides cof-fee, small-scale mining, especially of urao (carbonate of sodium and mag-nesium), enriched a select group of Mérida's merchants and miners.[27] For most of the nineteenth century the Andean states had a quasi-political and economic relationship with Maracaibo, and in 1866 they actually united to become part of the state of Zulia.

FALCÓN

The nearby region of Falcón, east of Lake Maracaibo, also found itself drawn into Maracaibo's orbit. To the north, the desolate peninsula of Para-guana juts into the Caribbean, forming an inverted body of land connected to the mainland by a thin strip of shifting sand dunes. The peninsula is constantly buffeted by strong Caribbean trade winds that disrupt most vegetation and disperse ample amounts of sand, providing only a brief respite from the searing tropical sun. Lacking an ample supply of water, most residents of the northern peninsula relied on fishing, some agriculture, and clandestine trade with Curaçao as their main sources of income. Isolated from the central regions of the country, Coro, the capital of Falcón, founded in 1527, interacted principally with nearby Maracaibo and Curaçao. In the interior, cool mountains with ample water provided a refuge for agriculture as well as cattle and goat production.[28] Throughout most of the nineteenth century and the early twentieth, Falcón had suffered an outmigration.[29] Opportunities there remained limited, and as news of employment in the nearby state of Zulia spread, residents quickly migrated to the oilfields in large numbers. Oil also increased migration within the state, since Falcón possessed oil deposits of its own. On the eastern edge of the state a British company uncovered an extremely productive field of light crude at La Mara.[30]

THE MARACAIBO LAKE BASIN

The daily course of activity in the vicinity of Lake Maracaibo on the eve of the twentieth century gave no indication of the monumental changes that would soon overtake the region and thrust it into the international limelight. Largely isolated from the rest of the nation, the lake remained the cornerstone of the economy and society of western Venezuela. It was the principal source of transportation in an area where natural barriers at times formed impenetrable obstacles to communication and formal roads remained nonexistent. Bounded by the Andean range, whose peaks reached elevations of over fifteen thousand feet, the lake was an immense reservoir 135 miles long and 60 miles wide, gathering water from the area's many rivers and streams. High in the Sierra de Perija along the Colombian border and throughout the Andean chain, rivers such as the Catatumbo, the Escalante, the Santa Ana, the Chama, and the Motatan collected the flows of dozens of smaller streams, forming expansive deltas as they drained into the lake.[31] In total more than 85 rivers and 100 streams emptied into Lake Maracaibo.[32]

As these rivers meandered through valleys and plains, they collected large amounts of silt and deposited them in the lake. A study commissioned by the Creole Petroleum Corporation and conducted by the Woods Hole

Oceanographic Institution in 1953 determined that the lake water tended to rotate in an "anticlockwise eddy," allowing "fresh water to remain in the lake on the average for about four years before escaping to the sea." Moreover, the study revealed "the existence of an unusual system of tidal motion in Lake Maracaibo which appears to be of importance in controlling the penetration of salt into the lake."[33] Driven by the prevailing currents, the centuries-old accumulations of silt formed a natural barrier at the straits where the lake water collided with the salty currents of the Caribbean. Increased lake levels during the rainy season and the existence of this natural bar limited access to salty ocean currents and ensured the persistence of this bountiful yet precarious body of freshwater. The sand barrier at the entrance to the lake impeded lake travel for vessels with drafts of over ten feet. Even with an experienced local captain, navigating the intricate maze of canals and sandbars from the seventeenth-century castle at San Carlos to the port of Maracaibo could take one to two days.[34]

The land and vegetation along the lakeshore presented a panorama of sharp contrasts. Miles of relatively desolate plains were dotted with low mesquite, cactus, and divi-divi trees whose seeds were used for dyes and tanning.[35] Where access to water permitted, these lands also supported the grazing of cattle and goats. Farther south, along the crescent outline of the lake known locally as "Sur del Lago," tropical vegetation, forests, and marshes provided the conditions for sugar, cacao, tuber, and plantain production. Rich clusters of mangroves and lush tropical palms that the inhabitants harvested for copra marked the area east of the lake.[36] Cardozo Galué has identified two subregions here: the coastal plains, whose principal port Maracaibo dominated commerce, and the agriculturally productive Andean piedmont which extended south into Colombia.[37]

These distinct lake regions teemed with life. White and red garzas (herons) and a wide assortment of ducks made the lake their home. Other migratory species of birds used it as a stopover on their long journeys between North and South America. Otters and other water animals also established residence in the lake and the numerous estuaries along its shores. A wide array of fish, especially a variety of the corbina and mullet (lisa), as well as shrimp, blue crabs, and other crustaceans, flourished in the lake.[38] The lake and its shores were by no means idyllic, however. Expansive swamps were breeding grounds for swarms of mosquitoes and venomous snakes such as the deadly fer-de-lance, or mapanare (*Bothrops lanceolatus*). Foreign travelers agonized over the clouds of insects that swarmed throughout the southern parts of the lake, resembling "a coal burning steamer. Millions of mosquito larvae are included in each cloud."[39]

At the mouth of the lake, Maracaibo, named—according to local legend—for the indigenous leader who had confronted the Europeans, had remained relatively small for most of the nineteenth century. The settlement there, established in 1529 by Welser's conquerors in the commission of the Spanish crown, had proved short-lived; facing sustained indigenous resistance and an arid environment, within months it had been abandoned. After another failed attempt in 1571, the Spaniards finally colonized the area in 1574 and established the port as Nueva Zamora de Maracaibo. In 1801 the state of Zulia had a population of about 100,000, of which the port city accounted for 24,000.[40] By 1891 the population of the city had reached nearly 40,000 while the entire state gained 45,000 inhabitants.[41] At various times during the colonial period Zulia had been governed by the *Audiencia* of Bogotá, and in 1777 it had passed to the Captaincy General of Caracas. At the beginning of the nineteenth century the province of Zulia was among the largest in Venezuela and included the Andean cities of Trujillo, Mérida, and San Cristóbal.[42] This arrangement was formalized in 1866 when the Andean states of Trujillo, Mérida, and Táchira became part of the sovereign state of Zulia. This situation continued, with certain modifications, until 1891, when the Venezuelan congress established the modern state of Zulia in its current physical configuration. Despite being formally separated from the Andean states, Maracaibo took advantage of its location at the mouth of the lake to become the center of trade for this broad region as well as the Colombian city of Cúcuta.[43] Speaking with a distinctive accent, the independent maracuchos (residents of Maracaibo) regularly complained about the domination of Caracas over their affairs.[44] In 1849 a movement to secede from Venezuela failed and its leaders left the country.[45]

Maracaibo's Baralt, Bolívar, and Urdaneta plazas delineated the center of the city and housed its principal merchants. Known to locals as "the city of palms," the port was characterized by a vibrant and chaotic mix of colonial whitewashed buildings, elegantly adorned two-story commercial establishments, stately quintas (residences), brightly colored rowhouses, and poorer dwellings made of bahareque (a local form of adobe) on the outskirts.[46] To those arriving from the lake the city resembled a mélange of red tile roofs and palm trees. Except for businesses and the homes of the élite, buildings seldom had more than one story. Temperatures that typically hovered around ninety-five degrees caused visitors and residents alike to describe Maracaibo as the "hottest place in the country."[47] The sun, in the words of one traveler, was "capable of disintegrating not only refuse, but also the minds and bodies of the citizens of the town."[48] To lessen the oppressive heat that engulfed the city after midday, many of the older neighborhoods such as El Milagro faced the water to take advantage of the afternoon breeze that occasionally blew in from the lake. Other neighborhoods, such as Bella Vista, became popular because their location at an elevation of 140 feet above sea level allowed unobstructed access to intermittent gusts. As was typical of houses in the Caribbean, most of the homes of the well-to-do included tall windows, usually barred, to induce an occasional breeze.

Differences in the urban landscape reflected the marked social distinctions that permeated Maracaibo's society. After 1830 the expansion of the coffee export economy had given rise to a new commercial élite. Composed mainly of foreigners, especially Germans, this group parlayed its international contacts in the Caribbean and Europe to become a new economic force. This new "counter-aristocracy," impeccably dressed in white suits, ties, and black boots, soon exerted influence over Maracaibo society, establishing its own circles and groups of eager followers.[49] The Club de Comercio, a private social club established in 1890, where they gathered, became the most powerful in the city.[50] It had over five hundred members, a salon, a library, a billiards room, and a bar and regularly hosted gala balls.[51] The port's commercial activity also supported bookkeepers, customs officers, lawyers, and others associated with the export economy. The vast majority of the population, however, did not benefit from these enterprises and lived in dire economic conditions on the outskirts of town. As Brian McBeth points out, Maracaibo possessed "rigid social rules and a defined class structure with a large pauperized population."[52]

An electric urban train system extending about seven kilometers connected the city to outlying neighborhoods such as El Milagro and the waterfront district of Los Haticos. A steam-powered train joined the Bella Vista suburb with the center of the city. A mule-driven train had previously carried passengers from the Plaza Baralt to outlying areas such as El

Empedrado.[53] Before the establishment of these rail lines, some residents from outlying neighborhoods arrived in the center of Maracaibo by boat.[54] The Maracaibo Electric Light Company, founded in 1886 and based in the United States, provided the city's power needs, servicing 3,200 houses and 231 streetlights.[55] Maracaibo had a few hotels and three commercial social clubs.[56] On the outskirts of the city approximately three hundred hatos, or ranches, provided the city with its basic foodstuffs. In addition there was a small but enterprising industrial sector, including several cotton mills, soap factories, candle makers, cigarette concerns, a tannery, a lumber mill, and a furniture factory. Germans operated two breweries, the Cervecería de Zulia and the Maracaibo.[57] The Curaçao Trading Company and the American Bazaar were the other principal commercial houses in the city. Important financial institutions included the Banco de Maracaibo, Zulia, and the Royal Bank of Canada.[58] By 1894 the various economic interests formed the Maracaibo Chamber of Commerce. A small but flourishing community of Arabs, mainly Syrian and Lebanese (referred to as Turcos by most Venezuelans), also engaged in trade.[59] Yet despite the expanding markets, life in Maracaibo at the end of the century exacted a heavy toll on its inhabitants.

Maracaibo's position as the commercial entrepôt of the region produced some unforeseen health problems. The presence of a significant number of mules and donkeys, which at times inundated city streets, gave the port a "semi-rural appearance."[60] More important, animal dung became a constant source of complaints. The town had an unreliable water supply for its size, and its drainage system proved totally insufficient. After heavy rains or increased lake levels, many parts of the city would periodically flood. One foreign traveler described Maracaibo's sidewalks as "steep tropical pavements" built high enough to avoid occasional floods.[61] The city's waste products usually made their way onto the streets and eventually into the lake's already brackish waters. One early visitor reported, "There is no sewer system, and, so far as one may judge from appearances, the streets are never cleaned."[62] Venezuelan commentators expressed similar concerns.[63] The arrival of vessels and the constant movement of people and animals increased concerns about the spread of tropical diseases such as yellow fever and malaria, which plagued the port throughout the nineteenth century. Displaying the western mentality of the period, one foreign traveler insisted that Maracaibo was "subject to enough ailments to reduce the most confirmed hypochondriac to a condition of violent revolt against pathology."[64] Aside from the peculiarities of the lake habitat, health conditions in Maracaibo paralleled those found elsewhere in Venezuela. As a result, life expectancy during this period hovered at around thirty years, and death rates almost equaled birth rates.[65]

Despite these conditions, Maracaibo was Venezuela's second-most important city. The large commercial houses, controlled in large part by Germans and their descendants, were its principal economic motor. These merchants bought and sold agricultural goods and functioned as importers and financiers for agricultural interests in the interior.[66] With family names such as Blohm, Boulton, Van Dissel, Breuer, Moller, Beckman, Zingg, Rahn, and Wolff, they controlled an active trade network that incorporated the Andean states of Trujillo, Mérida, and Táchira and extended to Cúcuta in Colombia.[67] Since the nineteenth century, trade in coffee and sugar had earned significant profits for the wealthy of the city.[68] The reach of Maracaibo's merchants extended into the Caribbean, where they traded with the Dutch-controlled islands of Curaçao and Aruba as well as with Europe and, to a lesser extent, the United States. H. L. Boulton and Company operated the Red D Line, providing regular service from Maracaibo to New York, a voyage that took about six days.[69] It also offered travel to London by way of Curaçao, which took approximately three weeks.[70]

For most of the nineteenth century Maracaibo had remained disassociated from events elsewhere in Venezuela. It was easier to reach Colombia or nearby Caribbean ports than Caracas. Travelers to Caracas had to set sail for Curaçao, clear customs, and await the arrival of a vessel destined for the nation's capital.[71] Curaçao was also the departure point for travelers to Margarita and the island of Trinidad. After arriving at La Guaira, the Caribbean gateway to Caracas, travelers confronted an arduous overland journey over towering coastal mountains, with frequent assaults by bandits. The journey became somewhat simpler after 1883 with the completion of the railroad from La Guaira to Caracas, which climbed over 3,135 feet, negotiating nine bridges and eight tunnels.[72] Construction of the railroad facilitated transport of goods but did little to shorten the time it took to cross the coastal mountains and reach the valley of Caracas.

A wide array of vessels, from tramp steamers to the smaller wind-powered piraguas, bongos, and schooners, regularly docked along the embarcadero at Maracaibo. Not counting boats powered by sail and oar, approximately 307 vessels were registered to transport goods in the lake at the turn of the century.[73] Lying under the shadow of Maracaibo's imposing customs building and its many warehouses, the vessels were the lifeblood of the city.[74] The port bustled with activity, as brokers, buyers, passengers, and the curious mingled, producing a jumble of sounds and smells. One German traveler described arriving at the port and disembarking into a huge open-air tropical marketplace.[75] Merchants kept a watchful eye as stevedores unloaded cargoes of coffee, sugar, cacao, plantains, dried beef, hides, coconuts, tubers, sugar, and an assortment of other products. Agricultural goods not consumed locally found their way to the Dutch West Indies.[76] Coffee, sugar, and cacao, the most important cash crops, were shipped to markets in the United States and secondarily to Europe. However, with prices dictated by capricious foreign markets and unpredictable Andean weather patterns, Maracaibo and the lake zone repeatedly experienced crises as prices for these goods contracted, supplies increased in the storehouses, and banks restricted credit.[77]

From Maracaibo the larger vessels typically made the journey to Encontrados, La Ceiba, and Santa Barbara, the lake's principal ports. The voyage from Maracaibo to Encontrados on a steamer such as *El Progreso*, *El Nuevo Fenix*, or *El Nuevo Mara* took three to four days.[78] *El Progreso*, a three-hundred-ton side-wheeler built in the United States, traversed the lake before navigating the treacherous waters of the Catatumbo River, where according to one foreign traveler the ship "slows down and jockeys about coyly trying to hit the channel without hitting a sand bar first."[79] At night passengers extended hammocks and tried to sleep to the rocking motion of the steamer. Swarms of mosquitoes and other insects accosted them as they approached the marshy entrance of the river.

The wind-powered bongos and piraguas made the journey up the smaller rivers on their way to towns farther inland.[80] During the last decades of the nineteenth century the Bobures, La Ceiba, and Táchira railroads connected the important agricultural areas in the interior and the Andean region with the lake and river ports. Providing access to the Maracaibo hinterland was the sole purpose of these railroads.[81] From Encontrados the journey by train to La Uraca, the terminus of the Táchira Railroad near the Colombian border, took between eight and ten hours. Departing from Encontrados, the train, one traveler from the United States wrote, included "an engine of the vintage of 1880 drawing several freight cars, two second class coaches for natives, and one first class coach, differing from the second class only in that you pay more in it, and that there the company is more select."[82] Other railroad lines in the Andes resembled the Táchira. From Santa Barbara the railroad traversed thirty-seven miles before arriving at El Vigia, from where a pack train of mules reached Mérida in about five days.[83] The Ceiba railroad, covering a distance of about sixty miles, went as far as Motatan. Muleteers and teamsters proved adept at leading as many as ninety animals carrying coffee to the railheads in the interior.[84] "Nothing is more characteristic of the Venezuelan mountain town," observed one traveler, "than the mule trains that constantly come and go on their journeys to and from the out country."[85] Not surprisingly, mules and donkeys remained in short supply throughout the Andes, and teamsters scoured the countryside deep into Colombia for animals in an effort to ensure deliveries.[86] A network of teamsters, muleteers, trains, and lake vessels connected Norte de Santander in Colombia and the Venezuelan Andean region to the communities surrounding the lake.

Political affairs in Zulia, as elsewhere in Venezuela, rested in the hands of a state president appointed by the central government or, after 1908, by Juan Vicente Gómez. What Gómez valued most was loyalty, and he made a practice of moving state presidents around to suit his political interests. Traditional political activity in the state was limited to small circles of powerful groups. State presidents had substantial discretion in political matters but did not always have a free hand.[87] It was not uncommon for interest groups to petition Gómez directly for redress of grievances, completely bypassing the state authorities. Thus there was a certain amount of accommodation and negotiations in the exercise of state and local power. In addition to Maracaibo, the state of Zulia at the turn of the century included eight other districts: Bolívar, Colón, Mara, Miranda, Páez, Perijá, Sucre, and Urdaneta.[88] With broad discretionary power, Jefes Civiles, or political bosses appointed by the state president, oversaw municipal matters.

COMMUNITIES ALONG THE EASTERN LAKESHORE

Colón, Perijá, and Bolívar were the largest districts in the state, but populations in these areas were small because of the difficulties of rural life, the prevalence of tropical diseases, and exploitative labor conditions, including debt peonage and even slavery. Situated a few feet above sea level and facing the constant threat of flooding, most eastern lakeshore communities lived at the mercy of the lake. At the same time they relied on it for fish and fowl, and in some cases for water and irrigation for agriculture. People typically owned land and gained access to water and grazing rights as members of an *ejido* associated with residence in a particular town.[89]

Houses built of bahareque, with dirt floors and straw or palm roofs, served as dwellings for the majority of the population.[90] One foreign traveler to the district described residents' use of "elevated flower and vegetable gardens . . . raised out of the reach of the hogs and goats which run rampant in this part of the country."[91] As in most of rural Venezuela, electric light was nonexistent, and night tended to engulf these communities in almost total darkness. The nearly total absence of illumination gave rise to many popular legends associated with the darkness.[92] Houses had only the most basic of furnishings, and many rooms included a hammock that served for sitting as well as sleeping. The smell of smoke emanating from the woodstoves permeated each house and penetrated the clothing of most residents.[93] Each structure typically included a small corral with an assortment of chickens, pigs, and goats that became central ingredients of the local diet. Subtle variations in housing arrangements belied social differences; those with whitewashed walls appeared only slightly better-off than those with simple earthen adobe walls. Basic services were lacking, and people improvised their own ways of acquiring water and disposing of human and household waste.[94]

Familial or extended social networks connected residents of most eastern lakeshore communities.[95] Typically *fiestas patronales*, or feasts in honor of patron saints such as the Virgen del Rosario, common to the eastern lakeshore, lasted upwards of a week and became reason for a community celebration.[96] Weeks before the event, funds would be collected for the festivities by raffling cows, pigs, or other animals. Decorations would adorn the town square or main street. A priest, who in most cases serviced the entire eastern region, and a traveling band of musicians would reside in the town for the duration of the festivities. A long sermon followed by a procession and dance culminated the week's activities. With the departure of the priest, religious activity in the towns once again revolved around separate lay societies organized for both men and women.[97]

The eastern district of Bolívar had three principal settlements: Santa Rita, the capital; Cabimas; and Lagunillas. Santa Rita had been founded in 1790, and its inhabitants survived by harvesting the abundant crop of coconuts that lined the water's edge, drying the shells, and selling the oil for use in soaps and other personal care products.[98] Residents tended small herds of goats, engaged in subsistence agriculture, fished in the lake, or harvested lumber from nearby forests.[99] Locals also harvested divi-divi seeds for use in the tanneries of Maracaibo. An assortment of piraguas and bongos visited the district's ports and carried these products to sell in Maracaibo, a distance of twenty-one nautical miles.[100] These vessels linked Santa Rita to the other Bolívar communities in the absence of roads.

At Punta Icotea, where the land abruptly jutted into the lake, the town of Cabimas, south of Santa Rita, dated from before the arrival of the Europeans. It drew its name from the copaiba balsam extracted from local trees by the indigenous people and used in paints and porcelains.[101] The Spaniards recorded the presence of Cabimas as early as 1579, and by the first decade of the eighteenth century Capuchin friars had founded a small mission at the site.[102] By 1774 a "Spanish" town with its own civil authority had taken shape at Cabimas, although the population remained small, never exceeding 230.[103] Most residents practiced subsistence agriculture along the lakeshore, harvested copra, fished, and extracted tar (*mene*) from several nearby natural outflows. The tar was used to caulk vessels and fuel lanterns, and even for medicinal purposes.[104] Some residents of Cabimas harvested straw and produced charcoal to sell in Maracaibo.[105] The production of straw had given rise to an artisan industry focused on the fabrication of woven baskets and mats.[106] A small group of merchants traded in these goods both in nearby Trujillo and in Maracaibo. By 1884 its population had increased sufficiently to make Cabimas a municipality, and by 1895 over fifteen hundred people resided there, in some 336 residences.[107] A single dirt street with an assortment of houses dispersed at intervals defined the semi-urban landscape.[108] The town had only one sustainable well, and drinking water during the summer months was a constant concern. The municipality also included La Salina and La Rosa, described by one chronicler as "scarcely a hamlet."[109]

Forty miles from Santa Rita, the town of Lagunillas remained much the same as when the first Europeans found it.[110] Located in a marshy area, it was built on posts (*palafitos*) over the water to escape dangerous vermin and insects. Structures in other lakeshore communities such as San Timoteo and La Ceiba also extended out over the water; an article in *Scientific American* in 1917 confirmed for foreigners what local residents had known for centuries: that this custom provided "freedom from the insect life that makes the shores unbearable."[111] An extensive network of rudimentary wooden walkways connected the houses to each other and to the adjacent mainland. The canoe remained one of the principal forms of transportation.[112] At high tide the adjacent lakeshore became inundated to a distance of three hundred meters, leaving the town isolated over the water.[113] In 1730 the Spaniards renamed the community Nuestra Señora de la Concepción de Lagunillas. Residents relied on fishing and seasonal agriculture for their livelihood. They regularly reported hearing subterranean noises, sounds that may have been occasioned by leaking gas and oil.[114] Geologists believed that the leaks may have caused the earth to settle and allowed the lake water to fill the vacuum.[115] According to local tradition, however, the town had been cursed by a Maracaibo priest who had been run out of Lagunillas by residents for his excessive moralizing during a celebration in honor of a local saint.[116]

At the southern crescent of the lake, Colon and Sucre included some of the most fertile but most isolated regions of the state. In Palmarito locals relied on the yearly migration of thousands of crabs to augment their subsistence. Under an unrelenting tropical sun, others in these districts labored in agriculture, growing plantains, maize, and sugarcane, or after the 1890s worked on the large cattle estates that dominated the southwestern part of the state.[117] Products from this region supplied the needs of Maracaibo and other lake communities.[118] Three navigable rivers—the Catatumbo, the Escalante, and the Zulia—traversed the territory, creating marshes and swamps as they approached the lake. As Peter Linder points out, distance from the principal population centers that surrounded the lake impaired the region's development and hindered access to labor. In 1911 the United Fruit Company considered establishing operations in the area, but it eventually discarded the idea, citing problems with transportation and the lake entrance.[119]

The Central Venezuelan Sugar Company, owned by the family of General Luis F. Paris, was among the region's most important enterprises.[120] In addition to their sugar operations they owned extensive herds of cattle and produced cheese. The company at times resorted to coercive methods to obtain labor for their plantations. Vicencio Pérez Soto, president of the state of Zulia and no friend of labor, contended that landlords such as Paris acted like feudal lords who "paid laborers poorly and treated them even worse." He characterized these actions as veiled slavery and eventually prohibited local authorities from tracking down escaped workers.[121] Other critics contend that many landowners made a habit of raiding nearby Guajiro villages on the peninsula and in Colombia to acquire indigenous laborers by force.[122] As late as 1928 the state government selectively intervened to free laborers who claimed to be working under slave-like conditions. Thus, for instance, in July of that year the state ordered that Ramón Nuñez, an indigenous laborer, be set free from the Hacienda el Milagro in Colón.[123]

THE RACIAL KALEIDOSCOPE

The lake region presented a racial kaleidoscope that included indigenous people, Africans, people of mixed race, and a few self-described blancos, or whites. After the formal abolition of slavery in 1854 Venezuelan authorities ceased to use race as a criterion in the collection of census data. Census records after this date, with some modifications, identified Venezuelans, foreigners, and the indigenous. When describing the indigenous, officials made distinctions between "civilized" (those who lived in established towns, if only minimally under the control of civil authorities) and "uncivilized" (those who remained autonomous). This not only made it difficult to ascertain the racial makeup of the population but also fueled the racial hierarchy that permeated society, in which blancos, or light-skinned people of mixed race, dominated positions of power.

The earliest inhabitants of the lake region were small groups of Arawak agriculturalists who were subsequently overrun by Carib immigrants.[124] Beyond these very broad general classifications, the indigenous groups that inhabited the area included Toas, Zaparas, Onotos, Aliles, Pemones, Bubures, Quiriquires (Kiri Kire), Jirajaras, Wayuu (Guajiros), and Bari (previously known as Motilones).[125] Not all these groups survived the brutality of the conquest, foreign diseases, and the burden of European expansion, and little is known about their cultures and societies. The Guajiros and the Bari survived the colonial period in significant numbers and continued to occupy the region.

The Guajiros inhabited the arid plains of the West and Northwest, extending into Colombia. Although they traditionally lived in a number of established communities on the peninsula that bears their name, they could also be found, either as indebted laborers or as slaves, on the haciendas around the lake. Some, especially women, brought their wares to Maracaibo and participated in the commercial life of the port. The Bari lived in the forest on the southern fringes of the lakeshore and westward toward the Colombian border, and had resisted both European and mestizo incursions into their territory. Occupying the area between Venezuela and Colombia, the Bari's territory defined the nebulous border between the nations. Neither country saw much importance in the region, thus allowing the Bari a degree of autonomy.

Not surprisingly, when discussing the indigenous people government reports and travelers' accounts tended to focus on the Guajiros, in particular on the women's ornate dresses and their custom of painting their faces with assorted colors. One such account, written in 1912 by a geologist from the United States, reported, "We saw a considerable number of Goagira [sic] Indians in the market at Maracaibo. These cousins of the Motilones are much more civilized than the latter—at least they wear clothes—are peaceful and acknowledge the sovereignty of the Venezuelan government."[126] While exoticizing the Guajiros, these accounts tend to deride the Bari as barbaric and uncivilized, "determined isolationist," or "fetters on development."[127] These depictions create a dichotomy between the acceptable indigenous such as the Guajiros, and the largely unacceptable and in some cases exterminable Bari.

As late as 1929 a government report on the Catatumbo region referred to the Bari as "hostile to Venezuela."[128] These stereotypical images, framed by their active resistance, masked the exploitation that indigenous peoples had suffered at the hands of foreign intruders bent on exploiting their labor and their land. The census of 1926 recorded 18,538 persons identified as indigenous, although it is not clear how the numbers were derived and, more important, they did not account for the district of Colon inhabited by the Bari.[129] In fact, in 1922 a United States consular report indicated in typical fashion that the "strength of the semi-savage tribes (Indios bravos) living in remote and unexplored regions was merely estimated by the census agents."[130]

During the prolonged period of Spanish colonial domination, approximately 100,000 enslaved Africans arrived in Venezuela.[131] The first official record of Africans in Maracaibo appears to be from 1604, when a slave ship ran aground in nearby Coro and the slaves were sold in Maracaibo. However, the anthropologist Miguel Acosta Saignes speculates that western Venezuela may have received slaves from Cartagena before this date.[132] Their presence in the port appears to have been constant, although the region did not receive as many enslaved Africans as the central cacao-producing states did.[133] Gibraltar and Bobures in the southern lake region, where cacao production had begun in the seventeenth century, remained the one exception in Zulia.[134] In 1617 the first shipment of enslaved Africans destined for the cacao plantations of Bobures and Gibraltar arrived in Maracaibo.[135] In addition, there is evidence that they were used as sailors aboard vessels plying the waters of Lake Maracaibo.[136]

Independence did not abolish slavery; it simply prohibited the importation of new slaves, which, as Federico Brito Figueroa points out, had already ceased in the final years of the eighteenth century. The beginning of the nineteenth century found only 3,734 legally classified slaves in the province of Maracaibo.[137] This small number of slaves should not obscure the much larger presence of people of African descent in the province of Zulia. Descendants of Africans, whether classified as enslaved, pardos, mulattos, free blacks, or cimarrones, represented 60 percent of the Venezuelan population at the turn of the century, a pattern that to varying degrees found expression throughout the lake region.[138] The wars of independence and the civil wars that followed initiated an exodus of whites and increased the incidence of miscegenation among the Venezuelan peoples.

Scholars such as Federico Brito Figueroa and Miguel Acosta Saignes have concluded that the departure of whites, and increased levels of miscegenation, minimized the ethnic and caste divisions of the Venezuelan population.[139] This conclusion must be understood as reflecting an agenda that minimized internal racial differences while privileging overarching and all-important class contradictions. While social distance may have diminished among the poorer classes, the same cannot be said for the remaining élite population, which clung to its traditional hierarchical views about race. It also does not address the persistence of a racial hierarchy and its influence over broad segments of the population. In fact, Acosta Saignes recognized that economic and political élites, including those of mixed heritage, maintained racist attitudes toward people of color. West Indian migration to mines at El Callao in the state of Bolívar and the southern districts of Zulia during the later decades of the nineteenth century reinforced these views.[140] As it did throughout Latin America, this outlook surfaced repeatedly in various government and élite plans to promote white European migration throughout the twentieth century.[141] Despite apparently differing political views, Venezuelan intellectuals such as Rufino Blanco Fombona, Pedro Arcaya, Alberto Adriani, Laureano Vallenilla Lanz, Arturo Uslar Pietri, and Mariano Picón Salas found common ground in their belief that the country needed to "improve" its racial stock.[142] Yet despite the persistence of marked racial divisions, many in the country continued throughout the twentieth century to promote the myth of Venezuela as a racial democracy. One influential geographer wrote that Venezuela had, without prejudice, "fused its three ethnic types." It had overcome "the restraints of social determinism and the struggle for liberation fomented this fusion."[143]

The idea of a racial democracy came to be encapsulated in the belief that Venezuela's racial makeup could be described as café con leche (coffee with milk). But the question was, How much black coffee and how much white milk? The mix determined the preferred national image, which always privileged lighter skin tones. A dilemma confronts any historian who critically examines this period: although it is relatively easy to find examples of racism in the historical record and judge them by contemporary standards, it is disingenuous to pretend that these beliefs did not shape social interaction, influence government policy, and marginalize entire groups of people. But what is worse is to ignore that racism existed or attempt to explain it as benevolent or simply as a reaction to a foreign presence, as if a purportedly enlightened white social group was forced to grapple with an uneducated and racially inferior rabble over which it needed to exercise control.[144]

Even as late as the 1930s, when other countries in Latin America had inaugurated cultural projects to incorporate, if only perfunctorily, the contributions of indigenous people and Africans to their society, Picón Salas was foremost among those who continued to believe that Venezuela had to transform its racial composition. In a letter to General Isiaís Medida Angarita in which he outlined the problems facing the nation, he argued that it was "necessary to whiten the country, just as Argentina had completely been whitened achieving one of the best races in the world."[145] To avoid the "problems" that Argentina had incurred he proposed developing a security service that would "weed out agitators and anarchists" among the immigrants.[146] Picón Salas was not alone in these views; they were widely shared by intellectuals and members of the emerging middle class who eventually opposed the Gómez regime.

The reservations expressed by élites concerning the Venezuelan racial character paled in comparison with the views articulated about the country by observers from the United States. The way they evaluated Venezuelans was framed by the moral codes, legal sanctions, and racial hierarchical practices operating within their own society. These preconceived notions of race, coupled with the dominant power relations that existed between the United States and Latin America, especially Mexico, influenced their view of Venezuelans. Not surprisingly one report published in the United States in 1924 concluded that "the major proportion of the population is degenerating in its thought, physically, morally, and mentally."[147] The reason for this decline was said to be miscegenation: the "amalgamation of white, negro, and several Indian stocks has tended to mongrelize the race. There is no fixed type, and the mixed unions constantly produce examples of reversions to original types."[148] Obviously this "degeneration" had consequences for the character of the Venezuelan, who was described by one official as "imitative but not inventive:" "He has no originality and [is] generally incapable of abstract thought. He has an exaggerated idea of his own importance. He is volatile and willful. . . . His mental processes are indirect and markedly different from those of the Anglo Saxon. The peons, or common people, are far more honorable than the higher classes."[149]

Venezuelan men received special attention from moralizing consuls and military attachés, who noted a "marked mental arrest on the part of the males, due to sexual indulgence while the organism is immature." Boys who had been very intelligent before maturity, it was reported, often became "stupid afterwards."[150] Of the small groups of élites it was reported that "[the] upper classes have not a single outstanding good trait, unless it is courtesy, and this is superficial only. The future of Venezuela must depend upon the value of the mixed blood, for not in this century, if ever, will there be a preponderance of the white element."[151] Even when referring to élites, officials continued to express an exaggerated preoccupation with purported

African traits. One military attaché commented in 1922 that a trace of "negro blood is to be found, however, in many families of the first class, who are apparently, of the purest Spanish strain."[152] These early views reflected the perspective not only of United States military attachés and diplomats but also echoed the sentiments of many who arrived to work in oil and for whom interracial mixing in Venezuela had "retarded national progress."[153]

Before the advent of the oil industry, development in Venezuela resembled socioeconomic patterns found in most of Latin America. The area was no more advanced or backward than many regions of the continent. Describing Venezuela as primitive betrays a bias toward western ideas and the sort of modernization typically associated with the arrival of the oil industry. This approach fails to consider that traditional or emerging class structures can be readily adapted to suit new economic and political arrangements without fundamentally altering social or power relations. Although the export economy may introduce a new order and way of life, which is incorporated by various groups, it never fully sweeps aside traditional society. Rather it created very distinct social realities and ways of life for different groups of Venezuelans. In sum, as E. Bradford Burns points out, societies can acquire the "veneer of progress" without in fact undergoing a fundamental transformation.[154] The existence of these distinct cultural, racial, and social conditions would continue to be a source of tension as Venezuela entered the era of oil production. Rather than fundamentally alter this reality, oil served to conceal these major contradictions.

At one level, pre-oil Venezuela can be characterized as a halcyon period, a time of relative social calm. In the hands of the Andean strongman Juan Vicente Gómez, a national political apparatus had just begun to consolidate its power over the country. In the East, where trade with Trinidad and other nearby Caribbean islands was the economic motor, Corsican and Venezuelan merchants in the state of Sucre engaged in the export of sugar and cacao. With Maracaibo as its center, most of western Venezuela participated in an active export economy centered on coffee production. A transport system consisting of railroads, teamsters, and a fleet of lakegoing vessels delivered the products of the hinterland to the port of Maracaibo and from there to markets in the Caribbean, the United States, and Europe. A merchant class composed of both Venezuelans and Germans benefited from these activities. Likewise, in the Andes a small élite composed of Venezuelans and recent Italian immigrants had monopolized the bulk of the fertile coffee-producing lands. The majority of the population continued to depend on agriculture for subsistence. Over the course of the nineteenth century, Venezuelan society had generated social, racial, and political relations which the emerging oil economy would have to alter, or with which it would have to contend or coexist.

CHAPTER 2

The Search for Black Gold

Oil has been present in Venezuela from time immemorial. Along Lake Maracaibo indigenous people used the tar that bubbled to the surface to waterproof their roofs, seal baskets, caulk their boats, light torches, trap animals, and in some cases cure various ailments. In the East campesinos extracted tar and heavy crude from huge lakes for similar purposes. The first confirmed export of oil occurred in April 1539, when Francisco de Castellanos, treasurer of Nueva Cadiz, sent a barrel of oil to the king of Spain as a sample.[1] Allegedly the Spanish monarch used the oil as an ointment to alleviate the gout from which he suffered.[2]

By 1914 Mene Grande was the first commercially viable oilfield operated by a foreign company, the Caribbean Petroleum Company, which eventually became part of the vast Shell conglomerate. Located inland of the southeastern shore of Lake Maracaibo, it was relatively isolated and therefore had a limited impact on local society. Nonetheless the process begun at Mene Grande set in motion profound changes throughout the country. Nearly a decade passed between the beginning of operations at Mene Grande and the next important stage in the development of the Venezuelan oil industry, the discovery of the Barroso no. 2 well at La Rosa in December 1922. This lapse in time underscores that the expansion of the oil industry in Venezuela was not an uninterrupted process. Rather, the industry regularly expanded and contracted with the vicissitudes of the international oil market, world conflicts, restrictive laws imposed by importing countries, and the complicated nexus of politics, society, and labor relations. These conditions led to the dramatic expansion of the industry and its contraction in the months preceding the Great Depression, when crude prices dropped 30 percent and the companies implemented concerted policies to curtail production.[3] The industry did not recover from this contraction until the mid-1930s.[4]

The developments at Mene Grande had their strongest impact on Maracaibo, where companies from the United States and Europe established their headquarters, and foreigners and Venezuelans came in search of work. The presence of the oil industry not only altered the urban landscape but also produced shifts in power relations, displacing the old merchant class and bringing about the rise of new social actors linked to the emerging oil economy. The internationalization of the city also introduced a myriad of new social practices ranging from diet and language to recreation and dress. As hundreds of males, either single or temporarily unattached, descended on the city, there was a marked expansion of the sex trade and the exploitation of women. And the presence of relatively well-paid oil workers produced a dramatic increase in the cost of living, worsening conditions for the average resident.

THE EARLY YEARS

Throughout Venezuela during the late nineteenth century, speculators had acquired concessions to produce oil but never undertook large-scale commercial production. Formal oil production did not begin until 1878, when Antonio Manuel Pulido, who owned a coffee hacienda named La Alquitrana in Táchira, uncovered oil seeps on his property. With several partners he formed the Compañía Petrolia del Táchira, and one of his associates traveled to Pennsylvania to purchase a derrick and other equipment to extract the oil. The rig arrived at Maracaibo, and muleteers transported it over the mountains to the well site.[5] Efforts to use the equipment proved disastrous, however, and Pulido soon discarded it.[6] He and his allies nonetheless initiated production, but this had little long-term effect on the development of the oil industry. Their well produced fewer than sixty barrels a day, barely enough to supply the household needs of local residents and nearby Cúcuta. Despite the meager production of the site, the literature on oil in Venezuela tends to include accounts of it, as if to establish the precedent of Venezuelan participation in the oil industry before the arrival of firms from Europe and the United States. At first glance the output of the Compañía Petrolia may not seem to merit much attention. However, the foreigner's penchant for claiming to be the first in exploring, drilling, and activating the oil industry establishes the context for the frustration felt by many Venezuelans. In the words of Efraín E. Barberii, "Petrolia has the merit of having been the first Venezuelan petroleum enterprise, created and administered by Venezuelans."[7] In a country where foreigners dominated oil production and Venezuelans found themselves excluded from positions of power, Pulido's activities and those of Petrolia de Táchira highlighted Venezuelans' role in developing their oil economy.

Shortly before the turn of the century there were other commercial ventures. After several desultory attempts and various owners, in the late 1880s the New York and Bermúdez Company set up operations atop the immense Guanoco asphalt lake in the state of Sucre.[8] This site resembled the Pitch Lake operated since the 1840s in neighboring Trinidad by economic interests from Britain and then the United States. The dense tropical forest complicated access to the deposits, and the company relied on the local caños, or tributaries, of the San Juan River to gain entry to the site.[9] Along these waterways the company transported heavy equipment from Trinidad, including a railroad engine, track, derricks, and the other materials needed to begin operations. A handful of managers and geologists from the United States grudgingly oversaw operations. Upon seeing Guanoco for the first time, one manager remarked, "Of all the Godforsaken places I ever saw, this was the worst, and it sure made newcomers feel like going back to the States."[10] Efforts to attract their families proved even less successful. One woman who came with her husband expressed culture shock and reported that their first impression of the "little native village lying on a hill side with only thatched roof, no streets, and an air of squalor" was "too much for the other bride" who arrived with her: she put her head on the woman's shoulder and wept.[11] The company recruited West Indian supervisors to direct Venezuelan laborers in the asphalt fields. In the oppressive heat of the tropical rainforest, the New York and Bermúdez Company employed about two hundred workers at Guanoco. Crews consisting of about thirty workers carved out blocks of tar weighing up to seventy-five pounds and deposited them in railroad cars for delivery to the docks for export.[12] A nearly perpetual rainy season, producing upwards of eighty-five inches of rain a year, severely hampered operations.[13]

A small settlement evolved at Guanoco, but its inaccessibility limited its impact on the region. Nonetheless its reputation spread in oil circles, and occasionally foreign tourists, including the camp manager's family members now residing in Trinidad, visited the site. The United States became the primary recipient of the oil and tar from this field. A dynamite explosion leveled most of the camp in 1911, and the company gradually rebuilt the facilities. The camp experienced a boom during the First World War, exporting 45,000 tons of asphalt.[14] The near total isolation of the site, the dense vegetation, the omnipresent tropical diseases, and the heavy weight of the crude increased the cost of extractive operations. Perpetual legal battles over the concession and accusations of political intrigue dogged the company, and although it continued production for several years the site was eventually abandoned. The difficulties confronting the New York and Bermúdez Company were a harbinger of those that oil companies would encounter throughout Venezuela. Although Guanoco did not fully meet investors' expectations, the experience alerted foreign oil companies to the potential that existed in Venezuela and especially to the existence of oil deposits in the eastern states of Monagas and Anzoategui. It also served as an example of the complex and at times thorny relations that might develop between the government and the companies.

Throughout the early twentieth century the Venezuelan government of Cipriano Castro granted several small concessions to Venezuelans and foreigners for the production of asphalt.[15] Since oil was not yet a proven export, most early concessions sought to extract asphalt and were only later expanded to include oil production. In 1907 the government granted four Venezuelans—Andrés Vigas, Bernabé Planas, Antonio Aranguren, and Francisco Jiménez Arráiz—concessions in excess of four million hectares in the states of Zulia, Falcón, and Lara.[16] In a pattern repeated throughout Latin America, by 1913 the concessions granted to Vigas and Aranguren as well as Rafael Max Valladares (in 1910 and 1912), initially obtained by Venezuelans with little or no capital to fund operations, had been transferred to foreign interests, in particular the newly formed Colón Development Company, the Venezuelan Oil Concessions (VOC), and the Caribbean Petroleum Company, all of which eventually became subsidiaries of Shell Oil. The concession that Valladares obtained on 2 January 1912 was sold two days later to Shell interests.[17] Two concessions eluded the Shell juggernaut:

the North Venezuelan Petroleum Company obtained the Planas grant and British Controlled Oil Fields obtained that of Jiménez Arráiz.[18] By 1913 European oil interests had acquired control of the vast majority of Venezuela's oil fields. Firms based in the United States, with their operations centered in Mexico, had been excluded from this initial phase. Castro has been attacked as an inept traitor by traditional political leaders such as Rómulo Betancourt, founder of Acción Democrática, and defended by many on the left as an early nationalist.[19] More recently the government of Hugo Chávez has called for a reinterpretation of Castro and other nineteenth-century figures. As Edwin Lieuwen points out, the contracts negotiated by the Castro administration "were more favorable to the government than [those] in Mexico, where the entire national domain was being alienated."[20] Castro's legacy has therefore been interpreted in terms not of the policies that he pursued but of the way his actions served contemporary political interests.

Historical debates aside, by 1911 scores of foreign geologists were feverishly surveying the land acquired in these various concessions. Among these, Ralph Arnold, with extensive experience in mapping sites from South Africa to California, oversaw a team of over fifty-two geologists that crisscrossed Venezuela. Although most members of the survey crew were from the United States or Europe, it included the Venezuelans Santiago E. and Pedro Ignacio Aguerrevere, who eventually graduated respectively from Stanford University and the Colorado School of Mines. From the perspective of many on the team, the geologists encountered two imposing obstacles, the physical environment and the assumed "backward" nature of the Venezuelan people. The reports that they wrote and later published as *The First Big Oil Hunt* depict an epic mission by the West against the tropical rain forest and a purportedly "primitive" society that did not yet comprehend the value of the wealth it possessed. Whether in Venezuela, Mexico, or the Middle East, this theme reemerges repeatedly in geologists' and oil company publications. In the end, according to this perspective, both the environment and the people had to be transformed in order to extract the oil and provide this valuable product to western society.

At Guanoco, besides describing the geological formations they encountered, the team also felt compelled to describe the people as "the worst group in Venezuela, made up largely of Negro escapees from Trinidad, Venezuelan undesirables waiting opportunity to escape to Trinidad, and occasional beachcombers always thirsty for liquor."[21] In addition to revealing their own biases, these descriptions provide insight into the tensions that emerged between foreigners and the multiracial Venezuelan population. Arnold doubled as something of an entrepreneur, taking detailed photographs of the flora, fauna, and people he encountered and offering these for sale in the United States.[22] Trinidad, still a British colony and the de facto regional headquarters for European oil interests, was a staging area for English-speaking geologists. Despite its multiracial composition (something that Arnold immediately noted), Trinidad was an English-speaking island that afforded foreigners a "refuge" from the unfamiliar Latin American culture they encountered on the mainland.[23] For many expatriates from Britain and the United States working in eastern Venezuela, Trinidad would continue to serve this function, as did Curaçao for those in the Lake Maracaibo region.

Contracted by John Mack, president of the General Asphalt Company of Philadelphia, which had acquired control of the New York and Bermúdez Company, Arnold reported that he was instructed to "find oil and bring it out of the ground" and "to discover and lay claim to every single piece of potential oil land in Venezuela."[24] The Venezuelan minister of development, Pedro Emilio Coll, took note of the foreign geologists' activities. His report to Congress in 1913 captured a prevailing sense of anticipation that oil would eventually provide an alternative source of income for the Venezuelan state. Coll said that he hoped to report in a few days "on a new source of income that shortly will be of major importance. Oil . . . that sought-after source of fuel . . . has ceased to be a treasure hidden in the bowels of the Venezuelan earth."[25]

With oil companies in fierce competition and a timetable established by the government for initiating operations, time was of the essence. Arnold's team amassed a wealth of information about conditions in Venezuela, pinpointing sites for immediate drilling and tracts to be claimed for future development. Eventually the General Asphalt Company lost its bid to produce oil, and later Shell acquired a controlling interest in the company and its Caribbean subsidiary. Despite extensive geological surveys, in the end the oil companies selected the eastern shore of Lake Maracaibo, where natural oil seeps dotted the landscape, and the area in eastern Venezuela encompassed by the Guanoco tar fields. Geologists for the Standard Oil Company of New Jersey described Mene Grande as the "largest area of oil seepage in the world."[26] George A. Macready, a geologist on the Arnold team, reported that "all the areas selected were made on geological examinations without the aid of drilling any well."[27] In the end the foreign experts recommended drilling on sites known for generations to the local indigenous and rural Venezuelan population.

MENE GRANDE

In 1913 General Asphalt began drilling at the Guanoco site. Bababui no. 1 became its first producing well, initially generating a hundred barrels of crude "so thick and heavy it could hardly be pumped."[28] This well launched the industry's transition from asphalt to oil production. Drilling operations soon followed on the Maracaibo lakeshore and inland at Mene Grande, in the present-day Baralt district. Arnold's crew had been favorably impressed by the site, reporting that the asphalt deposits were larger than any they had seen except for those at Trinidad and Guanoco.[29] Both the indigenous people and the Spaniards had commented on the abundant oil seeps in the vicinity of Mene Grande and nearby Misoa.[30]

Mene Grande, 120 kilometers southeast of Maracaibo, lies between the marshy lakefront and the tropical forest that enshrouds the slopes of the Andes. The site resembled a low mesa with scattered shrubs and small trees amid broad savannas.[31] In a pattern repeated throughout Venezuela, Caribbean began operating without obtaining formal ownership of the land. Given that the land had little or no previous value and boundaries were ambiguous, land titles throughout Venezuela were frequently in dispute, and the company exploited these conditions to its benefit. When a Venezuelan rancher named Clemente demanded that the company compensate him for the use of his land at Mene Grande, it responded, "If the limits of property were ever clearly defined . . . we would be glad to treat with him."[32] When disputes of this kind arose, the company naturally expected local government officials to intercede and support their actions.

Land title notwithstanding, near one of the seeps Caribbean's crews erected a rustic wooden cabria, or derrick, with a shed attached to house the equipment. Although controlled by British and Dutch interests, the company employed mostly oilmen from the United States to perform skilled occupations. It christened the well Zumaque no. 1 and began drilling in January 1914. The Star boiler employed on the rig was a constant source of concern for the company, which was afraid to use it near escaping gas.[33] Despite this danger, the crew completed exploratory drilling by April of that year, yielding, according to the United States consul in Caracas, ten barrels a day. Resentful of this success, the consul described the British as an invading army reaping profits in Venezuela.[34] On 31 July Venezuelan and United States operators of Zumaque no. 1 struck larger deposits of oil, and Venezuela entered a new era of commercial oil production.[35] Caribbean reportedly spent 17,733.47 bolívares before Zumaque no. 1 began to produce crude, and the cost of labor accounted for only a small fraction of the expenses incurred. During the course of the drilling the superintendent received 688.50 bolívares, the drillers and tool pushers 2,074.93, those employed under the category of general labor 198.15, and labor helpers 340.07, for a total of 3,301.65. Machinery, lumber, transportation, and living expenses accounted for the remainder of the well's costs.[36] For a well that consistently produced for over fifty years and sparked the discovery of a field that generated over 641 million barrels of oil, the costs were low by any standard.[37]

Remote from any significant population center, Mene Grande posed multiple challenges to the company. The region had no formal system of roads and relied primarily on waterways for transporting goods.[38] Supplies and machinery had to be imported from the United States and Europe and transferred in Curaçao to smaller freighters that could navigate the entrance to the lake; ships had to traverse the Maracaibo bar during daylight or risk running aground.[39] After clearing customs in Maracaibo, the materials were carried across the lake in small boats. Besides San Timoteo, which linked the lake region to Carora in the state of Lara, no formal ports existed where materials could be easily unloaded. To compensate for this situation, San Timoteo and the adjacent San Lorenzo and Motatan del Lago became a staging area for supplies arriving from Maracaibo. At first equipment and passengers left Maracaibo at midnight and arrived at San Timoteo or Motatan del Lago the following morning. With scarcely two streets, and a small church named in honor of San Benito, a popular Afro-Venezuelan saint, Motatan del Lago was the principal transit point for goods destined for Mene Grande.[40] Heavy equipment such as boilers had to be transferred onto flatbed wagons pulled by oxen or loaded onto mules to make the arduous journey. Caribbean's transportation department consisted of seven horses, thirty-four mules, 175 burros and seventy-two oxen.[41] The road, which at times disappeared into a swamp, was a constant challenge to teamsters and other travelers with heavy equipment.[42] As ballast, schooners arriving from Maracaibo carried rock and sand that the company used to fill in the coastal marsh and nearby streams.[43] Lighter materials might be reassigned to bongos or pole-driven flat-bottomed boats that took two days to make their way up the Motatan River to a place known as Motatan del Río, where the company kept an office.[44] From there they would be carried inland by bullocks, mules, or men.[45] The precarious dirt trails that led to the site became virtually impassable when it rained. Ironically, the oil industry whose fuel propelled the development of modern transportation and industry began by relying on animals and human porters to launch its own inauspicious beginnings.

At Mene Grande, Howard F. Nash, a recent Stanford graduate who spoke some Spanish, was at the outset the de facto superintendent and physician for a small crew of drillers and tool pushers from the United States, and Venezuelan laborers. He was subsequently replaced by Jack Stokes, also from California, and Roy Merritt, who "tended to engineering and liaison details with the Venezuelans because he spoke Spanish fluently."[46] The establishment of Mene Grande had the misfortune of paralleling the advent of hostilities in Europe, which severely limited access to foreign supplies and equipment. Moreover, to undertake and expand operations the company needed to secure a dependable labor force. The view that the discovery of oil at Mene Grande in 1914 immediately sparked a massive migration to the oil area is simply not sustained by the historical record.[47] News of the discovery of oil at Mene Grande filtered out only slowly to the surrounding communities. More important, people throughout the region had no experience with what employment in the oil industry might entail and therefore did not suddenly flood Mene Grande. The sparse population of the eastern lakeshore also contributed to the labor scarcity. To overcome these challenges, camp bosses from the United States relied on local political officials whom they referred to as the *Jefes Grandes* to recruit some two hundred workers.[48]

Among those drawn to Mene Grande was Luis Segundo Petit. Born in San Francisco in the state of Lara, in an area linked economically and socially to San Timoteo and the lake region, Petit had been working on a local farm when the news that foreigners were seeking laborers at Mene Grande reached him. He left for Mene Grande, arriving there in July and becoming part of the crew working on Zumaque no. 1. The oil camp, with the Cerro Estrella at the center, reminded him of an Indian rancheria.[49] Other early laborers included Petit's brother Samuel, Eusebio Sandrea from the lake port of Altagracia, and Joaquín Cardozo from nearby San Lorenzo.[50] From its inception, a few Afro–West Indians contracted on their home islands, primarily Trinidad and Curaçao, worked at Mene Grande side by side with the Venezuelans. Samuel Smith, a native of Curaçao, was among the first of them.[51] With only rudimentary tools at their disposal, Petit, Smith, and a small number of Venezuelan laborers cleared the dense brush, built rudimentary shelters, erected derricks, and fashioned earthen levees to store the oil produced by the wells. Other crews assumed responsibility for scouring the countryside for wood to power the boilers and kitchen stoves. Securing food became a full-time occupation for the camp. To supply vegetables, raised gardens were constructed to prevent foraging by animals. The company later brought in several Italian farmers and set up a produce operation and a small cattle ranch near the camp.[52]

Establishing a settlement was essential to the success of operations at Mene Grande. As Lewis Proctor, president of Caribbean, put it: "Our work in Venezuela has been located in uninhabited and wild sections of the country; almost the first requirement for the starting of any development work is arranging for the housing of our employees."[53] The first foreigners lived in primitive wooden structures with thatched roofs or canvas tents. Accommodations for the Venezuelan labor force proved even more rudimentary: hammocks were strung from polls in open-air structures, circular or rectangular, with thatched straw roofs, and workers kept their belongings in satchels or makeshift boxes on the dirt floor. At first acquiring food was a haphazard enterprise. To standardize the process, the company built and maintained a common mess hall that served daily meals to all workers. In this early phase little distinction existed between work conditions for Venezuelans and for foreigners. Petit remembers that the "jefes gringos. . . . worked without shirts, in typical llanero [plainsman] fashion in the suffocating heat."[54] As the camp evolved, this situation gradually changed, becoming a recurring source of tension between Venezuelans and foreigners.

The population and the requirements of production quickly diminished the existing water supply. To provide the town, the company built water facilities and pumping plants on several nearby streams and rivers.[55] Open-air latrines and the outdoors became common deposits of human waste and had to be regulated. Moreover, at both Mene Grande and San Lorenzo the marshlike conditions were a perfect breeding ground for malaria-carrying mosquitoes and for a multitude of other tropical ailments. Company officials appeared to have been distressed about the swarms of mosquitoes that inhabited the area, but more than this it was distrust of the ability of the Venezuelan labor force that framed company concerns. A report from early in 1915 reads, "All the men who were employed by us on this work were laid up with malaria. Although a few men were kept at work under native foremen, it was not thought wise to depend upon the native foremen to handle a large gang of men."[56] The company apparently worried about the ability of Venezuelan supervisors to oversee their fellow countrymen, preferring to rely on foreigners for this task.

Certain policies to improve sanitation, including the elimination of standing water and marshes, benefited the entire community. Other measures, however, continued to underscore the disparate treatment afforded to foreign and local labor. Foreigners who became ill with malaria or other ailments would regularly be sent to Curaçao to recuperate.[57] Venezuelans had no such option and either suffered with their illness or, in the worst of cases, succumbed to it. The newspaper publisher and social critic Bracho Montiel lamented that the homes of foreigners did not appear to suffer from mosquito attacks, since, after all, "mosquitoes were Venezuelan; it was the local's burden to bear."[58]

Montiel's mocking comments referred to company efforts to build what they called "mosquito-proof houses" for their foreign staff and to drain the pools of standing water that contributed to these maladies. Constructed with lumber imported from the United States and covered with screen meshes, the first structures at Mene Grande included separate sleeping facilities for two, office space, and a mess hall where the men took their meals. In reality the sleeping quarters were shared space with little privacy, used by alternating crews that worked different shifts. The arrangement soon proved untenable, since the noise from the mess hall made it impossible for crews to sleep. Eventually Caribbean found it necessary to build separate structures for drillers who worked different shifts.

Successful production from the Zumaque no. 1 well accelerated the pace of activity and increased Venezuelan migration to the area. Housing for Venezuelans continued to develop haphazardly, and many locals brought their families with them, with the result that next to the company facilities there arose, in the words of the camp superintendent, "quite a thriving native village with little stores that carried provisions, peon clothing, rum and beer."[59] Bars and other such establishments collected along Lara Street (named after the state from which many of the arriving laborers came). When the Zumaque no. 1 well entered production in July, Venezuelans and foreigners alike celebrated in these makeshift bars.[60]

Resolving the issue of transportation was central to the success of operations at Mene Grande. With more wells now under production, in 1916 the company decided to build a railroad and two parallel six-inch pipelines to the nearby indigenous town of San Lorenzo de Agua, significantly reducing the distance between Mene Grande and the outside world. The narrow-gauge line, with flat supply platforms and open-air passenger cars covered by canvas, resembled a long wagon train as it slowly rumbled from the coast to Mene Grande. A telephone line followed the rail line to San Lorenzo.[61] At the same time the company proceeded with the construction of a small refinery at San Lorenzo that had a capacity of two thousand barrels a day.[62] Iván Salazar recalled that a jubilant, Spanish-tinged "okay" rang out over the telephone line to indicate that oil from Mene Grande had reached San Lorenzo, marking the completion of the project. For storage the company built tanks that could hold 55,000 barrels of oil at San Lorenzo. It also operated a factory to produce metal containers to hold the refined oil. From the port, rudimentary wooden barges pulled by tugboats took the unrefined crude to nearby Curaçao, where the company had constructed refining and storage facilities.[63]

As the war in Europe waned and more wells began producing, operations at Mene Grande acquired a degree of permanence. In 1917, with a number of wells under production, Caribbean employed an average of 54 foreigners and 495 Venezuelans.[64] Four years later, in 1921, these figures were 83 and 991.[65] The category of "foreigners," presumably from the United States, Britain, and the Netherlands, was rather amorphous, also including significant numbers of West Indians and even Chinese from the Caribbean islands under British and Dutch control. At first most company records, either by omission or intentionally, failed to disaggregate the nationalities of their foreign employees. Venezuelan census records also do not clarify the matter, since they included only such broad terms as "British" and "Dutch." This issue inevitably became politically charged as increasing numbers of Venezuelans sought employment in the oilfields.

The nine hundred Venezuelans listed on company and government records as "peons" earned on average five bolívares a day, while others employed as artisans, technicians, and doctors could earn as much as fifty bolívares a day.[66] In comparison, the average wage of laborers was "three to four bolívares a day in the interior and about 25 percent less in the plains and the Andes."[67] Paid daily, workers could be easily dismissed if production slowed or if the company lacked supplies. In fact, employment during the course of 1921 fluctuated widely, from 745 in January to 1,288 in October.

With the dramatic growth of population and a significant labor force in its employ, Caribbean contemplated building a residential oil camp with distinctive housing areas for its Venezuelan and foreign laborers. First it sought to demolish the "native village" that had taken root adjacent to its facilities and now housed close to two thousand people.[68] This matter became a source of some dispute, and although it claimed to own the land, the company considered it best to "purchase" the houses from the Venezuelans and erect a new village some distance away.[69] These plans never materialized, since they would have seriously disrupted the lives of their employees: "so many laborers in addition to those previously employed in Mene Grande were required for extended operations it was not possible to dispense with the old village which it had been planned to demolish as the workmen had to have some place to sleep."[70] This decision reflects the company's awareness that it was advantageous to have a large reserve of unemployed laborers who could quickly be hired as conditions changed and who would help to reduce pressure on wages and undermine efforts at labor organizing. This pattern was replicated throughout the emerging oilfields even after company access to materials and production patterns became somewhat regularized and fields appeared to be in full production. Besides company policy, industry employment patterns were subject to the vicissitudes of the international oil market and political decisions in Europe and the United States.

Rather than destroy the established Venezuelan village, the company proceeded to build a "new village." The facilities at Mene Grande were a prototype for the many residential enclaves that would subsequently take shape in the Venezuelan rural landscape. As they evolved, the areas of the camp took on distinctive names; the first twenty houses that the company built became known as Las Veinte. Others followed, becoming known as Las Ochenta y Seis and La Cincuenta. After having acquired some stability, the neighborhoods received formal names: Las Veinte became Buenos Aires, Las Ochenta y Seis became Campo Alegria, and Las Cincuenta became Las Delicias.[71] The predominance of workers from Carora in Lara gave the camp a distinctive regional character, and by 1926 one section of the camp had become known among locals as Carorita.[72] Aquiles Ferrer, a laborer at Mene Grande, recalled that at first only skilled employees resided in these new facilities: common laborers continued to live in the old village in structures made of bahareque and thatch.[73]

In keeping with its policy of separate housing for foreign employees, the company built its senior staff residences on the slopes of the Cerro Estrella, now called Star Hill by the English-speaking population.[74] Cerro Estrella had been selected because the slight elevation provided access to a gentle breeze that effectively reduced the stifling tropical temperatures.[75] Beyond these, at a site called "Hollywood" by the foreigners, houses were constructed for the drillers.[76] With a panoramic view of the landscape below, expatriates from Britain and the United States congregated after work at the Star Hill Club to play cards, drink, and listen to music.[77] By 1922 Venezuelans and West Indians also had options; for distraction they could congregate in the bars along Lara Street, or frequent the new employee "club" built by the company, which included billiard tables and a film projector. In his report the minister of development, Antonio Alamo, alleged that the company had done a lot for "the peones."[78] Though at first there were minimal differences in working conditions and living arrangements between foreigners and Venezuelans, by the 1920s important distinctions had emerged as the formal residential oil camp took shape. Reflecting the prominent social and physical distinctions that now existed between the residential enclaves and broader society, one worker barred from the camp wrote on his suitcase, "Expelled from Mene Grande headed back to Venezuela."[79] Even during the early phase of the industry, differences in housing accommodations and wages were becoming palpable. Symbolically two Venezuelas were now evident, one which had existed before the advent of oil and the other defined by the industry.

The impact of the war in Europe and Mene Grande's continued isolation and limited size combined to forestall fundamental alterations of the social and economic dynamics of western Venezuela. Waves of Venezuelans and foreigners did not immediately descend on the oil camps. Information concerning the discovery of oil in 1914 spread gradually, by word of mouth through existing social and economic networks. Nor did Mene Grande spur an immediate oil boom in the region. As the anonymous author of *Venezuela and the Oil Pioneers* put it, "from 1919 until almost the end of 1922, not a well was drilled in Venezuela that fulfilled the country's geological promise."[80] Rather, exploration continued at a relatively unimpressive pace; between 1915 and 1916 the Colón Development Company struck oil at Las Cruces and later at its Tarra field in the homeland of the Bari near the Colombian border. British Controlled Oilfields began production at its lucrative El Mene concession. As 1917 came to an end, Venezuela was still exporting more asphalt than oil, and most Venezuelans, even in the Lake Maracaibo region, continued to rely on agriculture for subsistence.[81] The government's own reports seldom mentioned oil exports during this early period. Limited access to a tanker fleet and storage facilities hampered production, and most exploration and drilling sites operated with skeleton crews.

Although the war in Europe limited access to materials and curtailed markets, with the completion of the production site at Mene Grande and the refining and storage facilities at San Lorenzo, Venezuela had turned an important page in the development of its oil industry. As Germán Carrera Damas points out, oil spurred the movement of people and led to the formation of cities "frozen since the end of the eighteenth century."[82] The future remained uncertain, but developments were under way that would fundamentally alter the environment and the way of life of thousands of Venezuelans. By 1919 many observers believed that Venezuela was on the verge of a major discovery. Writing in the *Pan American Magazine*, the Protestant missionary leader and later diplomat Samuel Guy Inman asserted that "one of the world's largest oil fields would shortly be opened in Venezuela."[83] In 1922 a publication issued by Standard Oil assessed the development of the preceding decade and attempted to capture the sense of the approaching changes that foreigners expected. Capturing the racist sentiment of the day, it insisted that "neither the rigors of frowning nature nor the hostility of an irreconcilable native race can stay the forward march of industry, and already the walls of Jericho have been encompassed with the sound of trumpets and her defenses are crumbling with decay."[84] According to Standard, Venezuelans would, willingly or not, be expected to conform to the changes provoked by the oil industry.

THE BOLÍVAR COASTAL FIELD

With the end of the war, buoyed by their success at Mene Grande, the Caribbean Petroleum Company, the Colón Development Company, and VOC, by now all subsidiaries of the emerging Shell Oil conglomerate forged by Henri Deterding, expanded their drilling operations in the Lake Maracaibo region. In his classic novel *Mene*, Ramón Díaz Sanchez captured the arrival of foreigners in the Punta Icotea area on the eastern shore of the lake. Residents who observed the arrival of a Venezuelan warship initially feared that they would be fired upon. Instead "blond men" whom the Venezuelans called *musiúes*, dressed in khaki and carrying strange equipment, disembarked at La Rosa. At first the locals confused the new arrivals with the Germans who had traditionally sought to acquire copra there.[85] Whereas the Germans had produced no lasting impact on the areas where they visited, these foreigners did not leave; they settled on the outskirts of town and began drilling operations, forever changing the character of this once bucolic landscape.

The Shell subsidiaries succeeded in finding minor deposits on the eastern shore of Lake Maracaibo, but nothing that matched their earlier strikes in Mene Grande. In early 1917, however, VOC drilled at the site that would mark the next important turning point in the industry, the Bolívar Coastal field stretching from Punta Icotea in the North to Bachaquero in the South.[86] VOC's Santa Barbara no. 2 well produced upwards of 125 barrels a day.[87] Prompted by this early success, VOC went on to bore test wells near La Rosa, on the outskirts of Cabimas, and at the site of the Barroso no. 2, abandoning it as a dry well after reaching nine hundred feet.[88] As it resumed operations, the company hired sixty-nine workers, sixty-two of them Venezuelans.[89] Since no accommodations existed, it built a long house for its Venezuelan employees. This rustic structure had a rear wall, a thatched palm roof, and an open-air front covered with a screen mesh to lessen the tropical heat and, ostensibly, keep out the mosquitoes. To store the oil it erected a 55,000-barrel metal tank and a 250-barrel wooden structure.[90] A small pier carrying a narrow-gauge rail line extended out into the lake for loading and unloading supplies arriving from Maracaibo.

In July 1922 VOC revisited the abandoned wells at La Rosa. Crews at the Barroso no. 2, less than a mile from the lakeshore, decided to drill deeper into the earth's crust. By the first week of December they had attained a depth of 1,450 feet. At approximately 6:00 a.m. on 14 December they passed 1,500 feet, and the well began to flow at about two thousand barrels a day. The crew, unprepared for this occurrence, had failed to place a gate valve to control the flow of oil. As one driller at the site indicated, the "Maracaibo office had figured that they'd go down as far as 2,300 feet, so that at 1,400 they hadn't cemented in the casing."[91] In the early hours of the morning the ground shook and the well made a noise that "sounded like the passage of a thousand freight trains."[92] Working on the rig, Samuel Smith, who had earlier been at Mene Grande, remembers hearing the sound of thunder and seeking cover to avoid the rocks and other debris that descended on the laborers from all directions.[93] Another witness recalled, "with a roar that froze the blood, oil leaped from the well in a spout that towered 200 feet above the derrick and fanned out in the air like a titan's umbrella."[94] As news of the event reached the state capital, residents of Maracaibo reported seeing the gusher from their rooftops.[95] Flowing now at the rate of 100,000 barrels a day, oil saturated not only the crew but the entire town of La Rosa; it "covered the trees, coated the vines and in ever-growing streams flowed through the underbrush like black serpents."[96] Residents as far away as three kilometers reported oil splattering on their houses. Oil soon impregnated nearly everything in the vicinity of the gusher and blackened the waters of the lake.

VOC found itself with insufficient storage facilities and labor to contain the ever-expanding flow. It radioed headquarters in Maracaibo, which hurriedly summoned employees from as far away as Mene Grande, and more than five hundred were hired from La Rosa and Cabimas.[97] Equipment, including picks and shovels, was purchased at hardware stores in Maracaibo. Still short of personnel, the labor boss Felipe Scott sent crews to recruit laborers in Carora in the State of Lara and in nearby Andean communities, beginning a process of migration that would have long-term repercussions; in total voc hired over a thousand people.[98] At breakneck speed, workers dug earthen canals and vast open-air reservoirs to collect the oil before it reached the lakeshore.[99] Amid the intense furor that followed, a local priest declared that the company had drilled into the bowels of Hell.[100] Local adherents of San Benito approached Fred Brack, the superintendent of operations for the well. Along the lake region San Benito is venerated from 27 December to 6 January. The San Beniteros (devotees of San Benito) wanted permission to stage a ceremony at the well site and pray to San Benito to close the well. Brack scoffed at their request, insisting they would all perish in the attempt. Nonetheless, on the night of 22 December, led by a devotee of San Benito, a Mr. Arrieta, eight drummers and local faithful marched to the site of the well with an image of the saint. They stopped short of the well, erected the statue, and bathed the saint in crude. While the adherents of San Benito played drums, others prayed for an end to the calamity. Shortly thereafter the well collapsed on itself and shut down.[101] Brack was ecstatic and voc paid for a public celebration in Santa Rosa to honor the San Beniteros.[102] voc officials estimated that the well had spewed over 800,000 barrels of oil in nine days; the company managed to recover only about 350,000 barrels. Jack Lavin, an employee of Creole Petroleum Company, summed up the excitement, noting that with the Barroso, or el Chorro as most people called it, "the petroleum fever, the dance of millions had commenced."[103] Another Venezuelan writer commented that the much-sought El Dorado had finally been found.[104]

The massive eruption of Barroso no. 2 captured the attention of the nation and the world. The United States consul in Maracaibo reported on the event and sent pictures of the erupting well to Washington, lamenting that a European and not a United States company had made the discovery.[105] In contrast to the relative silence that had greeted the discovery at Mene Grande six years earlier, trade journals in Venezuela and newspapers in the United States enthusiastically publicized the developments at La Rosa. The *New York Times* described it as the most productive well in the world.[106] Citing the same source—Alfred Olavaria, the Venezuelan consul in New Orleans—the *London Times* also reported on the oil well at La Rosa, which it said was producing 120,000 barrels a day.[107] The *Lamp*, a Standard Oil publication, indicated that the center of gravity of the oil industry might shift from the North American to the South American continent.[108] Another publication, the *World's Work*, predicted that Maracaibo, like Tampico and Nome, Alaska, would soon become a household word in the United States.[109] As at Mene Grande, a fleet of wooden barges towed by tugs and, later, shallow-draft lake tankers collected the oil at La Rosa. The oil made the journey of 267 kilometers from the eastern shore of Lake Maracaibo to the Netherlands Antilles, principally Curaçao, for refining. One British traveler reported: "Some days there are as many as 42 ships lying in the ports of Curaçao."[110]

While international oil interests celebrated, the residents of La Rosa were left to take stock of the events that had occurred and to begin cleaning up the mess that the well had produced. voc crews hauled away oil for several months. With homes damaged and crops and livestock saturated with oil, the inhabitants demanded that voc compensate them for their losses. Unable to speak Spanish, voc's camp superintendent, Mr. Brack, hired Juan Texier Unda as a liaison with the local population. The company made an inventory of damages and purportedly provided compensation, although Texier considered some matters very "delicate." For the locals the issue went beyond immediate compensation, since land saturated with oil would remain unproductive for several years. Texier made it a point to communicate directly with President Gómez concerning his role in the proceedings. Whether writing at the behest of the company or hoping to curry favor with the general, his missive reveals that La Rosa's inhabitants were ready to pressure the company for their rights and that the government was willing to consider their demands.[111] This pattern of protest followed by artful negotiation was replicated throughout Venezuela as communities found their traditional way of life disrupted by the presence of the new oil industry.

UNITED STATES INTERESTS

United States interests proved to be relative latecomers to oil exploration in Venezuela. As Edwin Lieuwen points out, producers based in the United States, with ample domestic supplies and investments in nearby Mexico, at first did not pay attention to Venezuela.[112] The war in Europe and the ensuing increased demand for petroleum products changed this perspective. During 1918 Standard Oil dispatched several of its geologists to survey promising tracts and make recommendations.[113] However, by the time United States companies took notice of developments in western Venezuela, Shell subsidiaries had already acquired the lion's share of the land-based concessions authorized by the government. By the end of 1919 several United States companies registered in the state of Delaware, including the Mara, Perijá, Páez, and Miranda, had acquired important concessions. In the view of the United States economic attaché in Caracas, the presence of these companies marked "the entrance of new and purely American interests into the petroleum industry in Venezuela."[114]

After acquiring several smaller firms and engaging in personal negotiations with Juan Vicente Gómez, in 1921 Standard Oil decided to form its own subsidiary, naming it the Standard Oil Company of Venezuela (socv).[115] Having experienced dilatory tactics with various ministries and bureaucracies, with the assistance of the United States legation Standard's representative Thomas Armstrong opened direct negotiations with Gómez and set out to win his support with gifts. To curry favor, on more than one occasion E. J. Sadler, vice-president of Standard and also president of the Creole Petroleum Syndicate, sent Gómez hundreds of prize-winning roses, ornamental plants, and clinging vines. The company's representative in Caracas requested an audience with Gómez to present the gifts arriving at La Guaira. Gómez instead asked for the gifts to be unloaded at Puerto Cabello and sent directly to his hacienda at Maracay.[116] Gómez was not, however, won over with bribes or a few token gifts; British companies had already supplied him with several prize bulls.[117] Rather he appeared concerned about the growing power of British and Dutch oil interests, and the entry of the United States companies offered him the opportunity to introduce a counterbalance to the European monopoly. As McBeth emphasizes, Gómez, as a matter of policy, "wanted the country's oil resources to be developed by companies from different nationalities." In fact, Venezuelan consuls in the United States prepared brochures which they regularly distributed to oil interests there.[118]

Largely excluded from the lucrative land-based concessions along the eastern lakeshore, one United States holding company, the Creole Petroleum Syndicate, skillfully negotiated and acquired over-water concessions directly paralleling the property owned by the Caribbean and voc.[119] By 1928 Creole changed its name to the Creole Petroleum Corporation and entered into closer relations with Standard Oil of New Jersey, to which it sold a significant proportion of its stock.[120] Gulf Oil, which had formed a Venezuelan subsidiary, the Venezuelan Gulf Oil Company (later Mene Grande), also acquired lake concessions in what became known as the "kilometer strip." Their assumption that the oil deposits did not stop at the land's edge was to prove farsighted and permitted United States interests to establish a foothold in the lucrative Bolívar Coastal fields of Lake Maracaibo. Their actions would also benefit other United States interests, especially the Lago Petroleum Company, which had been established in 1923 and absorbed concessions granted to British Equatorial before acquiring its own lake properties.[121] Not only had United States companies been largely unprepared for developments in Venezuela but the United States military seems to have been woefully ignorant of conditions in the region. When asked to prepare a report on Curaçao and the coastal region of Venezuela, the military attaché Gary Crockett culled local Venezuelan papers for information to send to the War Department.[122] With the explosion of the Barroso, however, United States interests could not afford to stay out of Venezuela.

OIL AND THE BARI

While company operations on the eastern shore of Lake Maracaibo moved at a breakneck pace, the western shore presented difficult challenges. Caribbean and Standard Oil of Venezuela had uncovered several rich deposits, but their efforts were thwarted by the presence of hostile Bari, the indigenous group that inhabited the Perijá district. As it did for most of Venezuela, oil fundamentally altered the Bari's relationship with the national state and produced a series of efforts to incorporate their territory under the authority of the central government. Attempts by Colombia to settle its own side of the border, and oil concessions in the hands of the Colón Development Company, added urgency to the need to define the physical boundary with Venezuela. Between 1928 and 1929 several government commissions had been dispatched to ascertain and physically delineate the border between the nations.[123] For their part, the companies tried to cajole the Bari, offering gifts and other incentives, to no avail. Reportedly they also set booby traps under cooking fires, hoping to kill the Bari when they returned to their camps.[124] The Bari attacked oil crews with arrows, killing several Venezuelans and foreigners.[125] The *Tropical Sun*, an English-language newspaper published in Maracaibo, suggested gassing the Bari, who were seen as impediments to progress.[126] Armed guards accompanied work crews entering the Bari homeland, and to protect against arrows, work sites and sleeping quarters were enclosed with wire mesh.[127] Despite these efforts, neither the companies nor the government was able to demobilize the Bari. As late as the 1950s Creole Petroleum contracted with a group of Capuchin priests to conduct air drops of gifts from company planes in an attempt to woo the Bari. Monks that entered the area later were met with a hail of arrows. Clashes between the indigenous and oil crews, some violent and others not, continued throughout the early phase of the oil industry, not only in western but also in eastern Venezuela.

MARACAIBO AND THE FOREIGN PRESENCE

As news of the Barroso spread, hundreds of foreigners looking for work with the oil companies inundated Maracaibo.[128] The Venezuelan government initially imposed no restrictions on the number of foreigners who could seek employment in the industry. Ships arrived in Maracaibo daily, carrying outsiders seeking to secure their share of the wealth. One iconoclastic observer from the United States stated that Maracaibo faced "tropical bums, adventurous geologists, bewildered clerks, rough-neck drillers, and business magnates as rapacious as that other Morgan, the pirate, who had paid his visit some centuries before. The whole state of Zulia was floating on oil. You needed only to punch a hole in the ground and it would spout the black wealth, which made you king."[129] Other expatriates, fearful of "Aztecs shouting Marx," left Mexico's increasingly depleted fields and headed south.[130] A direct shipping line connected oilmen from the United States in Tampico with Maracaibo.[131] Many, like George Johnston, arrived in Venezuela in 1925 after having spent three years in Mexico.[132] Other cases abound, especially among Lago employees. Jeff Greable and Oswald Boyd came to Maracaibo from Tampico.[133] Arthur Proudfit, who began by working with Lago and rose through the ranks to become president of Creole, had worked in Mexico alongside his father, a driller for Huasteca Oil in Tampico, before arriving in Venezuela in 1928.[134]

Beyond drillers, a significant body of professionals, politicians, and speculators also moved from Mexico to Venezuela. Among these was William F. Buckley Sr., founder of the Pantepec Oil Company, who was expelled from

Mexico by President Alvaro Obregón and who in Venezuela acquired massive tracts of land and proposed building a deep-water port on the Peninsula of Paraguana that would have allowed him to monopolize oil exports.[135] Pantepec also employed Henry Osian Flipper, the first African American to graduate from West Point, whose surveys were used in a Supreme Court case that settled land claims on the border between Arizona and Sonora.[136]

The Mexican experience, according to Michael O'Shaughnessy, prepared personnel from the United States to operate in "tropical countries" and taught them the "Latin American game," by which he meant the process of acculturation and language acquisition that some of the drillers and mechanics had undergone.[137] His description points to the existence of a growing and mobile body of skilled and semiskilled oil workers who traveled between new discovery sites, including those in the Middle East, Mexico, Venezuela, and later Africa. One driller who worked on the Barroso said that he previously stood "on rigs in Mexico, India, and Oklahoma,"[138] and another reported that "a driller from Mexico whooped and shook hands with a driller from the Middle East, both recalling when they worked together on a well at Corsicana."[139] Although this group of oil professionals with international experience represented only a small segment of the expatriates, its numbers increased after the 1920s. Another important segment of the foreign population arriving in Venezuela originated from traditional oil-producing areas in the southern and southwestern United States.

From ports in the United States and Mexico most newcomers sailed first to Curaçao, where they shifted to smaller boats that could negotiate the shallow, treacherous entrance into Lake Maracaibo. One British traveler recalled, "From Curaçao, we seemed to have nothing but oil men on board, one became drenched and saturated in oil—in fact, I felt so inflammable that I was nervous about striking a match to light a cigar with, for I have always had a conviction, thought I have never revealed it, that I should burn rather well."[140] Upon their arrival in Maracaibo, foreigners were compelled by customs authorities to fill out a detailed questionnaire that was sent to the ministry of the interior.[141] The state of Zulia, with a population of 222,613, of which about 45,000 lived in the city of Maracaibo in 1920, now confronted the foreign onslaught.[142] By 1926 Maracaibo's population had nearly doubled, to eighty thousand. In 1928 alone the Venezuelan government recorded the arrival of 23,805 foreigners, the majority of whom settled in Zulia.[143] Reporting on the "oil boom," the *New York Times* asserted that "Americans in Maracaibo and the surrounding country are now numbered by the thousands. Fifteen years ago there was not one in the whole region."[144]

As an important port city and the gateway to the lucrative Andean coffee region, Maracaibo had always had a significant foreign population, including Syrians, Germans, British, Italians, and a handful of citizens of the United States.[145] These foreigners engaged in the export of coffee, commerce, and banking and interacted among themselves and with the Venezuelan élites. Members of the community, in the words of the United States consul, Alexander Sloan, "knew each other and gathered nightly in downtown resorts which served them as clubs."[146] The discovery of oil fundamentally altered the nature of the foreign community in the port and, more important, its relations with the Venezuelan people.

Among the arriving foreigners several issues tended to attract attention, including the oppressive heat, the port's racial composition, and the inadequate facilities. Jack Lavin, an employee of Creole Petroleum, complained that he could not even find respite in the shade, where temperatures continued to hover over ninety degrees.[147] Bathing in the lake offered little relief; as Jonathan Leonard reports, the water was so warm that a person swimming in it had "the sensation of being bathed in perspiration."[148] Though they eventually became acclimated to the heat, the foreigners of this early wave appeared bewildered and preoccupied by the diverse racial composition of the lake region. In the words of one perceptive New Englander, parts of the lakeshore were "Africa, with the chants and tom-toms of the Congo," and parts were indigenous, composed of Waraos, Guajiros, and Motilones (Bari).[149] The presence of Goajira women, with long colored dresses and colorfully adorned faces, initially confounded the foreigners. The purported white population, though limited in size, also came under scrutiny. One observer said, "A few of the Maracaiberos are white. The ones that are make a lot of it, but somehow they don't seem to fit the country any better than us oilmen."[150]

Travelers from the United States tended to depict Maracaibo as a dirty, sleepy port city transformed by the foreign presence.[151] At best this is an oversimplification; at worst it reveals the type of prejudice that prevailed among the foreign population. This prejudice is evident in the writings of one oil company employee from the United States, who described the port as a "filthy, stinking, fly-breeding town yawning restlessly on the edge of the lake grown slimy with waste and garbage."[152] Almost magically, however, the arrival of foreigners and the oil industry were viewed as having transformed the city and its inhabitants. One journalist from the United States wrote that oil changed "Maracaibo from old town to modern city in two years."[153] This magical transformation had less to do with oil than with the need to validate foreigners as agents of this purported modernization. Their cultural biases blinded them to Maracaibo's vibrant diversity and the contrasting rhythms of life in the port. Instead they highlighted what foreigners perceived as negative aspects of a tropical environment to which they were largely unaccustomed.

The other common depiction, fueled in part by Marachuco regional pride, was of Zulianos as different from other Venezuelans. In this view, the people of the lake region were "industrious, thrifty, and economically self sufficient," and oil development had "revived that spirit of independence."[154] Commentators, familiar with the so-called Pelaez oil protectorate in Mexico, considered the possibility that the United States might want to support the independence of Zulia, much as it had fomented the separation of Panama from Colombia.[155] The British also considered what such an arrangement might mean to their interests in light of the increasing influence of the United States in the area.[156]

Despite its role in the regional economy, Maracaibo was physically unprepared for the arrival of so many foreigners. Hotels such as the America, the Zulia, the Scandia, and the Detroit simply could not handle the incoming flood. In addition to formal lodging facilities, the newcomers overwhelmed the modest private housing available in the city. The United States consul complained that the group had monopolized all the available houses in residential areas: "congestion in the poorer quarters of the town is almost beyond belief. Rooms in the Chiquinquira area, in the Bolívar district . . . which contain no comforts of any kind and which are supplied with a bed and a few nails upon which to hang clothes, rent for $20 per month. In some of these rooms five or six people live, some on the floor and some in hammocks stretched above narrow cots with which the place is supplied."[157] In the view of one observer, Maracaibo had acquired an air of "insanity. . . . a mad carnival. . . . As fast as one batch cleared out of town and headed for the jungle oil camps, another trooped onto the docks, restless and eager after weeks at sea."[158] Maracaibo was simply unable to house the newcomers.

Beyond housing, foreigners, especially those from the United States, also had another impact on Maracaibo and the outlying regions. Their presence drew attention to their different lifestyle, encompassing clothing, food, music, and sports, and soon local merchants began to cater to the new clientele. A wide array of consumer goods from the United States and Europe were advertised and imported: Victor Records, spirits such as Black and White, Haig and Haig, and Buchanan scotch, cigarettes such as Chesterfields, drinks such as Orange Crush, and canned goods such as Libby's Corned Beef soon inundated the Maracaibo marketplace and became identified with the *petrolero* lifestyle.[159] Before long, other elements of society were also taking part in this new consumer culture. Newspapers such as the *Panorama* and others now made it a practice to carry the exchange rate between the dollar and the bolívar on their front pages.[160]

As the population of expatriates from the United States, Britain, and the West Indies grew, two English-language newspapers soon appeared: the *Maracaibo Herald* (1923) and the *Tropical Sun* (1926). The *Herald* promoted itself as the English paper published in the principal "oil metropolis of South America."[161] *Panorama*, Maracaibo's most important newspaper, produced an English-language section. Commercial establishments also adapted to the foreign presence, and enterprises with English names soon appeared throughout the city. Haunts such as the Cosmos, the Blue Book, the Bachelors' Inn, El Dollar, and Las Delicias became favorites of the hard-drinking petroleros. The Blue Book promoted itself as the favorite of Venezuelan high society and foreigners.[162]

Bernard and Casey Moran, twin brothers from San Francisco, California, had gone to Maracaibo to explore the possibility of establishing a publishing house. Casey Moran, who had also participated in the Alaskan gold rush, eventually took over operation of the paper and became an influential figure in the English-speaking community.[163] He regularly held court at the Rotary Bar in Maracaibo, where oil workers from throughout the lake region gathered to share news and gossip with him.[164] The *Tropical Sun* provided employment services for newcomers and reported having placed everyone from "office boys to engineers."[165]

The city served not only as the entry point for foreigners but also as the destination for oil workers seeking respite from work in the fields. On days of rest many would take the company boat to Maracaibo and partake in the night life there. As one publication reported in 1931, after successfully drilling a well in the Menito area, the oilmen came into town "to celebrate whoopee with their girlfriends in particular."[166] Away from their home country, one expatriate recalled, former residents of the United States appeared to undergo a transformation: "Something about the tropics, the distance from home, the lack of clerical exhorting, and the absence of group pressure, has melted away all the superfluous ones. Like the flame of wet wood, the American moral fervor dies out as soon as the draft is shut off. And minus morality, the individual American is a vastly more attractive person."[167] At times, expatriates inclined toward very heavy drinking. The *Maracaibo Herald* reported on the exploits of Frank Matlock, "who every night left another vale [a Venezuelan] at the cantina."[168] Other pastimes were significantly more dangerous. On more than one occasion oil workers commandeered the trolley that ran down Bella Vista Avenue and transformed it into an open-air bar or used it for bar-hopping.[169] On some days competing groups of oilmen staged trolley races and sped through the middle of the city en route to Plaza Baralt.[170] Thieves often took advantage of their inebriation to relieve them of their personal belongings.[171]

As incidents between Venezuelans and foreign oilmen became more frequent, United States officials worried about the consequences. Already one Venezuelan army officer had reportedly justified an assault on a British couple by saying he had thought they were from the United States. The head of the United States legation in Caracas, Willis Cook, recognized that citizens of his country were "a drunken and disorderly set, disrespectful of the local people, and with little regard to local law."[172] Beyond personal conflicts, Cook sensed a growing apprehension among some Venezuelans toward the foreign domination of the oil industry. He reported that Venezuelans not associated with the oil industry "rather resent the turning over of the oil deposits of the country to foreigners."[173] To defuse tensions and address Venezuelan concerns, Cook proposed meetings with the directors of the oil company to encourage them to exercise greater control over their employees. In 1926 the U.S. State Department wrote letters to the oil companies about the behavior of their men in Venezuela. One official suggested that it would be "unfortunate" for "relations with Venezuela to be disturbed by unseemly friction between oil employees and the native population."[174]

THE SEX TRADE

The new foreign presence also transformed and dramatically expanded the sex trade in the port and throughout the region. One observer lamented that "with five thousand Americans in town you had to look around a while before you found a girl that was not busy."[175] Purveyors of the flesh recruited unsuspecting young girls from the surrounding Andean states, the Goajira region, and Colombia, inducing or forcing them to become sex workers.[176] As the industry evolved, prostitution became a big business, attracting women from the Caribbean and as far away as France, Holland, and Belgium.[177] It also attracted the interest of local politicians such as the state governor, Santos Matute, who sought to monopolize this now lucrative activity.[178] Establishments like the Pavilion, a bar, dance hall, and brothel, became famous among the oilmen. Some men from the United States lamented the absence of "white" women, but Lavin comments that "it was not long before these critical musiús came to look upon the dusky females as luscious blondes."[179]

Aware of the sexual proclivities of their employees, some companies dispensed condoms; one former "office boy" at Mene Grande recalled that foreign employees had received an allotment of four each week.[180] One commentator from the United States speculated about what future archeologists might think when they unearthed an old oil camp and found so many contraceptive devices: "perhaps [they] will argue that it was deliberate race suicide that extinguished the asphalt culture."[181] Not all efforts at contraception succeeded: a few years after the oil boom the product of some liaisons could be found begging on the streets of Maracaibo. Leonard describes one fair-skinned child he encountered who went by the name of Opkeen—the only way he knew to pronounce his purported father's surname, Hopkins.

Before long city leaders took steps to limit and regularize the trade. They classified the activity of women, charged them a city tax, and subjected them to medical examinations every seven days.[182] Women active in the sex trade were required to carry a health card. In 1930 a special anti-venereal institute conducted a census of major towns in the state and required that sex workers who moved must report their whereabouts to the local institute office. Sex workers who catered to foreigners and upper-class Venezuelans contracted with private doctors for their regular exams.[183] Police and civil authorities ensured enforcement of these various decrees. An assortment of local remedies surfaced, pledging to cure sexual diseases; the Quintero formula promised to cure the "venereal assassin" that haunted large segments of the population.[184] Despite these efforts, the incidence of sexually transmitted diseases continued to increase. In 1935 the government decreed the first Sunday in September a national anti–venereal disease day.[185] In 1947 the government estimated that 64 percent of all persons requiring hospitalization in the country had contracted syphilis, and another 37 percent had other venereal diseases such as *chancro blando*. These patients spent an average of fifteen days in the hospital. The minister of health reported that his office had to maintain over three million units of penicillin on hand exclusively for the treatment of syphilis.[186] The spread of venereal disease became a major concern for the oil companies, who began testing their employees and using the results as a reason to dismiss those who were infected. Workers and later even labor unions took up the issue, demanding treatment rather than dismissal.

Since many of the bars and brothels occupied choice downtown buildings, the location of these establishments soon became a matter of public debate. Previously the sex trade had been low-key and not a cause for concern, but with the arrival of the free-spending oil workers, both Venezuelan and foreign, it began to offend the public's perception of morality. The city relocated the bordellos to an official district on the outskirts of town. From the point of view of the oilmen, the location could not have been better. The new red-light district now occupied a strip of land between the Shell and Lago urban camps, which continued to supply it with innumerable patrons. One keen observer from the United States who worked in the labor relations office of Creole believed that foreigners received greater public scorn from their brethren for socializing with Venezuelans than for frequenting the bordellos.[187]

THE COST OF LIVING

The influx of population, both foreign and Venezuelan, dramatically inflated the price of real estate, transportation, food, and basic services, impoverishing the majority of the city's residents who were not employed in the oil industry.[188] With oil companies paying employees in gold, some merchants refused to accept Venezuelan bolívares, the national currency. According to one resident, during the roaring twenties in Maracaibo "eggs tripled in price, and a fresh cabbage or a can of fruit cost a dollar."[189] The United States consul reported that prices on some basic goods had risen 500 to 600 percent.[190] In 1921, for example, a large chicken could be obtained for four bolívares, whereas now one cost ten bolívares. Likewise, oranges that had previously sold for two bolívares per hundred were now one bolívar for four.[191] The price of other products mirrored these increases, underscoring how dramatically conditions had changed in the port.

Foreigners alone could not be blamed for the high price of goods. Faced by recurrent droughts and new opportunities in the oilfields, many local farmers abandoned their plots, forcing Maracaibo to become more reliant on crops from the Andean states.[192] Moreover, shippers, brokers, and local merchants sought to cash in on the boom by inflating prices. *Excelsior*, a newspaper in Maracaibo, complained that some people had been forced to leave the city and seek refuge in the countryside, where costs had not risen as sharply. Others lamented that conditions had degenerated to the point where they had been forced to "eat rabbits and palomitas [pigeons], which were boiled three weeks before to preserve them until they could be sold at prices which the huckster fixes." According to *Excelsior*, "landlords and hucksters of articles of prime necessity" had "ruined" local residents' homes.[193]

Foreigners also felt the pinch in housing, transportation, and other services, and British consular officials constantly complained that exorbitant prices left them barely able to subsist on their allowance.[194] Likewise, when John Sanders, the United States consul, felt cheated by an ice vendor, he filed a formal complaint with the governor; in retribution, the merchant refused to sell Sanders any ice.[195] A group of British newcomers complained to their consul that they had contracted for a tour of the city at ten bolívares and that at the end of the trip the driver had attempted to charge them forty-five instead.[196] When the men refused, the taxi driver had had them arrested and jailed, inciting an international incident that involved the British consul, the Caribbean Petroleum Company, local police officers, and eventually the governor. These incidents reveal not only the impact of inflation and the role of speculators but the extrajudicial privileges that foreigners now expected from the Venezuelan authorities.

Concerned about the political consequences of spiraling prices, Gómez's government urged the governor of Zulia, Pérez Soto, to take an active role and prevent speculation. In uncharacteristic language, the minister of the interior, Pedro Arcaya, urged Pérez Soto to become "friend and protector of the consumer" within the limits of the existing laws.[197] Confronting new social ills, a raucous foreign population, and a cost of living that limited their purchasing power, residents of Maracaibo took stock of their situation. Bracho Montiel, editor of the Maracaibo weekly *El Norte*, recognized the changing conditions: "The dollar has become Venezuelan. The dollar in Venezuela is broker and colonizer. The national condition of any country has now become the dollar."[198] Other Maracuchos recalled with a certain fondness the period before the oil boom. Alexander Sloan, the United States consul, observed that people of all ages looked back to the time "before the foreigners began to exploit the petroleum treasures of their land as a halcyon period when life was quite different and business currents not quite so swift."[199] Just as important, the advent of the oil industry now served to demarcate how most residents of Maracaibo constructed time. The year 1922 and the discovery of the Barroso increasingly served to divide time into periods before and after the boom.

Venezuelans were not the only group to lament changes in their lifestyle and social position. Active since the mid-nineteenth century, the Germans were key players in the coffee trade in western Venezuela and enjoyed a privileged status within Maracaibo's commercial and social circles. As part of their role as coffee traders, they owned and operated pharmacies and other commercial establishments and functioned as trade agents in Maracaibo and the principal cities of the Venezuelan Andes. Many German men intermarried with local élites, forging important family connections.[200] Despite their importance to the regional economy and their ties to the local élites, their presence generated practically no long-lasting impact on Venezuelan society. The rise of the oil industry brought about the arrival of a large population from the United States and Britain that soon displaced the German community. Nothing exemplifies this better than the diminished importance of the Germans' Club de Comercio, Maracaibo's preeminent social club before the rise of the oil industry.

Soon after establishing their presence in Maracaibo, the oil companies founded their own private golf and country clubs on the lakeshore, with modern facilities. As gathering places for their senior staff, these institutions invariably acquired new social prominence, and Germans found themselves excluded from membership. They in turn retaliated, closing ranks and attempting to impose a German slate of candidates for offices of the Club de Comercio, in which they had been preeminent. Recognizing the newfound importance of the United States, a group of Venezuelan members opposed the Germans' actions and soundly defeated them. The United States consul viewed the event as a social and cultural watershed. He correctly surmised that since "many members of the German colony have married into Venezuelan families of high social position and wealth," this rebuff assumed "much greater importance."[201] The event foretold the diminishing importance of the Germans in commerce and an emerging shift in allegiance on the part of the Venezuelan élites and professionals, who sought to position themselves to benefit from the oil industry. It also exemplified the use of distinct strategies by German merchants and United States oil interests in shaping their relations with the local society, the first of which left no lasting legacy and the second of which continues to endure.

Besides displacing Germans, the discovery of oil recast Maracaibo's relations with the rest of Venezuela. A pattern of political conflict in the post-independence period and recurring civil wars at mid-century had limited the federal government's ability to control the interior provinces. Yet with the advent of oil and the presence of a sizable body of foreigners, the federal government could no longer allow an independent-minded region to determine how to make use of the nation's newfound wealth. Gómez's administration appointed a series of state presidents or governors, in most cases not natives of the state, to do its bidding in Zulia. Though some of the appointees were relatives of Gómez, their loyalty resulted from the independence they enjoyed to pursue their own lucrative ventures, acquiring land and forming partnerships with local élites.[202] Through these practices the federal government gradually pulled Maracaibo, known as the "Sultana of the Caribbean," firmly into the Venezuelan orbit and limited its ability to act independently.

Gómez's ability to exert control over Zulia and extend the power of the Venezuelan state over other regions rested on the unique relations that evolved between the foreign oil companies and his regime. Negotiating from a relatively weak position, he intentionally pitted British against

United States interests and extracted concessions from foreign interests by manipulating regional and local discontents. By closely managing relations with the foreign companies, Gómez acquired the symbolic power and needed resources to create "a national army, built a road system that initiated the economic integration of the nation, developed an effective state bureaucracy and filled its top posts with supporters, transformed rivals into allies by granting them status without power, and disposed of his enemies through exile, prison or death."[203] Financed largely by oil revenues, under Gómez the state bureaucracy expanded dramatically, from 13,500 in 1920 to 53,100 in 1936, an increase of 293 percent.[204] The lessons of the Gómez period were not lost on future generations of Venezuelan political leaders who assumed office after his death and who, at many levels, pursued similar policies to assure their stay in power.

The events of the period between 1914 and 1922 were a harbinger of what lay in store for Venezuela, but they did not immediately alter the social and cultural landscape for most people in the western part of the country. Except for a few laborers who migrated to Mene Grande, the conditions of life continued much the same as they had been throughout the nineteenth century. Although Mene Grande in 1914 was a prototype for future developments in the oil industry, it did not immediately transform the social or economic dynamics of the region. Waves of foreigners did not descend on Venezuela. The country continued to rely on agriculture, mainly cacao and coffee, to generate revenue.

The discovery of the Barroso in 1922 changed these conditions and established the importance of the Lake Maracaibo oilfields, triggering a veritable stampede of foreign oil companies. By the mid-1920s over one hundred oil companies were competing to claim and exploit potentially lucrative fields. As Standard Oil foresaw, the Barroso shifted the center of gravity of the international oil industry to Venezuela. Mene Grande and La Rosa provided important clues as to what Venezuelans could expect. Disputes over land and encroachment on common lands characterized this first phase, causing innumerable conflicts. Environmental degradation, a constant feature of the oil industry, took a heavy toll on the land, the waterways, and the health of the people; its long-term consequences remain largely unstudied. Likewise, clashes between traditional practices and the new order imposed by the industry became common, leading to confrontations between foreigners and Venezuelans. The establishment of the industry extracted a heavy price from Venezuelan communities near the new production fields.

Production at Mene Grande and La Rosa involved a foreign staff composed of supervisors and other skilled craftsmen, a significant number of Venezuelans employed as day laborers, and a larger body of unemployed at the immediate disposal of the companies if the need arose. Eventually the company moved to formalize housing arrangements and in the process exacerbated contradictions between foreigners and nationals by offering privileged accommodations to the foreigners. On the surface the events unfolding in Venezuela appeared no different from those experienced in Mexican and Chilean mining towns and rubber-producing centers such as Manuas in the Brazilian Amazon. The oil industry, however, did not remain limited to any one isolated region of the country. Word of oil production and of new sources of employment slowly reached communities connected to the Maracaibo lake basin. As geological teams fanned out across the land, most of Venezuela became a staging area for oil exploration. Before long, sections of eastern Venezuela in Azoategui, Sucre, and Monagas would experience developments similar to those witnessed in Zulia.

CHAPTER 3

La Ruta Petrolera

Learning to Live with Oil

Throughout western Venezuela, wherever oil companies engaged in extractive operations they repeated the pattern of development witnessed at Mene Grande. After 1922, however, operations occurred on a much larger scale and the impact of oil production was no longer confined to isolated areas of western Venezuela. It now reached into every corner of the country, directly or indirectly influencing most people's traditional ways of life. This chapter examines the haphazard and conflictive way in which the process developed and the new forms of production that the industry introduced. As it spurred migration, the industry broke down regional barriers and altered the way Venezuelans defined space and self. With few exceptions, the participation of Venezuelans in oil production reflected the earlier economic and social linkages between the new oil-producing region and the rest of the country.

Oil also dramatically reshaped the physical environment and existing communities while also giving rise to new settlements. As the industry hired hundreds of workers it introduced new patterns of labor relations, notions of time, and housing arrangements within the context of socially and racially stratified labor relations that privileged foreigners. Eventually mistreatment and inactions by local and national officials inspired labor organizing and political activity. To address conditions in every community where the oil industry developed would be a monumental undertaking. Therefore this chapter focuses on the most important communities

of their time, those in the area known as the Bolívar Coastal field, extending from La Rosa to Lagunillas. Throughout the lake region struggles over
land quickly emerged as local residents found their communities overrun
not only by foreigners but also by thousands of Venezuelan migrants. The
state increasingly became the arbiter of these disputes, and though at times
federal and state authorities sided with locals, in the majority of cases foreigners carried the day.

After the success of the Barroso, all eyes turned to the Bolívar Coastal
field, a zone that extended a kilometer out into the lake.[1] Hoping to repli-
cate the success of La Rosa, a host of companies began drilling operations
throughout the area. With voc and Caribbean dominating the land concessions, British Equatorial (subsequently acquired by Lago) drilled the first
over-water well in 1923 in the vicinity of La Rosa, inaugurating a procedure
that transformed the oil industry. In 1926 at Lagunillas, Venezuelan Gulf
Oil successfully drilled Lago no. 1, and Lagunillas quickly became the most
important production field in Venezuela. In 1928 Lago uncovered the lucrative Tía Juana field, second in importance to Lagunillas. By 1929, with multiple operations under way from Ambrosio in the North to Mene Grande
in the South, the magnitude of the deposits along the eastern lakeshore had
been confirmed. It soon became important to establish a nomenclature to
distinguish the different parcels being drilled. Company officials selected
names that reflected their own national origin (Superior, Michigan, Huron,
and Erie) and their far-flung experiences in Latin America (Gatún, Miraflores, and Petén).[2] An assortment of over one hundred companies operated
throughout the greater Lake Maracaibo area. Oil surpassed coffee as the
nation's principal export for the first time in 1926. Shortly thereafter, in 1928,
Venezuela became the world's second-most important exporter of oil.[3]

Once fields started to produce significant quantities of oil, the companies had to balance continued exploration with the demands imposed by
managing productive wells. This meant a transition to settled, established
operations at fixed points along the eastern lakeshore. There the companies confronted conditions very similar to those encountered during the
construction of the Panama Canal. Dense tropical forests, inhabited by
venomous snakes and voracious insects, engulfed the marshy area near the
lakeshore. One geologist with Standard of New Jersey described the conditions in epic terms: "Whatsoever things are designed by the gods for the

torture of the flesh and the subjection of the spirit, . . . are united to preserve inviolate these hidden treasures, and turn aside those who would profane the virgin solitude by the rude intrusion of a devouring industry."[4]

The task of clearing the trees and undergrowth was grueling. Shifts of men worked twenty-four hours a day, performing all the backbreaking work with axes and machetes.[5] They drained swamps, leveled the rainforest, con-structed docks, laid railroad track, and built aqueducts, power plants, and roads. Behind them other laborers laid pipe and built tanks at a feverish pace to store the considerable quantities of oil flowing from the new wells. The labor force not only waged a constant battle with nature but also confronted a host of tropical maladies, including yellow fever, malaria, and dengue. Industrial accidents—falls from oil platforms, drowning, severed limbs, and tetanus—were frequent. Workers proved expendable; if one complained or became ill, hundreds of others were ready to take his place. No labor unions existed, and no laws protected workers from the many calamities.[6] The con-ditions of this early era have been graphically captured by novelists such as the Colombian doctor César Uribe Piedrahita, who worked in the camps, and the Venezuelans Ramón Díaz Sánchez and Miguel Otero Silva.[7] This activity dramatically and permanently altered the physical environment of the lake region. The oil spills that occurred with increasing frequency even-tually covered large portions of the once pristine lake with a slimy film of oil; below the surface a thick layer of sludge obscured the bottom, devastat-ing the once abundant marine life.

LA RUTA PETROLERA

Venezuelans only gradually took notice of the developments along the east-ern shore of Lake Maracaibo. Before 1921 only a third of those migrating to the oilfields came from the rural countryside; the majority lived in urban areas.[8] The oil companies often complained about the absence of qualified workers. The U.S. Bureau of Labor repeated these concerns in 1922, report-ing that companies still faced "difficulty in securing sufficient unskilled la-bor for the work in the oil fields."[9] The question of labor proved much more complex than either the companies or the reports suggested, involving the way information about the oilfields reached the average Venezuelan and the extent to which people were free to move. The first wave of oil workers, who often returned to their hometowns, helped fuel the migratory stream.[10] In addition to local Zulianos, Venezuelans from the states of Lara and Falcón and the Andes were an important part of the first wave. Agricultural and cattle interests in the western regions of Lara, especially in the area of Carora, had previously traded with lake communities. Andeans arrived in the lake ports by mule or train and then took sailing vessels to Maracaibo. Falconianos traveled six to seven days on foot to the port of Altagracia and took a launch to Maracaibo from there. Workers from another important source arrived by sea; as seafarers, many residents of Margarita first heard about events at La Rosa from relatives who plied the waters of the Gulf of Venezuela to the north of Maracaibo.[11]

The historian Domingo Alberto Rangel argues that most migration occurred from the densely populated states, where there was ample surplus labor.[12] Lara, with a population of over 219,000, and Trujillo, with 178,942, were indeed two of the most densely populated states, and the populations of Falcón and Mérida exceeded 120,000.[13] Yet population alone cannot account for this internal migration. Other factors, including economic linkages, such as those that pervaded the lake region, and bleak environmental conditions, such as the scarcity of water in Falcón and Margarita, were also important.[14] Briceño Parilli and others offer somewhat questionable cultural explanations, including the purported rough nature of the Andean and the wandering spirit of the Margariteño seafarers, to explain their presence in Zulia. These stereotypes in fact emerged after workers had been employed by the companies for some time and therefore do not explain their initial willingness to migrate. No matter what their specific region of origin, however, for all Venezuelans work in the oilfields marked a sharp break with their previous practices and traditions.

Gradually, a migratory circuit, or *ruta petrolero* (oil route), took shape. With Maracaibo and the eastern shore of the lake as its center, it incorporated the Andes (Mérida, Trujillo, and Táchira), Lara, and Falcón, and extended to Margarita. During the 1930s Zulia saw its population soar with the arrival of 11,709 migrants from Falcón, 2,968 from Lara, 2,785 from Mérida, 4,727 from Margarita, and 10,659 from Trujillo. The same sort of circuit developed in eastern Venezuela when oil deposits were found successively in Monagas and Anzoategui. The states of Sucre, Bolívar, and Margarita provided the majority of migrants to the eastern oilfields. Migrants from Sucre in Monagas increased from 7,754 in 1936 to over 16,000 in 1940.[15] During this same period half the residents of Caripito, site of a Standard Oil refinery and oil depot, were recent arrivals from Sucre.[16] In some districts of Monagas, such as Colón, migrants accounted for 75 percent of the total population.[17] The existence of these two broad migratory circuits nourished the population of these areas, introduced new cultural practices, and cemented formal and informal ties between previously discrete regions.[18] In a pattern repeated throughout Latin America, the presence of economic enclaves drained population from the areas previously inhabited, ensuring if not their demise, at least their slow decline.[19]

Venezuelans had no established tradition of internal migration. Not since the wars of independence in the first two decades of the nineteenth century had Venezuela witnessed a significant movement of people. Moreover, a history of civil wars during the nineteenth century had accentuated regional differences. Most early laborers arrived at the Lake of Maracaibo with much trepidation. For many the journey represented the first time they had ventured from the familiar surroundings of their homes. Thrust into large bachelors' quarters, work sites, and villages, they came into contact with people who, although Venezuelan, were not always familiar; the Maracuchos spoke with a different accent, the Andeans seemed more formal and reserved, and the Easterners were more direct and outspoken. The migrants did not all eat the same foods, enjoy the same music, dress the same, or even pray to the same saints. No nationally shared diet existed: culinary traditions were regional in character. Even the *arepa*, the corn cake most closely identified with the contemporary Venezuelan diet, differed by region. Andeans preferred a flour variety, while others added local ingredients to make the dough. At one level the new encounters initiated a process of recognition, crucial to state formation and nationhood, but at another it produced friction as regional differences emerged.

Some of the early contradictions arose because of the lack of previous contact between Venezuelans from different areas. Most Andeans had little exposure to Afro-Venezuelans, and now had to adapt to their presence. Likewise, Maracuchos knew the Andinos only as the subject of the well-worn stereotype of the ignorant country bumpkin. One Andean who showed up at Mene Grande looking for work was asked by an animated Zuliano if he "vino enhuacalado de los Andes," the Venezuelan equivalent of having just fallen off the turnip truck.[20] Andeans knew Maracuchos as city dwellers eager to take advantage of their country brethren. Although these issues eventually dissipated, they were fertile ground for manipulation by opportunistic politicians and company officials eager to thwart an emerging labor movement.

The people who migrated to the oilfields included a broad cross-section of Venezuelan society rather than simply the poor illiterate "peons" or "irreconcilable native race" that early oil company publications described.[21] Fostering this view, Venezuelan authors such as Andrés de Chene erroneously assumed that locals lacked any skills and in the early phase provided only "brute force."[22] This perspective portrayed the migrant worker as a repository of backward cultural practices, Christian values deformed by fetishism and witchcraft, and only rudimentary concepts of "nation, family, and society."[23] Besides serving as an employer, it was suggested, the oil company had to bear the extra "burden" of stripping away these purported negative traits. The process was portrayed as an epic struggle between "two cultures: one primitive, rustic and untamed and the other modern, cosmopolitan, university trained and refined."[24] For the foreign oil companies and the emerging middle class, this portrayal underscored the backwardness of the country and the transformative role of oil for the nation and its institutions.[25] This was especially so to the extent that many in the middle class sought to represent Gómez's administration as incapable of administering the nation's newfound wealth. The industry was not only depicted as a driving force for modernization but assumed to be the eventual catalyst for political change, including democratization. This is the value that many early Venezuelan proponents of the oil industry expected, and it provided a point of convergence between these groups and the foreign oil companies.[26]

Inevitably, those who made their way to Maracaibo and the adjacent oilfields included a diverse assortment of agricultural laborers and campesinos, such as the poorly paid and exploited laborers of western Venezuela's haciendas, coffee, and cattle estates. The United States consul in Maracaibo noted that the local ranchers disliked the oil company for hiring away what they considered "their laborers."[27] As late as 1948 the economic development minister reported that the oil industry had indirectly freed the Venezuelan "peon" from the exploitative relations of the hacienda. On the face of it the claim appears doubtful; in the same report the number of people employed in the industry was reported at less than 2 percent of the national workforce while agricultural workers continued to hover at about 50 percent.[28] Agricultural production, as McBeth and others note, continued to rise during the first phase of the oil industry.[29] With various degrees of education and facing limited opportunities in family enterprises or businesses, the offspring of small and medium-sized landholders also sought employment with the foreign oil companies, and so did members of the emerging middle class and professionals such as doctors, lawyers, and other recent university graduates.

Although not as important in the first phase, over time, contacts with relatives, extended-family members, acquaintances, and fellow townspeople employed in the industry became the principal ways of acquiring employment. In 1926 the United States consul in Maracaibo reported that the scarcity of labor had been overcome. "The companies now report that the native labor, for practically the first time since the beginning of active operations in the oil fields is plentiful."[30] Edgar Campos, for example, a resident of Ceuta, learned about opportunities for employment in the foreign oil industry by word of mouth; he migrated to Lagunillas and subsequently to Mene Grande, where he worked for several Shell subsidiaries.[31] One Andino, the son of a small coffee producer, relied on an uncle employed by Caribbean to obtain employment at Mene Grande. One of eight children, he had previously worked with his father on their small finca in the state of Mérida.[32] Antonio José Sarache, from Mendoza Fría in Trujillo, had a cousin in Cabimas who told him about opportunities for employment in the camps. Sarache dropped out of high school and made his way to Cabimas, where he obtained employment with voc.[33] José Omar Colmenares, from Dividive in Trujillo, also used personal contacts to obtain employment at Mene Grande,[34] to which several people from Dividive had already relocated. Faced with limited prospects, his mother went with him to the camp, obtaining employment there as a seamstress.[35] The companies actively cultivated relations with their supposed "faithful" employees to recruit new workers. Company employment records confirm that family networks were essential for securing employment.[36] For the companies they provided an element of continuity and some degree of social control over employees.

The exodus of people from the countryside to the new production sites is usually one factor cited in the decline of traditional Venezuelan agriculture. The idea that the oil companies undermined agriculture is accepted by most Venezuelans. Briceño Parilli, for example, blames oil company imports of agricultural goods from the United States for undermining Venezuelan production, never questioning whether local producers had the capacity to meet the demand of the oil camps.[37] The oil companies went to great lengths to rebut this and similar views, by publishing pages of publicity and sponsoring lectures by "specialists." On the surface the notion that oil was responsible for the demise of Venezuelan agriculture seems plausible, but the reality is much more complex. The assumption behind this notion, that Venezuela had had a dynamic and productive agricultural sector before the discovery of oil, is difficult to sustain. Agricultural production suffered for most of the nineteenth century from a succession of civil wars, tropical diseases such as yellow fever, and a lack of adequate transport. Large estates, on which little or no innovation had occurred since the nineteenth century, dominated the countryside. Most agriculture remained regional, with specialization in crops such as coffee, cacao, and plantains. Small-scale operations or in some cases individuals produced most of the basic crops (corn, beans, and a variety of tubers). A congress of leading agricultural interests held in 1921 concluded that Venezuela "had no agriculture or farmers." It estimated that in a country of 2.5 million fewer than 50,000 people, "including elders over seventy years, women and children," were actually working the soil.[38] The participants judged agricultural production in Venezuela as "insignificant" and blamed this on the shortage of labor, prevalence of yellow fever, and lack of capital and adequate infrastructure. The report cited only three examples of productive estates—"the haciendas of General Gómez in Maracay, the Central Venezuela in Zulia and the haciendas of General Antonio Pimentel in Carabobo"—concluding that agriculture happened only "as God wants."[39] Though the arguments seem self-serving and aimed at securing greater government investment, they nonetheless underscored the difficulties continually faced in the countryside.

The issue of infrastructure loomed large at the congress, since in most cases the country lacked adequate means to bring its cash crops to market.

The coffee-producing regions of western Venezuela were an exception. The Andes gained access to international markets through the port of Maracaibo, and railroads connected Duaca in Lara to Puerto Cabello. Other districts, however, had no such networks. As several historians have discovered, in areas where production proved successful or campesinos could extract concessions, such as the northern portions of the state of Lara, people did not necessarily abandon the land or migrate to the oilfields.[40]

Along Lake Maracaibo, the companies limited their operations primarily to the immediate coast. As Fabiola Parra has argued, in these areas the industry did not displace agricultural producers but rather provided them with new markets.[41] In Mene Grande the oil company provided free shipping on its railroad to farmers willing to sell their produce to the oil camps.[42] Undermined by a succession of civil wars, monopolized by a handful of landlords, facing intolerable conditions of employment, applying limited technology, and lacking an efficient system of transportation, agriculture proved no match for the developing oil industry. The oil industry did have an indirect impact on the ability of producers to sell their goods abroad. As Coronil and others have pointed out, the strong Venezuelan currency, buttressed by oil-generated revenues, increased the price of Venezuelan exports and made it difficult to compete in international markets.[43] In particular, coffee interests faced higher production costs and international competition, especially from other producers in Latin America.[44] As agricultural production faltered and foreign reserves increased, by the 1930s Venezuela became a net importer of basic food products.[45]

CENTROS PETROLEROS (OIL COMMUNITIES)

Much as Maracaibo had been unprepared for the flood of Venezuelans and foreigners drawn by the oil fever, the communities of the eastern lakeshore found themselves overrun after 1922. In the words of an early oilman from the United States, "Maracaibo reeled momentarily under the impact of the boom, but was able to absorb it. Cabimas became a madhouse."[46] As several major oil companies (voc, Caribbean, Venezuelan Gulf, and Lago) initiated operations within its perimeters, the once-placid Cabimas, a town with a lone main street, became the first to experience the onslaught. The greater Cabimas area had previously included the smaller settlements in the area of Punta Icotea—La Rosa, Ambrosio, Punta Gorda, and La Salina, to name a few.[47] Even with limited production under way since 1914, the municipality of Cabimas in 1920 still only had a population of only 1,940 (1,030 women and 910 men). Although early on Caribbean and VOC had built some quarters and provided basic services for their own crews, outsiders quickly overran whatever local facilities existed, compelling the municipality to undergo drastic alterations.

As in Mene Grande, many newcomers never actually obtained employment with the oil companies and instead joined the floating population that characterized most oil towns. This "reserve army" of labor settled in the ever-expanding periphery of the formal settlement, becoming what some writers have labeled a "parasite community."[48] Occasionally its members secured work in construction along the docks, or performed menial service jobs while waiting for the chance to work in oil. By 1936 Cabimas's population had mushroomed to 21,753 (11,525 men and 10,288 women) and by 1940 the figure was 33,328 (17,070 men and 16,258 women).[49] That men were only slightly more numerous than women attests to the tendency of families and women to migrate as part of the first wave. Except for those from Margarita, for most migrant groups sexual imbalances gradually became less pronounced.[50]

Criminal records for Cabimas and the Bolívar district underscore the presence of a large floating male population and a dramatic rise in petty crime, including drunkenness, brawls, and the occasional swindler preying on unsuspecting oil workers. Reports during February 1926 demonstrate the diverse origins of the Venezuelans and even foreigners who descended on the oil towns. Among those arrested were Ramón Guevara from the state of Trujillo, Felipe Ramos from Margarita, Juan Yares from Falcón, Antonio Lugo from Mérida, Daniel Walter from the United States, and Joseph Malhogigg from Grenada. Of the twenty prisoners remanded for trial only five had actually been born in the state of Zulia.[51] Faced with this influx, Cabimas became, in the words of the early Venezuelan labor activist and journalist Jesús Prieto Soto, a "chaotic amalgam of humanity."[52] One observer from the United States commented that "choked with whites, yellows, and blacks, Cabimas became a hodgepodge of races and ambitions, a Babylon of tongues. It became a fantastic, tropical Klondike with all the attendant maladies that once hit Alaska and also California."[53]

In the wake of the Barroso and other subsequent discoveries, the companies engaged in a frantic effort to monopolize the remaining oil concessions around the lake and the nearby region. State archives and court proceedings verify tremendous activity throughout the lake region, initiated by both the oil companies and private individuals.[54] The prices of most existing structures, whether houses or shacks, soared much as they had in Maracaibo, becoming prohibitive for most newcomers. Residents in Encontrados, for example, complained that after the arrival of several exploration crews, houses that had once rented for fifty bolívares had increased to over eighty bolívares in a short time.[55] Before long people all along the lakeshore were demanding action by civil authorities to halt the speculation in housing and land. Although the municipal authorities regularly complained, state officials in Maracaibo repeatedly turned a blind eye to this worsening situation, insisting that the law did not permit them to regulate prices.[56]

Imprecise before the advent of the oil bonanza, property titles quickly became mired in legal controversy as land once worthless now acquired value. All the oil companies quickly established legal departments and hired Venezuelan lawyers to deal with these thorny issues. Where the oil company could not reach agreement with local owners it sought to gain access to the property by insisting that state authorities expropriate the land for a "public utility." To lay an underwater cable that would allow telephone service from its Bella Vista Camp at Ambrosio to Maracaibo, Venezuelan Gulf needed to cross land owned by Sylvia Melendez de Tinoco, who refused permission. Lago's efforts to erect lines from its installations in Lagunillas to its offices at La Salina encountered similar problems. Judson Wood, Gulf's representative, and Howland Bancroft, on behalf of Lago, complained to Governor Vicencio Pérez Soto, who ordered local civil authorities to grant the companies access to the disputed land.[57] When the Mara Oil Company found its work delayed because Carmen Beltrán refused access to her land, it called on the governor, who sustained its position.[58] Undoubtedly these and other landowners sought to benefit from their land's newfound wealth, but the oil companies' ability to use the purported law on "public utilities" gave them the upper hand.

Though at first voc and other companies sought to curry favor with local municipalities and landowners, after 1922 relations between these interests and the companies soured.[59] Dealings with local authorities over the use of municipal lands to drill or build company housing became a source of tension.[60] In a letter to voc in 1926, Carlos Dupuy of Santa Rita acknowledged the oil companies' control over production and in turn requested that the company recognize the municipality's authority to instruct the company where it could construct its facilities and to collect taxes on the property.[61] The same situation evolved in the district of Lagunillas, where voc sought to obtain concessions at Tasajeras del Sur. The municipality granted the request only after voc had agreed to recognize the *ejidos* (communal lands) in the area.[62] Despite this apparent truce, residents continued to complain about company-built fences and roads and the disasters produced by drilling operations within the municipal limits.[63] As companies attempted to drill in the proximity of already proven wells, the landscape quickly came to resemble a tangled web of drilling rigs, storage tanks, pipes, and makeshift jetties stretching over the land and the water. A maze of piers and other docking facilities severely restricted access to the lakeshore. Company-controlled docks crowded the shore, and residents in La Rosa and elsewhere complained that they no longer had access to the public embarcadero.[64] The lake, once a living resource that provided goods to the inhabitants, had become, in the words of one oilman from the United States, an "artery for traffic."[65]

Beyond access to the lakefront, drilling operations also occurred immediately next to established residences, and it was not long before this arrangement produced tragic results. One dramatic case occurred in 1928, when a well operated by Gulf Oil erupted in a ball of fire less than fifty meters from Ambrosio's principal street. The incident left several dead and injured and caused panic among the local residents. Later that year, a voc well erupted, scattering clouds of gas and sand that damaged nearby houses and coconut groves. On another occasion oil lines burst near the Botiquin "Sol de Oriente," harming the structure; the company offered the owner, Elías Borjas, 125 bolívares in compensation. The pernicious smell of escaping natural gas, a byproduct of oil production, and the ever-present odor of crude oil became part of daily life. Denying any responsibility, state officials blamed the avarice of local residents for having sold the companies the right to drill on their property.[66] The initial inaction on the part of the state and federal governments intensified an already volatile situation, directly pitting the local populace against the foreign oil companies. After repeated clashes, and with evidence of incipient labor organizing, the companies gradually recognized the need to make concessions to the adjacent communities and the labor force to avoid confrontations that could adversely affect production.

The environmental problems that beset the region were not confined to the land. As Lago developed its lake sites, crews first drilled near the shore, but increasingly wells moved out into the lake; Lago's LR 5 was 141 yards out. As these distances increased, the company had to address the issue of platforms and pilings to hold machinery and drillers; in a tropical climate with voracious wood-eating insects, timbers did not last long. Another problem was recovering the oil when a well blew, or began to produce. On many occasions the drillers were unprepared, and the oil simply poured out onto the lake. One driller from the United States rigged a series of canvas sheets with drum buoys with which he surrounded an escaping well.[67] Unfortunately the well flowed uncontrolled for six days, and a significant amount of oil floated on the lake surface and covered the shore. Throughout the Bolívar Coastal district oil stained the water and landscape. The United States consul in Maracaibo reported: "Oil is spattered everywhere on the vegetation and the houses, it is carried into the offices and dwellings on the shoes or the clothes of those who enter."[68]

Beset by dramatic changes in their way of life, environmental disasters, and the inaction or outright corruption of political officials, town residents along the lakeshore reflected on their condition. A group of "fathers and mothers of Cabimas" directed a letter to President Gómez lamenting that their towns, their pristine beaches, and the crystalline waters of the lake had been turned into an oil camp. The use of the phrase "fathers and mothers" in the letter and the inclusion of a significant number of women petitioners attested to the social disruption affecting the entire community. In the past, formal protests of this sort tended to be predominately male projects. The reference to a lost, idyllic past meant that for residents the very notion of the oil industry, once connoting development and progress, had become negative. According to the petitioners, the companies that built boilers, oil tanks, pipes, and fences had desecrated land the residents considered sacred (a reference to the well operated by VOC adjacent to the town cemetery).

More important, they argued, the companies had usurped their land, expropriated their lumber, erected fences, and run pipes over their property without their permission. Environmental issues were sources of concern, since the petitioners alleged that fires, explosions, and the scarcity of water had disrupted their lives: "water, the prime element of life is almost denied us, . . . company-provided faucets are few."[69] With few if any alternatives, some people had been forced to move from the countryside to the towns, and this had benefited both the company and the government. It had given the company unimpeded access to the areas where it had established drilling operations, as well as space to build facilities and construct camps for its employees.

The letter from the Cabimas residents drew the ire of the governor of Zulia, who chastised them for not having addressed the matter to him instead of approaching Gómez directly. To save face, in a communiqué to Gómez he minimized the events at Cabimas and Ambrosio.[70] Manuel Borjas Hernández, a promoter of the petition, attempted unsuccessfully to persuade the governor that the petitioners had appealed to Gómez because the matter involved the federal rather than the state government.[71] The indignation of the state governor was only one of the obstacles that the residents faced. Their demands reflected the concerns of small property and business owners who at one time had been influential in the affairs of the town. Undoubtedly the oil industry had disrupted their lives, but they also lamented their diminished social and economic standing and reduced political influence over their own affairs.

COMPETING INTERESTS

The thousands of migrants from throughout Venezuela who descended on the oilfields did not immediately share their concerns over land or property-related issues. Rather, those employed by the oil companies and other related industries worried about working conditions, wages, and housing. Other economic and social interests also proved less than sympathetic. Those involved in commerce benefited from the growth of the oil towns. The existing merchants, mostly owners of *pulperías* who supplied local residents, proved incapable of providing for the growing population. To meet demand, basic supplies arrived daily by boat from Maracaibo, where a few merchant houses benefited from the new expanding markets.[72] The docks at

Maracaibo, according to the British consul, were "piled high with materials mostly for the oil fields."[73]

Recognizing new opportunities along the eastern lakeshore, before long a host of new merchants acquired land on the ever-expanding main street of Cabimas and opened establishments. In some cases servicing the needs of workers employed on round-the-clock shifts meant that these businesses opened at all hours. The growth of the oil towns created conditions for new consumer markets, the introduction of foreign goods, and the development of a multinational merchant class. Within a short time Italians, Arabs, and Chinese established dominance over certain areas of the retail trade. While English could be heard at the work sites, Chinese, Portuguese, Italian, and Arabic speakers struggled to master Spanish and profit from their role in the commercial trade.

CABIMAS

In the Cabimas area the hundreds of outsiders quickly displaced the original residents, requiring the spatial and economic reorganization of the settlement and dramatically altering their environment. The oil worker, as the onetime resident Manuel Bermúdez Romero recalled, soon replaced the rancher on horseback on the streets of Cabimas.[74] Eventually the oil worker, with oil-splattered khaki clothes, an aluminum hardhat, boots, and a shiny metal lunch pail, became a common sight in every oil town in Venezuela. The first problem to face Cabimas was how to house and feed the newcomers. Residents with excess space opened their homes, renting rooms at premium prices, while others offered to cook meals for the mostly male migrants. Food preparation, once a private activity, moved into the public arena as street vendors with pushcarts crowded into the street to feed the hungry oil workers.[75] Cabimas's two main streets, La Principal and Rosario, which had housed a few shops and single-storied, whitewashed residences, experienced a wave of new and seemingly unplanned construction.

The urban boom overwhelmed the ability of the local municipal and state political structures to provide services to the expanding population. Water, lights, sewerage, refuse collection, police, and medical care either did not exist or were in short supply. Previously, a small number of wells, or *casimbas*, had supplied the population of Cabimas with some of its water. Teams of burros made the daily journey carrying water to these communities.

This source proved incapable of providing for the growing community, however.[76] Lack of access to water became a constant complaint among residents.[77] State and local officials pressured the oil companies to provide water. Since the water around the lake had been contaminated, the companies trekked inland and dug several new wells.

The companies' provision of basic services to the community was not simply a matter of corporate largesse; their drilling activities, their need for hundreds of workers, and the environmental damage caused by their operations had created the conditions that overwhelmed local municipalities. These activities, initially a response to local protests, became part of a broader strategy referred to by Standard Oil as "enlightened industrialism." Along with an array of other measures, they became part of the company's arsenal for winning over local communities, securing public support, and undermining potential challenges to their power.[78] Moreover, they linked the population not employed in the industry to the actions of the oil company. They also skewed local and national loyalties, since the population now looked to the foreign concerns and not to the municipality for services. The company supplied central water faucets for some towns from which people carried water back to their homes in tin buckets, usually discarded oil cans. These water facilities seldom kept pace with the demands of a growing population and also became a source of tension.[79] Facing political protests and labor disputes, the companies relented and offered other basic services such as electricity and in some cases access to medical care.[80]

The new physical appearance of towns such as Cabimas reflected their rather impromptu character. Unregulated construction produced a labyrinth of passages that eventually obstructed the movement of wagons and later automobiles.[81] Rodolfo Quintero commented that throughout the Lake Maracaibo region new makeshift settlements sprang up like mushrooms.[82] At many levels regionalism, still the prevailing unifying cultural force, determined how many newcomers congregated and where. The new barrios that arose near Cabimas and other oil towns bore the names of people's home states or some other region-specific identifier. Seeking some sense of security in this new, improvised society, migrants clung to their customs, traditions, and cultural symbols. Neighborhoods such as Corito, Los Medanos, and Punto Fijo reflected the origins of migrants from Falcón in the oilfields. Similarly, the appearance of several Caroritas along the eastern lakeshore spoke to the overwhelming presence of migrants from Lara.[83] Residents of Carora imported their traditional regional drink, cocuy, a local spirit made from a Venezuelan variant of the maguey plant.[84] Migrants from Margarita formed the nucleus of barrios known as El Cardonal and La Montañita. In Lagunillas they formed the basis of the Campo Rojo. In these and other neighborhoods they built shrines to the Virgen del Valle, patron of their island.[85] Zulianos and Andinos also congregated in distinctive neighborhoods and socialized with members of their home areas.

Mutual aid societies and social clubs, such as the Unión Mutua Falconiana (Falcón Mutual Aid Union), provided gathering places for people from the same state and raised funds to help developments back in their home communities. The Sociedad Pro La Guardia (Society in support of La Guardia), composed of migrants from Margarita, contributed to construction projects on their home island.[86] Framed by their concerns for mutual aid and sharing regional loyalties, these societies became the nucleus of early labor organizing.[87] Mutual aid societies proved incapable of addressing the multifaceted needs of the diverse population; rather they were a regional response to immediate community needs. Nonetheless, they played an important role and remained viable institutions even after trade unions had been founded.

Housing continued to be the most immediate need. Most Venezuelan newcomers slept in open-air accommodations referred to by Venezuelans as *caneyes* and euphemistically described as longhouses by the English-speaking population. In most cases these hastily constructed structures amounted to no more than a few wooden poles covered by matted straw roofs or sheets of zinc. These impromptu arrangements sprang up all over town, providing migrants a place to hang their hammocks and store their belongings.[88] Exposed on most sides to the tropical environment and offering little if any privacy, the caneyes were extremely insalubrious. Authorities in Cabimas described one of them as a twenty-one-square-meter structure in which twenty-four Venezuelans alternated sleeping on eight hammocks as they worked three shifts in the oilfields. Since men were not the only migrants, these open-air structures also served to house families. All ordinary household activities took place in the open air, including cooking and basic necessities. For one Venezuelan veteran oil worker, the mood of life in the caneyes varied from boredom to a constant commotion that reminded him of a human beehive.[89] Most structures did not have a single "bathroom, nor a drain, nor any manner of discharge on the entire property."[90] During periods of heat these conditions produced an unbearable stench, and when it rained they generated a lagoon that was a source of malaria. The caneyes became a breeding ground for diseases that quickly spread among the population. One long-time resident, J. A. Colina Nava, reported that it was not uncommon to find workers dead of malaria in their hammocks.[91] In one case, authorities lamented that two men who lived in a caney had already succumbed to the diseases.[92] With dozens of caneyes dispersed throughout Cabimas, raw sewage regularly emptied into the streets, a condition made worse with the advent of tropical rains. During the rainy season a network of raised wooden planks made some streets passable. Most waste eventually made its way to the shore, aggravating the contamination of the lake.[93]

LAGUNILLAS DE AGUA AND THE NEW LAGUNILLAS

In the pre-colonial town of Lagunillas de Agua, most people continued to live in houses elevated on stilts over the lake itself. The lakeshore, in most cases below sea level, constantly flooded, creating an inaccessible and inhospitable marsh in which insects and reptiles abounded. Though the town was connected to land by a series of creaky wooden causeways, most of its daily activities took place over water. People cooked on *reverberos*, or kerosene stoves, they used gas lamps for lighting, and although they lived over the lake they were obliged to buy their potable water in tin cans.[94] One traveling writer from the United States described Lagunillas as "a weird place, a jumble of galvanized iron huts perched on piles over oil-covered water. The streets are canals full of black floating timber. The sidewalks are precarious planks, slanting up and down tilting sideways . . . There are no smells but the clean antiseptic smell of the oil, for Mother Lake still carries away all sewage."[95] Aquiles Ferrer, an early resident, expressed the sentiment of many when he said that at Lagunillas "food was bad and sleeping worse, as if it were a Tropical Liberia."[96] Despite these grim conditions, Lagunillas became a magnet, an important destination on the oil route. As elsewhere, more people arrived than the companies could employ. Leonard reported that there were three times as many men in the village as were employed by the oil companies: "How they earn a living is a mystery."[97] The reality is that not everyone did find employment, and many people lived in poverty.

It was not uncommon for state and federal officials to receive petitions for assistance from the residents of Lagunillas. In July 1926, for example, Ana Cleotilde Sánchez wrote to Juan Vicente Gómez pleading for help. Her husband had become ill, and she found it impossible to care for and feed her eight children.[98] Her plight highlights the precarious conditions that many families faced, especially those dependent on a male breadwinner. Despite these and other problems, the population kept increasing. In 1920, at the onset of oil exploration, the population of Lagunillas included 982 residents (493 men and 489 women). With exploration by voc and Venezuelan Gulf under way, the town's population skyrocketed, reaching 13,922 by 1936 and 19,391 by 1941, not all in the over-water community. The male-female ratios mirrored those of Cabimas. Lagunillas residents now included 3,048 migrants from Trujillo, 2,650 from Falcón, 1,990 from Margarita, 1,190 from Lara, 278 from Mérida, 264 from Táchira, and 542 from other states. In addition to Venezuelans, over 785 foreigners now resided in Lagunillas and its environs.[99]

Incapable of absorbing the influx, the town witnessed the rise of a parallel community over portions of the reclaimed coastal wetlands. Building the community involved the monumental task of draining the adjacent coastal marsh, which lay several feet below sea level. To accomplish this task the companies constructed a dam along the coast and employed dozens of pumps operating twenty-four hours a day to empty the marsh, forever altering the environment of the area. On the reclaimed land they built their offices, oil storage tanks, and support facilities and constructed housing camps for their employees. Mene Grande (Gulf) built the Alegria camp in 1928 and Campo Rojo in 1930, the Shell companies built the Carabobo camp in 1929, and Lago (subsequently Creole) built the Bella Vista camp in 1930. Thus two communities, one founded by indigenous people and another by the oil companies, established an uneasy coexistence. The two Lagunillas, one built of timber and straw and the other of cement block and zinc, stood in sharp contrast, embodying the dramatic changes afoot in the oilfields.

For the oil companies the assorted over-water residences were a nuisance and an obstacle to their operations. A fierce struggle ensued between the residents of Lagunillas de Agua who wished to preserve their homes and the oil companies that drilled near the site. Townspeople distrusted Lago and Gulf, which repeatedly asked that the village be moved or at least reduced in size. A compromise in 1926 involved the placement of steel posts in the water to outline the boundary between the oil company's concessions and the town limits.[100] On numerous occasions residents warned of an impending disaster threatened by the pipelines that traversed the area around the town, the repeated oil spills, the escaping gases, and the density of the wooden structures. On two occasions, in 1928 and again in 1939, fire devastated the pre-colonial town.

The fire which destroyed over four hundred structures in 1928 had mysterious origins. There are those who insist that the companies, either directly or indirectly, had a hand in it. Oil regularly spilled from the nearby drilling sites and into the water below the town. The *Tropical Sun* in Maracaibo blamed a Chinese laundry worker who had tipped over a gas lantern for initiating the blaze.[101] After the fire, residents rallied support throughout the state and demanded the right to rebuild their community. In an urgent telegram in July 1928 Governor Pérez Soto reported to the minister of the interior that Lagunillas residents requested the immediate reconstruction of their residences, believing that they had "all the rights and preferences over any other interests," an allusion to the oil companies which sought to relocate the town.[102] Several statewide committees, including the Red Cross and the Maracaibo Chamber of Commerce, aided in raising funds for the victims of the Lagunillas fire.[103] As the leader of the Catholic Church, the bishop of Maracaibo became the titular head of one committee. Some of the most influential and economically powerful people in the state, including leading merchants, bankers, and even the oil companies themselves, donated funds and supplies. Among these, voc and Lago and members of the élite such as Guillermo París each donated five hundred bolívares. Others such as Caribbean and the shipper and merchant H. L. Boulton donated four hundred bolívares each.[104] In addition, hundreds of ordinary people from throughout the area contributed funds. Women were the recipients of the vast majority of the funds distributed to fire victims, underscoring their continued role as heads of households.[105]

While they publicly donated funds for the reconstruction, Gulf and Lago actively lobbied Pérez Soto and Gómez to dismantle what remained of the town.[106] Local merchants, including some with connections in Maracaibo, took the lead in demanding that the town be rebuilt. Many residences in Lagunillas had actually been converted into storefronts containing bars, brothels, restaurants, sundries stores, laundries, and other commercial enterprises. By March 1928 a forty-kilowatt diesel-powered generator was illuminating two thousand light bulbs distributed haphazardly throughout the town.[107] Denied access to the new, company-controlled Lagunillas, various economic groups had a vested interest in seeing the old town reconstructed, fearing the loss of the lucrative market represented by the oil workers. At one point they also sought advice from the governor concerning legal action against Gulf Oil and Lago Petroleum to recoup their losses, which they estimated at six million bolívares.[108] In a petition directed to President Gómez they outlined their position: "The residents of Lagunillas, the majority of whom are merchants damaged by the dreadful fire . . . urge you to proceed and reconstruct our houses in order to return to our dignified work and overcome the grave losses that have left us in misery."[109] The arguments they employed in the defense of Lagunillas ranged from its indigenous origins to the unhealthy conditions found on the mainland.[110] As was usually the case in these matters, Gómez operated behind the scenes. Concerned about the growing power of the foreign oil companies and wanting to extract concessions on the matter of communal lands, Gómez sided with the villagers.[111] In the end, either because they feared a public outcry or because they did not want to concede decision making to the companies, state and federal officials refused to dismantle the town and cede power to the foreign oil companies.

Versions of the origin of the fire that sealed the fate of the old Lagunillas in 1939 also differed widely. The *Esfera*, a conservative newspaper published in Caracas that favored the oil companies, blamed a woman named Luisa Mendoza for mishandling an oil lantern in the Bar Caracas and inadvertently starting the fire that left many dead.[112] In a report to the president, Manuel Maldonado, the governor of Zulia, also blamed Mendoza. The labor organizer and Communist Party member Jesús Farías sent a telegram to President Eleazar López Contreras identifying the accumulation of gas and oil from a nearby well as the source of the fire.[113] The oil companies again feared an avalanche of lawsuits, and the Shell subsidiaries requested a specialist from Curaçao to conduct an internal investigation.[114] They also pursued policies intended to curry favor with officials and the local population, offering medical assistance, providing housing at the nearby Bachaquero camp, and building a road to the lake edge to facilitate the movement of supplies and people.[115]

After this second fire, however, the balance of power in the area had shifted significantly. The existence of an established and fully functional land-based community undermined efforts to rebuild the over-water one. The companies had waged a protracted campaign with officials against the continued existence of the over-water settlement, claiming that it interfered with production at one of their most lucrative fields, and they now exercised significantly more power in regional and national politics. The federal government had limited the power of regional élites over even local matters. Many of the small merchants who had previously led the protest had ceased operations, and the concerns of local residents paled in comparison with the problems faced by many others throughout the region. Despite the unwillingness of most people to relocate, the government refused to accede to local demands for the reconstruction of Lagunillas.

Having little choice, a significant number of residents moved to Ciudad Ojeda, a few kilometers away. Founded by presidential decree in 1937, Ciudad Ojeda was the first formal city to be established by the government after the onset of oil production. According to the decree Lagunillas "constituted an imminent threat to health and well-being of its inhabitants," because the land beneath it was sinking and its current location forced its periodic rebuilding.[116] The government designated a million bolívares for the construction of the new town and named it for the Spaniard Alfonso de Ojeda, who had "discovered" Lake Maracaibo. Designed by the architect Cipriano Domínguez as a series of concentric circles around a central plaza, the city was expected to absorb the flow of people to the area, and it now became the district capital.[117] Despite the government's plan, by the end of the 1940s Ciudad Ojeda had still not evolved into the model city that had been envisioned.[118] The demolition of old Lagunillas, however, marked the end of an era for lake residents and underscored the growing power of the oil companies in government decision making.

NEW RELATIONS OF PRODUCTION

Venezuelans constituted the backbone of the oil industry's daily labor force. The new work regimen of the oilfields introduced Venezuelans to new patterns of work, relations of production, and especially ways of organizing time. For the average laborer arriving from the countryside, the experience of working in oil represented a dramatic break from the previous rhythms of seasonal agricultural work. The oil companies recognized this and attempted to "de-ruralize" the Venezuelan laborers and implant a new concept of time and a new work ethic. The process took time and initially required concessions to existing practices and norms. At first VOC, for example, established nine-hour split shifts to avoid the oppressive noonday heat and accommodate Venezuelan culinary customs and constructions of time. From May to October the workday for early VOC employees began at six and continued until eleven; workers then received three hours for lunch and were expected to return at two and work until six. From October to May workers began their day at seven, broke for lunch at noon, and returned to work from one to five.[119] Discipline and productivity were central concerns. The work rules established by VOC in 1915 reveal the types of behavior that they sought to "mitigate":

1. not being punctual in arriving to work during established hours
2. abandoning the job without prior authorization
3. carelessness in the execution of work
4. disobedience
5. gambling during work
6. drunkenness during work
7. "raterias" or theft of small items

These rules can be seen as falling into two major categories. The first four sought to impose control over a labor force that was considered disorderly and were aimed at regimenting the workday, establishing non-familial lines of authority, and limiting individual action. The last three rules assumed the existence of purported negative behavior and "cultural practices" that undermined the establishment of a work ethic and control of the workforce. In typical fashion, foreigners assumed the characteristic role of modernizers, confronted by a "backward" labor force that had to be transformed. Infractions of any of these work rules could result in a fine of between 5 and 25 percent of the wage or outright dismissal.[120] These rules relied on force for their implementation, and they expressed the relative power of the companies, which usually could count on the backing of the government.

Time did little to alter the early views of foreign companies concerning Venezuelan laborers. Despite almost twenty years in the country, Caribbean and other British-controlled interests continued to characterize the Venezuelan labor force as inefficient: "The Venezuelan workman has no social or any other kind of education and no esprit de corps, and consequently is unable to understand or properly make use of the provisions for syndicates and collective bargaining."[121] It would be a mistake to assume that these rules and the cultural assumptions underlying them were solely the product of insensitive foreigners. Many Venezuelan intellectuals, as well as Venezuelan business and agricultural interests, shared these beliefs about the labor force. A congress of agricultural, cattle, industrialist, and merchant interests in 1921, the first ever held in Venezuela, reflected much the same views about labor as voc's. Its final report included an assessment of Venezuelan labor as debased, addicted to gambling, inefficient, and lacking in morals and "fulfillment of their duty."[122] Business interests freely applied this characterization to both urban and rural workers. To deal with the ills ascribed to the workforce the congress proposed the development of business, agrarian, and artisan schools, but neither they nor the government addressed the root causes. At no time did the participants, who included members of regional and national élites such as Juan E. París, Alfredo Jahn, General Parra Picón, and Lisardo Alvarado, discuss the difference between urban and rural populations, the subsistence agriculture upon which people depended, or the abject health conditions under which most of them lived. At this level, the oil companies' policies actually mirrored the social, cultural, and class biases of the Venezuelan élite and the emerging middle class.

WAGE STRUCTURES

Labor relations in the oilfields reflected employment patterns marked by a multi-tiered social and racial hierarchy. Employees from the United States performed most professional and skilled functions, serving as tool pushers, riggers, machinists, carpenters, and fabricators. West Indians performed a variety of functions, from physical labor to office help. Asians were relegated to service positions, especially in the mess hall and the laundry. Venezuelans occupied a few office or staff positions as well as constituting the core of the unskilled labor force. To minimize costs and maximize profits, the foreign companies sought large numbers of workers regardless of their national origins.

With time, this structure underwent a series of changes brought about by the emergence of labor militancy, political changes, new company policy, and international conditions. At first, however, most Venezuelans in the employ of the companies were part of a daily bolívar labor squad, or cuadrilla, hired through intermediaries and overseen by a foreman who had the power to hire and fire them. The tenuousness of this situation undermined efforts at labor organizing and gave the company maximum flexibility with regard to its labor force. Both the company and the government classified most laborers on the daily bolívar roll as *peones*, a term that implied a host of negative cultural and social attributes including a rural outlook, illiteracy, and a lack of skills. Although they fiercely denied it, the companies were purported to have kept a list of workers not to be hired for political or other reasons. Since there was no national system of identification at the time, some laborers placed on the list could circumvent the process by altering their names. Officials of the various companies are known to have shared information that would invariably have included labor matters and personnel.[123]

Wages varied greatly by category and skill. For example, unskilled day laborers in 1915 received a daily wage of 3.50 to 5 bolívares. Blacksmiths received 6 to 10 bolívares, and carpenters 4 to 9 bolívares.[124] By the early 1920s the daily wage paid by voc, Colón, and most of the other companies had reached 5 bolívares, sometimes supplemented by meals and housing.[125] Lago's operation in the Bolívar Coastal oilfields provides insight into the company's operations and cost structure. By the 1930s Lago employed on average about fourteen hundred employees, principally in Lagunillas and La Salina, where it maintained over-water platforms, ground-support operations, and employee housing.[126] Total wages and salaries for December 1932 for a workforce of 1,423 amounted to $117,001.06, an average of 82.22 bolívares per employee. November wages had been slightly less, $115.497.91 for 1,421 employees, or an average of 81.28 bolívares per person. These expenses translated into production costs per barrel. For Lagunillas, Lago estimated the cost of a barrel of oil at $0.1286. The area of Cabimas had slightly higher costs, averaging $0.2833 per barrel. The average cost of production for all fields amounted to $0.1711, while the cost of a barrel on

international markets hovered near $1.00.[127] Labor therefore only consti-
tuted a small fraction of the costs necessary to produce a barrel of oil; other
factors such as transportation, refining, and profit margins exerted more
pressure on that price.

NEW HOUSING ARRANGEMENTS

Though voc and Caribbean took steps to expand the available housing,
their efforts were insufficient in the face of the ever-expanding population.
Most building materials, including construction-grade lumber, had to be
imported from abroad. Lago, a latecomer, faced a dilemma in that it had,
as one observer commented, "an oil field but no place for oilmen to stay."[128]
Many foreigners began by making use of whatever accommodations existed. Lago's first employees lived in rooms described as simple thatched-
roof huts.[129] At Lagunillas the first drillers lived in the over-water town and
later ones erected tents on the nearby reclaimed swamplands.[130] Describing
this situation and hoping to evoke a response from readers in the United
States, one journalist reported that foreign drillers had succumbed to the
allure of the tropics and gone "native," maintaining "palm thatched 'homes,'
mestizo women and jungle broods."[131]

Only a few foreigners actually pursued this arrangement. The majority made use of rudimentary housing in bachelors' facilities carved out of
the rainforest. Differences between the housing for foreign and Venezuelan
employees evolved gradually, becoming most pronounced after the 1930s.[132]
Even at the outset, however, screened longhouses constructed by voc safe-
guarded foreign workers from malaria-carrying mosquitoes, and crews of
cooks and attendants served their basic needs.[133] To control diseases, voc
sprayed oil on standing water around these structures.

Besides the longhouses, other, more formal quarters soon took shape.
Enclosed behind protective wire fences and built on stilts to protect against
flooding and contact with venomous snakes, these facilities were the first
separate housing arrangements in the area built exclusively for foreigners.
Lago eventually acquired land on a salt flat south of Cabimas, filled in the
lakeshore, and built its facilities and its first quarters for the largely bachelor
foreign crews. The one-story bunkhouses had six separate rooms, to each
of which four men were assigned, sharing a separate bathhouse that one
oilman described as a "community affair." Invariably one area in the bach-

elors' quarters would be designated the poker room.[134] Since the company had cleared the existing undergrowth, conditions at the camp resembled those in Cabimas; during the dry season it became a "dust bin, in the wet a quagmire."[135]

As the labor force increased, separate camps to house Venezuelan oil workers also became a necessity. Labor camps for Venezuelan workers steadily took shape all along the eastern coast of Lake Maracaibo—at Cabimas, Ambrosio, Tía Juana, Tasajera, Lagunillas, and elsewhere, with names such as Las 40, Las Delicias, La Salina, Miraflores, Las Cupulas, Campo Blanco, El Milagro, Rancho Grande, and Campo Altagracia (in Cabimas) and Campo Verde (in Tía Juana). Aquiles Ferrer described the first structures that voc made for housing families as small and surrounded by zinc on all four sides, not lending themselves to "comfortable or healthy conditions."[136] The voc camp at La Rosa, among the first built, provided access to water but employed a collective latrine or an outhouse separate from the structure.[137] Lago provided only small wooden shacks, roofed with the now-customary zinc. voc also built similar structures but painted the outside walls grey. Single male workers were housed in "caney-like structures, built with sheets of zinc that did not cover all sides and had a split roof." As they did throughout Cabimas, men strung up their hammocks from the poles that held up the roof.[138]

Workers throughout the oil-producing districts regularly complained about the lack of proper ventilation, the heat generated by zinc walls and roofs, and the utter boredom that followed a day's work. Faced by repeated complaints, in 1930 the government appointed a special commissioner of oil camps to inspect and report on conditions. After visiting the Standard Oil (later Creole) camp at Quiriquire in Monagas, the inspector concluded that Venezuelans "slept in overcrowded storage sheds . . . inevitably infested with mosquitoes."[139] A subsequent report from the office of the technical inspector of hydrocarbons in Maracaibo further confirmed workers' complaints, demanding that the Colón Development Company replace zinc roofs "in order to avoid fatal consequences" to the workers.[140] Other critics referred to camp houses as nothing more than corrugated "match boxes."[141] At Mene Grande, La Rosa, Cabimas, and Lagunillas, workers were critical not only of low wages and the high cost of living but also of the inadequate housing conditions. Even with the appointment of a special inspector of oil camps, in eastern Venezuela the situation did not appear to have been any better. Almost ten years after his original visit, at camps operated by Standard, including Jusepin and Quiriquire, workers complained of residing in "zinc prisons" in which the tropical heat was suffocating.[142] The history of labor-management relations in the oil industry is marked by a succession of local disputes over wages and housing dating from the early 1920s.

Views on the origins and significance of these camps reflect the ongoing debate concerning the assumed "modernizing" role of the oil companies in Venezuela. Briceño Parilli and many others insist that the "oil companies voluntarily provided advantageous housing conditions in oil camps in order to attract workers," but judging from early workers' complaints, company housing became a source of tension rather than relief.[143] The error of many foreign and Venezuelan observers is to equate living conditions in later periods, particularly after 1936 and the passage of labor laws that required companies to provide housing, with those present earlier.[144] Idealistic constructions of the past that focus on the allegedly benevolent role of the oil industry are simply not sustained by the record of workers' complaints. Once built, however, the new labor camps set the stage for the gradual transformation of the urban landscape. Moreover, they set in motion a process that had significant cultural and social implications for the formation of the working class in the oil industry.[145]

REDEFINING LEISURE

For both Venezuelans and some foreigners employed in the area, Cabimas was the principal center for leisure. As one early witness from the United States remembered, "When day faded into dusk, the conglomeration of hot, sweaty humanity was swelled by hundreds of professional girls, procurers, gamblers and foreigners all hell bent on a boisterous and happy evening."[146] Nearby residents found it impossible to sleep at night.[147] Since the companies paid employees in gold, hundreds of swindlers and con artists devised creative schemes to part workers from their pay. On Saturday nights "the main street of Cabimas was crowded from building line to building line with Venezuelan oil workers, all striving to spend their money."[148] Loan sharks preyed on the poor and the recently arrived, or on those who had gambled away their week's earnings.[149]

Inevitably, the predominantly male population supported recreational establishments such as bars, gambling dens, and bordellos. Sex workers from Maracaibo hired launches on Saturday afternoons to transport them to the booming oil towns, where workers lined the docks to greet them by name.[150] Gambling establishments and saloons opened adjacent "dance halls" for prostitutes, the owners having worked out arrangements with local officials.[151] Besides prostitution, district officials took note of the increased importation of liquor and the production and sale of local spirits from clandestine stills.[152] Facing political opposition, state and federal officials worried that opponents might manipulate the presence of thousands of workers in the oilfields. In 1923 the governor of Zulia, Santos Matute Gómez (who often used his maternal name Gómez to indicate a relation to the dictator), feared that a potentially explosive situation was developing at Mene de Bucivacoa in the nearby state of Falcón and at other camps in Zulia.[153] Steps were taken to install trusted civil authorities and adequate police forces in the camps. Newly appointed Jefes Civiles (civil officials), many of whom had economic stakes in illicit enterprises, applied their own brand of justice, at times siding with workers and at times with the companies, and took advantage of every opportunity to enrich themselves with private ventures.[154] For example, at the Altagracia camp the car owned by Mr. Fonseca had a monopoly on transport from a local store to the camp, and municipal officials, who received a commission, made sure that he had no competition.[155]

Beyond local independent ventures, the government appointed a commissioner to regulate gambling and oversee the operation of the bordellos.[156] In principle this official was to clamp down on illicit gambling and ensure the collection of taxes from legal operations. On more than one occasion commissioners raided foreign residential camps and sanctioned United States personnel. Chester Marvin Crebbs of Gulf repeatedly complained to the governor of Zulia that Valentín Barrios, accompanied by several policemen, had searched the Cabimas foreign camp, "surprising 5 or 6 employees playing poker" and "fining the offenders 30 bolívares." He insisted that the commissioner lacked a search warrant to enter what the company considered private property.[157] Despite his complaints, Barrios searched the camp again, this time citing four people playing bridge.

Officials of the nascent Department of Mines (Inspector General de Minas), such as Luis F. Calvani, took a dim view of these commissioners and the work they performed. In his *Nuestro máximo problema* he offered a scathing indictment of the relations between gambling and the local and company officials who benefited from it.[158] According to Calvani, the company benefited indirectly: gambling kept the workers broke and dependent on their next paycheck. At the same time, he suggested that workers who stayed up all night drinking, gambling, and engaging in other activities might in the long run "hurt production and undermine the operation of the oil companies."[159] Despite a chorus of criticism from a host of social critics, including unlikely allies such as the Catholic Church and the leftist press, gambling, heavy drinking, and prostitution flourished in the oil camps.

To provide alternative recreation for its employees, the oil companies sponsored open-air movie theaters projecting the celluloid images of Tom Mix, William Hart, and other Hollywood stars. Lago showed films at open-air facilities at Campo Rojo in Lagunillas, where "a considerable number of employees and workers of the oil companies gather to spend a few agreeable hours."[160] After the initial novelty of the films faded, some among the population lost interest in the attraction. Without Spanish translations, the film only reached a handful of people. Even with subtitles, it is doubtful that many workers, a significant number of whom lacked a formal education, could have read the captions. Moreover, the Lagunillas paper *El Bronce* repeatedly complained about the content and quality of films imported from the United States, lamenting that only the worst made their way to Venezuela.[161]

LOS GUACHIMANES (THE WATCHMEN)

The construction of company living facilities and the increasing value of foreign investments in the oilfields led the companies to address the question of security for their equipment and personnel. Fearing political unrest, on matters of security the oil companies and the state and federal government actively cooperated.[162] The local constabulary force, poorly trained and corrupt, was judged wholly insufficient to protect the new facilities. The oil companies hired and trained their own guards to control access to their installations, both production sites and residential camps. At first the new recruits, Venezuelans and some West Indians outfitted with distinctive expedition-like uniforms and large time clocks that they had to trigger on their designated routes, reported to supervisors of foreign origin, from the United States and elsewhere, but by 1936 some Venezuelans had been promoted to lead the guard units.[163] Through their presence and eventually their actions, the guards served as another layer in the refashioning of the Venezuelan labor force, ensuring through force that all understood the new social, cultural, and even racial order that operated in the oilfields.

The guard station at the entrance of a fenced housing camp, refinery, tank farm, or other installation marked the entry to the foreign oil company's property. The guards, or *guachimanes* as Venezuelans derisively called them, operated as the de facto law throughout the oilfields. The companies insisted that they simply provided "assistance to the outsider, and maintained the necessary discipline with incoming and outgoing traffic," but many Venezuelans viewed them as the protectors of foreign interests and as informants.[164]

Protest by local residents and oil workers against the guards became common. Rufo Antonio Mora wrote to President Juan Vicente Gómez to complain that they were "uncultured, sometimes bordering on barbarian," and "in several cases had seriously beaten an employee for the most insignificant reason, to the point of striking him with a club for asserting his rights." He continued, "Rather than correct these injustices the foreigners in charge of these companies regularly applaud their actions."[165] The newspaper editor and novelist G. Bracho Montiel wrote a scathing attack on the role of the guards that captured the prevailing sentiments with regard to this private police force, depicting them as shadowy figures, like vampires, that slept during the day and patrolled at night.[166] The historian Alí López, who attended school at the Tía Juana oil camp under a pseudonym, recollected that people seldom saw the families of the guards.[167]

By controlling access to the camps, the security guards actually kept track of the personal activities of workers and their families. According to Humberto Ochoa, a guard at the Concordia camp nicknamed "El Zorro" would lock the gate at nine o'clock sharp and record any late arrivals, reporting them to the camp staff for termination.[168] At Tía Juana as elsewhere, the guards patrolled on foot at first and later drove around in carts, inspecting the fence. Inquisitive Venezuelan youths who congregated around the fences to watch the foreigners play golf or observe activities at the social club, including 4th of July celebrations and Halloween, often became targets.[169]

By and large, foreigners held a much different view of the security guards who patrolled the camp facilities and served as a metaphoric thin blue line between the foreign enclave and the Venezuelan community. For them the guards allowed Venezuelans in to work, kept out "undesirables," and protected residences while the men were working. That some West Indians served in the security force and could communicate in English facilitated interaction between the camps' foreign residents and the guards.

Increasingly the guards became the focus of dissatisfaction in the community and among workers, and the labor and leftist press aggressively criticized them. Attacks against the guards, whether verbal or physical, embodied the host of tensions that existed in the oilfields. The enmity that many people felt toward them surfaced in the aftermath of the death of Gómez in 1935. During this turbulent period, groups of people set out to settle scores with those in power, and many officials and guards fled. Some foreign employees and their families took refuge on Lago tankers in the middle of the lake until order was restored. One unfortunate former guard in the employ of Lago decided to arm himself and hold out in the Lago offices. Despite his efforts he fell victim to roving bands of workers, who surrounded him, stabbed him to death, and threw his body into a local incinerator.[170]

Beyond physical attacks, which were relatively uncommon, a campaign in the press was mounted by *Petróleo*, a leftist paper distributed in the oil camps. It described one guard, Adeli González, as a "despotic and servile mercenary, a faithful servant of the yanquis and one of the most repulsive beings that workers encountered." It went on to argue that the company must consciously recruit these undesirables in order to promote terror among the workers.[171] Although there is some evidence that they manipulated regional differences in hiring security forces, in fact the companies recruited from the same group of workers who had migrated to the oilfields from throughout Venezuela. In some cases local officials also recommended individual workers for the job.[172] The firms established training programs and attempted to create esprit de corps within their security forces. In the end, however, the companies could not rely solely on the guachimanes to control conditions in the oilfields. Their presence increasingly became a political liability, an outward sign of foreign control over the larger Venezuelan population. Though the security forces were eventually scaled back, the term "guachiman" became politically charged, applied, as Brancho Montiel has pointed out, to anyone who did the bidding of foreign interests.[173]

Beyond its economic impact, by the mid-1920s the oil industry had begun to make its presence felt in the Venezuelan social and cultural landscape. Though they continued to explore for new fields, the oil firms had thousands of acres, both on land and over water, under production. Internal migration, drawing upon diverse social groups, swelled the ranks of an international labor force that congregated in and around the burgeoning oil towns. Migration also produced a significant floating population that further enlarged the ranks of the newcomers and either constituted a reserve army of labor or became part of the service sector that attended to workers' needs. Migrants maintained links with their communities, attracting relatives and friends, and setting the stage for continued migration to the area.

Draining marshes, relocating communities, and despoiling the waters of Lake Maracaibo, the oil industry dramatically altered the physical environment of the region. Existing communities such as Cabimas and Lagunillas found themselves overrun by the oil companies, who did not respect municipal boundaries, and by waves of newcomers who settled in and around the towns. The cost of living soared, traditional housing proved insufficient, and most basic products had to be shipped in from Maracaibo and beyond. To survive, people erected caneyes and adapted to the new hardships. Regionalism and previous ties to a community helped nurture mutual aid societies that provided a basis for future political action. Early residents banded together and resisted these new challenges, but their traditional way of life was forever altered. Municipal authorities proved relatively powerless to halt these changes. Bars, gambling establishments, and bordellos soon proliferated, and their owners sometimes operated in collusion with state and local officials in preying on the oil workers.

Within the industry, a working class gradually took shape and began to define their interests. Few laborers had any experience with the new demands of working in oil. Their adaptation was gradual and involved concessions on both sides. Their relocation accelerated but did not cause the decline of traditional agriculture, which began sometime earlier. Overwhelmingly, in this early period the companies relied on coercion to mold the new labor force. The need to regularize their workforce and exercise greater control compelled them to begin providing housing. Differences quickly emerged between the housing and benefits provided to foreign and Venezuelan laborers, and these differences, coupled with the presence of a social racial hierarchy in the workforce, contributed to tensions in the oilfields. Faced with this volatile scenario, over time the foreign oil companies developed comprehensive alternative strategies that did not rely on force to maintain order in the oilfields and camps.

CHAPTER 4

Oil, Race, Labor, and Nationalism

By the first decades of the twentieth century, the presence of an internationally controlled oil industry and a significant number of foreigners brought concerns about Venezuelan nationalism, race, and identity to the forefront. The United States and British interests that were the owners of the oil industry did not necessarily become the principal targets of Venezuelan nationalism. Rather, it was immigrants of color, particularly Afro–West Indians and Chinese, who became the objects of opportunistic politicians and others who sought to manipulate and direct the emerging nationalist sentiment.[1] The treatment of West Indians and other immigrants and their eventual expulsion from the country brought to the surface deep-seated racial attitudes in Venezuela, further challenging the myth of racial equality.

The foreign-controlled oil industry is critical to any comprehensive understanding of issues of race, identity, and nationalism in Venezuela. The industry played an important role in promoting transnational migration to Venezuela, and this dynamic stamped the foreign policy of the regime of Juan Vicente Gómez and the early national discourse on race and identity, influencing future generations. Traditional interpretations of Gómez's administration have portrayed his government as incapable of comprehending the changes introduced by the oil industry. A careful examination of its responses to the presence of foreigners reveals a much different picture. Oil production forced Gómez to adopt an assertive international policy seeking to influence the course of public opinion in the United States and throughout the region. The manipulation of middle-class and élite concerns about race demonstrated a nuanced understanding of Venezuela's social and racial hierarchy and bridged the political differences between the Gomecistas and the emerging forces that opposed the dictatorship.

The literature on migration in Latin America is extensive, but it overwhelmingly focuses on efforts by élites, influenced by prevailing positivist thinking, to "whiten" the population by attracting European immigrants.[2] Since the 1980s, however, circum-Caribbean scholars have been exploring how interregional immigration promoted by an international export economy influenced the discourse on nationalism and racial identity.[3] The works of these scholars focus attention on élite fears of a supposed "darkening" of the population as a consequence of the Afro–West Indian immigration generated by the activities of foreign entities such as the United Fruit Company.[4] In Venezuela the scapegoating of Afro–West Indians and Chinese immigrants reflected not only economic fears about the foreign-controlled oil industry but also prevailing racist sentiments among élites, intellectuals, and elements of the emerging middle class.

Despite the existence since 1918 of racially inspired restrictive immigration laws that prohibited "the entrance to Venezuela of all foreigners. . . . not of the European race or an insular Yellow race of the Northern Hemisphere," the discovery of oil in Venezuela attracted Afro–West Indians and Chinese from throughout the Caribbean.[5] The colonial relations maintained by the British and the Dutch inspired most of this early migration. Oil companies such as Caribbean, VOC, Lago, and Standard used Trinidad and Curaçao as staging areas for their operations, hiring labor there to work in Venezuela. Curaçao and Aruba also served as sites for refineries. As a consequence, people from Trinidad, Grenada, and Curaçao and from as far away as Mexico, Asia, and the Middle East flocked to Venezuela seeking to share in the newfound wealth. This dramatic movement of people created a cauldron in which a host of tensions began to ferment, all under the watchful eyes of complacent government officials and bosses from the United States and Britain who were sometimes pitiless in their disregard of the contradictions generated by this massive relocation of people.

Before the oil boom Trinidadians and Venezuelans in the states of Sucre, Monagas, and Bolívar shared a long history. The earlier Spanish colonial experience had facilitated commercial and social exchange between the regions, one that continued even after the British occupation of Trinidad in 1797.[6] Throughout this period the towns along the Gulf of Paria engaged in trade with Trinidad. From the muddy banks of the San Juan River near the town of Caripito, the nearby British colony received cotton, cacao, fruits, and cattle.[7] Furthermore, the relative proximity of the Venezuelan mainland to the island led to extensive smuggling.[8] The imposition of a 30 percent surtax on trade with Trinidad during the government of Antonio Guzmán Blanco fueled the growth of contraband, and the presence of Trinidadian and Venezuelan fishing vessels in the Gulf of Paria facilitated its transport.[9] Contraband was not the only concern of the British and Venezuelan authorities. On repeated occasions Trinidad was a safe haven for Venezuelan political exiles seeking to avoid persecution or planning rebellions.[10] The British authorities constantly manipulated the presence of Venezuelan dissidents on Trinidad, viewing them "as a salutary check to the hostile attitude of the Venezuelan Government to British undertakings" and "a powerful lever in defence of [their] interests."[11] In western Venezuela, Curaçao played a similar role, and Gómez's regime closely monitored the presence of Venezuelan workers and immigrants in Curaçao and the other islands controlled by the Dutch.[12]

Beyond serving as a refuge, Port of Spain, the capital of Trinidad, was an important economic and social nexus for many eastern Venezuelans. Remote from Caracas and lacking a viable overland system of roads, they inevitably looked to Trinidad. Many families in Sucre, Monagas, and Margarita sent their children to schools in Port of Spain to receive a British education. In some cases entire families temporarily moved to Trinidad; their children born on the island subsequently found it difficult to reclaim Venezuelan citizenship.[13] Marriage and family linked many Afro-Venezuelans to the social life of Trinidad. Angelina Pollak-Eltz found that older residents at Güiria, in the state of Sucre, still preserved Trinidadian customs and traditions, especially those associated with food, language, and music.[14]

Afro-Trinidadians were also an important component of the labor force in eastern Venezuela. British authorities in Caracas estimated that over three thousand West Indians labored on the cacao plantations between Carupano, Yaguaraparo, and Güiria.[15] The discovery of gold at El Callao in the 1850s also attracted Trinidadians, as did mining activity at Imataca, both in the present-day state of Bolívar. When the New York and Bermúdez Asphalt Company began operations at the Guanoco tar pits in Sucre, it also recruited Trinidadian laborers.[16] As oil discoveries increased in western Venezuela, the British consul in Caracas predicted in 1914 that thousands of West Indians would flock to the country, because they were "more trustworthy and hardworking than Venezuelan labourers."[17] In this he not only discerned the course of future developments but also framed the social and racial arguments that would be used by foreign oil companies in opting to hire West Indians over Venezuelans.

Trinidadians were the largest group of West Indians in Venezuela. Increased foreign immigration to their island, especially from Asia, competition for employment, and depressed wages provided the impetus for many to seek work in Venezuela and throughout the Caribbean.[18] One British traveler observed, "The oilfields . . . are a great attraction throughout the islands, and in Trinidad, it is most difficult to retain skilled builders, who are offered higher wages in the oilfields."[19] The immigrant stream also attracted a few white Trinidadians and British expatriates who faced difficult conditions on the island and sought a better life in Venezuela.[20] Though some previous contact had occurred, mainly in eastern Venezuela, most Trinidadians knew little about Venezuela. The *Guardian*, a newspaper published in Port of Spain, viewed Venezuela as an "unexplored country" and lamented that most people in Trinidad relied on "traveler's tales for news."[21] Afro-Trinidadians making their way to the oilfields had only a partial view of what awaited them in Venezuela.[22]

As Venezuelans flocked to the oilfields, foreign companies increasingly found it necessary to explain their preference for West Indian labor. The most commonly used rationale echoed Spanish and British colonial justifications for the introduction of African slaves or indentured labor, among them the purported lack of skills of the Venezuelans, their supposed feeble physical condition, and their insufficient numbers. The companies' arguments had a familiar ring and reflected decades-old stereotypes about "indolent" or "lazy" Latin American mestizo laborers unable to work in the searing tropical climate. Contrary to foreign stereotypes, most Venezuelans proved quite adept at performing their designated duties: stripping away the dense tropical growth, draining the swamps, felling trees, transporting supplies, digging trenches, constructing roads, and erecting oil derricks and other structures. One observer from the United States believed that Venezuelans, if given the opportunity, could perform all but the most technically skilled operations. In an unusual expression of candor, this foreign traveler concluded, "The companies won't teach the natives all the tricks of the trade. They're afraid if the natives get to know it all these countries down here will kick the Americans and the English out and run the fields themselves."[23]

When Standard Oil of New Jersey contemplated building a refinery in Aruba, it described Afro–West Indian workers in the same stereotypical terms that it had earlier used to describe Venezuelans. It also found that many Arubans had previously deserted their island to work in nearby Venezuelan oilfields.[24] Its internal memos lamented not only their insufficient numbers but also their supposed lack of skills and "malnourished state."[25] In reality, neither Afro–West Indians nor Venezuelans had had any significant previous experience in the oil industry; both groups had to acquire new skills and adapt to new methods of production and new relations of labor.

In the face of these negative assertions, an examination of internal oil company documents reveals very different reasons for hiring Afro–West Indian labor, or what one Standard official called "British Negroes." The company described the West Indian worker as follows: "He is thrifty, home loving, and industrious, and has an excellent temperament, with few of the Latin characteristics, such as excitability, irresponsibility, etc. The young Arubans have had the advantage of better schooling and more easily learn our ways and methods. The young ones have a greater sense of responsibility and are more regular in their attendance on the job."[26] Evidently the belief that West Indians had these cultural and social attributes played a significant role in the oil company's decision to hire Afro–West Indian labor, especially from British- and Dutch-held colonies. Beyond these alleged social characteristics, the ability of West Indians to speak English and their experience with the British colonial administration and educational system increased their social value in the eyes of the oil companies. Moreover, previous relations with Europeans increased the expectation that West Indians would accommodate to the demands of their new employers and be less likely to join Venezuelan labor unions.[27]

The oil companies also sought skilled West Indians and Asians with previous experience as accountants, typists, bookkeepers, or members of the general secretarial staff. The United States consul in Maracaibo reported that the "822 British subjects reported as coming into Maracaibo during 1924 were negroes from Trinidad." The men were employed in the oil camps, some as clerks and stenographers.[28] Cecil Aleong, a Chinese immigrant from Trinidad, had worked twenty-nine years as a bookkeeper at Lagunillas, La Salina, and finally Maracaibo before retiring in the late 1950s.[29] Fluent in English, with limited Spanish skills and minimal ties to the local community, West Indians and Chinese were considered unlikely to divulge private internal matters, a concern that surfaced again years later when companies finally began hiring Venezuelan office staff.[30]

Besides filling clerical positions, Afro–West Indians acquired employment as electricians, mechanics, carpenters, sheet-metal workers, mariners, drivers, and materials transporters. A Trinidadian named Eduardo Elcock, who arrived in Venezuela in 1921 and after several years found employment in the oil industry, is an example of this pattern of migration and employment. Elcock worked as a "de facto" nurse in oil camps throughout the country that lacked formal medical services, and his ability to prescribe home remedies for common illnesses earned him the nickname "El Brujo."[31] Another Trinidadian, Stephen Joseph, who immigrated to Venezuela in 1927, worked his entire life in Creole's materials department while his compatriot Theophilus Wickham Jones worked in the metal shop.[32] Gordon Wildman arrived from Port of Spain in 1929 without speaking a word of Spanish and obtained employment with Lago, first as a telephone operator in Lagunillas, then in the electrical department, and lastly as a dispatcher in the materials warehouse.[33] Other Afro–West Indian workers followed the same pattern. Joseph Modest arrived from Grenada in 1924 and found employment with Standard Oil at Las Palmas, later making the transition to Creole.[34] Morain O. C. Bruno, also a native of Grenada, immigrated to Venezuela in 1925 and worked in the metals department at La Salina for most of his career.[35] Other Grenadians, such as William James Linton, soon followed and also labored for several decades with Creole before retiring.[36]

Not all West Indians occupied office or skilled positions in the oil company hierarchy. Many found employment only in the kitchen, in the laundry, or in housekeeping and were sometimes pejoratively labeled "houseboys."[37] Along with Venezuelans and Asians employed in this capacity, they cleaned the foreign employees' quarters, especially the bachelors' facilities, did the laundry, and performed other such duties. Agricultural interests in the southern Lake Maracaibo region also had an interest in Afro-Caribbean labor. United States consular records in Maracaibo and in the French West Indies reveal plans to import Martinicans to work on the sugar plantations of the Central Venezuelan Company in the Bobures region. According to Walter S. Keineck, United States consul in Martinique, on 4 August 1926 a contingent of over one thousand laborers embarked at Fort de France destined for Venezuela.[38] In 1929, while maintaining racially restrictive policies, the government nonetheless authorized the introduction of five hundred Martinicans to work on the estate of General Juan E. París in the state of Zulia.[39] Not all Martinicans found employment in the cane fields, and a significant number obtained employment as "house servants" in Maracaibo and the surrounding communities.[40]

DOMESTIC WORKERS, ALWAYS MUCHACHAS

Beyond the oilfields, some families from the United States hired Venezuelan or Trinidadian women to perform their housework. The United States consul at Maracaibo reported that "it is a great hardship for an expatriate woman to live in Maracaibo without at least one servant."[41] The perception of local women reflected the prevailing stereotypical view of Venezuelan laborers. One publication directed at women from the United States described the Venezuelan maid as "an alpargata [sandals]-shod gal just in from the Andes or the llanos, she'll have two hands but you will have to explain to her just about everything she'll do with them."[42] A Venezuelan government commission found that "many of the British, Dutch and Americans who desired English speaking help [maids] employed Trinidadian women for whom the company initially provided separate bungalows."[43] Gladys Joseph from Trinidad worked as a cook and housekeeper for five single Europeans who lived in the Socorro staff houses in Caribbean's camp. When she left their employ, the men wrote her a glowing letter of recommendation. Georgina Millete, from Grenada, worked in the house of Charles Rider for three years before seeking employment elsewhere.[44] Both the United States vice-consul and the British vice-consul in Maracaibo employed West Indian women as housekeepers.[45]

Domestics, either West Indian or Venezuelan, were among the few workers not from the United States or Europe who could enter the inner sanctum of the foreign senior staff camp. As a woman from the United States who resided in the Creole camp in Quiriquire described them, "Native cooks and nursemaids for the American colony are seen slap-slap-slapping down the sun baked road in their woven sandals [alpargatas], minus shape or heel."[46] In the early 1930s Standard Oil actually tested all "family servants for Kahn and amoebic dysentery."[47] To assist new arrivals in selecting "suitable *muchachas*" (maids), several women from the United States organized a registry.[48] More formal publications, such as Mary George's *A Is for Abrazo*, served as a social primer for newcomers.[49] Creole and other oil companies also published guides.

Life for Trinidadian women was just as arduous as for their male counterparts. Homes for foreign staff members did not provide living facilities for housekeepers; most lived in the Venezuelan makeshift communities that arose outside the barbed-wire fences surrounding the United States camps or in nearby cities such as Maracaibo. Many of the single women shared living spaces with other women, relatives, or fellow Trinidadians, to save money and take advantage of support networks. Working in what one observer from the United States described as a "country club suburb" and living in subsistence conditions provided a poignant reminder of their distinct social position.[50] The single Trinidadian women who left their immediate families and friends behind and began new lives in Venezuela inspired relatives to make the journey. For example, after working as a cook for a year in the house of Bryan Jones, Clarestina Hunt sought permission to bring her sister to Venezuela. She received a letter of recommendation on Caribbean Oil Company letterhead, addressed to the president of the state of Zulia, in which Jones agreed to hire her sister Hustina as a housekeeper.[51] In May of the same year Leonora Harley petitioned to bring her sisters Margaret and Clara from Trinidad to work as cooks in the home of her employer, who worked for Caribbean.[52] Egerton Goddard, a native of Trinidad employed as a mechanic by VOC, attempted to secure employment for his wife, Rosalie.[53] Booker Tennyson Wilson, who had worked for Caribbean for three years, sought permission to bring his twenty-six-year-old cousin Waaltna Fountene from Trinidad.[54] This pattern was repeated throughout the oil industry wherever West Indians had secured employment.[55]

Housework was not the only arena of employment for West Indian women; many also initially secured employment with the oil companies, but they tended to be limited to service jobs such as those of laundress, cook, or seamstress. For example, Doris Arthur worked washing clothes for Caribbean in 1929.[56] In May 1930 the Lago laundry facility at La Rosa employed thirty-five laundresses and three laborers, who washed a monthly total of 34,763 pounds of clothing and materials used in industrial operations.[57] Formal employment outside the oil industry proved more difficult to secure for English-speaking West Indian women. Some, such as Florencia Marcial, a native of Trinidad, used their personal skills and worked as seamstresses in Maracaibo, catering to the foreign community.[58] Some Trinidadian women worked in bars or even operated brothels. The Washington Hotel and Bar in Maracaibo employed Daisy Assang as a waitress attending to the English-speaking patrons, and in Caripito, Laura Fullerton—or Doña Lola as she was affectionately known throughout the community—operated one of the town's best-known bars and bordellos.[59]

People from Trinidad, Grenada, and Curaçao, who constituted the largest Afro–West Indian community, tended to congregate in their own ethnic enclaves. In Cabimas one neighborhood was named Curazaito.[60] In this and similar neighborhoods, immigrants from throughout the Caribbean recreated the customs and traditions of their island homes. On weekends cricket teams that were organized separately for white British and Afro–West Indians played a game alien to most Venezuelans except in its vague resemblance to baseball. Cricket spread among West Indian immigrants, and eventually teams were formed in most of the oil camps throughout the lake region. The formation of formal leagues with teams from Lagunillas, Cabimas, and other areas soon followed. In 1941 the Campo Rojo (Red Camp) cricket team of Lagunillas defeated all rivals in Zulia and was crowned "Lake Maracaibo champions." In the evening the sound of steel drums and Caribbean tunes filled the night air. On Sundays Methodist ministers, some of whom had come from Trinidad, preached to the faithful.

Excluded from formal white British organizations—the British Masonic lodge in Maracaibo, for example, invited only "English white brethren" to attend its meetings—and sometimes at odds with Venezuelans, the West Indians often established their own social clubs.[61] When forming organizations, West Indians sometimes created branches of existing white-only organizations. For example, the Pearl of La Rosa Lodge in Cabimas had a white British and an Afro–West Indian branch. With limited funds, however, many of these fraternal organizations found it difficult to build and maintain their own centers where members could congregate and socialize. At the urging of a sympathetic visiting British consular official, in 1945 the members of the Cabimas West Indian Masonic lodge attempted to form an independent social club "open to all British West Indians of good repute."[62] British authorities surmised that "if they demonstrate their worthiness by forming a cultural society or club for respectable West Indians, H.M.G. [His Majesty's Government] should help them get a good start by providing some money."[63] West Indians had often been depicted as a troublesome group by the white consular officials forced to deal with their predicament. Thus to receive support from the British authorities, the community had to demonstrate its worthiness and good repute to the very consular officials charged with representing its interests. The distinction being made concerning "good repute" also speaks to important social differences emerging between the "respectable" West Indians in the employ of the oil companies and others who worked in the informal or service sector. In the end this distinction did little to improve the chances of the community's petition for support; the Foreign Office decided that its colonial counterpart should handle the request.

TRANSNATIONAL TIES

West Indians in Venezuela maintained close ties to their homelands. Vacations afforded opportunities for regular visits, and a stream of immigrants kept the population informed of events in their island nations. By 1929 Egbert Searly, a native of Trinidad, had worked for three and a half years at the Venezuelan Gulf marine terminal in the Bella Vista district of Maracaibo. Eager to see his family, he requested permission to visit Trinidad. The superintendent of lake transportation for the company wrote to the president of the state of Zulia to secure travel documents for Searly. He assured state officials of Searly's good conduct and indicated that he would return to work upon completion of his visit.[64] The constant movement of West Indians fostered an exchange of cultural knowledge, including social and culinary practices, between Venezuela and the Caribbean. Many Trinidadians in Port of Spain incorporated Venezuelan foods such as *hallacas* into their Christmas festivities.[65] A newspaper in Caracas reported that Christmas in Trinidad included the "traditional Anglo-Saxon customs with a touch of Venezuelan flavor."[66] For their part, Venezuelans also incorporated West Indian condiments into their foods; goat meat prepared in a spicy curry sauce became a favorite of Venezuelan workers in Monagas and on the desert peninsula of Paraguana in the state of Falcón.

Although residing in Venezuela, some West Indians preferred that their children be educated in their homeland. Employed in Creole's accounting office, Cecil Aleong nonetheless sent his daughter to study in Trinidad.[67] His compatriot William James also had two children in school in Port of Spain.[68] Others returned to the islands to seek spouses. The desire that their children obtain a British education did not preclude their establishing deep and sometimes permanent roots in Venezuela. A number of single West Indian men married Venezuelan women and raised their children as Venezuelans. When they retired, those with Venezuelan families remained in the country. Augustus Wharwood, a native of Grenada who arrived in 1929, referred to Venezuela as his second country.[69] Horatio Baptiste, also from Grenada, married María Lourdes, had four Venezuelan children, and after almost three decades of working in the oil industry retired and stayed in Venezuela.[70] John Dickson, a Trinidadian by birth, married Elvina Inciarte, a Venezuelan woman, had six children, and became a naturalized citizen.[71]

In 1936 the Venezuelan Ministry of Interior reported that West Indians, especially Trinidadians, had the highest rate of naturalization among all immigrants. After 1936 West Indians were required to become Venezuelan citizens to retain their employment. This was as a result of a hard-won struggle by Venezuelans that forced the companies to ensure that 75 percent of their white- and blue-collar employees be native Venezuelans. The policy became a source of constant conflict, with the unions complaining that the companies were failing to implement the policy and the companies claiming that they were doing so.

The government's actions further exacerbated these matters. The citizenship requirement permitted government officials to issue naturalization papers selectively to West Indians. One document from the Ministry of the Interior in December 1938 underscored its intent to "resolve this issue in favor of Venezuelans" by rejecting requests for naturalization.[72] In Maracaibo, *Petróleo* censured the oil company policy, insisting that if West Indians had to become citizens, the same policy should be applied to employees from the United States and Britain. Why, it asked, "are offices in Maracaibo full of white foreigners that have access to houses, food, clubs, clean clothes and earn upwards of 150 dollars a month?" Recognizing how the oil industry had racialized social relations, it appealed to the West Indian reader as "Black Brother," arguing, "we are with you in your time of pain, in your desperation, and as you are orphaned; without knowing it for some years you sold out to the Rockefellers and the Morgan . . . and now they have thrown you out onto the streets."[73] Besides revealing the extent to which the struggle in the oilfields had been racialized, this purported defense of Trinidadians also exposed the persistent tensions that continued to surround the presence of West Indians in Venezuela.

CHINESE IMMIGRANTS

The Chinese presence in Venezuela has been largely ignored or cast in terms of racist and cultural stereotypes. A special section of *El Nacional* devoted to immigrants who settled in Venezuela asked: "Why are there no Chinese buried in Venezuelan cemeteries?" In addition to repeating well-worn stereotypes, the article asserted that the first Chinese immigrants arrived in 1856, when the government of José Tadeo Monagas contracted to bring six hundred agricultural laborers, and that another group arrived from Cuba ninety years later.[74] Otherwise the article reduced the Chinese presence to its role in introducing the modern laundry and in founding several restaurants. It concluded that Chinese are not buried in Venezuelan cemeteries because older immigrants who accumulated wealth inevitably returned to their native land. Although several thousand resided in the country, the Chinese were still largely viewed as a foreign population that married foreign brides but seldom integrated into Venezuelan society. Their role in the formative years of the oil industry was equally ignored.

Shortly after the start of the oil boom, Chinese who had previously journeyed to the Caribbean joined the migration stream to Venezuela. As they did elsewhere in Latin America, once in Venezuela immigrants were conduits for other family members from mainland China, Taiwan, and Hong Kong. George Kingland arrived in Trinidad from Taiwan in the early 1920s and, contrary to traditional depictions of non-assimilating Asian immigrants, married Juana Reyes, a Venezuelan from Yaguaraparo in the state of Sucre. When the opportunity arose he went to work for Standard Oil as a cook in Pedernales, in the Delta Amacuro region. Using his knowledge of English to improve his employment opportunities, he moved from the isolated Pedernales camp to El Tigre in the state of Anzoátegui, where he obtained employment in the foreign staff dining hall. Juana, who had learned English in Trinidad, facilitated communications between her English-speaking husband and children and the larger community. Although Kingland's social circle included some Venezuelans (the family had twenty-two children), he continued to socialize with fellow Asians, who regularly congregated at his home outside the camp.[75]

Arriving in Venezuela in 1924, Henry Ching Fong established himself as a merchant on the Calle del Comercio in Maracaibo. In 1929 he solicited permission to bring to Venezuela Lee Woo, a thirty-eight-year-old fellow countryman originally from Canton and then residing in Trinidad. In his petition Ching Fong indicated that he would make use of Lee Woo's assistance in his business, promising to be responsible for Lee Woo's good conduct and to explain to him the "good customs and laws of the country."[76] Similarly, by 1929 Ramón Ho had become a successful merchant in Cabimas. After two years he requested permission from Zulia's governor, Vicencio Pérez Soto, to expand operations and bring relatives from Cuba and Canton to assist in his business. Ho's request reveals the extent to which the Chinese diaspora encompassed broad social and economic networks that connected Asia and Latin America. Ho had two sons, three brothers in Canton, and two more brothers in Havana. To support his claim he presented a letter from the local municipal authorities of Cabimas attesting to his good conduct.[77] Petitions similar to these appear throughout the records of the Zulia historical archive.

In 1920 the general consul of the Chinese Merchants Association of Chicago requested information from United States diplomats in Maracaibo concerning the possibility of organized Chinese migration to Venezuela. The consul's response underscored the legal prohibition against Chinese immigration while also signaling that powerful agricultural interests, particularly the sugar producers, could "secure suspension of laws."[78] Although nothing appears to have come of this communication, it nonetheless underscored the extent to which Venezuela had surfaced in discussions concerning Chinese migration to Latin America.

Most Chinese continued to rely on family networks and their own initiative in migrating to Venezuela. The records of ships arriving at Maracaibo document a small but steady stream of Chinese passengers disembarking at the port. Departing from Curaçao en route to Maracaibo in February 1928, the *Flora* carried six Chinese immigrants among its passengers.[79] Throughout March and April the numbers remained relatively consistent. Plying the waters from Curaçao and Maracaibo, the *Atlas* also included Chinese among its passengers.[80] The great majority of Asians who worked for the oil companies found themselves relegated to jobs as cooks and bakers or to the laundry. Chan Fai, for example, performed his duties as "first cook" for Caribbean at the San Lorenzo mess hall on the shores of Lake Maracaibo, and John Fui and Jaime Chen also worked with him there.[81] Kenneth Afoon performed similar duties at Caribbean's camp in Cabimas.[82] Pue Car Ye was a cook for Lago, as was his relative Vien Chu Lee for voc. Ton Con Mo worked in the laundry for Lago.[83] At the Creole camp in Tía Juana, Eddie Sie Hong gained a reputation among the foreign and Venezuelan women residents of the staff camp, who lined up outside his kitchen door every day to await fresh bread.[84]

As they did throughout Latin America, Chinese not employed by the foreign companies turned their energies to the new consumer markets that flourished in the oil towns. Vicente Ching, for example, operated a well-known laundry in Lagunillas that catered to oil workers and the community at large. His business dealings put him in contact with important commercial interests in the state, including members of the París family of Maracaibo, who wrote him a letter attesting to his standing in the community.[85] Economic censuses for Zulia, Monagas, Anzoátegui, and other oil-producing states reveal Chinese involvement in varied forms of commercial activity. In Lagunillas Andrés Fan Fung operated a grocery store, Emilio Yo owned a tailor shop called the Half Moon, and San Lee claimed to have the best restaurant in the district.[86] In Caripito the Hung family operated a bakery and a grocery store, and sold lubricants.[87]

This pattern of ownership could be found throughout the small oil towns of western and eastern Venezuela. Although Asians established a foothold as merchants, they confronted stiff competition from other groups. Italians, Spaniards, and Arabs also opened retail operations in the oil towns, and immigrants from the Middle East gradually came to dominate certain areas of retail commerce, especially electronics. The United States consul in Maracaibo termed them "Syrians" and estimated that about six thousand had immigrated to Venezuela by 1927, while the number of Spaniards and Italians hovered at about seven thousand.[88] A Venezuelan government commission studying the camps in the late 1950s reported that in the state of Anzoátegui "all small commerce with an average capital of 6,000 bolívares is almost totally in the hands of the Lebanese."[89] Similarly, in Caripito several Middle Easterners controlled the sale of fabrics and haberdashery and South Asians operated jewelry stores that catered to the foreign and Venezuelan middle class employed by Creole Petroleum.[90]

LABOR AND THE MEXICAN CONNECTION

Besides West Indians and the Chinese, oil companies that had previously operated in Mexico also recruited and brought to Venezuela a small number of their skilled Mexican employees to serve as translators and perform other administrative functions. Others worked in the oilfields as intermediaries between the drillers from the United States and the Venezuelan laborers. Bernardo Calero, a Mexican citizen, worked as a translator in Lago's land and legal department in Maracaibo; classified as a "Gold Roll" employee, he was paid in dollars.[91] A letter from the Secretaría General del Estado de Zulia in 1928 reported that Pan American, Pantepec Oil, and Lago had recently recruited a number of former Mexican oil workers. Judging from payroll records, however, the number of Mexicans employed by these companies remained small and never equaled the number of West Indians.[92]

The presence of Mexicans is apparent from the cultural and political reactions they evoked. United States diplomats stationed in Zulia claimed to have detected the use of Mexican slang by Venezuelan laborers. They focused on certain offensive phrases used to describe people from the United States, phrases that in their view could only have been learned from Mexicans. Some expatriates from the United States reported that by 1925 Venezuelan laborers had begun to refer to them with common Mexican obscenities while adopting a belligerent attitude toward many foreigners. According to the United States consul in Maracaibo, Alexander Sloan, drillers who had formerly worked in the Tampico oilfields had told him that "within the last few months certain obscene expressions which were common in Mexico" had become common in the oilfields: "The courteous Venezuelan peon has changed his attitude toward the foreigners [and] it is now quite common to hear muttered comments when a foreigner passes.[93] Having previously interacted with supervisors from the United States, Mexican employees apparently ignored their efforts at intimidation, and this gained them the admiration of many Venezuelan workers.[94] United States diplomats and company officials surmised that the presence of Mexicans had had a negative influence on the previously "docile, uncomplaining, fairly efficient laborer that he was a few months, or at least one year ago."[95]

The attitude of the Venezuelan laborers had undoubtedly changed since the inception of the oil industry. As early as July 1925 Venezuelan workers employed in the Mene Grande transportation department staged a work stoppage. Discontent over the authoritarian actions of the Dutch camp superintendent had been building for some time, and the strike erupted when he ordered workers to clear brush around the camp, without providing further compensation.[96] The work stoppage succeeded in extracting concessions from Caribbean, including an increase in pay and a reduction of the ten-hour day.[97] Labor protests also spread to La Rosa and Cabimas, where workers also went out on strike over similar issues. One incident dramatically illustrated the growing resentment of Venezuelans and oil workers over conditions in the fields. During a game of baseball between employees from the United States on 4 July 1925 at La Rosa, several Venezuelans rode their donkeys onto the playing field and refused to move. Pressed by authorities to leave, the men refused, stating "they were Venezuelans, [and] that this was their country, and they intended to ride where they pleased."[98]

To attribute increased labor militancy to Mexican influences is to overlook the deplorable conditions that Venezuelans encountered in the oilfields and their own ability to organize. Venezuelan workers faced constant pressure in an atmosphere driven by intense competition between companies attempting to bring new wells under production. The policy of blaming labor radicalism on outsiders had been employed previously by Gómez's administration, as it was throughout Latin America during this period.[99] In nearby Colombia, labor militancy among banana workers in Magdalena was also blamed on Mexican agitators.[100] It was insensitivity and discriminatory company policy, not the Mexicans' presence, that instigated labor radicalism and negative attitudes toward foreigners. Moreover, oil workers from the United States, many with years of experience in the Tampico oilfields, commonly used Mexican slang and obscenities around the Venezuelan labor force.

The Mexican influence among United States oil workers is clear in the pages of the *Tropical Sun*, an English-language weekly newspaper published in Maracaibo that catered to the expatriate community. Articles and advertisements repeatedly made reference to Mexico, highlighting the experiences of drillers who had worked in both countries. One advertisement for the McDevitts Hotel, a favorite watering hole for foreigners, made claims for what it called the best chile con carne in the Maracaibo area. This dish, uncommon in Venezuela, had been a favorite of oilmen from the United States working in Mexico.[101] The paper also reported on the affairs of United States drillers who had stayed in Mexico, including deaths, retirements, and other social news. In one story it reported that Shaddy McGrath, who had previously been in charge of the charcoal station in Tampico, had retired to San Antonio, Texas. Finding life in San Antonio dull, McGrath reportedly "set off firecrackers occasionally so he could yell "Viva la Revolución!"—an allusion to his experiences in Mexico during the period of armed conflict.[102] As late as the 1950s some staff members from the United States with previous experience in Mexico still belonged to a group called the Mexican Pilgrim Society, which held its annual reunion in Venezuela on 12 December, in commemoration of the feast of the Virgin of Guadalupe.[103]

Assigning blame for nationalist sentiments or labor militancy to Mexicans served several purposes. It provided a convenient way for the companies to minimize the grievances of Venezuelan laborers. From the Caribbean fields in Mene Grande to the British Controlled Oil Fields in Falcón, laborers had been complaining about pay, housing, medical services, and discrimination. Neither the companies nor the government seems to have prepared for these developments. On many occasions Gómez opted to manipulate labor militancy to exact concessions from the foreign oil companies. On others he opted for inaction, forcing the foreign companies to come to terms with their laborers.[104] Nonetheless, beset by increased labor militancy and by middle-class reformers seeking employment in the industry, Gómez took advantage of the Mexican threat to portray opponents of his regime as alien anti-Venezuelan provocateurs.

The presence of Mexicans in Venezuela became highly charged and politicized. In the aftermath of the revolution of 1910, some Mexican political leaders looked critically at the Venezuelan government of Juan Vicente Gómez. José Vasconcelos, rector of the National University of Mexico and subsequently minister of education, called Gómez the "Porfirio Díaz of Venezuela," a theme later repeated by publications such as the *New York Times* and the *Nation*, and dozens of travelers' accounts.[105] The United States attaché in Mexico City recalled that Vasconcelos used the Fiesta de la Raza (held, appropriately enough, at the Simón Bolívar amphitheater) to make "a virulent attack upon the Gómez regime in Venezuela."[106] Opposition leaders in Venezuela, including the poet and activist Andres Eloy Blanco, kept Vasconcelos abreast of developments in the country.[107] Mexico also served as an informal base of operations for Venezuelans opposed to Gómez's regime, and in 1928 exiles formed the Partido Revolucionario Venezolano in Mexico City.[108] In 1931 an "invading" force of over a hundred Mexicans recruited as laborers left Veracruz for Venezuela aboard the ship *Superior*. The organizers manipulated the Mexicans and instead pretended to stage an invasion that was easily squashed by Gómez's military.[109]

Though individual Mexicans such as the labor leader Luis Morones and others supported the struggle against Gómez, the government kept its distance. When Vasconcelos called Gómez "the last tyrant in Spanish America, the most monstrous, the most repugnant, and the most despicable of despots of our unfortunate race" and a "human pig that dishonors our race and dishonors our humanity," the government of Alvaro Obregón quickly disavowed his comments, and he called its position "servile."[110] Salvador Guzmán, the Mexican chargé d'affaires in Caracas, who was married to a Venezuelan, expressed regret over the incident.[111] In the aftermath of this affair the Venezuelan government, through the governor of Zulia, issued circulars that warned the local authorities in oil-producing areas to monitor the activities of the Mexican oil workers, since they were citizens of "an enemy country of Venezuela" in which communism had sunk roots and was expanding. At the end of 1928 Pérez Soto forbade Pan American Petroleum to recruit technicians and workers in Mexico.[112] For his part, Obregón allegedly lent moral and financial support to Venezuelan exiles attempting to overthrow Gómez.[113] Venezuelan exiles sought refuge in Mexico, where they associated with intellectuals and political figures in the capital. Doña María Tapia de Obregón, the president's wife, organized a group of women to write to Gómez asking for clemency for jailed political prisoners.[114]

The relocation of dozens of companies from the United States and Britain to the new Venezuelan oilfields frustrated Mexican officials and probably also fueled the attacks on Gómez.[115] Confronted by these criticisms, Gómez had Venezuelan agents shadow Vasconcelos when he traveled abroad and report on his speeches. Pedro Arcaya, Venezuelan ambassador to the United States, wrote an account of Vasconcelos's visit to Washington, branding his pronouncements as "socialist, almost anarchist or even Bolshevik."[116] According to Domingo Alberto Rangel, the oil companies also placed their "entire intelligence network" at Gómez's disposal, a network which included not only local agents but also access to information that they received from various "chancelleries and various secret police." Gómez regularly received information at his offices in Maracay from Standard and Shell, which subsidized police forces in various western countries.[117] Operating on information received from various sources, in September 1923 the Venezuelan government denied a Mexican theater company access to the country, labeling their activities "undesirable."[118] The owner of the enterprise, Miguel Wimer, had a Venezuelan partner who had criticized Gómez during a recent performance.[119] The Mexican theater union took up the issue, and its leaders publicly attacked Gómez. The official reasons for the exclusion centered on the extended period of national mourning occasioned by the assassination nearly three months earlier of Juan Crisóstomo "Juancho" Gómez, the president's brother. Not content with this subterfuge, the government also floated the idea that foreigners might have been involved in the assassination.[120]

The acrimonious relations exploded into the open at a meeting of the Pan American Union in Washington on 3 October 1923. Ambassador Arcaya took the opportunity to make a violent, defamatory attack on the government and people of Mexico. He assailed the plans to hold a forthcoming inter-American meeting in Mexico City, calling the schools in Mexico "a nucleus of rebellion and savagery." Felícitas López Portillo believed that the United States secretary of state, who spoke no Spanish, did not understand the verbal exchanges. Once translated, he asked that they be stricken from the official record of the meeting.[121]

The incident received widespread publicity in the Mexican press. In September 1924 the Mexican government closed its consular offices in Venezuela.[122] The news media in the United States took advantage of the rupture to further their criticisms of Obregón, charging him with an inability to manage Mexico's affairs.[123] The Venezuelan press took comfort in favorable articles and editorials that appeared in the *Washington Post*, insisting that the media in the rest of the country supported Gómez's position.[124] The United States military attaché in Caracas expressed surprise at the "connection" that seemed to have been established "between the Venezuelan Legation at Washington and the editorial offices of the *Washington Post*" and entitled his report to Washington "*The Washington Post* as an agency for Venezuelan propaganda."[125]

Arcaya wrote a spirited if self-serving defense of the Venezuelan position in a small pamphlet that was translated into English and published in Washington in 1924 as *New Notes on Political History*. In it he defended Gómez's regime against its critics, including Venezuelan exiles, Samuel Gompers of the American Labor Federation, and of course Vasconcelos, who had become his personal nemesis. He accused Vasconcelos of stirring up rebellion throughout Latin America but reserving his most "gratuitous hatred" for Gómez.[126] What was most revealing about the publication of the brochure in English was the extent to which the Gómez regime had become concerned about its perception in the United States and throughout Latin America and willing to publicly challenge its international critics. By openly playing on fears of Mexican infiltrators, Gómez's government played to concerns expressed by United States government officials. Oil had introduced a new reality within the once closed political system, forcing Gómez to justify his actions to outsiders. This view of Gómez breaks from traditional interpretations of the regime as isolationist and unconcerned with world affairs.[127] Instead it is clear that oil compelled the regime to adopt an assertive foreign policy, and to address emerging relations with other Latin American nations, the United States, and Britain.

Despite the rupture in relations, accusations continued to fly between the Mexican and Venezuelan governments. Government-sponsored publications promoted the advantages of Venezuela, highlighting that "Maracaibo is 240 miles nearer to New York than is Tampico, Mexico."[128] Contending that Mexicans functioned as "Bolshevik agents," in 1928 Gómez ordered their expulsion from Venezuela and prohibited any future immigration.[129] Yet despite the formal acrimony between the two governments, many Venezuelan workers continued to admire Mexicans for their apparent resistance to intimidation by their foreign bosses.[130] During the 1940s and 1950s Mexican films proved quite popular among Venezuelan oil workers and caused concern for officials of the United States embassy, who feared competition and the nationalist content of the Mexican cinema.[131]

IMMIGRANTS IN THE MIDDLE

West Indians and Chinese employed in staff or skilled positions found themselves in a contradictory situation. Many held significantly different posts from most Venezuelans and represented an intermediary stratum between the local labor force and supervisors and drillers from the United States and Europe.[132] The presence of foreign laborers further complicated the already difficult process of union organizing, especially as it concerned relations between West Indians and Venezuelans. The United States consul in Maracaibo claimed that the Trinidadian could be "insolent and overbearing" and looked upon the Venezuelan as his social inferior.[133] The basis of the consul's belief may be more complicated than it appears, reflecting his own perceptions of race and embodying a distinction that many foreigners drew between Venezuelans (as "docile peons") and West Indians.[134] It fails to capture the thorny role that Trinidadians played in the emerging labor hierarchy and power relations, a role that pitted them against Venezuelans. Undoubtedly some Trinidadians and other West Indians exploited this asymmetrical relationship to their advantage and identified with their foreign supervisors. This attitude, as Judith Ewell points out, led many Venezuelans to think that West Indians could be "as arrogant in their attitudes as the white American and English bosses."[135] This social distance quickly became a source of tension between the two groups.

The inability of the West Indians and Chinese to communicate fluently in Spanish and their positions within the company social and racial hierarchy drove a wedge between them and Venezuelans. In 1927 Venezuelan workers employed by British Controlled Oil Fields at Mene de Mauroa in the state of Falcón drafted a long list of grievances and presented them to the state governor. Besides the usual demands for wages and conditions, they sought the firing of an arrogant "negro antillano" who "treated the Venezuelans very badly."[136] Unfamiliar with English, Venezuelans referred to the West Indians as *mainfrends*, derived from "my friends," a term frequently used by Trinidadians to address locals.[137] This term eventually extended to encompass all West Indians. Inevitably, people of Asian background became known as *chinos* regardless of their ancestry.

Repeated incidents between West Indians and the police and military further marred relations. British consular records reveal a lengthy list of complaints filed by West Indians who felt abused or harassed by the Venezuelan authorities. The record of those arrested at oil camps such as Lagunillas would occasionally include a significant number of West Indians. In Lagunillas, for example, the local authorities reported on 10 September 1929 the arrest of ten West Indians for "desacato a la autoridad" (defiance of local authorities).[138] It is impossible to ascertain what crime, if any, the men had committed, since the police operated with a certain degree of impunity and the West Indians usually did not speak Spanish. To secure their freedom, on the following day the men paid a fine of 25 bolívares each, the equivalent of a week's wages.[139] Beyond the oilfields, Afro–West Indians throughout Venezuela encountered problems with the authorities. In 1933 a policeman killed Joseph Cook, a native of Trinidad who sold "ice and sweets" on the streets of Caracas. An investigation revealed that a police officer shot him three times for not moving from the locale where he sold his goods.[140]

Beyond tensions with Venezuelans, early oil camp society reproduced the virulent racism present in the United States. Segregation permeated labor relations and deeply influenced social life in most oil camps. At first these attitudes led to the establishment of segregated bathroom facilities, drinking fountains, mess halls, and social clubs, officially separating white foreigners from employees of color. As Robert Vitalis points out, during this period "segregation in the oil industry was still the norm within the United States."[141] At one company administrative office in Maracaibo there was a sign reading: "Toilet only for Americans."[142] Thus West Indians, Asians, and Venezuelans initially confronted strict color barriers that drew clear lines between them and their American supervisors.

Language differences limited communication between the foreign bosses, West Indians, and the Venezuelan laborers. Early on, many expatriates from the United States simply refused to learn Spanish. One oil worker lamented that a "large number of hard headed Americans stubbornly refused to even attempt to learn the language." One in particular, the chief accountant for Standard, "insisted that Venezuelans who worked for him had to learn English."[143] He once gave instructions to an "office boy" to go "dos [two] doors down the hall to another office," and when the young man questioned his instructions he yelled, "Can't you speak your own language?"[144] Daniel Bendahan, who worked as an office boy at Standard Oil, described his often amusing experiences with his supervisor, a Mr. Walter Schoroclaw of the United States, a "musiú [foreigner] who had been in Venezuela for almost thirty years and still had not learned one single phrase in Spanish."[145] The unwillingness of some supervisors to learn even rudimentary Spanish reveals the hierarchy that many foreigners assumed in their treatment of Venezuelans. Not all, however, adopted this course of action. According to Bracho Montiel, drillers from the United States, especially those with previous experience in Mexico, "gave orders in a mixed language, half English and half Spanish, with extravagant corruptions that formed their own slang."[146] Oil camp "Spanglish" included adaptations such as *ohquei* (okay), *pagerol* (payroll), *overol* (overalls), *socates* (sockets), *swiches* (switches), *tipiando* (typing), *gut bai* (goodbye), *guachiman* (watchman), *ol rai* (all right), *taima* (time out), and a host of other terms that soon became quite common in Venezuelan society. In many cases the foreigner's inability to speak Spanish served to promote the use of Spanglish. In trying to communicate with a Venezuelan, a mechanic from the United States who did not know the Spanish word for "winch" explained to a worker, "Esto es un winche."[147]

English curse words such as *chit* and *sanabebiches* also quickly became part of the oil workers' vocabulary.[148] As they became familiar with English idioms, some Venezuelans increasingly referred to foreigners in positions of authority as misters or *mistercitos*.[149] The term had a double meaning, however, for although it seemed to be a formal salutation it also became a way of mocking offensive or racist behavior.[150] English-speakers adopted many Spanish words, especially those associated with local foods or practices. Language also expressed the relations of power operating between Venezuelans and foreigners. Symbolically this meant, in the words of the leftist newspaper *Petróleo*, that Venezuelans regularly "received orders in English while suffering in Spanish."[151] An example of this relationship can be found in the terms that foreigners used to refer to Venezuelans. In particular Venezuelans resented the use of *muchacho* or *chico* (boy) to describe an adult male. Carlos Ramírez Paris, who started as a laborer for Lago in the 1930s, recalls being regularly called "Chico Ramírez" by his British foreman.[152] This view found expression in the formal labor categories that Venezuelan men often occupied. Caribbean classified some of its Venezuelan employees as "store boys" and "customs boys."[153] The novelist Miguel Otero Silva, author of the classic *Oficina N.1*, set in the oil camps of Anzoátegui, argued that adult Venezuelan men were always "boys" in the eyes of the foreigners.[154]

Social, racial, and national distinctions found expression in wages and salaries. Companies such as Caribbean, voc, Lago, and Standard Oil maintained separate payrolls for their United States, West Indian, and Venezuelan employees.[155] They used a monthly dollar salary for their United States employees and a monthly bolívar payroll for the handful of Venezuelans who occupied staff positions.[156] In eastern Venezuela, Standard kept a separate classification, the "Trinidad Payroll," for its West Indian employees.[157] The majority of the Venezuelans employed by the company found themselves relegated to the often tenuous daily bolívar payroll. Beyond this, salary structures reflected the inequitable social and racial hierarchy that influenced interpersonal relations in the oil camps.[158]

The contentious intermediary position of the West Indian in the social and racial hierarchy is represented in many early Venezuelan novels that depict conditions in the oilfields.[159] *Mene,* by Ramón Díaz Sánchez, *Guachimanes,* by Bracho Montiel, and *La mancha del aceite*, by César Uribe Piedrahita, sympathetically depict the ostracized Trinidadian, without family and friends, facing racism because of the color of his skin.[160] Díaz Sánchez's novel tells the story of one Trinidadian man, Enguerran Narcisus Philibert, who suffers from a stomach ailment and mistakenly uses a "white only" restroom. After being reprimanded by a boss from the United States, he loses his job and is placed on the infamous "blacklist." Refused employment in all the fields along the eastern lakeshore and not wanting to return to Trinidad in disgrace, he takes his own life by jumping into the oily water of Lake Maracaibo.[161] There are accounts of Chinese confronting similar conditions. In 1934 the Cabimas paper appropriately named the *Taladro* (the Drill) reported that a distraught Chinese immigrant had apparently hanged himself.[162]

The number of West Indians or Chinese employed by the oil companies is difficult to determine. Companies submitted regular reports to the government that among other things included the number of foreigners they employed, but these reports loosely categorized employees as foreigners and Venezuelan, not always distinguishing among the various nationalities. Before the discovery at La Rosa, a notice from Caribbean in 1922 simply indicated that in October it had employed 243 foreigners and 1,033 Venezuelans.[163] Likewise, a document from Lago in 1939 included a generic classification of 268 foreigners and 3,119 Venezuelans.[164] The technical inspector of mines, Luis F. Calvani, argued that these reporting practices concealed the conditions facing the Venezuelans. According to Calvani, Caribbean's report in 1926 indicating that the company employed 3,337 Venezuelans and 1,233 foreigners, and Gulf's claim that it employed 3,323 Venezuelans and 742 foreigners, intentionally obscured the status of local workers: Of the "6.600 Venezuelans that appear as employees only 2%, at most, are actually in staff positions while 98% serve as simple laborers that receive a daily wage."[165]

Placing West Indians in the category of "British citizens" or "British colonials" also prevented an adequate count of their numbers. This practice skewed some early Venezuelan censuses that recorded West Indians in the same manner. The census of 1926 recorded 2,840 British, 257 French, and 422 Dutch colonials in Venezuela.[166] Payroll records, where available, provide insight into the number of West Indians, Venezuelans, and other foreigners employed by particular companies. In January 1933, for example, Standard Oil of Venezuela had 2,427 people on its payroll. Of that number, Venezuelans accounted for 1,924 (79.4 percent), British West Indians 248 (10.2 percent), citizens of the United States 141 (5.8 percent), and Chinese 18 (0.7 percent). The remaining employees included a smattering of Germans, Spanish, British, Polish, Italians, French, and other Latin Americans. By 1940 the numbers had changed significantly. In January of that year Standard employed 4,906 workers, of whom 4,406 (89.8 percent) were Venezuelans, 397 (8.1 percent) were from the United States, 25 (0.5 percent) were British West Indians, and only 7 (0.1 percent) were Chinese.[167] Standard's employment practices do not of course represent the entire industry, but they do indicate that West Indians had a significant presence in the initial phase of the oil industry, followed by a gradual and steady decline throughout the 1930s. The massive layoffs that occurred in the industry after 1928 accelerated the trend. This tendency also reflects the growing pressure on the part of Venezuelan workers, the middle classes, and the government to increase the employment of local labor.

Labor organizers and a host of social critics argued that the oil companies' policies exacerbated tensions between Venezuelans, Afro–West Indians, and Asians.[168] During the period of contraction that the industry underwent in the late 1920s, some oil companies kept foreigners as service employees and dismissed Venezuelans who performed similar tasks, arguing that Chinese and West Indians had been retained because they possessed "greater skills." In 1927 Lago discharged several dozen Venezuelan *"sirvientes"* (servants) at Cabimas and Lagunillas while keeping their Chinese counterparts. Lago insisted that the Chinese were "specialists" in their fields, and it felt no obligation to provide the Venezuelans with severance pay.[169] The same month, when voc removed twenty-one "servants," including cooks, kitchen helpers, and dishwashers, it contended that it "had only used the services of Chinese as cooks or kitchen helpers and other inferior positions and never in important posts."[170] In the 1930s, when dismissing several Trinidadians, Lago openly pitted West Indians against Venezuelans; when it fired Robert Bayley, for example, it gave as an excuse the need to hire more Venezuelans.[171]

Despite being forced to compete with one another in employment and pay, Venezuelans and West Indians confronted similar conditions on the job. Occasionally examples of labor solidarity surfaced. Joseph Nesfield, described by voc officials as an *Antillano de color* (West Indian), signed petitions circulated by Venezuelan workers protesting their dismissal.[172] Workers sent complaints to Zulia state officials and forwarded petitions to President Juan Vicente Gómez, who ordered an investigation into the matter.[173] Other Trinidadians also joined the incipient labor movement with their Venezuelan counterparts. Francisco Sotillo, a Trinidadian, became a founder of the Sociedad de Auxilio Mutuo de Obreros Petroleros (SAMOP), established in 1933 under the direction of the communist labor leader Rodolfo Quintero.[174] According to Quintero, even some United States employees of voc lent moral support to the emerging labor movement.[175]

Such instances of cross-racial and cross-ethnic solidarity proved rare. Pressures against labor solidarity in the oilfields seemed pervasive. Opportunistic politicians exploited racial and cultural differences between Afro–West Indians, Asians, and local labor. The nascent middle class pressured the government for access to the staff positions held by some West Indians. Although Venezuelan politicians and intellectuals openly promoted welcoming immigrants to increase population, they viewed blacks and Asians with suspicion. The Venezuelan constitution and numerous proclamations from the Ministry of the Interior specifically prohibited the immigration of blacks and Asians. While serving as minister of the interior in 1930, Pedro Arcaya reported that "under the pretext of labor shortages," the oil companies were seeking to flood the oil-producing region with "inadmissible individuals brought from the Antilles," increasing the number of Venezuela's groups and complicating its population question.[176] While professing that Venezuela remained open to all immigrants, Arcaya underscored the view that the racial makeup of newcomers must increase the country's "physical, intellectual and moral standing." He added, "Numerical increases without selection retards progress" and reported that his office exercised constant vigilance to prevent blacks and Asians from entering the country.[177]

IMMIGRANTS AND CAFÉ CON LECHE

Some scholars have asserted that Venezuelan immigration policy was not overtly racist but rather reflected broader social and cultural concerns.[178] Race and culture in this context appear largely indistinguishable, however. Despite the popular view of the nation's racial heritage as "café con leche," historically the Venezuelan upper classes, intellectuals, and even elements of the nascent middle class disdained people of color.[179] Intellectuals of the stature of Arturo Adriani, Mariano Picón Salas, Rufino Blanco Fombona, and Arturo Uslar Pietri repeatedly warned of the dangers of "colored immigration" and the need to "whiten" Venezuela.[180] These racial beliefs pervaded cultural attitudes and found expression throughout Venezuelan life.

While reporting on the progress of Maracaibo's aqueduct, for which he was responsible, the engineer Pedro José Rojas took the opportunity to complain about what he saw as West Indian "religious prejudices and depraved private customs." In the Antilles, he said, West Indians form cults and commit mysterious crimes. In Cuba "they sacrifice young and robust whites to save the lives of old, wretched and ailing Blacks."[181] Alleging that young white children had begun to disappear in Maracaibo, Rojas called on the authorities to take action. His view resonated with those who considered West Indians a black mass that was prepared to absorb Venezuelan society.

After the death of Gómez in 1935, Venezuelan intellectuals pondered the country's future and proposed plans to modernize the nation's institutions and culture. Arturo Uslar Pietri firmly believed that Venezuelans retained a "primitive temperament adverse to modern mentality."[182] Repeating age-old arguments framed by nineteenth-century positivism and reinforced by notions of the Protestant work ethic, Uslar Pietri critiqued the three elements of Venezuelan society—the Spanish, the indigenous, and the African. While he belittled the Spaniard for the lack of a work ethic and the indigenous as indolent, he reserved the worst condemnation for the African, who he said did "not benefit our race in any way."[183] In assessing immigration during the Gómez period, Mariano Picón Salas expressed his belief that "the only immigrants that arrived in Venezuela had been some Antillean Blacks, a backward and morally degenerate element, who brought us their sensuality, cruelty, and primitive superstition."[184] It was Rufino Blanco Fombona, as customs officer at Güiria, who expressed the greatest fears of a supposed Black Trinidadian "invasion": "Facing the Afro-English island of Trinidad, Güiria a few years back had a flourishing Caucasian population. Today only a handful of white men remain. The Trinidadians . . . have in the course of a few years transformed its ethnic character. What has happened in Güiria in a short period of time could happen in all of Venezuela. Anyone who does not see this has no eyes. Immigration, dense and multiple waves of European immigration, is the only remedy, the only salvation for all of us."[185] Blanco Fombona's comments appear as a footnote to a book on Simón Bolívar set during a period of the independence struggle known as the War without Quarter of 1813–14. His work originally appeared in 1941 as a succession of serialized articles in *Esfera*, a daily publication in Caracas known for reflecting the views of the oil companies. The Venezuelan Ministry of Education subsequently reproduced the articles as a book in 1969 and distributed it for free.

Despite protestations to the contrary, the concerns about West Indians reflected deep-seated and persistent apprehension about the sizable number of Afro-Venezuelans and the possibility that the presence of West Indians would alter the nature of relations with them. The governor of Zulia articulated this sentiment when he informed Gómez's government that he feared the formation of distinctive black neighborhoods in Maracaibo. He affirmed his support for Gómez's policies to "defend the race" from outside influences that represented a "lamentable regression" to Venezuela's "ethnic nucleus" and "grave prejudice" to Venezuelan society.[186]

Leading Venezuelan intellectuals of the period, including Blanco Fombona, Picón Salas, and others, publicly expressed their uneasiness about the nation's racial composition. In making the argument for European immigrants to General Medina Angarita in 1937, Picón Salas remarked, "Around Caracas and all the of the nation's coastal mountain range we need more white population. Our Republic's capital, and as a consequence the soul of its masses is today more café than leche." While Caracas teemed with blacks, the Andes and Mérida, Picón Salas's birthplace, were the "grand reservoir of the white race for the Republic."[187] His comments underscore that despite efforts to portray Venezuela as a country that had undergone widespread miscegenation, embodied in the ideal of café con leche, some élites still preferred to manage the racial mix to ensure a lighter outcome. Even as late as 1937, Picón Salas and other influential intellectuals and political figures believed that white European migration was needed to improve the country's racial stock. This belief prevailed among broad sectors of the population, not just intellectual and political élites. In the 1950s one French traveler reported remarks by his Venezuelan host, a Creole engineer, to the effect that Venezuela still needed to attract European immigrants: "All we want is to whiten our race . . . Most foreigners are Italian but that's OK because Italians are born builders and hard workers."[188]

SCAPEGOATING IMMIGRANTS

The Chinese also experienced anti-foreign sentiment. Newspapers took note of their increased role in some areas of commerce. The *Panorama*, the leading Maracaibo daily newspaper, pointed to the gains that Chinese had made since their arrival: "The evolution or metamorphosis of these silent yellow men known as Chinese appeared notable. Previously, the children of the Celestial Republic had been defined only as laundry men. Now they have abandoned their irons and have installed themselves behind counters and bars as if they were in Peking."[189] Not surprisingly, this criticism resurfaced wherever the Chinese managed to make inroads in commerce and competed for the growing consumer market. Chinese who owned small shops also came under attack after the passage in 1936 of the nation's first comprehensive labor law, setting minimum wages for certain jobs. In Maracaibo the leftist *Petróleo*, usually sympathetic to the plight of West Indians and Asians, chastised Chinese laundry owners for trying to pay Venezuelan women less than the official four bolívares a day.[190] Officially, however, not all Asians became the targets of Venezuelan prejudice. In 1924 the minister of development confirmed to the United States military attaché in Caracas that only Chinese were legally prohibited from entering the country. The United States attaché commented: "Under this interpretation of the immigration law, Chinese are excluded from entering Venezuela as immigrants but Japanese are permitted to do so." Japan, he surmised, was regarded "as one of the great powers of the world with an army and navy capable of enforcing respect for her nationals in any part of the globe," while China was looked upon as "a decadent and inferior nation of pacific inclinations and customs."[191] Although the number of Japanese in Venezuela remained minuscule, it is doubtful that most Venezuelans made distinctions between different groups of Asians.

Conditions for foreigners (that is, those not from the United States or Britain) worsened in 1929 when the government ordered the expulsion of all Afro–West Indians and Chinese. The *London Times* reported: "The President of Venezuela has decided forthwith to prohibit coloured immigration into Venezuela, even when immigrants are provided with passports. Coloured foreigners already domiciled in the country are obliged to carry a certificate from local authorities. The decision will have a serious effect on the regular flow of West Indian immigrants to the Venezuelan oil fields."[192] The *New York Times* also took note of the Venezuelan decree.[193] The decision by both papers to report on the issue underscores the importance that Venezuela had acquired in world affairs.[194] Several factors appear to have influenced the government's decision on this issue. Gómez's administration had received numerous complaints from the Venezuelan middle class and working people concerning the role of foreigners in the oil industry.[195] As it had with the Mexicans, the government used the presence of West Indians to deflect attention from its own failings. Moreover, the Gomecistas could manipulate the figure of the West Indian and the Chinese as a subtext to address élite and middle-class concerns about Venezuela's own racial configuration. The West Indian and to a lesser extent the Chinese thus served as the "other" against which some elements of Venezuelan society measured themselves. In practical terms, even if all the West Indians in administrative or skilled posts had been dismissed, it would not have substantially increased employment for Venezuelans. The impending economic crisis of the late 1920s and 1930s would do more to diminish the presence of foreigners than the implementation of restrictive measures on the part of Gómez's regime. The announced expulsion of Afro–West Indians and Asians was part of a continuing effort by the government to redirect and defuse the internal pressures that it confronted.

The government directed consular and port officials to prevent the arrival of "undesirable aliens." State officials in Zulia requested that Lago and other companies gather information about "undesirable aliens" in their employ. Likewise, the federal government asked Lago to prevent "undesirable aliens" from boarding its ships in Curaçao and Trinidad.[196] With upwards of a thousand ships arriving in Maracaibo every month, the task of limiting so-called undesirable aliens proved next to impossible.[197] In addition, many local officials illicitly augmented their pay by issuing documents to "aliens." As Blanco Fombona pointed out, it was common knowledge that West Indians "with a few bolívares purchased the benevolence of the local authorities in the coastal areas."[198]

As a result of the edict, however, West Indians and Chinese already in the country now had to carry certificates of employment and good conduct issued by oil company officials and local authorities in order to travel or change occupations. Even before the presidential proclamation, West Indians and Chinese had begun to request such documents. The historical archives of the state of Zulia contain hundreds of petitions. Joseph Sylvan, for example, sought and received a certificate of good conduct from authorities in Lagunillas in July 1929.[199] Chan Fai carried a credential provided by Caribbean attesting to his honesty and good character.[200] A. Thompson, a native of Trinidad, retained a letter indicating that Caribbean employed him as a typist.[201] To avoid confusion, when Caribbean hired white Dutch or British employees living in Curaçao or Trinidad, it had to provide authentication that they were Caucasian and possessed Dutch or British citizenship.[202]

The need to secure documents compelled some people to identify them-selves by color. Increasingly the terms negro (black) and amarillo (yellow), labels that had been absent from government records since the abolition of slavery in 1854, became commonplace. When Jeremiah Julian requested a letter of good conduct from Gulf Oil Company, his former employer, it carried the formal designation of "negro."[203] A request for a work and travel permit by Helen Daniel, a native of Trinidad, also carried the designation "negra."[204] When George Henry wrote in support of travel documents for José Quan, who resided in Curaçao, he described himself and the applicant as "amarillo."[205] The new law that forced "undesirable aliens" to carry travel documents racialized this group and increasingly distinguished its members not only by nationality but by color. Although it is difficult to ascertain how these developments affected popular culture and discourse, it is clear that among intellectuals and government officials Trinidadians, and by exten-sion all West Indians, had become a racialized group that could be easily scapegoated for economic woes and chastised for allegedly "darkening" the population.

Neither the need to carry travel or good-conduct certificates nor the prohibition of immigration deterred West Indians or Chinese from enter-ing Venezuela. The application of presidential mandates by state and local governments varied considerably. Moreover, some local officials considered West Indians not immigrants but temporary laborers who would return to their homeland once their employment ceased. Motivated by monetary gain or pressure from the oil companies, government officials continued to approve requests by West Indians seeking work.[206] As late as 1940 the Brit-ish consul in Caracas reported that Venezuela's coasts "remained open to islanders, who continually arrived in search of work and markets, and were as regularly rounded up and after a period of admonitory detention in labor camps, deported."[207]

The enactment of the new repressive regulations continued to fuel anti–West Indian sentiment. A headline in the Maracaibo newspaper *Panorama* in August 1936 proclaimed: "El Peligro Negro" (The Black Threat). The un-named author of the article lamented the number of "Antilles Blacks who daily obtained [Venezuelan] citizenship as if it were a bond issued in the stock market." If the government did not put an end to this practice, he said, Venezuelan identity would soon be extinguished.[208] Not all Venezuelans supported the government's actions against West Indians. The leftist newspaper *Petróleo* railed against this scapegoating and rebuked the *Panorama*, insisting that the danger was not black "but white." To *Petróleo*, what Venezuelans feared was not Afro–West Indians or Chinese workers but "white imperialist *musiúes*, who exploit native workers and workers from throughout the world." Imperialism and its national allies, it argued, were the principal enemy.[209]

Many Venezuelans denounced the public campaign against the West Indians even while demanding that oil companies hire more locals in staff positions. When Lago attempted to replace a Trinidadian supervisor in the transportation department with a Venezuelan, the laborers protested and defended him. According to *Petróleo*, Venezuelans cared more about the treatment they received than making "racial distinctions between Chinese or Japanese."[210] Venezuelans repeatedly defended foreigners who they believed had been mistreated by the oil companies. When a German immigrant found himself without employment, Venezuelans at Mene Grande took up a collection on his behalf.[211] In January 1947 the *Maracaibo Herald* reported that laborers at Mene Grande had also demanded the reinstatement of Vern Goldstein, a boilermaker from the United States, asserting that he had joined their union.[212] Conversely, when confronted by ill treatment, workers publicly expressed their dissatisfaction. In May 1936 over two thousand laborers staged public demonstrations to protest the unfair treatment they received from a West Indian named Phillips and a Mexican named Canales.[213]

The presence of West Indians, Chinese, and others in Venezuela attests to the role of foreign capital in dislocating populations and encouraging international immigration throughout the Caribbean. Between 1920 and 1940 the practices of foreign oil firms gave rise to a complex social and racial division of labor in which Dutch, British, and United States citizens monopolized most managerial positions as well as drilling and other technical operations. West Indians for the most part held clerical positions, while others occupied much-sought-after skilled jobs. Chinese found themselves consigned to relatively menial positions or sought new opportunities in local commerce. Overwhelmingly, Venezuelans were relegated to the tenuous position of day laborers. This social and racial hierarchy also found expression in the allotment of salaries, benefits, and housing arrangements. Conditions in the oil camps invariably attracted the attention of politicians, intellectuals, an emerging middle class, and an incipient labor movement that sought to channel, direct, and manipulate a growing discontent. With racially based employment practices, housing arrangements, and wage differences, the oil industry further racialized Venezuelan society and reinforced existing patterns of racism.

Beyond simply anti-foreign sentiment, the political conflicts that erupted in the oilfields embodied class differences and diverse political agendas. Strategies employed by labor and the middle class to resolve their problems with the oil companies reflected distinct class orientations. The oil industry transformed politics as well as the Venezuelan social and cultural landscape. First, it forced the Venezuelan government to abandon its previous insularity and defend its perceived interests both in the region and in the United States. Second, the congregation of thousands of Venezuelans in the oil camps produced levels of social interaction not experienced since the wars of independence and created a new social environment for workers accustomed to a reality framed largely by regional political and economic forces. Beyond all the practical challenges inherent in this new setting, they also grappled with the contradictions arising from their participation in a new national industry controlled by foreign interests.

Increasingly, regional distinctions became secondary to the common political and social conditions affecting diverse groups of Venezuelans. Moreover, opposition to the apparent privileges afforded to foreigners united Venezuelans from various social classes, providing a new common ground for political action. Labor militancy, often blamed on foreign provocateurs, became a constant feature of life in the oilfields.[214] Confronted by a near total foreign monopoly over their principal natural resource, some Venezuelans indiscriminately lashed out against the West Indians. Oil company policy only exacerbated these circumstances. The presence of a foreign population of color also exposed the virulent racism present throughout Venezuelan society. Attacks by intellectuals and political figures on West

Indians and Chinese became a way of surreptitiously addressing white concerns about the population of color in Venezuela. Despite company actions, government scapegoating, and language and cultural differences, however, West Indians, Chinese, and Venezuelans overcame their differences and developed family and social bonds that endured.

CHAPTER 5

Our Tropical Outpost

Gender and the Senior Staff Camps

As oil operations stabilized, and the required tour of duty for employees from the United States involved prolonged stays, the companies pursued new cultural and gendered strategies in dealing with their foreign employees. Several factors were at play in their decision. A predominately single male labor force occasioned complaints about boredom, excessive drinking, and other social behavior that the companies considered inappropriate. Likewise, married men without their families produced discontent, estrangement, and pressure to return home. Both conditions were viewed as disruptive to the stable conduct of operations. Concerned about dissatisfaction in their ranks and about retaining their foreign employees, company officials had often debated the merits of an all-male labor force and concluded that they would get better results if their white employees from the United States were permitted to bring their families to Venezuela and have them in the field with them.[1] They surmised that providing housing for them would eventually pay for itself by producing a stable labor force. Although it may have alleviated some of the immediate problems for the foreign staff, the construction of separate living facilities for them served to accentuate social differences between the foreigners and the Venezuelan labor force.

The companies also considered other factors; their employees' public conduct directly influenced relations with the local community, and by extension with Venezuelan authorities. On many occasions the actions of male employees had led to negative incidents and even outright clashes with Venezuelans. To ensure smooth operations and to buttress relations with the Venezuelan community, the company opted to recruit an increasing number of married employees and relocate their entire family to the oilfields. This new cultural strategy would have far-reaching consequences not only for oil company operations but also for the social and cultural norms of the residential camps and the outlying communities. Besides social practices, the foreign presence also promoted new patterns of consumption, introducing a diverse array of products from the United States and creating markets for Venezuelan products. For middle-class Venezuelans employed in the industry, the cultural norms and social practices of the married couple from the United States were a constant reminder of how they were expected to conduct themselves if they were to advance in the industry.

As they began to recruit foreign employees with families, the oil companies had to attend to the needs of their residential compounds for married couples. Although bachelors' quarters and the traditional mess hall continued to be a feature of the staff camps, they increasingly shared space with the formal residences for employees and their spouses and children. To accommodate their needs, schools had to be built, teachers hired, hospitals and medical staff expanded, and recreation centers enlarged. This expansion had the effect of recreating, in the residential enclaves of rural and urban Venezuela, important features of everyday life as it was lived in the United States. Bounded by protective fences and guarded by a detachment of guachimanes, the foreign camp housed the foreign community and isolated it from unwanted contact with Venezuelans. While the predominantly male labor force left the camp to work every day, the fences circumscribed the activities of unemployed married women. Not all conditions for foreigners were equal, and camp life reflected social distinctions based on rank and status in the company.

INCREASING FOREIGN PRESENCE

By the mid-1950s the number of foreigners in Venezuela had increased; by one estimate, United States citizens numbered about 35,000 and the British approximately 10,000.[2] Though not all of the foreigners worked in oil, the industry remained the principal reason why foreigners came to Venezuela.[3] The camps in which most of the them lived represented islands of United States culture and society in the broader Venezuelan landscape. In the words of one resident, the camp resembled "a self sustaining colony born of the quest for oil and strangely at odds with the surrounding primitive country."[4] Since the camps evolved as the exclusive domain of largely white employees from the United States, they embodied the racial mores and social prejudices prevalent in the United States. Oil camps with names such as La Rosa, Tía Juana, La Salina, Concordia, Miraflores, and Bachaquero lined the eastern shore of Lake Maracaibo, and the foreign areas within them soon acquired English names such as Hollywood, Sunset, Star Hill, Victory, and Tortilla Flats.[5] At many levels the camps were self-sustaining enclaves in which United States employees and their families sought to recreate the norms and customs of their previous homes. Where possible this also meant reproducing culinary traditions, social practices, and national and religious observances. In the larger camps, celebrations for the 4th of July, Halloween, Thanksgiving, and Christmas became extravagant expressions of United States culture in which all camp residents were expected to participate. That the Venezuelan society and culture engulfing them remained foreign to most residents of the United States only heightened the importance to them of the celebrations as a way to retain their identity.

The senior staff camp also housed Venezuelan professionals known as the "junior staff," mostly doctors, lawyers, and lower-level administrators. Though these two groups coexisted within the residential enclave, power relations clearly favored the foreigners, and cultural exchanges occurred within the context of a dominant United States social and cultural environment. The experiences of the camp exercised a powerful influence on the emerging Venezuelan middle class that shared this unique space. To advance in this environment the members of this middle class found it necessary to incorporate elements of the lifestyle of the United States: language, diet, fashion, sports, and holidays. Framed by the dominant role of the oil industry, United States culture and practices acquired a new cachet and defined modernity for many in the Venezuelan middle class. Invariably the United States residents underwent a limited adaptation, incorporating elements of the Spanish language into their vocabulary and adopting some Venezuelan culinary practices. In the end, the senior staff camps were a distinct social and cultural space, in which United States citizens lived apart from the Venezuelans who inhabited the area outside the fences.

RECRUITMENT OF MARRIED MEN

Company policies at first favored hiring single men, in the belief that married employees would be more costly and that family needs would place greater demands on the all-male workforce. During the early period of the industry, the difficult conditions in the Venezuelan countryside in fact favored the hiring of single employees, since few if any services existed and housing remained primitive. As early as 1915 Caribbean had begun to grapple with this issue, but it remained essentially unresolved during the early years of the oil industry.[6] As the initial boom subsided and the need to retain able and well-trained employees acquired importance, particularly after the Depression, the idea of hiring married workers became more attractive. Throughout the 1920s protests by Venezuelans alerted the companies to the nature of the problems they faced with single men.[7] In the 1930s increased pressure from labor, the middle classes, and the government resulted in limits on the number of foreigners employed by the firm. These changes and the shifting political climate placed a premium on the quality of foreign employees and forced the companies to become more selective in the acquisition of personnel.

The companies had their own reasons for hiring married men. Single employees often proved unreliable, and turnover rates were high. Standard found that many applicants were "seeking foreign service to escape from some undesirable local situation, such as excessive indebtedness, domestic difficulties, failure to advance or to get along with their supervisor."[8] In 1936 its directors took up the issue at their annual board meeting. The minutes of the gathering summarized the shift in policy: "For many years we felt that foreign-service was acceptable to single men and concentrated our efforts to secure such. This of course, put a serious limitation on our selection, and with improved housing and living facilities in the field we now lean toward married men as we find in the long run they are more satisfied to grow with the local organization."[9] The move toward the employment of married men parallels the shift in the industry toward a greater degree of professionalization and away from reliance on traditional roustabouts who would work without preference for any company.

After the Second World War, with a significant number of professionals returning to the labor force, companies actively recruited university graduates or highly experienced specialists. Creole and Shell offered liberal benefits packages to entice families and paid for their relocation to the oilfields and, by the mid-1950s, yearly vacations back to the United States. For its part, Creole advertised the salary that it paid to its foreign employees—in dollars deposited in a United States bank—noting that in most cases it was exempt from United States income tax. Many camp residents tried to live on their monthly living allowances and have their entire salaries deposited to United States accounts.[10]

The company also lauded its "longer vacations with travel at Company expense." After a year of service employees and their families received "29 days of vacation each year during the first four years of service and 30 days per year thereafter,"[11] with travel time not counted as part of the vacation. Return trips to the United States often meant a voyage on a company tanker, a Grace Cruise liner, or, for those willing to spend more, a rather circuitous flight on Pan American Airways with multiple stops en route.[12] By 1940 Pan American offered six weekly flights between Miami and Venezuela.[13] After the Second World War direct flights between Caracas and destinations in Texas facilitated travel between the two countries.[14] Vacation time could also be accumulated, so that the employee after two years could take sixty days in one year. To attract candidates, Creole published brochures with titles such as "An Oil Well with an Interest in You" and sent recruiters to Oklahoma, Texas, and Louisiana.[15] Advertisements in major newspapers announced visits by Creole recruiters operating from local hotels. One person recruited during this time recalled, "If you wanted to be in the oil industry, Venezuela was the place to be."[16] The chances of promotion seemed better overseas than in the home divisions of the oil companies, and gradually skilled specialists replaced the early roughnecks.[17] The companies expected that hiring people with university or professional training would also yield other, nonmonetary dividends; these employees would prove more tolerant of cultural differences and would adapt to work in a foreign country with greater ease.

Concerned about the rising tide of nationalism evident after the Second World War, Creole forewarned its employees that they would be seen as de facto "ambassadors" of the company and the "American way of life," that their "ability to get along with nationals, both employees and outsiders, and efforts to promote a social and economic development of Venezuela" were key factors in the company's industrial and public relations.[18] Sensitive to changing political conditions, the company required new and returning expatriate employees to acquire a working knowledge of Spanish, the laws and customs of the country, and the policies and operations of the company.[19] By the mid-1940s foreign employees faced an eight-week course with five hours daily of Spanish instruction under the direction of a "drillmaster" and two hours of history and "customs." Before establishing these mandatory courses, companies such as Standard Oil (later Creole) hired Berlitz language instructors and assigned them to its camps.

In Maracaibo classes at Bella Vista camp promised to teach foreigners about the "mentality of the Venezuelan" and promote "camaraderie between the native and the foreign worker."[20] In the words of a former industrial relations official with Creole, at best the classes sought to keep the expatriate from "put [ting] his foot in it all the time."[21] In Caracas classes were held at the Creole headquarters with the co-sponsorship of the Centro Venezolano Americano, an English-language cultural center founded during the war with support from the oil companies, the United States government, and Caracas élites.[22] Perturbed by the prospect of long classes, in some cases over two hundred hours, many United States expatriates typically referred to these programs as company "indoctrination sessions."[23] Though the employees received a basic formal introduction to Venezuela, their families never underwent a similar process. In 1956 Creole Petroleum produced a color film entitled *Assignment Venezuela* for prospective employees that stressed the proper role for United States citizens and their families in the country. In the long run, however, little could be accomplished in a required training session that lasted only a few weeks, and those who arrived in Venezuela continued to reflect the views of race and culture that prevailed in the United States.

GENDERED STRATEGIES: INCORPORATING WOMEN AND FAMILIES

From the point of view of the company, the very idea of incorporating women into camp life was linked to the perceived role that women played in the social reproduction of society. The assumption was that by their presence they would exercise a regulatory influence upon the unruly male labor force. Embedded in this assumption was also the notion that women and the family would serve to ensure continuity abroad of United States culture. Women were not, however, the only source of United States culture and norms. The expatriate population had many methods at its disposal for maintaining contact with the United States. The company commissaries sold an assortment of food imported from the United States, mostly canned. In the evenings countless shortwave radios tuned in to stations relayed throughout the Caribbean from the United States and Britain and kept abreast of news and other developments. Newspapers such as the *Diario de Occidente* in Maracaibo published an English-language section listing the shortwave radio bands and the programming for the week.[24] At times the entire family would gather to listen to the radio. Some women in eastern Venezuela religiously followed British radio soap operas emanating from Trinidad.[25] Departures and arrivals of staff to and from the United States served as cultural conduits, introducing the latest fashions and musical releases.[26] Magazines and novels published in the United States made the rounds from one home to another. English-language newspapers such as the *Maracaibo Herald* and the *Caracas Journal* (later *Daily Journal*), as well as the English-language section of *Panorama*, also disseminated news and cultural and sports information from the United States. By the 1950s enterprising families in eastern Venezuela erected towering television antennas to receive English programming from nearby Trinidad. Increasingly the United States population in eastern Venezuela also looked upon the British colony of Trinidad as a vacation spot.

A series of unspoken patriarchal assumptions informed the expectations that accompanied women's presence in the camps. Although they had participated in social functions associated with their husbands' employment in the United States, they had mostly lived in separate neighborhoods there. The enclosed camp dramatically constricted women's freedom of movement. The constant interaction imposed by camp life now added a new subjective factor to the evaluation of employees: the extent to which family members appeared to be team players fully participating in camp life. According to one spouse, women were expected to be "social assets" to their husbands.[27] This practice reflected the assumption that a poorly integrated person might prove socially corrosive and imperil camp cohesion. This was an extra burden for the wife, since now her actions directly influenced the evaluation that her husband received from the company.

From the point of view of the company, women also had other roles to play, in particular providing the company with a human face and the appearance of a settled community integrated in some way with Venezuelan society. The company hoped that these women would become involved in local community work and that their actions would reflect positively on it. Participants in a Standard (New Jersey) board meeting in 1939 discussed their expectations of how the spouses of executives from the United States would behave in Venezuela: "Wives of executives in foreign countries especially play a big part in forming public opinion. Many are marvelous missionaries, but some are hell raisers." Because of this variance, the company made an effort to promote a model of behavior. For example, the chairman of the Standard Oil board of directors praised the supervisor Jim Clark's wife in Maracaibo for having "attracted attention by the intelligent way in which she has carried on community work" and asked that Mr. Clark convey to her the "board's appreciation and thanks."[28]

The wives of executives and other officials typically used their "authority" to help sponsor charities and other community work in which other camp women participated. Most women quickly understood that acceptance in camp social circles and opportunities for promotion for their husbands were tied to their participation in these "service" activities. Company publications actively promoted the work of "wives' committees" on behalf of orphans, fundraising during Christmas, and other charity work. Standard Oil expected that all its employees and family members would participate in the mission of "selling the company."

Invariably the company's male employment hierarchy replicated itself among the spouses; a woman's social standing in the camp reflected her husband's position in the company. By their very positions, the wives of executives were sought after as friends and allies, since they wielded a certain degree of authority within the social circle of the camp. Moreover, invitations to morning coffee gatherings, bridge games, or formal parties became command performances for anyone whose husband was interested in a promotion. This ever-present social hierarchy fueled animosity and tensions. Most remained muted, but occasionally they would erupt when a person at a gathering had consumed too much liquor, and invariably the outburst would be blamed on the excessive drinking.[29]

To facilitate the transition of new families, by the 1950s many camps had orientation manuals with instructions on everything from the appropriate manner in which to display the Venezuelan flag, the schedule of church services, how to send mail, shopping in local facilities, commissary rules, and even the best way to pick and eat tropical fruit.[30] Previously this information had circulated mostly through word of mouth and by ad hoc welcoming committees that greeted new arrivals. In addition, more formal booklets such Mary George's *A Is for Abrazo* served as primers for women newly arrived from the United States.[31] Columnists such as Anne Sutton, Mona Caldwell, Panchita Mack, and Dorothy Kaymen-Kaye retold their experiences in the camps and, along the lines of "Dear Abby," dispensed advice to newcomers.[32] The *Caracas Journal* maintained a network of female correspondents in the camps who reported in tremendous detail on their daily activities.[33] With names such as "Lagunillas Lowdown," "La Salina Letter," "News N'Views," "Quiriquire Quips," "Caripito Chatter," and "Maracaibo Report," these columns shared news and gossip throughout the English-speaking population of Venezuela.

At the same time, the paper ran a regular woman's column that was eventually entitled "The Woman's Angle." The column, written by Kaymen-Kaye, proved equally popular among men. Eventually the newspaper compiled a number of articles and published them as two books, *Speaking of Venezuela* and *Caracas Everyday*. These publications were well received among foreigners, especially women, as they made the transition to life in Venezuela.[34] Women in the camps also published weekly and monthly newsletters such as *La Salina News*, the *Caripito Courier*, and the *Judibana Pelican* that detailed the social life of the camps. The camp bulletins reported on arrivals and departures (especially of unmarried men and women), births, travel plans, recipes, garage sales, and upcoming events. These pamphlets, books, and articles ran the gamut from teaching foreigners how to eat their first mango and how to get along with their housekeepers to providing comfort for the homesick and scolding those who refused to adapt. Several addressed the reluctance of foreigners to learn Spanish: "Americans and Englishmen, cast off your shame, you have nothing to lose but your accent."[35]

The social world of men was framed primarily by their careers in the company and the social and professional obligations of their employment. By the 1950s the majority of the workforce consisted of Venezuelans, with most expatriates holding skilled, supervisory, or administrative positions. Men from the United States became the primary interface with the Venezuelan labor force and the local population outside the camp, but friendships between them and their Venezuelan counterparts were the exception. According to Edwin J. Drechsel, who lived in Caripito, few if any of the "foreign employees had off the job contacts with Venezuelans."[36] Harold Lieberman, employed by Creole as a labor relations officer, recalls being told that he was "going native," because he frequently interacted with Venezuelans.[37] By socializing with Venezuelans Lieberman crossed over established boundaries that formally separated musiúes from Venezuelans.

Camp life for men, as well as for women, depended for the most part on their marital status. Married men became drawn into the social life of the camp and the club activities, the regular games of golf, baseball, and, for the more adventuresome, occasional fishing and hunting outside the camp. Though bachelors also participated in some of the camp's social activities, they were perceived as a potentially disruptive force and thus tended to socialize among themselves. Their life was punctuated by visits to the club and incessant games of poker, as well as drinking and sports. One bachelor described the daily routine that confronted some single men at La Salina: He awoke every workday at 5 a.m., had breakfast at 5:30 in the mess hall, and literally ran to the nearby boat dock by 6:00 to board a launch that took him to the drilling site on the lake. The mess hall staff regularly prepared sack lunches for bachelors to eat during the day. The launch returned with the men at 6:00 in the evening, and they hurried to the mess hall for dinner before it closed at 7:00. Those who arrived early usually played a few hands of poker before dinner. After their meals they played poker or a poker dice game called *chingona*.[38] Some visited the nearby red-light district, and venereal disease was common. Bachelors euphemistically referred to the disease as the "snakebite."[39] The life of the bachelor appeared more alienated and less connected to existing social networks operating in the oil camp.

Relations between Venezuelan and foreign women in the senior staff oil camps remained complex, not lending themselves to generalization. Although élites made efforts to bridge differences, fomenting cultural exchanges and social networks, their efforts proved limited.[40] Undoubtedly there were strong bonds of friendship between some United States and Venezuelan families, usually when educated, white middle-class Venezuelans socialized with foreigners who had similar social and class values. Matters of culture, however, proved a common source of friction. The reaction of Venezuelan middle-class women to their neighbors from the United States originated from conflicting perspectives concerning lifestyle, fashion, etiquette, and social behavior.

Despite living in the same social milieu and interacting regularly, the two groups functioned largely in different worlds. At social functions or at the camp club it was not uncommon to find Venezuelans and expatriates socializing with members of their own nationality. There existed two rumor mills in the residential camps, one focused on residents of the United States and the other on Venezuelans. Even as late as the 1950s, when their numbers in the enterprise had increased, Venezuelan professionals resented the privileges afforded to United States expatriates, such as higher salaries and better housing, as well as disparities in the application of justice. Middle-class Venezuelans disliked having "bosses" whom they considered lacking in "proper manners" and a "formal education." Social attire was highly valued by members of the Venezuelan middle class, who regarded it as a characteristic that distinguished them from the lower classes. Therefore it is not surprising that the behavior of women and men from the United States at various social functions should have become fodder for the rumor mill among Venezuelans.

Most of the criticism centered on the casual behavior of some foreigners, their table manners, poor social skills, and above all their wardrobe. In remarking on the attire of a woman from the United States at a formal reception, a Venezuelan woman commented, "The gringa wore the same simple dress that she uses to go to CADA [commissary] every day."[41] On these matters Venezuelan women believed that they "set the standard in fashion," insisting that "nobody liked how the gringas dressed . . . wearing short skirts, shorts or dressed in western fashion."[42] They attributed this distinction in style to the fact that many of the Venezuelan women in the camps were from Caracas and reflected the fashion trends prevalent in a cosmopolitan urban center. In contrast, they tended to stereotype their counterparts from the United States as provincial. Ironically, these perceptions seldom surfaced in the public sphere, and most United States expatriates were largely unaware of the biting critique to which they were subjected from the Venezuelan women with whom they interacted in the camps. For Venezuela's middle class, highlighting distinctions between themselves and the expatriates was one way to redress the asymmetrical power relations that pervaded social life at the camp and in urban settings.

Single expatriate males married Venezuelan women with some frequency. For example, Frederick (Freddie) Hill Evans, a native of Long Beach, California, arrived in Venezuela in 1926 to work as a tool pusher for Gulf. He eventually settled in Cabimas, where he met and married Ramona Edilia Mora González, a native of Coro. Hill Evans wrote a poem that conveyed his sentiments:

I am a gringo, my brothers,
But not by choice,
I was born that way,
All I know is that I am a brother,
Of that valiant and dignified race,
Those that are my Venezuelan brothers.

When he wrote this poem Hill had already been in the country for forty-three years and married to Ramona for over thirty-five years.[43] By demeaning his so-called gringo roots, Evans sought social acceptance by his "Venezuelan brothers." His poem underscores shifting loyalties and his effort to identify with his newly adopted country. Of the dozens of oilmen who arrived with him from the United States in 1926, Evans recalls several others who married Venezuelans and permanently settled in the country. With a significant number of single expatriates employed in the industry, there were United States men married to Venezuelan women in almost every oil camp.

Women from the United States, however, were not as easily inclined to marry Venezuelan men, and these sorts of relationships occurred with less frequency. When they did occur, the intercultural social ties had often been established at universities in the United States. Carlos Rojas Davila, for example, obtained employment with Creole after receiving his doctorate in mathematics from the Central University of Venezuela; while pursuing further studies at the University of Oklahoma he met a fellow student, Calibee Feaster, whom he eventually married.[44] Life in the camps for these binational and intercultural couples was challenging. Besides having to straddle cultural and social differences they had to negotiate resistance and in some cases open hostility from both the United States and Venezuelan communities.

CAMP LIFE

Men like Harold Lieberman, hired in the 1930s, viewed the opportunity to work in Venezuela as a way out of the unemployment pervading the United States during the Depression. He wrote to all the oil companies operating in Venezuela and was eventually employed by Creole. Like most employees from the United States hired by the oil companies, he had "no idea" what he was getting into.[45] Like the men before them, women and children from the United States were unaware of what awaited them in Venezuela.[46] Some families brought their pets, mainly dogs and cats, to help facilitate the transition for the children. In preparation for the assignment to Venezuela, Morse Travers paid a visit to the local library and read books: Erna Fergusson's *Venezuela* (1939) and Y. T. Ybarra's *Young Man of Caracas* (1941).[47] Travers proved to be the exception, since few people bothered to prepare for their assignment. One woman hired as a teacher thought that she was going to "live in a tree house."[48] The theme of expatriates living in the jungle proved quite common in the travel literature. William Burchfiel, a Navy lieutenant and a native of Tennessee, described the Caripito camp as an "American Tropical Outpost deep in the Venezuelan jungle." Anne Rainey Langley, who lived for several years in the Quiriquire oil camp, wrote an article for *National Geographic* in 1939 entitled "I Kept House in a Jungle."[49] Henry Allen, invited to visit the Creole oil camp in Caripito, expected to find people living in tents and sleeping in hammocks and wondered how canvas tents would afford protection from the tropical snakes he had heard so much about. Rather than describe the camps, these accounts tell us more about the stereotypes held by their writers. When he arrived at Caripito, Allen reported that to his utter surprise, the staff camp looked like a country-club suburb in the United States: "An attractive golf course, modern houses many of which had new, streamlined finish to them, green undulating lawns, glorious flowery shrubbery, tropical fruit trees, well laid-out drives and sidewalk, a new church, a large hospital on a neighboring hill, a big commissary building, a group of modern offices set in the midst of tropical landscaping, a club house with wide-open doors, windows and a verandah made an amazing picture."[50] Though not all camps resembled Caripito, referred to in company publications as one of "the most attractive oil communities of Venezuela," many had similar amenities.[51]

Not all the facilities in the camp were equally available to all residents. New employees, whether married or not, invariably arrived as bachelors. The probationary period allowed the company to determine if the employee could adapt to camp life before incurring the expense of bringing his family to Venezuela. Once in the camp, an employee's ranking in the company hierarchy determined his assignment of a residence. The upper echelon of the company lived in the largest houses; in some parts of the country these homes rested on ten-foot stilts to afford greater ventilation in the humid tropical climate. Seniority and family size also played a significant role: newer employees sometimes had to wait for residences to become available. The interiors of the houses did possess a certain sameness, since the company provided most furnishings (usually some kind of rattan furniture).

A staff camp usually had a club that served as the center of all public social activity. In the words of one early camp resident in Caripito, every afternoon "many of the employees, expatriates and Venezuelans, married and single, went there to sit, talk and drink or play billiards. The bar did a constant business until closing time and beyond."[52] The clubs appeared to reinvigorate the expatriate community. The inauguration of the Caribbean Club at the Cabimas camp in 1928 led to a celebration that drew over five hundred expatriate men and women from throughout the lake region. The *Tropical Sun* reported that "Home Sweet Home" played until 4:00 the next morning.[53]

Clubs tended to acquire amenities gradually. The first experience with a swimming pool at the Caribbean Club was a fiasco. The camp relied on Maracaibo lake water to fill the pool, and because of the silt in the water it became unusable. Eventually a pump had to be used to remove the silt and impurities.[54] At the club, or dispersed throughout the camp, the company also maintained baseball fields. In 1955 camp residents were able to cast ballots for the major league All-Star game.[55] By the 1950s most clubs had a bar, a soda fountain and grill, billiard tables, tennis courts, a swimming pool, and a nine-hole golf course, usually carved out of the rainforest.[56] They would also have a small library of well-worn books and magazines.[57]

Most public celebrations took place at the clubs. Musical performances, dances, and a weekly selection of films from the United States provided entertainment for the expatriate community. As one expatriate recalled, the latest movies arrived by plane twice a week.[58] Once a movie arrived, neighboring camps, even from competing companies, shared it until it had made the rounds of all the local facilities. In the stifling heat of western Venezuela, films became open-air affairs; moviegoers sat in folding chairs and viewed the latest Hollywood productions on a large outdoor screen. At the soda fountain they could order Coca-Cola, ginger ale, root beer floats, hamburgers, french fries, and hot dogs. Parties at the club usually included the typical American "steaks, beer, beans, potato salad, and pies."[59] Beer, in most cases the Venezuelan brand Polar, and local brands of rum, especially Santa Teresa, became the most popular. Imported Scotch whiskey was the drink of choice for visiting dignitaries or company officials. Repeated exposure to these consumer products, either in the clubs, at mixed social gatherings, or at the company commissary, gradually influenced Venezuelan habits and customs. Venezuelans remain among the most prolific consumers of Scotch whisky in the world, drinking more eighteen-year-old scotch than any other country in Latin America. One national publication concluded that drinking whisky mixed with ice and water was akin to a "criollo ritual."[60]

The camps had ample and well-kept park-like areas, shade trees, flowers, and lush green lawns seeded with grasses imported from the United States.[61] Maintenance of the camps also entailed controlling tropical diseases. After the Second World War the U.S. Army sent specialists to Caripito to combat malaria and other tropical maladies.[62] The lessons learned during the war in the Pacific were applied in the Venezuelan countryside. As a result Creole began to spray DDT throughout the camps and adjacent neighborhoods. Outside the camps, the DDT crews stenciled numbers on the houses that they sprayed; the designation became a home's de facto address. The sight of company trucks spewing hazy chemical clouds, with children unwittingly running behind, became common in some camps.

Each camp also had an elementary school that offered classes through the eighth grade, after which the children would normally be sent to boarding school in the United States or to live with relatives while they attended high school. Teachers, recruited in the United States, taught classes in English that incorporated both the Venezuelan curriculum and that which would prepare students to attend high school in the United States. For the youth of the camp, life revolved around activities at the club, such as sporting events, swimming, and games. During the summer the return of the older high school students enlivened camp life. Besides attending school, children were encouraged to belong to the Boy Scout and Girl Scout troops that formed in most camps. Religious services tended to be nondenominational. Although Catholics could easily attend services in nearby Venezuelan churches, few if any ever ventured out of the camp to worship. The presence of Catholic nuns as nurses in some company hospitals allowed for worship at these facilities.

Hospitals, initially staffed by medical personnel from the United States and subsequently by Venezuelan doctors and nurses, operated in all the camps. Shopping took place at a company-subsidized commissary that stocked basic products as well as an assortment of brands from the United States, mostly canned goods. In addition, there was a mess hall where single employees took their meals. To maintain their facilities in pristine condition, the companies employed an army of Venezuelan cooks, gardeners, and maintenance personnel.

Lago's monthly reports provide insights into the complex tasks performed by the camp staff, which catered to the needs of what amounted to a small town. In the vicinity of Cabimas, Lago maintained staff camps at Ambrosio, La Salina, La Rosa, Punta Gorda, and a location named Lot 66. A camp foreman directed a Venezuelan and West Indian staff that included, according to company documents, "house boys," mail carriers, a sanitation gang, yard laborers, peones, office-building janitors, security, laundresses, watchmen, and schoolteachers.[63] The camp staff cleaned the bachelors' quarters and club facilities, prepared meals, collected trash to be burnt in an incinerator, sprayed crude oil on nearby vegetation and standing pools of water to control mosquitoes, maintained the yards, and delivered ice and water to the camp residences. During the month of May 1930 the kitchen staff prepared 16,099 meals at La Salina.[64]

The company attempted to provide its foreign employees and their families with all their basic physical needs. As part of the compensation package, the staff employee received housing, furniture, electricity, and in some cases natural gas. The company gardeners kept the lawns perfectly manicured. Although common in the United States, the idea of homes with lawns remained foreign to most Venezuelans. The staff also attended to most home repairs, including, according to one spouse of a former Creole employee, changing their light bulbs. When a woman who did not know how to drive needed to go to the commissary, a company driver picked her up at the door.[65] Besides camp staff, many expatriate families employed maids, often West Indians or Venezuelans. As one woman from the United States who had lived in eastern Venezuela candidly admitted, the "lazy Americans went to Trinidad to get help so they would not have to speak or learn Spanish."[66] Although this may not always have been so, this practice did mirror experiences observed in foreign enclaves in Central America and the Caribbean.[67]

URBAN PETROLEUM DISTRICTS

The oil companies operated not only in the rural countryside but also in Maracaibo, their original base of operations, and in the national capital, Caracas. At first the largest companies, among them Caribbean, voc, Lago, and Gulf, established their operational headquarters at Maracaibo and maintained hospitals there for their staff. Lago first located its facilities at Los Haticos, near the wharf, and later moved to the newly formed section of Bella Vista. Standard Oil Company was based at La Arriaga, the Shell group at Los Haticos.[68] Employing an ever-growing army of managers, administrators, and support staff, the companies gradually created the equivalent of urban oil districts within the city limits. By 1935 the Lago camp in Maracaibo had, besides the main company offices, "three bachelor quarters buildings housing some forty employees, about twenty houses for married employees and their families, a mess hall for the singles and official visitors, a club with full bar, music room, with piano, billiard room, library that doubled as a part time barber shop, outdoor tile dance floor, swimming pool and open air movies twice a week."[69]

As it had in the countryside, the presence of the oil companies in an urban setting transformed the use of space. Creole Petroleum, for example, viewed the construction of offices to expand its operations in Maracaibo as the precursor of new urban development that would include the nearby Hotel del Lago, frequented by oil personnel, the Coromoto Hospital, and the "beautiful residential zone known as Bella Vista."[70] The presence of corporate headquarters and adjacent support and residential facilities in major population centers such as Maracaibo and Caracas led to the formation of what Henry Vicente labeled urban "petroleum districts."[71] The new petroleum district in Caracas, Vicente recalled, was south of the river Guaire, bounded by the Creole Building at Los Chaguaramos (now Bolivarian University) and the former Shell Offices at Chuao. A new phase of urban development in the capital city saw the construction of the Valle Arriba Golf Club, the Hotel Tamanaco, a Sears store, the CADA supermarket, and the Las Mercedes residential area, all catering to professionals and the middle class employed by the industry. The river Guaire, which previously marked the southern limits of the city, was now an important marker separating the new "modern" petroleum district from the older traditional neighborhoods of Caracas.[72] The new districts, characterized by a contemporary architectural style, became endowed with the same notions of modernity that defined the oil camps in the rural areas.

LIFE BEHIND THE BARBED-WIRE FENCE

Far from the large major cities, rural camp life appeared tranquil. The general homogeneity of a mostly white population from the United States and the pervasiveness of camp culture reduced potential sources of conflict. Most people never locked their doors or windows. Parents allowed their children to walk to school unsupervised and to play unimpeded throughout the camp, in the knowledge that the facilities remained fully enclosed and protected around the clock. Outside the camps the National Guard protected the camp and looked after the facilities and the well-being of the foreigners. This sense of protection extended beyond the camp, and there were few incidents of crimes against foreigners. One woman who lived in Quiriquire described her existence in the camp as life "in a bubble, a fairy way of living."[73]

For others, despite the relatively tranquil setting, camp life was stifling and alienating. While men left to work every day, unemployed women remained behind, constrained by the very fences that protected the camp. The fences soon acquired symbolic meaning: "no matter where you looked," said one woman, "the fences were always there." A woman whose husband had worked for Gulf wrote that she had lived for twenty-five years behind barbed wire.[74] Another resident of San Tomé in eastern Venezuela poked fun at camp life and referred to residents as "Santomaniacs."[75] In many cases the perceived restrictions were self-imposed, reflecting a preference for the safety of the familiar and fear of the Venezuelan world outside the camp fences.

Many women seldom stepped outside alone. Groups of women who lived on the eastern shore of Lake Maracaibo organized monthly trips into Maracaibo by company launch to shop at the large emporiums such as the Curaçao Trading Company, returning in the late afternoon. By contrast, Venezuelan women in the Judibana oil camp organized bus tours to Caracas to visit family and shop. To escape the heat, expatriates and Venezuelan employees vacationed in the nearby Andes, where Creole maintained facilities at the Hotel Guadalupe, near La Puerta in the state of Trujillo.[76] Despite their distance from any production sites, areas such as La Puerta and many others throughout Venezuela increasingly grew dependent on the oil companies and their employees for their economic well-being. Travel to this region increased during the Second World War, when it became almost impossible to leave Venezuela. The absence of viable infrastructure in eastern Venezuela, which had previously isolated the local population, also had an impact on foreign employees of the companies. Expatriate families did not have access to large urban centers such as Maracaibo for shopping or recreation. To break the regular routine, expatriates in Caripito, Quiriquire, and Jusepín in some cases organized getaways to Trinidad, where in addition to shopping they sought out British-trained ophthalmologists and dentists, specialists not usually found among the company's medical staffs.[77] Facing the Port of Spain racetrack and cricket fields, Queens Park, a hotel dating to the colonial era and regarded as "the most noted of the hotels in the British West Indies," became a favorite haunt for visiting expatriates.[78] Creole operated an airport at Cachipo and maintained its own fleet of planes with almost daily flights to nearby camps and frequent trips to Port of Spain. Pan American Airways also used the Cachipo field for flights between Caracas and Trinidad. Amelia Earhart made use of these facilities on her final trip around the globe; Creole officials welcomed her at the airport and held a dinner for her at the Caripito staff country club. Despite the occasional excursions and the visits of dignitaries and celebrities, the reality is that most families rarely ventured out of the security afforded by the camp.

Camp life tended to privilege couples with children, who would form support networks and socialize regularly. Not everyone could make the transition. Incidents of separation, divorce, and spouses returning to the United States shortly after arriving were not uncommon. One childless woman wrote to Mona Caldwell, a columnist for the *Caracas Journal*, complaining about her situation: "In the morning we start out either someone comes to my house or I go to a friend's house and then several of us gab and have coffee. Then I have to go home and have lunch alone because most of my friends have husbands who come home for lunch. In the afternoon we start meeting somewhere in someone's house and play cards and have tea. Often in the evenings, there are barbecues and my friends invite me. I simply hate life here. I simply cannot stand it any longer. I feel like I will burst inside."[79] Caldwell had little sympathy for this woman's plight, though she readily admitted that camp life was not for everyone.

For families with children, school established a daily regimen marked by the start and end of the school day. One woman reported that among her acquaintances breakfast represented their first chore, after which they dispatched their children to school. Then, by ten o'clock, different circles of women would gather at predetermined homes or at the camp club and play bridge or canasta, knit, raise funds for some social project, or engage in some other activity. Housework, for those who had the resources, was attended to by Venezuelan or West Indian housekeepers.[80] This was the routine day after day. The simple reason for so much activity, another woman stated, was "that there is no place to go outside of the company property for recreation."[81] In the evenings, parties or other social activities took place in individual houses or the club. Social gatherings invariably became gendered events, "the men on one side of the room talking shop, the women on the other side comparing maids or talking about their children."[82] For most residents, especially women, what was most difficult was, in the words of one woman, "the damn monotony of camp life that drives everyone crazy."[83] Movies at the club and parties marked the weekends. Liquor flowed freely at these social events and took its toll on both men and women.[84]

Food preparation was a major area of concern for expatriate women accustomed to the selection of products found in stores in the United States.

With tropical heat and the scarcity of refrigeration, offerings at the camp commissary tended to be limited to a predictable assortment of canned foods. Fresh milk simply did not exist, and the powdered variety (the most popular of which was the KLIM brand) could be found in every pantry. The expatriates also had to learn to use Venezuelan cuts of meat such as *lomo* and *lomito* in place of the familiar top sirloin or porterhouse.[85] The commissary did sell a variety of tropical fruits, such as mangos, papayas, and pineapples, that were foreign to most expatriates. Some worried about eating local foods, which they thought might be laced with "amoebas." The *Caracas Journal* quoted one doctor from the United States as saying that while in Venezuela he would always recite a "silent prayer at a party before eating salad or fruits. Don't get me this time."[86] He recommended that in the privacy of their homes, expatriates should take a vitamin rather than eat fruits or vegetables. Newcomers would be quickly instructed on how to boil and filter drinking water and how to treat Venezuelan fruits and vegetables by washing them in water containing a Halazone tablet. Though the tablets proved effective, they also left a chemical residue that altered the taste of fruits and vegetables, and they quickly lost their effectiveness in the humid tropical climate. In the end it was peace of mind, rather than amoeba-free food, that the expatriates achieved by using the tablets. Drinking liquor was also suggested as a way of killing "amoebas and preventing dysentery."[87]

The absence of foods and fruits typically found in the United States increased the desire for these products. Anne Rainey Langley, a resident of Quiriquire, describes her excitement over an apple: "I had never lived on canned foods for weeks, counting the days until the next boat would bring us fresh vegetables from the States."[88] In eastern Venezuela the arrival of tankers that on occasion brought produce from the United States was cause for celebration among the expatriates.[89] The camp grapevine quickly relayed information concerning the arrival of produce. In the words of Myriane Marret Woolen, who also lived in the Quiriquire camp, the arrival of these goods meant that for the next two weeks there would be a round of parties.[90]

In an effort to adapt to the local food supply, camp women produced a series of cookbooks which they sold, usually donating the proceeds to a local charity. In anticipation of the frequent parties, women "pored over their cookbooks, looking for the one recipe that would be different from what they'd eaten at the last party."[91] The inspiration for these books was the first

English-language cookbook published in Venezuela, *Buen Provecho*, sponsored by the British War Charities in 1943,[92] which women from both Britain and the United States helped to produce.[93] With names such as *Amuay Cooking Capers, Recipes along the Venezuela's B.C.F.* (Bolívar Coastal Fields), and *Pruébalo [Taste It]: We Cook in Maracaibo*, cookbooks published by the women's groups demonstrated how they had adapted the culinary traditions of the United States to their Venezuelan setting.[94] The appearance of these cookbooks did not mean that the expatriates had developed new bicultural culinary practices, but rather that they had simply been forced to adapt to the available supply of foods. Children exposed to Venezuelan food since birth developed a fondness for certain dishes such as the arepas, local soft drinks, and sweets.

Despite these adaptations, the culture of the United States continued to pervade social practices in the camp. The predominance of Texans and other Southwesterners meant that their customs exercised more influence over camp life than other traditions from the United States. Many of the expatriates hired by Creole Petroleum had been previously employed by Carter Oil in Oklahoma and Humble Oil in Texas.[95] Some expatriates assumed that Texans and Oklahomans had been hired because they had experience with hot weather.[96] Others, especially those from the Northeast, found themselves obliged to adopt a Texan drawl and learn to cook differently to become socially acceptable. Outdoor affairs, especially the traditional barbecue, became quite common, and invariably guests would have to listen to some variation of "Deep in the Heart of Texas."[97] One woman from New England reported that she had learned to cook southern food in Venezuela, preparing okra, grits, and gumbo for the first time.[98]

An assortment of formal and informal social gatherings tended to dominate the life of women. At San Tomé, a Gulf Oil camp, Ann and Paul Hogan hosted a party for sixteen guests "for no good reason except they felt like having a party."[99] In Maracaibo the "ladies of Creole Maracaibo held a get-together tea at the home of Mrs. Allen Owen in honor of the ladies of Richmond Exploration now living in the Creole camp."[100] For staff employees from the United States, constantly subject to transfers, social life consisted of an interminable series of welcoming and farewell parties, as well as receptions for company and political dignitaries. Many women dreaded these parties. The *Maracaibo Herald* described them as a voluntary racket: "Every one in Venezuela has been here for 44 years except you and is now retiring. You should shell out $20 to buy a gift. Doesn't matter that he works on the other side of the country, has never heard of you and has been earning $100,000 yearly for the past 18 years."[101] In the view of another commentator, "conspicuous celebrations" seemed to have several purposes, one of which was "to welcome what the invaders refer to as visiting firemen or jefes that is, individuals from the homeland tribe (U.S.) whose presence is somehow considered advantageous to the group." The irritation with constantly having to attend parties for visiting company officials was compounded by the social hierarchy in the camps. In the words of one woman, class distinctions were "not founded on intrinsic worth but on position in the economic order."[102]

UNITED STATES CELEBRATIONS IN VENEZUELA

In addition to attending a never-ending succession of social functions, women were expected to assume responsibility for ensuring traditional celebrations associated with the political and liturgical calendar of the United States. The presence of women and children provided the context: it is doubtful that without them these holidays would have been celebrated with the same level of exuberance. National holidays and religious festivities often became campwide celebrations. Observances of Valentine's Day, St. Patrick's Day, Easter, the Fourth of July, Halloween, Thanksgiving, and Christmas involved weeks of long preparation by women's groups, and participation, although voluntary, was expected. Separated from homes and families, expatriates assigned special significance to these festivities and celebrated them with an exuberance not usually witnessed in the United States.

Since Venezuelan Independence Day falls on 5 July, expatriates normally staged long celebrations in honor of both it and the Fourth of July. The practice of celebrating both holidays served to mute overt manifestations of United States patriotism that might provoke a nationalist reaction from the Venezuelan population. Holidays without explicit political content were of less concern. Halloween, a celebration that Venezuelans knew nothing about, took on a festive air for both adults and children. The *Maracaibo Herald* reported that at the Creole camp in Lagunillas the witches rode broom sticks, the jack o' lanterns had been carved, and children attended elaborate costume parties. There was no fear of letting children run free throughout the camp, since guards afforded constant protection. In the evening adults staged costume dances at all the camp clubs. The Creole camp at La Salina sponsored a so-called Indian affair for which the mostly white participants painted their faces and dressed as local indigenous Guajiros.[103] Likewise, Thanksgiving in some camps became a community celebration. At San Tomé in 1946 all eight hundred residents ate together.[104] Some expatriates took advantage of these customs and set up turkey farms outside the camps in the hope of earning extra cash during the holiday.

Christmas, complete with pine trees imported from Washington and Oregon and the figure of Santa Claus, took on a tropical flair. Creole employees strung multicolored lights in the shape of Christmas trees on the oil derricks that surrounded the camps.[105] The communications department at La Salina attached speakers to the oil derricks and serenaded the camp every night with Christmas music from Helen Traubel, Bing Crosby, and Fred Waring.[106] To supply the needs of the camp residents, local businesses began to carry an array of products made in the United States. One paper reported that local businesses had sold their entire supply of Christmas trees and assorted ornaments, but that few people had bought or displayed the traditional Venezuelan *pesebre* or nativity scenes.[107] During Christmas the camp, decorated with brightly colored lights, resembled a middle-class neighborhood in the United States. Anne Sutton, who lived in Maracaibo, explained that the "festive lights and colorful fountains made the grounds of the Lago or Caribbean club look like a fairyland."[108] In addition to Christmas trees, the camp commissaries and even some local businesses carried an assortment of holiday seasonal items. United States customs and traditions not only played a role among the Venezuelan junior staff that inhabited the camps but also began to influence consumer patterns and celebrations among middle-class elements in the surrounding communities.

SPORTS, RECREATION, AND CAMP FOLKLORE

To entertain themselves, men and women in the camps played softball, baseball, golf, and bowled, forming teams that competed with each other and with teams from other camps. Women's leagues played at the regional and national levels.[109] Sports also became an opportunity for various expatriate communities to interact. The Caripito Golf Club organized a tournament with the Saint Andrews Gold Club in Trinidad; departing from the Creole airstrip at Cachipo, a Pan American DC-3 plane took twenty-one players across the Gulf of Paria to play golf in Port of Spain.[110] The British returned the favor every other year, traveling to Caripito to play the Creole expatriates.[111] A series of parties, teas, and banquets marked the end of the tournament. Boy Scout troops in eastern Venezuela also interacted with their white counterparts in Trinidad. In May 1940 a scout troop from Trinidad visited Caripito and enjoyed a barbecue in its honor attended by the nearby camps of Quiriquire and Jusepín.[112]

To break the boredom, expatriates also engaged in some rather unorthodox sporting activities. Unconventional variants of sports included something commonly referred to as screwball golf, in which players faced unusual obstacles. On one hole they teed off from a mattress, on another tee they would place one foot in a bucket, or they would play an entire hole with only one club or be forced to hit the ball through the center of a tire. Besides traditional baseball and softball, natives of the United States staged games of what they called "burro baseball": players mounted a burro and batted, fielded, and ran the bases while riding it.[113] At Tía Juana the game between married and single men attracted large crowds. As one expatriate from the United States put it, these were "silly things, but there was nothing else to do."[114]

Inevitably the enclosed nature of the camp and the close proximity in which people lived meant that gossip became a popular pastime, rivaling any organized sport. Accounts of what people had done, real or not, would accompany them from camp to camp. This process gave life to folklore about sexual matters, extramarital affairs, single residents, and drinking. One former resident candidly described the camps as a "marriage market" for singles, mostly teachers, nurses, and engineers. The *Caracas Journal* reported in September 1945 that United States men at San Tome were eagerly awaiting the arrival of Catherine Reed, Lucille Zuendt, Mary Ardein, and Ruth Curtis, teachers newly assigned to the camp school.[115] Single women—teachers or nurses who had not found a partner after a few months—came under suspicion, not concerning their sexual orientation but rather the possibility that they might be having an affair with a married man. The same sort of suspicion followed bachelors, though promiscuity among single men did not always lead to the same sort of reproach. Accounts of employees from the United States marrying former Venezuelan sex workers appear regularly in descriptions of camp life.[116] Beyond these more typical encounters, the camp rumor mill always included tales of extramarital affairs and sex parties. The most common and most widely repeated tale involved swapping partners under the pretext of various sexual games, including "spin the bottle."[117] Yet despite these apparent indiscretions, marriage remained a necessary precondition for full participation in camp activities and social life.

THE EXPATRIATE COMMUNITY AND THE MEDIA

The expatriate community in Venezuela inevitably attracted the attention of the media and the entertainment industry in the United States. James Tuck, a columnist for *Cosmopolitan*, wrote a mocking account of camp life to which residents reacted bitterly. He called the expatriates who worked for the oil companies some of the highest-paid employees in the world and described their routine as follows: "Bright and early Monday morning, they stroll out of their luxurious house or apartments, wearing oil-splattered clothes and are picked up by their white coated chauffeur who drives them in their limousines to the airport where they catch a plane to the fields."[118] Women were reported to be living in swanky country club districts with two servants and to be paying fifteen dollars for nylons. Venezuelans fared no better in the article, being stereotyped in the worst possible way. Tuck's article hit a nerve among the expatriate community. The *Caracas Journal* defended camp residents, and to curry favor with locals, attacked the article in *Cosmopolitan* for its negative portrayal of Venezuelans.[119]

By the 1950s, influenced by the Latin explosion in the United States, a host of entertainers began to incorporate Venezuela into their repertoires. Musicians, novelists, and filmmakers portrayed the experiences, real or invented, of the foreign "petroleros."[120] The singer Burl Ives recorded "Venezuela," a generic account of an expatriate and a Venezuelan whose lyrics typified the prevalent stereotypes of the time:

I met her in Venezuela with a basket on her head.
And if she loved others, she would not say,
but I knew she'd do to pass away the time in Venezuela,
to pass away the time in Venezuela.[121]

Venezuelans and women did not fare any better when represented by Caribbean singers such as Harry Belafonte, who recorded a calypso song called "Sweetheart from Venezuela" that also described an encounter with a local woman named, typically enough, Juanita. To a calypso beat, Belafonte sang:

Juanita my Darling, you sure you love me, Si si Señor,
You feel in your heart you will marry to me, Si si Señor,
You promise to love me the rest of your life, Si si Señor
I love Juanita, my sweetheart from Venezuela, Si si Señor
I will teach you to habla in English like me, Si si Señor
I will take you to padre and marry you now, Si si Señor[122]

Other musicians, such as Guy Lombardo in 1958, also recorded tracks on Venezuela.[123]

Writers such as Sterling Silliphant wrote mythical accounts that drew inspiration from the oil industry in Venezuela. In 1955 Silliphant published his novel *Maracaibo*, which was subsequently made into a movie starring Cornel Wilde, Jean Wallace, Abbe Lane, and Michael Landon. The movie's steamy poster had Wilde kissing Wallace while an oil derrick burned on Lake Maracaibo in the background. In typical Hollywood fashion, Wilde, the main character, faced the challenge of putting out the fire, or else the city of Maracaibo would be lost.[124]

At many levels expatriates shared a deep sense of alienation, a feeling of not belonging either to life in Venezuela or to that in the United States. Having been away, in some cases for a decade, they had missed the important events that help mark a generation in the United States and were reduced to the position of outside observers of developments both there and in Venezuela. Upon returning home many felt a deep sense of estrangement and longed to recapture the life they had left behind, reflecting upon their experience in Venezuela as the "best days of their lives." In the United States others experienced a significant change in their social status. The privileges, security, and status that characterized the senior staff camps in Venezuela informed this nostalgic portrayal of the past.

In the end, the senior staff camps had an impact well beyond their residents' attempts to recreate the lifestyle of the United States. Their presence dramatically altered the panorama of the Venezuelan countryside and even major urban areas, inaugurating new residential prototypes, consumption patterns, and forms of social organization, influencing fashion, leisure, sports, and diet. Initially intended to alleviate problems within the all-male labor force, the presence of spouses and families became part of the oil company's cultural strategy, aimed at both its expatriate and Venezuelan employees. For companies like Creole (Standard Oil), whose board of directors privately discussed the matter, women were seen as important cultural agents, serving to regularize expatriate camp life and also establishing a social model of behavior that Venezuelans hoping to advance in the industry were expected to incorporate. The emerging Venezuelan middle class was soon adapting these practices in and outside the camps. Paradoxically, most United States expatriates in the camps remained unaware of the role that they played in this broader social and cultural process.

CHAPTER 6

The Oil Industry and Civil Society

As the boom period of the industry subsided, and the companies learned from their experiences, they adopted new strategies to integrate the Venezuelan labor force. As this process evolved, Venezuelans employed by the industry underwent a profound process of social and cultural acculturation. This adaptation entailed adjusting to a new urban landscape that through the use of ordered space sought to reorient traditional behavior patterns to suit the new industrial model. Beyond reformulating the use of public and private space, the oil camps recast regional differences, altered conceptions of work and time, introduced distinct lifestyles, and promoted new consumer patterns among Venezuelan workers and the middle class. These practices had an impact on both men and women and eventually shaped a generation of Venezuelans who were offered conditions of life and an opportunity for regular advancement largely unattainable outside the oil industry. Though dramatic at first, over time the oil camp experience became normalized, evolving into a set of social assumptions and class expectations that defined those employed in the industry and against which other elements of society could measure their own status. Those employed in the oil industry became models of social interaction and behavior in both the residential oil camps and throughout broader society. The residential camps therefore provide an opportunity to examine the effects of the oil industry on the lives of Venezuelans and foreigners, and the construction of a distinct model of political participation and a concept of citizenship that favored its interests.

The oil companies recognized that they could not simply attempt to influence the outlook of their immediate employees. The development of the oil industry generated important national expectations which the companies themselves had helped to feed. Yet the number of people who benefited directly from the industry by employment or subsidiary industries remained exceedingly small. The foreign companies responded with a corporate project that extended well beyond their employees, reaching broadly into civil society. Fearful of the rising tide of nationalism throughout Latin America and recognizing the expectations that the industry generated, by the late 1930s the largest oil companies began to develop a new, far-reaching model of corporate citizenship. As Terry Lynn Karl has observed, "the export of oil fosters especially powerful organized groups with very real interests in maintaining this model."[1] Nowhere did this process resonate more than with the Venezuelan middle class, for which the possibility of work in the oil industry dramatically expanded opportunities. Moreover, by the mid-1930s corporate practices coincided with the interests of political leaders and their intellectual allies, who viewed the foreign oil companies as instruments that could help them refashion the traditional political and economic order. After Gómez's death in 1935, according to Coronil, Venezuela's new political leadership sought to portray the country as a modern oil nation unpolluted by the past twenty-seven years of one-man rule.[2] Accomplishing this task required the assistance of the oil companies, which continued to be portrayed as agents of modernity that permitted Venezuela to break from its purported backward political past and enter a new modern era. If oil represented progress for the country, then the lifestyle associated with the oil industry and the social stature that it conveyed became a model for broad segments of Venezuelan society. Over time, intellectuals, academics, and artists actively participated in formulating a national social and cultural project that identified the economic interests of the foreign oil companies with the welfare of the nation. The long-term success of these company-sponsored programs can be judged from the extent to which various elements of the population appropriated these practices as their own, and the extent to which the practices penetrated political discourse.

As is typical of extractive enterprises, the oil industry never employed a significant portion of the Venezuelan labor force. In 1941 the number of people on the payrolls of all the major oil companies accounted for 1.9 percent of the labor force, and by 1948 it had peaked at 4.5 percent.[3] In 1948 Creole employed 20,483 workers, Shell 17,890, and Mene Grande (Gulf) 10,342, while several smaller United States firms employed an additional 9,054.[4] This employment pattern persisted throughout the 1950s and 1960s.[5] In the 1970s improvements in technology diminished the need for workers in the industry, except for those with superior skills. Yet the downward trend in employment did not in any way diminish the role that oil and employees of the industry played in the economy or society. The impact of the oil industry must therefore be measured by its strategic position in the national and world economy and the influence that it exerted on political actors and on the social and cultural norms of the country.

A NEW ORDER

Marked by visible social and racial distinctions, segregation in housing arrangements, the reorganization of public and private space, and the promotion of particular consumer patterns, the oil camp exerted a significant influence over the people who resided within its boundaries.[6] Inclusion in the camp implied the physical removal of Venezuelans from their previous communities and their reinsertion into a new and discrete urban and social order. Creole's publications stressed the way the composition of the camp influenced the socialization of its employees: "When you visit our camps, the most impressive feature that you observe is the strict order that pervades the settlement; this order permits everything to function . . . everything operates in concert with each other."[7] The camps displayed defined urban schemas, streets formed by precise blocks, and the inclusion of open and closed spaces around houses and schools. This arrangement introduced a relatively new concept to most Venezuelans: homes surrounded either by private or collective manicured lawns and gardens. The *Tropical Sun* proudly announced that Caribbean and other companies had begun the practice of planting lawns, grown from imported United States seed, at several of their camps.[8]

The new order characteristic of the camps contrasted sharply with the largely unplanned and unregulated character of nearby Venezuelan towns and communities, overrun by recent migrants. Though in many cases they had the same name, the oil camps and the nearby communities stood for two distinct realities. William Burchfiel, the navy lieutenant from Tennessee who described Caripito as an "American Tropical Outpost," saw it as two communities, "a white camp for foreigners and a pueblo village for natives," contrasting sharply in structures, environment, and standard of living.[9] The racial distinction that he made remained a subtle but important subtext of the new urban reality in the oil camps. Beyond housing differences, foreign employees were almost always white, the professionals and middle managers included few Venezuelans of color, and the laborers represented a racial cross-section of the country.

The camp at La Salina, operated by Creole, and the nearby community of Cabimas embodied these urban and racial distinctions. Cabimas had a population in 1950 of 42,294, of whom nearly 2,500 were Creole employees.[10] Its buildings numbered nearly 9,800, scattered among "main streets, water lines and the fringes of the oil camp." Cabimas still had only one paved street, Calle Principal, and its utility company, the Compañía de Utilidades Públicas, purchased power from the nearby Creole power plant. Water, drawn from the lake and high in salt content, reached only the urban center; a significant number of residents purchased potable water sold in tin cans from burro-drawn carts throughout the town. Sewage disposal remained the responsibility of individual residents, most of whom relied on septic tanks or the nearby lake.[11]

The camp at La Salina provided a dramatic contrast to the conditions at Cabimas. Creole employed 2,854 bolívar-paid employees, of whom 50 were staff, 320 intermediate employees, and 2,484 daily employees; 33 of the staff, 273 of the intermediate employees, and 1,983 of the daily employees were married.[12] Among the employees considered married were a large number of those whom the company referred to as "concubines."[13] Residents of the camp, regardless of their marital status, enjoyed an array of basic services such as electricity, potable water, sewage disposal, paved streets, and trash collection as well as access to medical facilities, schools, and a social club for leisure activities. The physical appearance of the camp and the availability of services there further accentuated its differences with the local community, engendering envy and bitterness. Thus the camps were more than an established housing arrangement: they were an ideal organizational structure, a model of the modern class and social relations that the companies sought to foster among the workers and their families.

The rhythm of activity at a nearby refinery or oilfield imposed a new conception of time on social and economic activities at most camps. For example, in Caripito, an oil storage and refining center, the sounds of daily life were punctuated by the refinery's steam-powered whistle, which could be heard throughout the camp and the adjacent town, announcing the start of the workday not only for the company employees but for many town residents. The stream of men dressed in standard-issue khaki uniforms making their way toward the gates of the refinery marked the beginning of the workday, just as the echo of the afternoon whistle and the returning stream of workers marked the end. Local merchants, street vendors, and nearby bars in the adjacent La Sabana eagerly awaited the sound of the afternoon whistle, and families knew when to expect their returning spouse. The sound of the whistle at any other time of day usually meant a fire or some other disaster at the refinery, and families from throughout the camp and the town would anxiously congregate at the main entrance to await news of loved ones. Companies not only influenced the work habits of their employees but shaped the constructions of time for the people in the town and adjacent communities.

Oil camps, where people lived in immediately adjacent residences of relatively uniform size, shape, and color, disarticulated Venezuelans and their families from their previous lives. Whether they came from the older cities, where the Spanish colonial construction of space prevailed, or from the rural countryside, the new housing arrangements required a remarkable adaptation. The new living quarters were small, usually on the order of 115 square meters, accentuating the dramatic changes that the workers and their family now experienced. The interior space of the houses usually contained two small rooms, a kitchen, a living room, and an exterior wash area.[14] The exterior of the building, usually a simple whitewashed structure of brick or cement block covered with a zinc or asbestos roof, contrasted to the local bahareque and thatched or tile-roofed houses outside the camps. Complaints about the lack of ventilation and limited living space were quite common.[15]

Though residing in new, "modern" structures, workers and their families retained their customs and traditions. When entering a camp house it was not uncommon to find hammocks suspended in the bedrooms, or chickens kept for fresh eggs.[16] Nonetheless, the design of the new living arrangements undermined traditional practices. By establishing a series of formal rules and regulations, the companies sought to "de-ruralize" their new laborers and recast their relationship with the land, producing modern laborers who depended on the company for their wages. Faced with small accommodation and no possibility of growth, camp life also recast the family and weakened the extended networks that pervaded Venezuelan society. Eroding the basis of the extended family and its multiple levels of authority emphasized the role of the male, and so did limiting women's ability to engage in independent productive activity.[17] Though invariably this process accentuated the role of the nuclear family, it would be wrong to think that women were relegated to the domestic sphere. Camp life defined household responsibility to extend to the entire camp, with social obligations that extended beyond the physical home. Life in the oil camps thus served to forge a new laborer while also reconstituting familial relations.

Confronted by these conditions, some families opted to live in nearby villages instead of a camp.[18] The number of those living outside the confines of the camp varied significantly. Of the 2,854 employees at La Salina, only 1,304 seem to have resided in the various camps maintained by the company. These figures may be deceiving, since the employees who did not occupy company houses included 565 single men who lived with relatives in the camp and 168 who had been assigned to nearby Tía Juana or Lagunillas and resided in the camps there. This left nearly 1,000 married employees who resided outside the camp and to whom the company paid a total of 4,000 bolívares as a housing allowance.[19]

Reasons for living outside the camp varied significantly and ranged from the employee's eligibility for housing and its availability to the size of the household and the desire to remain in the community and participate in local economic activities. Francisco Moreno, a twenty-year veteran at La Salina, moved out because he found the camp too restrictive.[20] Housing in the camps permitted the immediate reproduction of the nuclear family but little else; there was no space to cultivate a garden, raise animals, or engage in other economic activity, practices common among rural Venezuelans. Indeed, pursuing these activities ran counter to the interests of the companies, which wanted employees to focus exclusively on their employment and participate in camp-sponsored activities. Those who opted out often sent their children to camp schools and participated in camp activities, such as the social club and sporting events. In some cases families passed relatives' children off as their own so that they could attend the better company-operated schools.[21]

Formed in many cases by groups with no established familial bonds, the camps forced people to develop new social contacts in an environment in which the foreign oil company exerted an ever-present influence as both employer and provider of housing, education, and recreation. Creole and Shell were conscious of the fragility of these new associations: they promoted the image of a broad corporate family to which workers and their families belonged and on which they could rely for social and personal support. The company publications that announced marriages, births, baptisms, graduations, and other events and the camp's bulletins sought to create the sense of an extended corporate family while at the same time promoting a set of social practices and norms that the company found constructive.[22] That the oil workers were highly mobile, subject to constant transfers between camps, made it necessary to establish broad solidarity among them. As part of this project, and to ensure the diffusion of their ideals, the companies promoted the concept of the nuclear family. According to a Creole publication: "The spiritual level of the family determines the spiritual level of the community and the nation. When we mention spiritual we refer to a complete set of social practices, habits, beliefs and ideals that influence an individual's character. The home is the central place where these spiritual qualities take shape."[23] In keeping with these objectives, life in the camp revolved around a daily routine that involved not only the worker but the entire family in a set of activities that encompassed sports, social functions, night classes, and even religious instruction.

THE CHURCH AND THE OIL INDUSTRY

The Catholic Church played a key role in legitimating the oil companies' activity in the country and promoting their broader socialization project, forming a holy trinity with the government and the military that legitimated the model of development and social vision promoted by foreign oil interests in Venezuela. Everett Bauman, the director of Creole's Public Relations department, stated: "[The company has always] favored extension of church influence in our operating areas, feeling that religion provides a cohesive and beneficent force among our workers and is one of the basic elements in securing a better community life."[24] Church policy and company policy coalesced on many levels; both promoted a gendered order expressed in the nuclear family and both encouraged wholesome social practices hoping to deter social behavior such as excessive drinking, gambling, and prostitution. Attempting to promote its own moral vision, the church supported company policies aimed at creating a disciplined labor force and instilling a new work ethic.

Church and company policy also coalesced at another, more political level: both had an antipathy for leftist political forces. Companies like Creole saw the Catholic Church as a vehicle to prevent the spread of leftist influences among workers. In the words of the Creole executive Siro Vázquez, "We are alert to promoting the Christian philosophy to combat [communism's] spread."[25] Sharing grounds on multiple fronts, the large companies such as Creole and Shell typically helped to subsidize church activities in the oil camps. In many cases construction of the local Catholic Church near the camp was financed by the company and the priest received a formal stipend. In a manner reminiscent of the Spanish colonial era, the Catholic Church was also called upon to help the oil industry in dealing with the indigenous populations. In western Venezuela they unsuccessfully attempted to be a liaison with the Bari indigenous populations. In eastern Venezuela Creole facilitated the work of the Capuchin monks among indigenous populations that inhabited the various caños flowing into the Orinoco and the Caribbean. Close relations with the foreign companies presented unforeseen challenges for the church. Monsignor Ramón Lizardi stated that having local camp priests drive around in a company car with the Creole emblem on its side reduced the cleric to "another paid employee of the company."[26] The priest and by extension the church, in the view of the monsignor, had simply become "ministers of the sacrament" rather than the traditional counselor of the local population. In the eyes of many, the church in the oil camps had been transformed into an appendage of the company.

GENDER AND THE OIL INDUSTRY

The oil industry is assumed to be a gendered enterprise; most images revolve around the roustabout, the roughneck, the driller, or the tool pusher, positions that traditionally evoke strong masculine images. Yet from their inception oil operations in Venezuela also involved women. Some fulfilled traditional domestic functions while others were directly or indirectly employed by the industry. Generally overlooked, women are central to understanding industry operations, as well as the residential life of the communities.[27] Women were expected to play multiple roles within the industry. At one level the oil industry accentuated the role that women played in the social reproduction of the family and in the social life of the camps. The presence of women, according to one company report, increased the social commitment of the male worker, ensured the stability of the family, promoted social cohesion, and thus favored labor peace.[28] At another level women were essential to the efficient operation of the companies, working in such diverse functions as geologist, nurse, laboratory technician, administrator, bookkeeper, accountant, teacher, and the ubiquitous secretary. Invariably, given complex and multifaceted corporate structures, the companies had to incorporate women to work alongside men in offices and other arenas. The introduction of women into the workforce was projected as an outcome of the discourse on modernity and progress applied to gender relations. In the process the oil companies engaged, though never fully challenged, the traditional male-dominated culture that restricted women's role in society and their participation in the workforce.

Camp life did not restrict Venezuelan women to the confines of their homes; they were expected to participate in both traditional and nontraditional aspects of residential life. Class and national origin largely defined women's familial and social obligations within the camp structure. In addition, the companies developed programs to socialize women and increase their contribution to the corporate enterprise. Besides local committees, social clubs, and sports programs, women of the campo obrero, or laborers' camp, were expected to attend special "educational programs."[29] In 1948, for example, Creole established home economics schools in Las Salinas, Lagunillas, and Tía Juana in which some one hundred wives enrolled.[30] In these schools Venezuelan women received instruction in homemaking, time management, social skills, fashion, and other matters and at the same time were exposed to new consumer patterns and fashions.

Venezuelan middle-class women were entrusted with a different set of social obligations that included welcoming parties, retirements, birthdays, weddings, and visits from company officials.[31] One longtime camp resident at Judibana reported that whenever she heard the sound of a car horn on her block, she knew it was a delegation from the women's committee collecting for a baby shower, or an arrival or departure party.[32] Social functions were important in affirming the norms and values associated with the professional class. The relative isolation of most camps, their dimensions, the physical proximity of the residences, and the small size of the population compelled people to attend most social functions. Company publications even advised women how to select the appropriate attire for these activities, suggesting, for example, that "a decorative hat and a black dress provide great decoration for cocktails and an early dinner."[33]

The companies' pamphlets addressed not only women's position within the family but also their civic role in the country and the industry. As early as the 1940s the opportunity of employment in the oil companies modified, if only slightly, traditional gender relations and women's employment patterns. In 1940 Creole employed only 111 women, but by 1949 that number had increased to over 1,500.[34] By the 1950s a small number of women, mostly foreigners, worked in administrative or professional positions. The single woman geologist in the Creole laboratory tired of being on exhibition every time a group of dignitaries visited the facilities.[35] In the great majority of cases, however, women found themselves limited to traditional occupations such as nursing, teaching, or clerical work. As the number of women employed in the industry increased, the companies were forced to address their role in the labor force.

Since the 1930s issues of women's rights and equality had been addressed at various inter-American conferences. Middle- and upper-class Latin American women, some of whom were from Venezuela, had participated in these activities promoting the cause of universal suffrage and child care at meetings in Cuba and Mexico.[36] In Venezuela the death of Gómez inaugurated a period of limited political openness that benefited all social movements, including women's.[37] In 1940 Caracas was the host for the first official Congress of Venezuelan Women.[38] Creole's *El Farol* joined the debate on women's issues with its own articles, one of which, "Lucha por la liberación de la mujer en Venezuela," promoted the idea that the "modern woman works, thinks, and struggles in peace and in war because she is just as capable as any man. That is why women in the U.S. refuse to blindly follow men."[39] Framed by wartime concerns, the publication sought to link its version of women's liberation with ideas of modernity and progress borrowed from developments in the United States.[40] In 1944 Venezuelan women gained suffrage at the municipal level, and by 1947 they could vote in national elections.

The values implicit in this version of women's liberation appeared to have been aimed at a middle-class audience, but at the same time the companies promoted a version of the model female employee aimed at their own labor force. The company objective was to normalize the role of women in the labor force, not challenge traditional notions of patriarchy. As part of this campaign, a Creole publication interviewed Ana Victoria, who worked in the laundry at the Amuay refinery and saw "no contradiction in working in an all-male environment since she knew that the company appreciated her services." Though it generally paid women less, the company cast itself in the role of protector, holding women's work in high esteem even if it did not receive approval from the broader patriarchal society. According to the interview and a host of other articles, women employed by the industry had not forsaken their traditional domestic tasks, or their role as nurturing mothers.[41] Thus the companies' idea of women's independence was not intended to challenge the traditional male order.[42] Women's participation in the labor force was framed by the industry's need for an ever-expanding labor force, particularly in the service sector. Within the industry certain jobs would eventually be identified as women's work. Participation in the oil industry, even within this initially limited arena, nonetheless created new public spaces for women.

CORPORATE CULTURE AND SPORTS

The companies paid particular attention to the social life of their workers. To avoid practices that could generate social disorder, companies such as Creole and Shell sought to involve workers in what they considered appropriate forms of entertainment. They attempted to include workers in activities that would strengthen their "moral character" and ensure their loyalty to the company. One industrial relations official working for Creole in eastern Venezuela candidly described the sports program as an instrument of the company's broader labor strategy.[43] Many workers complained that opportunities for economic advancement were linked to their participation in company-sponsored activities. One persistent critic of the industry, Rodolfo Quintero, argued that the companies were seeking to "create a new oil culture" in which workers and their families would be completely absorbed by the company-sponsored activities.[44]

The perceived concerns of a "modern society" again informed what was considered appropriate behavior by the company. *Muscle*, a publication sponsored by the Sport Caripitense, pointed out that "sports are the way that individuals in modern society establish bonds of solidarity."[45] The identification of sports and modernity was not accidental but rather sought to draw distinctions between what the company considered appropriate behaviors favorable to their operations and inappropriate "traditional" behaviors such as cockfighting and gambling. To promote this effort, the companies gradually established sports directorates in the camps whose task it was to involve the workers and their families in organized athletic events. These sporting activities began at the local and regional level and evolved into a sophisticated network of intercamp and intercompany rivalries that culminated in a national competition patterned after the Olympics. These competitions involved men and women as well as children. Most sports programs were aimed at the Venezuelan working classes and not the professional class, where other forms of socialization prevailed.

Although Creole and other companies sponsored a wide range of sports, baseball quickly surpassed all others in popularity. The first recorded baseball game in the country was played in Caracas in May 1895; Venezuelans and expatriates from the United States and Cuba took part.[46] The sport quickly spread throughout the country, though in many ways it remained an "aristocratic" game played by members of the upper and middle classes who could afford the equipment. Promoted by the oil companies who supplied the equipment and built stadiums at almost all their large camps, the game began to sink roots among workers who previously had been observers. Players who demonstrated athletic prowess received special treatment and could aspire to become part of the company-sponsored professional teams. Games played between rival camps attracted hundreds of workers who filled the stadiums, ensuring its wide diffusion among all social classes. After championship games Creole donated the trophy and the individual medals, and its public relations department publicized the activity in its local bulletins and national magazines.[47] Baseball became widely popular in Venezuela and remains the national pastime.

THE MODEL VENEZUELAN WORKER

Sports proved to be only one means of fashioning the ideal worker. For companies such as Creole, the life of the ideal employee revolved around a complex web of work and family obligations. The model employee arrived at work early every day, and returned home after the end of the shift to help with domestic duties, spend time with the family, take part in functions at the camp's social club, or attend a baseball game. Time management and the work ethic were central features of this model worker: "Punctuality, loyalty, efficiency, and interest in work are at the heart of the covenant between the worker and the employer. These are the things the worker gives up for his weekly paycheck. Under these conditions work ceases to be a dull routine and becomes an ultimate goal."[48] Regular meetings between workers and management were an opportunity to promote this behavior.

The work ethic also translated into family life; the model employee (initially male) lived within his means and opted for a small family, usually not exceeding two children. The life of José Domingo Casanova was portrayed by the Creole public relations department as "a biography of personal achievement": he was described as living in Temblador "with simplicity and modesty, in the company of his wife and two daughters providing a living example of what personal determination and enthusiasm can accomplish."[49] The model employee sought to advance his career through personal initiative and sacrifice rather than through collective means. As one Creole publication put it, "individuals build themselves."[50] The company openly frowned upon employees who took part in leftist political activity or publicly criticized company policies; radical or socialist ideas were the subject of repeated attacks in company publications.[51]

With control over their work environment, housing, and recreational activity, it was relatively simple for the companies to evaluate the behavior of their employees. The camp labor relations department typically maintained a web of informants, consisting of minor government officials, police, National Guard officers, and other employees, who regularly provided reports to company officials in an attempt to curry favor.[52] Monthly camp reports provided a detailed accounting of employees' behavior and political activity. For example, a report from Standard Oil on operations in Temblador indicated: "the attitude of the employees toward the company appears to be very satisfactory, with the exception of one monthly bolívar and seven daily bolívar employees who reputedly have exhibited radical tendencies."[53] (No action was taken against these employees, since it appeared that they had not managed to influence their co-workers.)

Companies regularly held out as examples those workers who relied on resourcefulness to overcome adversity, and they encouraged individual initiative with training programs and scholarships. Under the guise of a "good investment," Creole publicized the case of an employee who "was at home studying for his night classes at the Chávez School in Cabimas." This employee had advanced, the company continued, from being an anonymous apprentice earning 5 bolívares a day to an assistant and then a first technician in the laboratory, where he was performing work that for others had required years of training.[54] By publicizing the advantages of individual ambition, Creole sought to establish a model of behavior that it hoped others would emulate. It emphasized that its employees were parties to a social contract, and that by adhering to this contract they would achieve a level of compensation and benefits unmatched in the Venezuelan private sector and contribute to the "advancement" of the nation. Promoting itself as an agent of development and modernization, the company hoped to avert nationalist sentiments.

Creole also experimented with policies that the U.S. State Department employed in Europe during the cold war. During the 1950s the State Department regularly encouraged visits to the United States by European labor and business leaders. Exposure to the society and business practices of the United States was seen as a tool for advancing policies in Europe and Latin America. For its part, Creole organized "foremen visits" to the United States for two months, with all expenses paid. Visitors not only inspected Standard Oil company facilities but toured an automobile assembly line, a steel mill, a coal mine, a cattle ranch, and a General Electric factory, and attended a New York Yankees baseball game. The company indicated that it selected the foremen Esteban Olivares, Rafael Alonso, José Romero, and Braulio Rodríguez because of their "work performance, position in the community, and capacity to interpret their experiences."[55] Proficiency in

English was not a prerequisite; the company provided a translator for the group. Creole's participation in these programs of the cold war era speaks to the close relationship between business and United States government interests throughout Latin America. Creole hoped that the foremen would return to Venezuela convinced of the superiority of the lifestyle and business practices of the United States and share their opinions with their fellow workers.

VENEZOLANIZATION

Venezuelans accounted for the bulk of the industry workforce, yet their presence in the upper ranks of the oil companies was at first limited. Throughout the 1930s and 1940s the oil companies began to hire Venezuelan engineers and professionals trained at universities in the United States and Venezuela. Guillermo Zuloaga and Siro Vázquez, who began their careers in government ministries, attained important positions in Creole's management. At the outset, however, it was mainly foreigners from the United States and Europe who filled the higher administrative and professional positions, with a small number of West Indians in lower-level clerical positions. The oil companies insisted that Venezuelans lacked the necessary skills to perform most operations. In the legal department the companies were obliged to hire Venezuelans, since foreigners could not represent them in court, but even here the upper echelons of the legal departments tended to be filled by foreigners.

Despite these obstacles, Venezuelans with university degrees and other professionals eagerly sought general administrative or junior staff positions. Confronting criticisms from the middle classes and an organized labor movement demanding better conditions and wages, the foreign oil companies modified their policies and slowly began to hire Venezuelans into positions previously reserved for foreigners. The departure of United States personnel during the Second World War also opened some positions in engineering and middle management. By the mid-1940s a strategy known as Venezolanization—the hiring and promoting of Venezuelans to most positions in the company—became official company policy. Companies such as Creole believed that hiring Venezuelans would yield many positive results. At one level doing so allowed companies to replace unpopular administrators and managers from the United States who had been associated with the policies and practices of the Gómez years, thus appearing to cleanse the enterprise and to bring it into line with the positions of the new political leadership.[56] At another level, hiring Venezuelans provided an important outlet for the Venezuelan middle and professional classes, creating "a local stake in the success of the companies' operations" which would help mitigate "extreme nationalistic attacks upon it." In addition, Standard Oil expected that eventually its former employees "would pass over into the government . . . bringing with them an informed and professional knowledge of the oil industry."[57] The foreign companies envisioned a revolving door similar to the one they experienced in the United States, with former employees serving in government posts and former government officials obtaining employment in the company, thus assuring the company's long-term interests. Although at first they resisted the change, in the end the foreign oil companies saw no contradiction between middle-class or nationalist demands for inclusion and their own interests. The newly hired members of the professional and administrative staff were expected to be important advocates of the foreign oil companies to the broader society, whose presence would shield the foreign enterprise from nationalist critics.[58]

THE CORPORATE LADDER: OFFICE BOYS AND THE SECRETARIAL POOL

The oil companies' social hierarchy had senior staff employees from the United States and Britain at the top, lighter-skinned Venezuelan junior staff in the middle, and usually mixed-race Venezuelan office boys and secretaries at the bottom. The distinction between senior staff and the other categories embodied other important differentiations. The foreigner was assumed to be the purveyor of knowledge, while the Venezuelan was considered the neophyte expected to implement company policy.[59] Over time this distinction would be modified to account for a select group of Venezuelan professionals who ascended through the company ranks and acquired positions of power. Differences between foreigners and Venezuelans found expression in salaries, benefits, housing, and the use of public and private space in the oil camps. The larger oil camps had separate social clubs for their senior and junior staffs and for their other workers. A policy of racial separation reminiscent of Jim Crow stamped rural camp life and most oil company administrative units in Maracaibo and Caracas. This social and at times racial stratification was important not only in the oil industry but in Venezuelan society at large, where it reinforced prevailing views on race.

Between the entry-level daily laborer and the skilled professional were two categories that Venezuelans could aspire to: office boy and secretary. Both were open to people with an elementary or high school education. Many office boys and secretaries were students who worked during the day and attended school or university at night. The office boy or secretary was a helper, messenger, or assistant in a specific company department, while also playing the role of "native informant" for the foreign supervisor unfamiliar with Venezuelan culture and society. Daniel Bendahán, who began his career as an office boy, recalls the multiple functions he performed for his bosses, such as running errands, finding him a *criada* (a domestic worker) from his home town, and bribing local officials who had been offended by the actions of the foreigner.[60] Venezuelan women hired to secretarial positions within the oil companies began by working in a large "secretarial pool" that most companies kept at regional or central offices. Secretarial positions were valued as entry-level positions. One Venezuela woman who had previously worked for the Curaçao Trading Company recalls that securing employment as a typist with an oil company was popularly known as the equivalent of "trabajar con papa dios" (working with the good Lord).[61] The office boy and secretarial positions became the principal source of training and administrative employment for many adult males and females. In keeping with corporate culture, Creole regularly reminded new hires to say not that they worked "at" Standard Oil but rather "for" Standard Oil.[62] Although subtle, the difference sought to ensure a sense of identification with the company and loyalty toward it.

The very first issue of Standard Oil's new employee magazine *Nosotros* described the exemplary career of Braulio Rodríguez, who began as an office boy and climbed the corporate ladder to become director of his department, overseeing eighteen other office boys.[63] This article and a host of others encouraged the belief that office boys could easily ascend within the company.[64] For example, a later commentary extolled the progress made by the former office boy Luis M. Barrios, who started to work for Creole in 1936 in the materials department at Caripito and by 1947 was secretary of the transportation division.[65] Invariably the lesson these articles imparted was that this sort of personal advancement occurred as a result of individual initiative, perseverance, hard work, and loyalty to company. The corporate culture promoted the ideal that employees who exhibited these superior characteristics, even if they started out as office boys, would be rewarded.

Besides acquiring necessary practical skills, one of the principal lessons that many former office boys and secretaries received was the importance of *superación personal*, or personal improvement and initiative. If they expected to advance, employees had to prove resourceful and loyal. As one former office boy recalled, "I arrived early, left late, and sought to associate with and learn from the professional staff."[66] Contrary to the notion of meritocracy that the industry propagated, a broad network of personal contacts with foreigners, family, and friends was critical to an employee's ascent in the company hierarchy. Former office boys and secretaries recall how the friendships they established with foreigners and other Venezuelans served them and their families.[67]

NEW WAYS OF SHOPPING
AND CONSUMER PATTERNS

The corporate culture promoted a middle-class lifestyle like that of the United States.[68] Faced with a rising cost of living and mounting labor pressure, the large companies eventually agreed to establish and stock commissaries at camps where more than 250 persons were employed. They subsidized the costs of what they termed "national items," usually thirty basic consumer goods such as rice, flour, sugar, corn, and meats, and stocked other, non-subsidized products, such as toiletries and an array of canned and packaged goods from the United States.[69] Once established, the commissaries reoriented where people purchased their foodstuffs and what products they consumed. For a population accustomed to acquiring goods directly from local producers and small merchants, the transition to shopping in the new commissaries initially generated some resistance. Workers at Jusepín complained that Creole's policies prevented local campesinos from selling their goods in and around the camps, thus obligating the workers to shop at the commissaries.[70] Despite early apprehension surrounding the commissaries, their presence in the oil communities expanded markets for a host of Venezuelan manufactured products emerging in the 1950s, assuring that they became well-known brand names in the camps and for a generation of Venezuelans. Among these were an assortment of goods such as Yukery juice, HIT and Dumbo cola, Polar beer, Mavesa margarine, the chocolate drink Toddy, the pound cake Panque, canned meat diablitos, Imperial coffee, and the precooked arepa mix P.A.N. For many products entering the Venezuelan market during this period, the commissary provided access to an important new consumer market.

Beyond brand identification, the commissaries revolutionized the way Venezuelans of all social strata in the camps shopped for food, as the local open-air public markets gradually gave way to the private, enclosed, modern, sanitary commissary. Initially goods at the first commissary were dispensed by clerks standing behind a counter. This practice was soon replaced by self-service commissaries that "functioned as modern supermarkets" where customers walked the aisles, selected their own goods, and placed them in shopping carts.[71] Venezuela's first modern chain of supermarkets, CADA, financed by Rockefeller investments, extended the self-service model to the general public.[72] One company publication reported that "with Creole's encouragement, a chain of supermarkets extends to the large oil industry areas."[73] The introduction of supermarkets modeled after those in the United States had an unintended consequence. As Judith Ewell has noted, the novelty of walking down aisles filled with an array of United States and Venezuelan products compelled middle-class women to do their own shopping rather than dispatch their housekeeper as they had typically done.[74] The availability of these products altered consumer patterns for those employed in oil and for the urban middle classes, but did not necessarily reach the Venezuelan population largely unaffected by the oil economy. Among the middle class, however, it established a pattern of conspicuous consumption closely aligned with that of the United States.

SEMBRANDO PETRÓLEO

In July 1936 Arturo Uslar Pietri optimistically suggested in an article published in the Caracas daily *Ahora* that the "wealth produced by the destructive mining system should be invested in creating agricultural wealth, reproductive and progressive: oil should be sowed."[75] No other statement so galvanized political discourse as the suggestion that oil profits could be reinvested and, like agricultural products, be harvested. Before long the foreign oil companies, political parties such as Acción Democrática, military leaders, and intellectuals had co-opted the position that oil revenues could be invested to diversify the economy and promote social policy.[76] The idea of "sowing oil" soon found its way into industry and government publications, and the slogan adorned public edifices, rendering it meaningless except for its propagandistic value. The idea that oil could be harvested influenced the policies of the oil companies, which used it to align themselves with the mildly nationalist sentiment that it embodied.

The public relations campaigns of the companies not only appropriated the ideal of sowing oil but gave it a new meaning. It quickly became associated with efforts to modernize the country, and the large oil companies projected themselves as the key agents in this process. Before oil, the argument went, Venezuela was a backward nation of illiterate campesinos and feuding caudillos. Oil offered it the opportunity to join the advanced nations of the world. The companies were not alone in making this argument. In a speech to the Creole Coordinating meeting in Caracas in 1951, the minister of mines and hydrocarbons, Santiago Vera Izquierdo, advanced this belief: "Before oil operations started in this country we were only concerned with a few sacks of coffee, coco nuts and things like that, and right now we find ourselves in a position of importance in the trends of the whole world."[77] Many accounts of traditional Venezuelan historiography also argued that before oil, the country had been largely stagnant since the eighteenth century.[78] This perspective even found its way into works for school-age children and youth. One described Venezuela as a poor country, isolated and spent by the wars between caudillos, and continued: "Everything changes with oil."[79] Progress in this view depended on preserving the role of private oil companies in the Venezuelan economy. Any critique of this arrangement or the social order that it engendered was categorized as "ignorant," "retrograde," or "antiforeign" and therefore harmful to the nation. Not surprisingly, throughout this period outwardly pronationalist movements failed to generate much support within the middle class. The national discourse on development and modernization was framed by an acceptance of the importance of oil to the country and the role that foreign companies played.

An ongoing and ever-evolving publicity campaign stressed the foreign companies' role in "sowing" Venezuelan oil to benefit the nation. The campaign found regular expression in corporate and government publications, such as a report by the National Planning Association that described Creole's role in modernizing Venezuela. Walter Dupouy of Creole echoed these sentiments in 1949 when he underscored that just as the Spanish colony "had depended on the Guipuzcoana Company [the Caracas Company] to modernize, in our epoch the modernization of the country is the result of the stimulus of the powerful oil industry. Thanks to their efforts we have achieved or are trying to achieve the progress that stamps our century."[80] The idea of sowing oil became the point of consensus between the foreign companies and Venezuelan élites and political figures who believed that oil revenues would transform their nation and sustain their standard of living. In an article entitled "The Company and the Nation" published in 1964, Creole's president Harry Jarvis wrote: "Our 45 years of experience . . . give us the hope for a future of sustained prosperity for the nation and the company."[81] The link between the progress of the nation and the oil companies appeared firmly embedded not only in corporate culture but in the minds of middle-class Venezuelans who directly or indirectly depended on the oil industry for employment and social standing.

SELLING THE COMPANY:
THE WORK OF PUBLIC RELATIONS

Social investments in cultural and social programs for employees proved important, but they only reached a small share of the population. By the early 1940s Standard Oil of New Jersey and Creole Petroleum, its affiliate in Venezuela, found it necessary to establish public relations departments aimed at broadly influencing Venezuelan public opinion. Public relations became the full-time job of Creole's president Arthur T. Proudfit, who had "no operational duties and spends exactly all of his valuable time on relations with the Venezuelan government and the Venezuelan people."[82] Shell developed similar operations under the leadership of José Giacopini Zárraga, who emerged as a key figure. For the company this new enterprise attested to shifting social and political conditions they had confronted beginning in the 1930s and leading up to the Second World War. For Standard the formation of a public relations department had several sources, one associated with developments in the United States and the other with the shifting political climate in Latin America. First, during the pre-war period and even during the conflict, the public in the United States perceived Standard Oil as insensitive. A report presented at Standard's board meeting in 1944 described the company's public image as often "greedy, monopolistic, [and] selfish."

The report continued: "The charge too often goes unchallenged that we have put financial gain even above patriotic duty."[83] The company was accused of "having schemed and connived with foreign powers to bring about the Second World War for reasons of financial gain," and when participants in a poll were shown a list of major companies and asked if their feeling was "not so friendly" toward any one of them, Standard "was the outstanding choice."[84]

A second set of factors which reflected the changing political conditions in Venezuela and Latin America was framed by the death of the Venezuelan dictator Juan Vicente Gómez in 1935 and the nationalization of Mexican oil in 1938.[85] With the death of Gómez, the foreign oil companies, to paraphrase Stephen Rabe, "lost their shield" and could no longer simply rely on the national government to suppress social protest and protect their interests.[86] In addition, by the late 1930s nationalism had become a potent political force, and countries such as Bolivia and Mexico moved to assert control over their oil industries. Addressing a meeting of the Standard Oil Coordinating Group in February 1946, the State Department's former director of the Division of American Republics, Laurence Duggan, stressed that nationalism in Latin America had "taken the form of antipathy for foreigners, especially to large business enterprises carried on by foreigners." These firms, he said, were attacked as "imperialistic economic leeches sucking away the life blood."[87] Accustomed to the protection of either the United States or the British government or reliant on the strong-arm tactics of Gómez's regime, some foreign oil companies initially resisted change. Shell, for example, according to Giacopini Zárraga, initially refused to engage in public relations, yet being continuously depicted as a "disproportionate giant involved in every major event in the country" finally convinced the company of the need to influence public opinion.[88] Buffeted by changing political winds and no longer able to rely on Gómez, the oil companies now sought to develop a more sophisticated and complex shield that could protect their long-term interests.

Faced by these interrelated new political and social realities and seeking to reverse these negative perceptions, Standard Oil established public relations departments that sought to transform public opinion by focusing on information, education, identification, affirmation, and representation.[89] In addition, Shell sought to promote behavior and "model institutions . . . that serve as examples for other economic activity in the country . . . as well as for the state."[90] Though the Creole and Shell public relations departments worked separately, they had a common goal: identify the foreign company's interests with those of the nation.

Creole pioneered polling activity in Venezuela, regularly tracking popular sentiment toward the company and its activities. Beyond simply monitoring attitudes, the company sought to directly influence public opinion, energetically courting reporters and news agencies. Rubén Sader Pérez, the one-time president of the Venezuelan Petroleum Corporation, recalled that in promoting their views the oil companies nurtured relations with "writers, newspapermen, commentators," who though not on their payroll were "subject to a siege, at times implacable, at times artful."[91] The Caracas newspaper *La Esfera* was considered a mouthpiece of the oil industry because of its fervent support of the foreign companies. Creole also employed a staff of industry and academic "experts" who regularly gave lectures on important issues to ensure that the company's position received widespread coverage in the local media. Creole and Shell subsidized faculty appointments in universities, assigned company experts to science departments, promoted exchange programs with North American universities, offered scholarships for studying abroad, and financed work by well-known writers and artists.

The public relations departments for Creole and Shell in Venezuela served multiple functions; internally they helped foster practices deemed useful among foreign and Venezuelan employees, while externally they served as the companies' public face. These tasks were not mutually exclusive, since the companies saw their employees as their ambassadors. At the Coordination Committee Group Meeting held in Miami in 1946, Standard's director, Chester F. Smith, addressed this issue: "In working out your business problems, you must constantly be an example of the way South Americans and North Americans can work together and live together in harmony."[92] The newly formed public relations departments, both in the United States and in Venezuela, proved effective instruments in promoting the companies' views.[93]

CIVIL SOCIETY

The oil companies' influence extended beyond their own employees and involved Venezuelan society at large. The companies employed a broad array of modern public relations tools to reach Venezuelan society. To promote their efforts, Creole contracted with professional firms such as McCann Erickson "to open a local office in Caracas" in 1946 and help introduce "local color" into advertisements.[94] At a time when few national media outlets existed, the two largest companies, Creole and Shell, sponsored radio programs and published cultural magazines and educational literature. Creole's "Esso Reporter," a radio program broadcast in the two largest cities, Caracas and Maracaibo, offered a mix of news and corporate views on issues facing the country. In addition, Creole sponsored a weekly program, "Aplauso al Merito" (Praise for Merit), on which plaques were presented to Venezuelans who had made a contribution to the nation. By sponsoring this and other programs Creole sought to identify itself "with the deeds and achievements which have enriched the nation's culture, expanded its knowledge and enhanced its way and means to enjoy a better life."[95]

At a Standard board meeting, one adviser recommended making extensive use of radio as well as film: "These two media do not require literacy on the part of the audience. In underdeveloped areas they are far more effective in getting across an idea than the printed word. Every *pueblecito* [small town] in Latin America has a radio, and with the new cheap projectors coming on the market, every *pueblecito* will have its cine . . . I am sure, however that Donald Duck can do more to correct misinformation than tons of printed literature."[96] By the mid-1950s, with the appearance of commercial television in Venezuela, the company developed national television programs such as "Farol TV," hosted by the broadcaster Renny Ottolina, and the influential nightly news program known as the "Observador Creole."[97] Broadcast during prime time on Radio Caracas Television, the "Observador Creole" was seen by 66 percent of viewers.[98] For its part, Shell Oil transmitted a weekly radio program entitled "Hoy y Mañana" (Today and Tomorrow), featuring talks by Venezuelan scientists; copies of the program were made available to local high schools. Shell also sponsored short films that ran on Venezuelan television highlighting its company activities and contributions to Venezuela.[99] The United States government also maintained an active campaign to influence Venezuelan public opinion. The United States Information Program supplied "output" to all sixty-three radio stations and the three television channels as well as the important newspapers. They also provided direct assistance to a wide array of private institutions, among them the Centro Venezolano Americano in Caracas.[100]

Both Shell and Creole also engaged in extensive philanthropic and cultural efforts. Shell established the Servicio Shell para el Agricultor in 1952 and in 1955 began to publish a monthly magazine, *Noticias Agrícolas*, "hoping to be useful to farmers."[101] It established the Fundación Shell in June 1959 to "promote and assist with activities in the natural sciences, education and culture in Venezuela."[102] The Fundación Creole, begun in October 1956, was an important philanthropic institution providing financial support for cultural, educational, and scientific projects as well as building schools and training teachers.[103] The foundation stated that its main purpose was to "contribute to the social and economic progress of Venezuela."[104] It provided funds to academic and scholarly institutions in the United States to conduct research in Venezuela.[105] Creole also attempted to identify with other segments of Venezuelan society, waging campaigns and advertising its support for business and merchants. Its Creole Investment Corporation provided start-up funds for new and small businesses.[106]

The companies' public relations departments propagated throughout Venezuelan society many of the values that they promoted to their employees. Central to their perspective was the need to remake the Venezuelan character—to promote a western concept of time, labor, and management and to purge Venezuelans of "negative traits" stereotypically associated with Latin American culture. The western idea of punctuality and efficiency became paramount. In 1944 one Creole publication that circulated nationwide underscored the company's view: "Today! This word is the paramount symbol of men who triumph in life. 'Mañana' is the word that condemns men to an existence of lamentable sterility. If we become accustomed to saying mañana I will do this; mañana I will begin this or that thing, we will soon reach old age without having accomplished anything of importance for ourselves, or for our nation or for humanity."[107] The article made clear that by emphasizing "today" the company typified modernity and progress. Venezuelans and Latin Americans in general were hopelessly mired in the past, and only by adopting the attitudes prevalent in the United States could they hope to uncover the path to modernity. One employee who worked for Shell recalled his department's motto: Either you are five minutes early to a meeting or consider yourself late.[108]

Besides time management, efficiency, individualism, and respect for authority, the companies also promoted morality, religion, and their own views on politics and union organizing. These themes acquired new importance after the nationalization of Mexican oil in 1938, which made Venezuela the only country in Latin America that permitted the presence of foreign oil companies. In company publications and works by Venezuelan writers, Mexico quickly became associated with a declining economy and a reliance on credits from the United States for survival.[109] After 1938 the need to promote a political outlook that favored the extraction of oil by United States enterprises acquired a new urgency. Increasingly Creole sought to associate itself with the very existence of the nation. The nation depended on Creole, and Creole depended on the goodwill of the nation.

For the oil companies, preserving their investments in the nation's oil production was their most important policy concern. They appeared less worried with the form of government that operated in Venezuela and proved quite adept at working with dictatorships, military strongmen, and even purported nationalist middle-class governments. One of the principal tools in the Creole public relations arsenal was its national magazine *El Farol*, its name being a translation of *The Lamp*, the publication of Creole's parent company, the Standard Oil Company of New Jersey. (Shell published the *Revista Shell* and the Mene Grande Oil Company published *Mene*.) Originally aimed at employees when it was founded in 1939, by the mid-1940s *El Farol* was adapted to the company's new public relations strategy and increasingly sought a literate, middle-class audience. Distributed free of charge and with a production run of seventy thousand by 1952, it proposed to "give preference to everything Venezuelan, to promote our traditions, our folklore whether in literature, art, science or history."[110] The staff included the Zulia historian Juan Besson and incorporated a number of highly acclaimed Venezuelan writers, academics, and intellectuals. (The historian Gustavo Morón became editor of the *Revista Shell*.) The content of *El Farol* initially reflected the important cultural and social literary movements stirring throughout Latin America.

During the 1940s authors who wrote in *El Farol* were influenced by the indigenismo and negritude traditions prevalent in Latin America. Its glossy color pages regularly featured indigenous and African representations, Caribbean folklore, bucolic panoramas, and artistic renderings of oil production and workers. After almost thirty years of one-man rule in Venezuela, the state and its cultural institutions were relatively weak. The oil companies stepped into this void and portrayed themselves as promoters of a national culture. *El Farol* published articles about Venezuela's indigenous legacy, the historic role of Afro-Venezuelan culture, the origins of Carnival, and recipes for *hallacas* (a Christmas dish that has some similarity with tamales) and *arepas*. That Venezuelans would have to be instructed about the importance of one of their staples may on the surface appear odd. However, the article by the famed essayist Mariano Picón Salas explored the indigenous roots of arepas, their regional variants, and their popular literary usages in Venezuelan culture. It highlighted how urbanization had altered the traditional preparation of the arepa. Long identified with the hearth and home and cooked over a traditional *budare*, or griddle, it now became a commercial product sold at food stands throughout Caracas. (What could be more authentic than eating an arepa at the Caracas arepera named Alma Llanera, after Venezuela's unofficial anthem?) These portrayals linked the nation's various culinary traditions, incorporated changes, and established the arepa as the preeminent national dish.[111] Moreover, these and other efforts parallel moves by commercial interests to produce and sell a series of consumer products, such as industrially prepared arepa corn flour, previously prepared in the home.

El Farol dedicated significant coverage to the various regional manifestations of Venezuelan culture. For important segments of the Venezuelan population the efforts of *El Farol* and a wide array of other corporate publications united the experiences of the plainsmen (llanero), the way of life of the Andes (Andino), and the cultural traditions of the East (oriental).[112] Local experiences ceased being simply manifestations of isolated regional cultures and became elements of a national Venezuelan culture. This venture developed in close association with important groups of Venezuelan intellectuals who viewed the oil company's magazine as a "Venezuelan cultural enterprise."[113] In keeping with this orientation, throughout the 1960s Creole also issued a publication with the nationalistic title *Defendiendo lo Nuestro* (Defending What Is Ours); thus the foreign oil companies purported to promote and nurture expressions of Venezuelan culture. Just as importantly, by "defending what is ours," implying the partnership between the companies and the state, the foreign companies professed to protect the nation against factors that might affect the price of Venezuelan oil, including challenges from protectionist forces in the United States or producers in the Middle East.

During the late 1940s and the 1950s the magazine created a new public space for Venezuelan writers and essayists who by and large opposed the government of the military ruler Marcos Pérez Jiménez (1948–58). The presence of these intellectuals in the magazine implied a balancing act and a degree of self-regulation between their political views and their largely literary or cultural function. They were usually free to write about various topics as long as they refrained from directly addressing political issues that the company or government might find sensitive. As one former magazine editor acknowledged, authors knew the range within which they could operate and seldom violated it.[114] While featured authors avoided political issues, the magazines' editors faced no such limitations. The publications openly attacked the left and organized labor while lauding capitalism and the free market system. While acknowledging his "genuine concerns" for the poor, one article provided a damning critique of Karl Marx and the inapplicability of his ideas to Venezuela.[115]

El Farol during the 1940s and 1950s contained works by such notables as Mariano Picón Salas, Arturo Uslar Pietri, Juan Pablo Sojo, Ramón Díaz Sanchez, Miguel Acosta Saignes, Armando Reverón, and Héctor Poleo. Sojo wrote on black ancestors and Miguel Acosta Saignes on the Timoto Cuica, an indigenous group that inhabited the Venezuelan Andes before the arrival of the Spaniards.[116] The very same intellectuals who two decades earlier had criticized the oil companies now published in their magazines. Díaz Sánchez, author of the highly acclaimed novel *Mene*, which disparaged the exclusionary and racist actions of United States oilmen, was serialized on the pages of *El Farol*. Creole also promoted work by noted Venezuelan artists and in 1955 began sponsoring the annual Armando Reverón prize in painting.[117] The participation of a distinguished group of Venezuelan intellectuals in the cultural programs of Creole and Shell lent credibility to the activities of the foreign companies and facilitated their identification with the nation's economic and cultural progress.[118] By the late 1950s the new Venezuelan state and various sectors of civil society moved in and gradually filled the cultural and social space once occupied by the foreign oil companies. However, rather than imply a growing separation, as Coronil points out, when the "Venezuelan state took up the functions previously performed by the oil companies, the two states in effect merged into one, at once increasing the national state's apparent unity and intensifying its internal conflicts."[119]

The persistence of racially and economically segregated oil camps throughout Venezuela increasingly clashed with the industries' broader social and cultural discourse. The oil camps highlighted the immense profits that the foreign oil companies obtained and the unique and distinctive lifestyle that they provided to employees. Over time the camps had become symbols of the widening rift in Venezuelan society between those employed in the oil industry, Venezuelan as well as foreign, and the majority excluded from its benefits. Social critics and the left railed against the privileged lifestyle of the camps and the impoverishment of the towns that had emerged around them. A decade later, the protest singer Alí Primera reflected this sentiment when he composed "Perdóneme Tío Juan," in which he described the poverty surrounding an oil camp as an open sore, an affront to Venezuelan society: "You [tío Juan] have not visited an oil camp, you do not see that they take what from the land what is ours, and all they leave us is misery and the sweat of the worker."[120] Yet it was not only the left that criticized the oil camps. Business interests also resented the self-contained nature of the camps, where company commissaries provided employees with most basic necessities, thus making it difficult for them to compete. The Venezuelan government also worried about the existence of population centers that operated largely outside the emerging national civic culture. Even United States government officials recognized that the higher standard of living evident in the "isolated US-type villages" angered most Venezuelans.[121] By 1950 even Creole officials believed that "the modern communities we create behind cyclone fences—literally compounds—present a very undesirable contrast to the towns which invariably spring up outside the fences."[122] Creole's President Harry Jarvis believed that no one was "happy with the oil camps."[123]

Faced with mounting political pressures and the rising costs of maintaining the camps, by the mid-1950s the oil companies began the process of allowing residents to purchase their own homes and incorporate their neighborhoods into the surrounding municipalities. Employees at the Bella Vista camp in Maracaibo were among the first in Venezuela to experience this type of integration. Symbolically, in 1954 the Maracaibo municipal authorities demolished the gates that had historically marked the entrance to the Shell and Creole camps, making them accessible to pedestrian and public traffic.[124] Despite these changes, most residents continued to work for the oil companies, and the area maintained its physical urban distinctiveness. This approach was not uniformly applied to all camps: geographically isolated areas such as Caripito and Quiriquire maintained their independent camp structure until nationalization.

Though no longer physically separated from the nearby communities by gates or fences, the employees of the company still lived worlds apart. The sense of privilege and status associated with employment in the industry did not diminish. The fences had never been decisive in separating oil employees from the rest of the population. Social and economic distinctions and access to important benefits, not physical borders, separated oil camps from the nearby communities. The elimination of boundaries did little to alter the class divide that persisted between the former oil camps and the municipalities that eventually incorporated them.

Nowhere was this more evident than in Judibana, on the Paraguaná peninsula, where important changes were under way. In the shadows of the huge Amuay refinery Creole constructed the "modern city of the future," to be inhabited by fifteen thousand residents who would live without fences and in their own homes.[125] The mantle of the model oil camp, ascribed to Caripito during the 1940s, now passed to Judibana, which in Jarvis's view would not be "one more of these isolated self-contained fenced in communities which are known throughout Venezuela as oil camps."[126] Creole envisioned Judibana as an independent municipality able to govern its own affairs; instead of an oil camp it was called an *urbanización*, the term used to refer to middle-class neighborhoods throughout Venezuela.[127] The urban schema resembled a typical planned suburban middle-class neighborhood in the United States, with spacious homes, garages, manicured lawns, public parks, a church, a movie theater, and a modern supermarket. These areas stood in stark contrast to the traditional neighborhoods of adjoining houses that characterized most pre-oil Venezuelan cities. In developing Judibana as a model community, Creole, according to its president, had "the blessing of the national government."[128]

In deciding to integrate its camps into the local communities, the company never publicly acknowledged that housing in camps such as La Salina, built in the 1930s and 1940s, had, in the words of one Creole official, been "gradually becoming sub-standard."[129] The company had to decide whether to incur significant costs to improve the older camps, or develop alternatives. Shell had already embarked on a renovation project at its Lagunillas camp, making residences for Venezuelan drillers "equivalent" to the accommodations that Creole provided for senior staff in Caripito. Hoping to offset future costs, the company opted to coordinate and expand its existing home-ownership programs, which it expected to engender additional benefits. Homeownership was expected to produce results similar to those generated by the earlier strategy of Venezolanization. One Creole executive believed that allowing employees to purchase homes would "give more people a stake or personal interest in the welfare of their community."[130] Employees would be able to acquire fifteen-year home loans similar to those offered in the United States, for amounts equivalent to twenty-six months of their basic salary, at an annual interest rate of 2.4 percent.[131] These special types of credit arrangements were inaccessible to the rest of the Venezuelan labor force and virtually nonexistent elsewhere in Latin America.

By the mid-1950s Creole and Shell no longer needed to operate and maintain many of their camps. The disruptive period of the industry, characterized by waves of immigrants needed to sustain an ever-expanding labor force, was a thing of the past. Hiring practices became institutionalized, and technological innovations permitted using fewer workers to maintain normal production levels. More important, oil production, under way for over thirty years, had begun to decline in some areas, forcing Creole to fend off rumors concerning the imminent closure of certain camps.[132] In many areas the communities adjoining the oil camps had expanded dramatically, becoming permanent cities and providing many of their own basic services, although to a certain extent they still depended on the oil industry. Collective bargaining with unions helped to normalize relations with labor. At many levels Creole's industrial relations supervisors preferred dealing with labor unions, since in the words of one official, the "alternative was chaotic."[133] Political and judicial structures had become sufficiently institutionalized to play a mediating role. Manufacturing and local commerce could fulfill the basic economic needs of the community. Creole could now formally disengage from these areas, since, as Jarvis put it, the company wanted to "run an oil business, not a town."[134] Though the camps were gradually integrated, the social and economic expectations that they generated endured.

Beyond its economic function, oil fundamentally altered the Venezuelan social and cultural landscape. Venezuelans employed in the industry confronted different conceptions of time and work, as well as new social and cultural expectations driven in large part by United States culture. The oil industry also provided the basis for a new level of social interaction between people of diverse social status. The camp experience introduced a new lifestyle, altered the use of public and private spaces, and established new consumer patterns. It also reformulated the role of the Venezuelan family and accentuated the position of the nuclear family and male patriarchy. Aware of the fundamental changes under way in the oil camps, the companies incorporated the family into their structure and paid attention to the role of women as agents of change. This does not mean that those employed in the industry simply became passive recipients of a United States way of life. Venezuelans from different social classes responded in various ways, from resistance to adaptation and even accommodation. What it did mean, however, is that these groups now had a material interest in preserving the economic and social model that generated their distinct lifestyles and social positions.

Initially oil exploration and production increased employment opportunities for thousands of previously rural laborers. Over time, employment opportunities diminished and familial relations and personal contacts increasingly determined who obtained jobs in the industry. Although many Venezuelans remained relegated to the lower socioeconomic strata, constant pressure by labor and an emerging middle class eventually provided them with access to other employment. The companies took steps to provide opportunities for their employees, educate those who were illiterate, offer extensive training programs, and promote workers into supervisory positions. Creole and Shell established model worker campaigns that rewarded loyalty, efficiency, and dedication.

Employment in the oil companies expanded the economic base of the middle class, and for an entire generation of Venezuelans the country's Standard Oil subsidiary became affectionately known as "Mama Creole." Political conditions allowed the oil companies to find willing allies among some middle-class political groups and intellectuals that accepted them as an important agent of change. The experiences acquired in the oil industry influenced several generations of Venezuelans who after 1960 took the reins of power in the country. The model of the nation that they promoted remained rooted in the oil industry, and in the ideals of citizenship and political participation that it generated.

CHAPTER 7

Oil and Politics

An Enduring Relation

No discussion of oil in Venezuela would be complete without an assessment of the industry's impact on the political process. Moreover, an examination of this legacy provides a prudent way to evaluate the extent to which the oil economy influenced not only the social discourse but also the decision-making process. For Venezuela the oil export economy had important political consequences. It firmly situated Venezuela in the sphere of influence of the United States, compelling political actors to pay close attention to developments there. Preserving the structure of the profitable export economy also lessened the likelihood of dramatic economic or political shifts. The maintenance of good relations with the United States became naturalized, accepted by various social classes as an inevitable outcome of the oil economy.

For the foreign oil companies the ability to adapt to political changes, or in some cases influence the course of reforms in Venezuela, proved central to their successful operations. Beyond their economic function, oil companies were an important component of the foreign policy of the United States toward the region. The U.S. State Department closely monitored relations between the Venezuelan government and the foreign oil companies. Venezuela played a still greater role in foreign policy considerations after the nationalization of Mexican oil in 1938, during the Second World War, and during the cold war. In the words of the U.S. National Security Council, "oil operations, are for all practical purposes, instruments of our foreign policy towards these countries."[1] Thus Venezuela was not only an important and profitable source of oil but an important economic and subsequently political model that the United States actively promoted throughout the region and beyond. By the late 1940s, as *Fortune* magazine put it, "if there had been no perfect illustration of what United States technical and capital resources could do for the world's 'underdeveloped areas,' it would have been necessary to invent the Republic of Venezuela."[2]

Conventional approaches to the history of the relations between the foreign oil companies and various Venezuelan governments stress important ruptures in the nation's struggle to gain control over the industry and the leading role of Acción Democrática (AD) in the political process. According to this interpretation, foreign corporations benefited from the policies of the dictator Juan Vicente Gómez (1908–35), opposed the reforms initiated by AD during the Trienio (1945–48), and resumed their cozy relationship with the military under Marcos Pérez Jiménez (1948–58). Only after 1958 did the democratic forces undertake a sustained process of reform, increasing revenues though not challenging the basic model of production that allowed foreign companies to control the industry. Intent on legitimating political outcomes after 1958, this approach fails to consider how the oil export industry skewed social class alliances, forging an important nexus between the foreign interests and the middle and upper classes that depended on oil revenues to maintain their status.[3] Rather than ruptures with an immediate past, policies adopted before 1998 reflect a significant degree of continuity.

The election of Hugo Chávez Frías in 1998 marks an end to the traditional political arrangements pursued by previous governments. Central to Chávez's policy was an effort to complete the nationalization of the oil industry, closing the loopholes left by the 1976 law and reasserting state control over the petroleum industry. Establishing state control over PDVSA and attempting to renegotiate the agreements signed with foreign oil companies during the so-called *apertura petrolera* of the early 1990s became a central component of this undertaking. Invariably these actions brought the government into conflict with the very social and political forces that had previously benefited from the oil industry. At one level the dispute between Chávez's government, the oil company hierarchy, and the oil workers' unions regarding the future of the oil industry was a struggle for the economic purse strings of the nation, a battle between the new PDVSA, aligned with the social priorities of the government, and the old model. At another level the dispute was a symbolic contest over the nation's identity, its model of citizenship, and a definition of modernity and progress previously defined by élite and upper-middle-class concerns.

FOREIGN OIL AND THE CHANGING POLITICAL LANDSCAPE

Juan Vicente Gómez, Venezuela's longtime dictator, died peacefully in his sleep in December 1935. Though he skillfully manipulated political conditions in Venezuela, his twenty-seven-year rule had been assured by his relations with the foreign oil companies and the United States government. As Stephen Rabe argues, on multiple occasions the United States moved to "strengthen" Gómez's regime by deploying navy ships to Venezuelan waters, sharing intelligence on dissidents, and dispatching dignitaries to visit the dictator.[4] His dealings with foreign oil interests and the resources that the government received from the export of oil provided the symbolic power and revenues needed to expand the state, limit the power of regional élites, and harness political opponents. Supported not only by the United States but also by England and Holland, Gómez became the first Venezuelan ruler no longer beholden only to local or national political interests to guarantee his hold on power.[5]

Gómez's successor, General Eleázar López Contreras (1936–41), introduced some political liberalization, restricting the presidential term to five years and permitting labor unions and political parties to function openly.[6] His administration also marked the advent of a new era in the nation's economy. Venezuela's transformation from an agricultural exporter to a mono-exporter of oil, begun under Gómez, accelerated, and the nation became a net importer of food, a condition that continues to this day.[7] In matters of oil policy, however, López Contreras did little to break with the past. As Gómez had done before, he privately assured United States oil interests of continued good relations even as members of his administration were involved in sensitive negotiations with the companies.[8] In 1941 López Contreras designated General Isaís Medina Angarita as his successor. Medina Angarita gained popular support by freeing political prisoners, legalizing political parties, including the Communists, and instituting an important petroleum reform law in 1943. Yet his attempt to impose a successor led to his downfall. A group of young military officers known as the Union Patriótica Militar (UPM) formed an alliance with Acción Democrática and staged a coup in October 1945.[9]

The foreign oil companies were not completely unprepared for the events of October 1945. Paralleling debates in the State Department concerning the Good Neighbor Policy, Standard Oil and its affiliates in Venezuela prepared for changes in the political climate.[10] By 1937 its directors recognized that "a growing feeling of nationalism and its inevitable reaction of antagonism to foreigners [had] made it imperative for any foreign company operating in Latin America to give more attention to industrial and public relations."[11] By 1940 they had concluded that "by cooperation, and not unyielding opposition" private industry would do more to mold the trend of modern legislation in foreign countries, especially Latin America.[12] Standard's strategy was a sign of business acumen, given that new social actors had arisen in the region and their social agendas could often be co-opted to avoid fundamental change. At a meeting of their Coordination Committee in February 1946, Laurence Duggan, serving as a consultant to Standard Oil, echoed the views he had earlier expressed in the State Department: "At the risk of repetition, may I again state my conviction, that the political reality throughout Latin America today is the emergence of new political elements representing the people who, under semi feudalistic society, had no chance for expression.... It is necessary to base policy judgment on this political reality, whether you like it or not, and forget 'wishing for the good old days' when these days are gone forever."[13] Though they learned to adapt to changing political and social conditions evident in the region, United States companies nonetheless sought to protect their basic economic interests. In Venezuela their policy continued to be framed by the desire to limit the rise of a militant independent labor movement, deter Communist influence, and avoid the nationalization of oil as had occurred in Mexico.

Within a week of the coup of October 1945, the three largest oil companies—Creole, Shell, and Mene Grande (Gulf)—met with Rómulo Betancourt, who was described by the United States embassy as being "in the driver's seat." A company official summarized the results of the meeting as follows: "Received [the] impression junta will be realistic and that no change is contemplated in the oil law and concessions contracts.... They feel, therefore, be wiser concede everything reasonable at once instead of have measures forced on them later, including collective contracts they would have opposed had nothing changed."[14] Hoping to avert any fundamental changes to their operations, the companies agreed to mild labor reforms and tax increases.[15] Standard Oil's internal documents acknowledge that "in view of the general labor attitude prevailing, it was absolutely necessary for the Junta to take certain steps in favor of labor," and considered the agreement of 8 December 1945 "a conservative step under these circumstances."[16] To prevent strikes that might disrupt production, in January 1946 the junta prohibited labor stoppages and mandated arbitration for work-related disputes.[17]

Besides preemptively acceding to milder reforms, oil company officials pursued other long-term strategies to assure their economic interests. Standard Oil instructed "Company's affiliates [Creole Petroleum] do their utmost to cultivate acquaintance and friendship with the growing middle class and the labor movement."[18] Company officials believed that the middle class and well-compensated oil workers would provide a buffer against leftists and radical reforms that might threaten their business model. By adopting policies that favored this segment of the population, the oil companies sought support among a group that they viewed as a long-term ally in maintaining social and political stability.[19] Moreover, they attempted to establish a clear connection between the well-being of these interests and the economic objectives of the United States firms. Creole in particular often reiterated that there was no contradiction between its objectives in Venezuela and the well-being of the nation and its various social classes. It sought to be "foreigners in name . . . not in interest and in action."[20]

As a matter of policy, Standard Oil and its affiliates, in this case Creole, sought close relationships with their employees, "developing as many channels of contact with them as possible for better mutual understanding and to improve free exchanges of information on company-worker problems." This policy, it concluded, would "reduce the need for outside assistance of either the labor authorities or the syndicates."[21] Despite having signed a new labor contract with the Oil Workers Federation that improved the economic conditions of workers, in the end Creole management felt that "all attempted encroachments on management's prerogatives [hire, fire, and lay off] were denied."[22]

Oil company policy had correctly anticipated the new political climate in Venezuela. Interviewed by the industry's *Oil and Gas Journal* shortly after the coup, the new minister of development, Juan Pablo Pérez Alfonzo, reassured foreign investors: "The defense of our national economy and the necessity of using foreign capital for the development of our national resources can be harmonized without trouble. . . . It is in [the country's] best interest to permit development of its oil petroleum resources under the present arrangement of foreign capital and technicians. There is no intention to nationalize the industry or to expropriate properties."[23]

Pérez Alfonzo's assurance against nationalization became an article of faith among military and democratic government officials, as well as leading intellectuals.[24] In describing the situation in Venezuela, Tom Barger, an official for Aramco who had previously been stationed in the country, indicated that "all politicians inveigh against [the oil companies] but no party coming to power, however revolutionary, wants to kill the goose that lays the golden eggs."[25] AD's position contrasted sharply with Creole's own internal polling data of the Venezuelan population, which in 1947–48 indicated that "82% of the [university] students as a group were for nationalization of the industry, while the national average was only 72%."[26] It should therefore come as no surprise that Standard's president asked the United States ambassador to thank Betancourt for these assurances. The ambassador refused, indicating that the United States government should stay "out of the forefront of the oil picture" in order not to fuel anti-Americanism.[27]

Central to AD's oil policy during this period was the idea of "no more concessions." (It did not, however, apply to the transfer of existing "exploration concessions.")[28] The policy, in the view of Pérez Alfonzo, was neither "overly nationalist, nor anti-imperialist or emotional" but simply reflected Venezuela's economic dependence on oil.[29] Simply stated, the country would not offer the companies any new tracts of land for drilling. Instead it would attempt to ensure collection of taxes on existing grants and the honest calculation of federal revenues accruing from royalties.[30] Leftist critics argued that AD's policy excluded smaller United States firms in favor of the three oil giants, Creole, Shell, and Mene Grande, that already controlled the majority of proven oil reserves.[31]

Since the 1920s the Venezuelan government had become increasingly dependent on oil revenues. From 1917 to 1936 oil made up 29 percent of state revenues, from 1936 to 1945 it made up 54 percent, and from 1945 to 1958 it made up 71 percent.[32] These conditions, according to a report by the National Security Council, gave rise to a symbiotic relationship between the oil companies based in the United States and the Venezuelan government, since anything that diminished the profits of the companies "also reduced the income of the sovereign."[33] One business publication in the United States went further, arguing that this purported "interdependence" diminished popular support for labor disputes, since they deprived the state of funds and negatively affected the status of the middle class.[34]

The three large companies continued to hold substantial tracts of land, most of which remained unexplored. Among these the Standard affiliates held 65 percent of the industry's proven reserves.[35] In return for an increased share of revenues (16 $^2/_3$ percent of royalties) and the construction of re-fineries in Venezuela, the much-heralded Petroleum Law of 1943 extended company concessions that would have expired in 1960.[36] One company of-ficial estimated that it would take the companies upwards of five years to develop the newly acquired tracts.[37] Even without any new oil concessions, production was expected to rise 20 percent over the next five years. Ac-cording to the United States embassy, the "principal impediment to higher production" continued to be "the shortage of Venezuelan labor and the dif-ficulty in obtaining steel pipe . . . not the policies or practices of the Ven-ezuelan government."[38] Despite public protestations to the contrary, AD's policy of no more concessions did not undermine the position of the three large oil producers. Rather than open conflict, AD and the United States oil companies spent the next three years in a "truly cooperative—if arm's length—relationship."[39] United States business, *Fortune* wrote, found "allies among reformers who were given to calling themselves socialist."[40]

For the AD leadership, Venezuela's dependence on oil precluded national-izing the industry outright, as Bolivia had done in 1937 and Mexico in 1938.[41] On repeated occasions Venezuela's democratic leaders distanced themselves from Mexico's policies, insisting that the country lacked the refining capac-ity, an adequate tanker fleet for transportation, and a marketing network. One analyst with Standard Oil suggested a different perspective: "We have to admit that the Latin American governments, at least one or two of them, have demonstrated that they can operate petroleum properties."[42] Intent on consolidating its tenuous hold on power, AD feared the sharp drop in production and the even sharper drop in revenues that would have followed nationalization; it needed recognition from the United States to consolidate its power and keep political opponents at bay. Moreover, it desperately needed oil royalties to expand the state apparatus and develop a patronage system that linked the interests of the growing urban middle class with the powerful oil workers. The United States ambassador offered the following assessment of Betancourt: "[The president is] astute enough to realize hopes of putting into effect [AD's] economic and social programs upon which its popular support relies depend upon oil revenues. There is every reason to expect that Betancourt appreciates Junta's basic interests are thus similar to those of the oil companies and that will treat them with kid gloves unless pressure from labor becomes too great."[43] In December 1945, however, the government decreed an end-of-year tax on oil to recoup profits, and in November 1948 it implemented a 50/50 profit-sharing agreement. It should be noted that leftist critics such as Salvador de la Plaza considered the 50/50 agreement a ruse that actually benefited the foreign enterprises, since the oil royalty was now included in calculations of the overall taxes paid by the oil companies.[44] In assessing the income tax, Coronil asserts that what "had been designed by Medina's 1943 law as a tool to capture for Venezuela all surplus profit, now became tied to a formula that obliged the state to share it with the oil companies."[45] In the end, despite the nationalist rhetoric that surrounded the enactment of the 50/50 formula, the policy limited the state's ability to obtain additional revenue from surplus profits.[46] This policy of "wise nationalism" expressed the limits of AD government policy.[47]

After Mexico's nationalization of oil, Venezuela acquired strategic political as well as economic importance to the United States and the foreign oil companies.[48] Since 1928 it had achieved the status of the world's second-largest producer and the first exporter of oil, and now it was the only nation in Latin America that permitted "large-scale production . . . of oil by private companies" with "no restrictions on the outflow of dollars."[49] Creole's investment in Venezuela, according to one business source, was the largest overseas expenditure by a United States company in a single country. Furthermore, 48 percent of Standard Oil of New Jersey's dividend income from affiliates was derived from Creole profits.[50] In addition, not wishing to deplete its own strategic reserves, the United States government considered Venezuela the "keystone" of its "petroleum war production needs outside of the United States in World War II."[51] Reserves in the Middle East and elsewhere in Latin America had not been fully developed. As a result, the United States government and the oil companies repeatedly promoted Venezuela as an economic model for Latin American and the Middle East. One State Department official even suggested the 50/50 profit-sharing arrangement as a model for a solution to United Fruit Company's problems in Guatemala during the early 1950s.[52]

During the Trienio AD also invited sources of foreign capital to participate in the nation's development and granted new non-petroleum mineral concessions. Bethlehem Steel and U.S. Steel procured rights to explore rich iron ore deposits in Guayana. The Venezuelan embassy in Washington began to publish an English-language *Venezuelan Newsletter* to furnish "the business and financial sector of the United States public with accurate information regarding trade and investment prospects and benefits in Venezuela.[53] According to Sergio Aranda, United States investments, once limited to oil, under AD began to penetrate other important areas of Venezuela's economy.[54]

THE NEW SECURITY APPARATUS

Fear of Communists in the labor movement further encouraged cooperation between AD and the large oil companies. In its fight against Gómez's dictatorship, the Communist Party had gained considerable support among students, intellectuals, and labor. After Gómez's death, López Contreras's and Medina Angarita's governments built up the state security apparatus to repel challenges, real or imagined, from the left. Conditions in the oilfields, the minister of the interior stated, gave rise to "disturbances of all classes" that the local police and municipal authorities could not handle.[55] To buttress internal security and "protect" the rural oilfields, the government created the Guardia Nacional (GN) in 1937. Throughout the industry it quickly became known as the Guardia Petrolera (the Petroleum Guard). In the more remote areas, such as Temblador in eastern Venezuela, members of the Guard lived in the workers' camp at the company's expense.[56] Eventually, under the government of Medina Angarita in 1944, the Guard was reorganized and became part of the national military apparatus.[57]

In 1938 the Caracas government established a political and social bureau within the city's police force to contend with the increased political activism. Then in 1941 Medina Angarita's government authorized a national identification card (cedula de identidad), a move widely applauded by the oil companies because it facilitated identification of their workers. Concerned about the left in 1947, the junta, controlled by AD, formed the Seguridad Nacional (SN), described by the U.S. State Department as an "FBI-type organization."[58] Many SN agents received advanced training in Spain, while directors were sent to the United States.[59]

Most foreign oil companies also developed an internal security apparatus to gather intelligence on potential threats to their interests.[60] Within Creole Petroleum the industrial services administrator was "responsible for developing and executing policies and programs for protection of corporate assets amounting to 2.2 billion against loss or damage."[61] Below the national director, two regional supervisors in western and eastern Venezuela oversaw "the company guard force, professional and volunteer fire department, investigation of crimes, third party liability, land invasions, and other confidential matter wherein the company is or may be a party of interest."[62] In some cases the expatriates who staffed security offices had previously been employed by law enforcement agencies in the United States. Typically cloaked in secrecy and the subject of endless rumors, the company security director in the camps was known as the local "Dick Tracy."[63]

The Office of Industrial Services screened all Venezuelan and foreign employees.[64] The former Central Intelligence Agency operative Philip Agee indicated that he regularly conducted background checks of employees for foreign oil companies operating in Venezuela and elsewhere in Latin America.[65] In addition, the office gathered intelligence and cooperated with the Venezuelan military and police "on matters of mutual interest."[66] As one United States intelligence report indicated, "information on oil workers, communist activities, suspected sabotage or subversive groups, and other matters of mutual interest is exchanged between the FAC [military], SN, and company officials. All three groups maintain information nets."[67] To protect oilfields during the Second World War, United States military attachés developed contingency plans that included the landing of United States troops in the event that production was threatened.[68] In 1948 the Venezuelan Armed Forces, the oil companies, and a United States government team conducted a "security survey" of oil installations.[69] The survey recommendations were subsequently implemented by the United States companies and the Venezuelan military. United States intelligence agencies also kept track of developments in Venezuelan oilfields, and their records indicate the existence of a web of informants that reported on union activities in Caripito, Quiriquire, and Jusepín as well as the other oil camps.[70]

At times the chain of command between government forces assigned to protect the oilfields and the foreign oil security forces became blurred. According to Creole's internal memos, the Industrial Services representative in eastern Venezuela was responsible for the "effective use, placement and support of the 265 Guardia Nacional assigned to the protection of Creole property."[71] To ensure support from local authorities, Creole's security directors regularly fielded requests from military officers for housing, cars, and other favors.[72] In an attempt to curry favor with local officials, the Creole superintendent in Caripito, a Mr. Calhoun, regularly invited military officials to participate in activities organized by the senior staff club, and during Christmas he went to great pains to order individualized gifts for them from the United States. When he presented a local official with a box of expensive Cuban cigars, the suspicious agent replied: "¿A quien hay que joder?" (Whom do you want taken care of?).[73] Company employees were also expected to report information considered adverse to their employer. On one occasion Manuel Pérez wrote a letter to the Lagunillas security office reporting that he had seen a fellow worker painting "Viva Fidel, Cuba Si, Yankee No" on walls adjacent to the company commissary. After requesting anonymity, Pérez indicated that he provided this information because he knew that such slogans were contrary to company "norms and wishes."[74]

Despite these measures, United States government and business interests continued to express concern regarding the presence of Communists in the labor movement. On one occasion in 1946, fifty United States businessmen in Caracas presented a petition to their ambassador urging the State Department to "combat the rising Communist influence in Venezuela."[75] Publication of the letter by newspapers in the United States produced a storm of controversy in Venezuela. In Caracas the Communist Party organized demonstrations against interference by the United States in Venezuela's internal affairs. Despite fueling nationalist sentiments, the episode, in the view of one observer, had one positive outcome: increasing the antipathy between AD and the Communists. United States Ambassador Corrigan reported to Washington Betancourt's pledge that in the event of a war with the Soviet Union, "Venezuela would support the U.S. 100% and would imprison all militant communists."[76] Clashes between the two groups continued during the Trienio, and Betancourt pledged that as long as he was president "there would be no Communists in the cabinet."[77]

In 1948 the Central Intelligence Agency concluded that Betancourt's regime in its last months and Gallegos's newly elected administration had shown increasing concern regarding the Soviet threat, and that as a result Venezuelan policy had moved increasingly into "the orbit of the United States."[78] Maintenance of the existing oil export model required that Venezuelan political leaders be attentive to Washington's policy concerns. Beyond adopting the politics of the cold war, operating in the orbit of the United States had broader political and social implications. It meant that the country was often the subject of visiting delegations sent from the United States to study and make recommendations concerning Venezuelan institutions, including military, justice, commerce, and even education. These visits often generated specific recommendations that the Venezuelan government was expected to implement.[79] In 1935, for example, Professor George I. Sánchez arrived in Venezuela as a "general technical advisor" to the Ministry of Education and director of the National Teachers College. He maintained his relationship with the ministry of education for over twenty-five years.[80]

AD IN POWER

In December 1947, in the first free and direct elections in the country's history, the esteemed novelist Rómulo Gallegos, AD's candidate, won with over 70 percent of the vote.[81] During this period AD established a national apparatus that survived Pérez Jiménez's dictatorship. Wolfgang Hein described its policies as aimed at developing "close ties between the party and the labor movement on the one hand and between A.D. and the industrial bourgeoisie on the other."[82] The newly organized Comité de Organización Política Electoral Independiente (COPEI; Christian Democrat) and the Unión Republicana Democrática (URD; center left) objected to its blatant use of the government apparatus to build a patronage system.

The presence of Communists in the labor movement remained a frequent subject of discussion between AD, the United States, and the oil companies.[83] In one meeting the new United States ambassador, Walter Donelly, informed President Gallegos of purported Communist influences in the industry, "giving him facts and figures on infiltration [by] Communist labor syndicates in strategic operations, including transportation ports, pipelines, power plants, and refineries." The ambassador complained that Communists had made inroads because AD labor leaders seldom visited the rural oil camps. Gallegos promised to have AD labor leaders visit the interior of the country and have the army "remove dangerous communist elements from strategic points."[84] A CIA memorandum applauded AD's efforts, indicating that the party appeared "determined to remove Communists from the labor field and from the petroleum industry in particular."[85]

Political intrigue marked the Trienio and the subsequent democratic interval. In the words of Pedro Estrada, director of the SN, the Trienio was characterized by "never ending conspiracies."[86] Relations between the military and AD remained tenuous at best; neither side fully trusted the other. The U.S. army and naval attachés stationed at the embassy in Caracas had anticipated a coup as early as December 1947. The United States cooperated with the AD government to find possible conspirators. The FBI and the Justice Department investigated Venezuelan exiles in the United States and concluded that several Dominicans and United States citizens had participated in a plot to procure weapons illegally and overthrow the Venezuelan government. The United States government derailed several other attempts by limiting access to weapons but refrained from prosecuting those involved for fear that the publicity would be "detrimental to inter-American relations."[87]

Support by the United States for AD did little to quell internal opposition to the government. Claiming that AD sowed dissension within its ranks, the military finally ended the democratic experiment in November 1948.[88] Shortly after being toppled, AD blamed the United States and the oil companies for its overthrow. Playing to nationalist sentiments, Gallegos dispatched a letter to President Harry Truman condemning the presence of United States military attachés at the Caracas army barracks during the revolt.[89] Although little evidence existed to substantiate these charges, some in AD also accused the United States oil companies of having instigated the revolt against Gallegos. Oil companies such as Creole had cultivated relations with AD and did not stand to gain by promoting a coup.[90] United States interests appeared satisfied with AD, since, as one business source put it, it had "stopped the Communist movement in its tracks."[91] Rather, the military found allies among "conservatives and wealthy business men, industrialists, large landowners, some government employees and professional men," who feared change.[92] Despite AD's having received 70 percent of the popular vote in the recent election, as reported in the *New York Times*, there was "no popular opposition to the military's action."[93] After the coup, most political parties adopted a wait-and-see attitude, while some openly cooperated with the military.

PÉREZ JIMÉNEZ, FOREIGN OIL, AND THE UNITED STATES

The rise of Pérez Jiménez coincided with a favorable international climate for Venezuelan oil, allowing the dictator to reap massive revenues from petroleum. During the 1950s demand in the United States for oil increased as the country sought to replenish the strategic reserves used during the war. Throughout the 1950s the conflict in Korea, the nationalization of Iranian oil, and the Suez crisis also spurred demand for Venezuelan oil.[94] Continued reliance on oil caused concern in some international business circles. Standard Oil projected various scenarios for Venezuela if Middle Eastern oil again became available and a postwar depression materialized in the United States.[95] Other observers went further, underscoring the point that if Venezuela did not confront its dependence on oil the "country [would] be little more than a glorified filling station."[96]

During the 1950s United States oil companies launched new explorations, reopened old fields, and located new deposits in Guatemala, Colombia, Ecuador, Peru, and Bolivia.[97] Conditions were developing under which no single oil-exporting nation could hold a preferred position in the international trade in oil.[98] Increased competition from oil-exporting countries in the Middle East compelled Venezuela to take an aggressive role in defending its perceived interests. It had already dispatched a top-level mission to Mexico and Canada "to bring about a closer understanding between Venezuela and other oil producing countries."[99] In a move that predates the founding of the Organization of Petroleum Exporting Countries (OPEC), in 1949 a Venezuelan delegation visited Iraq, Iran, and Saudi Arabia. The British ambassador in Caracas indicated that the visit was intended to "gather information so that the Venezuelans could appraise the future impact of Middle East petroleum production on the markets for Venezuelan oil and encourage the Arab States to increase royalties and taxation so as to raise Middle East production costs and improve Venezuela's competitive position."[100] Failing to fully recognize the significance of the trip, the oil companies provided some of the logistics for the Venezuelan delegation while in these countries.[101] Despite these actions, Venezuela slowly ceased being the world's leading exporter of oil, and its share of total world trade in petroleum declined from 46 percent in 1948 to 33 percent by 1958.[102]

Relations between Truman's administration, big oil, and Pérez Jiménez quickly improved. When tariffs imposed by the United States threatened the flow of Venezuelan oil, the two governments negotiated a new trade agreement. Nelson Rockefeller and Creole's president Arthur Proudfit personally lobbied Washington for a new treaty.[103] This incident highlights the symbiotic relations that had developed between the foreign oil companies and the Venezuelan state. On the surface it appeared that Creole's lobbying efforts in Washington sought to defend Venezuela against restrictive measures, and the company was glad to be seen in this light. Yet in fact it sought to protect its own investments in the country, investments that could have been negatively affected if Venezuela retaliated against higher tariffs. In spite of criticism from oil producers in Texas, the United States negotiated a new agreement with Venezuela ensuring continuation of the old tariffs. In return for this Venezuela reduced duties on goods exported from the United States, including cars, radios, televisions, planes, and trucks, offering advantages to "practically every important group of U.S. exporters."[104] Pérez Jiménez's administration, like AD before it, continued to depend on oil profits and appeared willing to sacrifice internal markets to maintain existing revenue levels.

Imported consumer goods from the United States reached an all-time high of $695.4 million in 1957, with an additional "half a billion spent on freight, insurance and other services."[105] Continued access to petroleum reserves was only one factor that the United States considered when it agreed to a new treaty. The National Security Council (NSC) insisted that a new agreement with Venezuela was vital because it "provided the basis for stabilizing relations between oil companies and other governments, particularly in the Middle East."[106] Internal Creole documents echoed these sentiments: "The Venezuelan example is, we hope, beginning to make an impression."[107] Peru, Colombia, Cuba, and Guatemala adopted oil laws that reflected the

50/50 formula.[108] Implicit in this assessment was the belief that Venezuela would compensate for the higher tariffs by altering the 50/50 formula, precipitating new demands by other oil-producing nations.

With the exception of 1956 and 1957, Pérez Jiménez's government largely followed the policy of no new concessions, and as before the arrangement posed no immediate threat to the three major companies. Arthur Proudfit summarized the effect of the policy: "We are not concerned. . . . This policy contributes to the orderly exploration and development of the large concessions now held."[109] Even without new concessions, crude production in 1955 exceeded previous records: the companies produced 2,157,216 barrels a day, compared with 956,000 during the war years.[110] Creole maintained its position as the industry leader, operating 3,000 wells, employing more than 14,000 people, and pumping close to half the nation's output, 982,365 barrels a day. In 1954 it paid $232 million in taxes and royalties to the government.[111] Shell continued as the second-largest producer and Mene Grande (Gulf) remained third. Besides these principal corporations, a number of smaller companies began to expand or establish operations in Venezuela. During the 1950s companies such as Socony-Mobil, the Texas Company, Standard of California, Sinclair, Richmond, Pantepec, Phillips, and Atlantic increased their presence in the country. In addition, United States drilling and oil service companies such as Halliburton operated in Venezuela.[112]

Government oil profits collected from 1948 to 1957 totaled 25 billion bolívares, more than US $7 billion at prevailing exchange rates.[113] Government expenditures were invested in major population centers, where a series of mega-projects would produce the greatest political effect. Oil profits physically transformed Caracas: the capital's population more than doubled by 1957, reaching 1.2 million.[114] Caracas élites set out to transform their city, adopting modernist architectural styles that left little room for tradition.[115] The opening in 1955 of a Christian Dior boutique, the first in Latin America, affirmed Caracas's new status. Figures compiled by Chase Manhattan Bank showed that construction activity in Caracas reached record levels, with expenditures on public works from 1948 to 1953 amounting to $1.3 billion. During the fiscal year 1957–58 public investments reached US $685 million, providing ample opportunity for government corruption in the issuance of contracts.[116]

Boom conditions continued well into the mid-1950s. Although government expenditures on public works reached new peaks, "a large budget surplus was turned in."[117] The excess funds acquired during 1956 were for the most part obtained from increased oil production extracted to compensate for the closure of the Suez Canal. For the first time since 1943, Pérez Jiménez granted new concessions to the oil companies, filling the administration's coffers. In one sale the government awarded over 793,000 new acres to the companies, netting US $668 million in revenues.[118] Sale of new tracts occurred again in 1957.

By 1958 the reopening of the Suez Canal increased production from the Middle East, creating an oil glut on international markets.[119] Standard Oil of New Jersey estimated that in the Western Hemisphere alone there was a "spare producing capacity of 4 million barrels a day."[120] A report by the State Department in 1950 predicted that the development of oil in the Middle East and western Canada constituted a long-range threat to Venezuela's oil market.[121] Diversification did not hurt oil industry profits, however; on the contrary, they improved. Standard Oil reported that "as a result of diversification of operations, Standard's earnings are up, by 1959, 20% over equivalent months in 1958."[122] Venezuela was not so fortunate. By 1957, as world oil supplies increased, *Barron's* reported that Venezuela's "gusher was in trouble."[123]

In the United States independent oil producers, threatened by a world oil glut and a looming recession, increased pressure on President Eisenhower to impose quotas on imported oil.[124] Hoping to stave off mandatory restrictions, United States companies in Venezuela adopted "voluntary" ones.[125] Venezuela regularly shipped 40 percent of its oil to the United States.[126] Shrinking markets in Europe and talk of oil quotas in the United States frightened the Venezuelan élite and Pérez Jiménez. Headlines in leading Caracas newspapers blasted the "Yanquis" and threatened retaliation if the United States adopted quotas.[127] With good reason, the U.S. State Department worried about the "growth of anti-Americanism in Venezuela."[128] Officials in Pérez Jiménez's government and business leaders recommended scrapping trade agreements with the United States.[129] Pérez Jiménez adamantly opposed the restrictions and threatened reprisals. *Barron's* reported that talk of restrictions by the United States might lead Venezuela to alter the 50/50 profit-sharing arrangement: "The wrath of the Pérez Jiménez government may fall hardest on the very United States oil companies which, because they have producing wells in that country, have been seeking to protect Venezuelan interests." Oil restrictions, in the words of the ambassador, would cause the United States to lose "the outstanding example of good oil company–government relation" and "forfeit its showroom for [the] USA system in Latin America."[130] Plans by Pérez Jiménez to construct an oil refinery also caused concern; the United States considered them a significant departure from "the government's stated policy of private industrial development."[131] Washington also disapproved of efforts by Pérez Jiménez to purchase sophisticated weaponry from Italy, France, and England; the NSC worried that Pérez Jiménez did not recognize the "great danger of allowing communists and ex-communists to control any labor activity."[132] In 1956 the NSC formulated a plan for removing or isolating purported communist labor leaders in Venezuela and presented it to Pérez Jiménez. The dictator's unpredictability was now a matter of continuing concern.[133]

In 1957 Pérez Jiménez attempted to extend his rule by means of a plebiscite, and by midyear the opposition was openly calling for his removal. The fraudulent plebiscite was a catalyst for the formation of the Junta Patriótica; though it was founded by members of URD and the Communist Party, it eventually became a multiparty organization that sought to coordinate opposition to the regime. The junta demanded adherence to the constitution, an end to presidential reelection, and the establishment of a democratic government that would respect civil liberties.[134] Important elements of the military began to distance themselves from Pérez Jiménez. By the late 1950s opportunities for promotion had declined for younger officers, and Pérez Jiménez had become identified with his old Andean counterparts (Gómez, López Contreras, and Medina Angarita). Winfield Burggraaff argues that "the problems of maintaining loyalty in the younger generations of academy graduates, unsolved by Medina Angarita, remained to plague Pérez Jiménez."[135]

THE OUSTER OF PÉREZ JIMÉNEZ

As the events of January 1958 unfolded, the leaders of Venezuela's three main democratic parties were in New York. During a meeting at the New York Athletic Club, they agreed to form a "Great Civic Front" to avoid political strife.[136] Valmo Acevedo, a reporter for the Venezuelan magazine *Bohemia*, wrote: "All present agreed that political cannibalism, sectarianism and intolerance by the parties and their respective leaders were factors that could propel a coup."[137] The parameters of what has since been called the Pacto de Nueva York became apparent. The three parties excluded the Communist Party and agreed to respect each other's interests while trying to develop joint strategies. Moreover, the signers agreed not to call on the military to settle their disputes.

The overthrow of Pérez Jiménez did not take long. The growing influence of the Junta Patriótica convinced many officers that they must act quickly in order to play a role in a new political order. On 1 January 1958 air force pilots were the first to act. They strafed military installations and government buildings in Caracas but failed to oust the dictator. On 10 January the defense minister launched another unsuccessful attempt. Pérez Jiménez tried to appease opponents by replacing his security chief, Pedro Estrada. But on 22 January a general strike called by the Junta Patriótica paralyzed the country. When Pérez Jiménez called out the military to crush the strike, they did not respond. The dictator hurriedly left the country, leaving a suitcase full of money on the airport runway where he boarded the plane that took him into exile in the Dominican Republic. Once in Venezuela, the three democratic parties formalized and broadened the earlier understanding reached in New York; they called their agreement the Pacto de Punto Fijo, using the name of Rafael Caldera's house, where the document was signed. The pact was immediately assailed by various political forces for "deforming the unity aspirations of the Venezuelan masses," undermining the possibility of a consensus candidate, and privileging the political parties and their individual candidates.[138]

As the political tide in Venezuela turned against Pérez Jiménez, economic forecasters in the United States showed a surprising lack of concern regarding the fate of foreign oil in the country. Not one major business publication expressed fear of impending disaster, nationalization, or expropriation. The oil companies were affected neither by the general strike that preceded the ouster of Pérez Jiménez nor by the political turmoil that ensued. In the words of the *Oil and Gas Journal*, "If Venezuela's oil industry even faltered during last week's revolt, it was not perceptible to the eye."[139] Conscious of the need to secure recognition from the United States, the new junta moved to reassure the foreign oil companies that the new regime would "protect investments."[140] According to Ambassador Charles Burrows, the leader of the interim government, Wolfgang Larrazábal, had sought Washington's opinion on legalizing the Communist Party and requested support for a new "secret political investigative bureau" that would focus on communism.[141]

Throughout January and February 1958, industry sources insisted that "conservatives" and not "revolutionaries" dominated the new junta. The *Wall Street Journal* reflected the prevailing business mood: "Venezuela continues to be the brightest spot in the United States foreign investment picture in Latin America. Communism has nothing to do with its recent revolution and although it is now openly active, its role so far seems to be of little importance."[142] Investments by United States oil companies in Venezuela echoed this confidence. In February, a month after Pérez Jiménez had been overthrown, Mobil Oil of Venezuela announced plans to invest US $28 million for the construction of a new refinery, and both Shell and Creole augmented the capacity of their refineries.[143]

The status of United States oil in Venezuela during 1958 and 1959 contrasted sharply with its fate in another Caribbean nation during the same period. Whereas Venezuelan insurgents had left oil installations untouched, Cubans had not. A month after the ouster of Fulgencio Batista, industry sources warned of a campaign by Cuban rebels to destroy oil installations on the island. Already one refinery operated by Esso (a subsidiary of Standard Oil) had reportedly been bombed.[144] The radical program of the Cuban rebels struck a responsive chord in Venezuela, and Caracas newspapers closely followed events on the island.[145] As they had reacted to the Mexican nationalization in 1938, oil interests and the United States government now worried about the impact that the Cuban revolution might have on foreign investments in Latin America.

As they had with AD and Pérez Jiménez before, foreign oil companies came to terms with the new Venezuelan government. Creole was among the first to affirm its faith: H. W. Haight, its president, asserted "that the petroleum industry would continue to contribute to the aggrandizement of the nation and its citizens." As the representative of all United States companies in Venezuela, he informed Larrazábal, "For our part, we wish to assure you that the Venezuelan oil industry will conduct its operations always cognizant of the important role that they play in the country, and will always cooperate fully with the government authorities in charge of the nation's oil wealth."[146] Shortly after the revolt, Creole replaced Haight as president of the company with Arthur Proudfit. Haight had become a political liability; his public criticism of the government's oil policy broke with company practice and earned him the enmity of Venezuela's new rulers, who ordered him out of the country.[147] Proudfit had been president of Creole during the Trienio and had extensive ties with the Venezuelan leaders who assumed power after 1958. Pressure also mounted for the United States to assign a new ambassador to manage relations once Pérez Jiménez was out of the picture. United States interests in Venezuela lobbied President Eisenhower to appoint a new "conscientious and courageous Ambassador," or "we are largely lost before we start."[148]

A month before the provisional junta turned over power to the newly elected president, Rómulo Betancourt, it unilaterally altered the 50/50 arrangement and increased the government's share to 60 percent of oil profits.[149] As startling as this may seem, the decree did not represent a dramatic departure from existing practices. Momentum for a change in the law had been building for quite some time. In a memo to President Eisenhower in 1958, Brigadier General A. J. Goodpaster warned that "strong pressure [was] rising in Venezuela for basic change in oil policy, including revision of 50–50 profit split."[150] Allen Dulles, the director of the CIA, reported that Betancourt favored a formula closer to a 60/40 split rather than the 75/25 advocated by some nationalists.[151] The new 60/40 split appeared acceptable to Washington, since, Dulles wrote, by "application of all revenue and exchange measures Venezuela now receives about 56% of the net income of the oil industry."[152] A report by the United Nations Economic Commission on Latin America in 1960 concurred with this assessment, indicating that the "total taxation paid by many companies . . . had in any case reached or exceeded 50 percent of assessable profits."[153]

BETANCOURT AND THE UNITED STATES

After the ouster of Pérez Jiménez, politics in Venezuela became synonymous with Betancourt. His views became the litmus test for democracy in Venezuela, and debates in the U.S. State Department, Congress, and the popular press centered on his political beliefs.[154] Cold warriors in the United States fiercely attacked Betancourt's record. The State Department, however, had a different view: "Mr. Betancourt's political orientation may be best described as nationalistic, leftist, non-communist, and frequently outspokenly anti-Communist.... When in power he co-operated with the United States.... It is believed that he is basically friendly towards this country."[155] Betancourt's leadership of AD and his tenure as president during the Trienio had established him as an acceptable representative of Venezuelan democracy. Despite his early nationalist and leftist rhetoric, after 1948 Betancourt traveled in the United States and nurtured ties with AFL-CIO leaders, elected officials, the State Department, the press, and academics.[156] His lobbying yielded positive results, and he received letters of support from throughout the United States. Many of these letters never reached Betancourt, since they were intercepted by United States intelligence, which, enmeshed in the cold war, turned them over to Pérez Jiménez's security forces. One such letter, sent by the historian Edwin Lieuwen in 1957, commented on the favorable review he had written of Betancourt's *Política y Petróleo* for the *Hispanic American Historical Review*. Lieuwen stressed that he considered Betancourt's work the "Bible" for understanding contemporary Venezuela.[157]

On the eve of national elections political conditions remained volatile, and the United States worried about the rising tide of nationalism and the outcome of the elections scheduled for December 1958. For his part, Betancourt had already assured the oil companies that future changes in the nation's oil policies would occur only through "careful discussions between the parties."[158] A foreign polling company commissioned by United States and Venezuelan companies predicted that Wolfgang Larrazábal, the interim junta president, would win the presidency by a comfortable margin.[159] Larrazábal's national coalition, which included the URD, independents, and the Communist Party, projected itself as a national unity ticket. Since its rhetoric appeared decidedly more radical than that of the other parties, the United States did not want to see Larrazábal elected.[160]

Guardedly, the United States did what it could to support the election of Betancourt and to a lesser extent Caldera. The adoption of oil import restrictions by the United States loomed as the principal issue that might inflame nationalist sentiment and force even the centrist parties to adopt a more militant stance. As they had done in the past, United States policy makers soft-pedaled the issue and stressed consultation with Venezuelan officials rather than unilateral action. The State Department sent a delegation to Venezuela to discuss the proposed restrictions.[161] The governor-elect of New York, Nelson Rockefeller, vacationing in Venezuela at his private estate, reassured Betancourt and other political leaders.[162] Secretary of State John Foster Dulles repeatedly stressed that the United States no longer saw the need to adopt restrictive oil measures.[163] Despite these assurances, pressure mounted in the United States for a more restrictive oil policy. However, in order not to provoke hostility toward it and possibly undermine the campaigns of Betancourt and Caldera, the United States withheld until after the election of 7 December public disclosure of a tentative cabinet recommendation that the "voluntary oil imports program" be revised. A State Department memo explained that disclosing the recommendation would give the Communists "an almost insuperable political advantage" and "would seriously undermine the campaigns of Admiral Larrazábal's two opponents for the presidency," either of whom was considered acceptable.[164] In the end Betancourt easily defeated Larrazábal in the presidential contest.

In March, a month after Betancourt assumed office, President Eisenhower's administration, citing national security concerns, announced the imposition of mandatory controls on oil imports, potentially reducing earning for the Venezuelan state. Hoping to mute Venezuelan reaction, Eisenhower sent a personal communiqué to Betancourt citing joint interest in maintaining "established trade patterns" without disruptions.[165] At the urging of the State Department, which sought to avoid a "shift toward nationalistic oil policies that could adversely affect U.S. oil interests," Washington moved in December to grant Venezuela special status and limit disruptions in sales.[166] Just as importantly, they sought to remove an issue that might radicalize the political environment in Venezuela and force Betancourt into a difficult position.

Despite Eisenhower's assurances, Venezuelan political leaders remained concerned about the threat of restrictions from the United States, and about the inroads that Middle East oil was making in European markets.[167] Faced with these new conditions and the decline in the price of oil provoked by the unilateral actions of the foreign oil companies, policy makers in Venezuela recognized the need for concerted action by oil producers and exporters. Hoping to address these issues, in the spring of 1959 Pérez Alfonzo, the Venezuelan minister of hydrocarbons, traveled to Cairo to attend a meeting

of Arab oil exporters establishing the basis for future joint cooperation between Venezuela and Middle East oil producers. The second meeting of
this group, held in Baghdad in September 1960, led to the founding of the
Organization of Petroleum Exporting Countries (OPEC) of which Venezuela was an original member. In the words of Pérez Alfonzo, "the governments of the consuming countries never believed that Arabs, Iranians and
Venezuelans could agree on anything. All their computers were unable to
calculate this equation."[168]

LA GRAN VENEZUELA AND THE NATIONALIZATION
OF THE INDUSTRY

During the 1970s, while neighboring countries experienced prolonged and
debilitating guerrilla conflicts and a legacy of brutal military dictatorships,
the Venezuelan economic model appeared to produce sustained political
peace and economic prosperity.[169] During the period known as La Gran
Venezuela, coinciding with the Arab oil embargo, the country experienced
a stunning influx of petrodollars.[170] Awash in oil profits, the government
earmarked funds for impressive mega-projects, new economic ventures, and
the expansion of existing patronage networks. Cases of corruption also increased exponentially. In 1976 the government of Carlos Andrés Pérez of
AD (1974–79) formally nationalized the oil industry, compensating United
States and European interests and creating a new national corporation,
Petróleos de Venezuela (PDVSA). The legislative process leading to nationalization, which allowed foreign capital to participate in the nationalized
industry, remained mired in controversy. As Terry Lynn Karl points out, the
adoption of "perhaps the single most important law in Venezuela's recent
history" bitterly divided congress, with most parties, including those on the
left, voting against the bill.[171] Despite the political rancor the event was
marked on 1 January 1976 by a ceremony at the Zumaque no. 1 well in Mene
Grande that helped launch the industry. In a symbolic act, Pérez raised
the Venezuelan flag over the well to signal the creation of the nationalized
petroleum industry.

From its inception PDVSA functioned largely as a holding company, preserving the operating structure and more importantly the corporate culture
of the previous foreign companies; Creole became Lagoven, Shell became
Maraven, and Mene Grande became Meneven.[172] Despite nationalization,

the former United States and British oil companies continued to supply foreign personnel, primarily in technical and advisory posts. With production oscillating between two and a half and three million barrels a day, after nationalization the United States remained the largest recipient of Venezuelan oil. PDVSA executives and managers took responsibility for implementing oil policy and provided the government with the resources needed to pursue policy initiatives. In return, they were left to chart the course of the corporation and attempted to insulate themselves from rancorous public debates by framing oil industry policy as the exclusive preserve of an élite group of qualified oil experts. After the nationalization of the industry, political parties and leading intellectuals, including those on the left, largely lost interest in oil matters.[173] For their part, the directors of the enterprise increasingly viewed politicians and the populace at large as a potentially disruptive force. Furthermore, in keeping with modernizing discourse that framed earlier interactions with the foreign firms, PDVSA executives promoted themselves as a model of efficiency and success in contrast to a corrupt and inefficient government bureaucracy.

RISING SOCIAL DISCONTENT

During the last half of the 1980s the purported Venezuelan "miracle" began to unravel. As the price of oil plummeted on international markets the government devalued the currency. Social inequality, a persistent and neglected feature of the society, increased dramatically, becoming visible in the remarkable growth of the informal economy and the poor neighborhoods that ring most urban centers. Charges of corruption, mismanagement, and favoritism, previously muted by oil profits and the political consensus forged in the 1960s, surfaced with increased frequency. Public faith in the Venezuelan political system, the leading political parties, and the oil conglomerates began to diminish. But nothing prepared Venezuelans for the events of February 1989, when the government of Carlos Andrés Pérez, in its second term (1989–92), sought to implement a series of foreign-inspired austerity measures known as the *paquetazo* that included increases in the price of gasoline and the elimination of subsidies for basic foodstuffs. In protest, thousands of Venezuela's poor descended from the hills that surround Caracas, and the government, fearing a loss of control, unleashed the military to repress them. Beyond the hundreds who perished in the

Caracazo, the main victim was the Venezuelan political process and the image of the nation as a democratic model. The headlines in various publications in the United States expressed dismay that South America's "most stable democracy" had exploded.[174] Demonstrations became generalized, and one student leader recalled that during Pérez's presidency the country experienced thousands of street protests.[175]

In February 1992, as popular discontent mounted, disgruntled military officers led by a young Hugo Chávez Frías staged an unsuccessful coup. Although the officers who participated were imprisoned, their action drew national and international attention to the failures of the Venezuelan political system. In 1994 a series of banking and insurance company failures, caused in part by corruption, mismanagement, and financial deregulation urged by neoliberals, worsened the plight of thousands of Venezuelans. Street protests by retirees who had deposited their life savings in these banks became a daily occurrence. Against the backdrop of crisis and a weakening national government, PDVSA sought even greater autonomy. Nowhere was this made clearer than in the naming of Luis Giusti as president of PDVSA, an appointment that President Rafael Caldera (1994–99) had twice opposed. Arguing that it would increase efficiency and develop a single corporate culture, Giusti moved to integrate PDVSA's operating affiliates, and Lagoven, Maraven, Meneven, and several other companies were absorbed by the oil conglomerate.

PDVSA's autonomy increasingly became evident during Caldera's administration, when the oil company promoted a series of joint ventures with foreign oil companies that culminated in what became known as the *apertura petrolera* (oil opening). This policy permitted the participation of numerous foreign companies, which as PDVSA partners would be able to bid on fields not fully explored or other "mature" oilfields that had been previously abandoned. Another component of the apertura involved the opening of new concessions along the Orinoco basin, an area with tremendous heavy crude deposits. According to one leading newspaper in Caracas, the bidding by 131 companies on these fields, a lavish production hosted at the most luxurious hotels in Caracas and widely reported in the press, once again transformed Caracas into the "petroleum capital of the world."[176] Venezuela appeared destined to repeat the heydays of the earlier oil boom.

The apertura generated increased expectations of a new petroleum boom, and rents for houses in formerly forsaken oil communities in eastern Venezuela and elsewhere skyrocketed. As hotels in Caracas, Maracaibo, and Maturín filled with petroleros, the foreign presence again became palpable in Venezuela. Bidding for these new concessions filled the PDVSA coffers with millions of dollars for which the conglomerate never provided a full accounting. For some observers this policy was part of a strategy aimed at the eventual privatization of the enterprise, and a special eight-page advertising section in the Latin American edition of *Time* floated this idea as a trial balloon. The supplement concluded: "The hard work in the future lies in convincing a nationalistic public to accept what is almost inevitable—in the future PDVSA will be privatized."[177] In their haste and perhaps arrogance, PDVSA officials had failed to consider the valuable lessons learned by the foreign multinationals that operated in Venezuela in previous decades. From their own bitter experience, after clashing with labor, business, and even the government, these foreign firms had recognized the need to engage broad sectors of the Venezuelan populace and gain their support before pursuing new initiatives. Though it functioned as a "Venezuelan" enterprise, PDVSA's relative autonomy had estranged it from large elements of the Venezuelan population and fostered antipathy toward the values that it embodied.

Some oil labor unions and members of the middle and upper classes continued to view the oil company as a necessary counterweight to the state, a brake on populist demands, and a defender of their interests and way of life. The PDVSA president and its board of directors increasingly represented a political power parallel to the elected president and the legislature. Other groups, however, worried that PDVSA's contributions to the national treasury had dwindled and complained that resources were being absorbed by the company's growing bureaucracy and its new international ventures. Some also feared that many PDVSA officials considered themselves part of a global managerial petroleum network whose decisions reflected international rather than Venezuelan interests and pointed out that the state had little control over the conglomerate's finances.

For a great many Venezuelans PDVSA embodied much of what had gone wrong with the nation—a legacy of squandered wealth and a managerial class and privileged labor élite whose experiences stood in sharp contrast to the lives of ordinary people. As the number of poor continued to grow it became difficult to rationalize the special privileges afforded to oil industry employees. The immense revenues that PDVSA had generated in the almost twenty-five years since nationalization were a constant reminder of the prosperous way of life that had eluded most Venezuelans. In an article entitled "El parasitismo petrolero," Uslar Pietri argued that between 1976 and 1995 the country had generated and largely squandered billions from oil sales and argued that this should be the main topic of national debate.[178] In light of this stark economic reality, suggestions that the oil industry continued to embody the country's hope for development rang hollow among the poor who made up the backbone of the population and the lower middle class that had seen its situation deteriorate in the past two decades.

Elections in 1998 revealed the extent to which the political landscape in Venezuela had changed. Distrust of the traditional parties had increased to such a degree that independent candidates, and not those nominated by the traditional dominant parties, drew the most interest. At the beginning of the year it appeared that the former Miss Universe and mayor of Chacao, Irene Saez, had a commanding lead. Chávez, the former lieutenant colonel who had led the coup of 1992, remained behind in the early polls. Out of touch with the popular sentiment, AD nominated Luis Álfaro Ucero, a long-time party boss. Saez's association with the former president Luis Herrera Campins (COPEI, 1979–84) and her inability to articulate a comprehensive program lost her support among the population. With a decidedly anti-party and anti-establishment discourse, Chávez's candidacy tapped into the growing popular discontent. As the campaign intensified, the traditional parties rallied behind a new unity candidate, Enrique Salas Rohmer, the former governor of the state of Carabobo. In the end, however, their efforts proved unsuccessful and Chávez won a resounding victory.

When Chávez's government assumed office in 1999, oil prices hovered at less than $10 a barrel. The government immediately took the initiative, attempting to stabilize world prices, forging a working consensus within OPEC while at the same time enhancing the role of the Ministry of Mines in PDVSA, placing its personnel in management positions. These policies (especially the latter) brought the government into immediate conflict with the PDVSA apparatus. The passage of a new national constitution in 1999 and special laws in November 2001 that applied largely to new oil contracts placed the administration on a collision course with the PDVSA.

Not surprisingly, those employed in oil quickly organized to defend their interests. Their slogans proved quite telling, reflecting traditional values nurtured by the oil industry since its inception. Company employees christened the courtyard in front of the PDVSA building the "Plaza of the Meritocracy" and others formed a group called Gente de Petróleo (People of Oil). In protest marches, the slogan "PDVSA es Venezuela" was used to buttress the perception of an efficient and able managerial class being subverted by a populist and inefficient political class—PDVSA representing modernity and prosperity, the government representing inefficiency. This slogan and its embedded message did not resonate broadly among the population. After repeated crises in the 1980s and 1990s, it had became obvious that Venezuela had changed and that the political and social model associated with the traditional oil economy was unsustainable. The Venezuelan population had expanded dramatically since the 1960s, when important segments of the economy appeared to benefit from the nation's oil revenues. The suggestion that the oil economy could raise a large share of the population into the middle class lost credibility among the disenfranchised. Instead, the widespread perception was that oil only ensured the success of a small, privileged part of society directly associated with the enterprise or its affiliates.

Many Venezuelans applauded Chávez's efforts to rein in the oil conglomerate and use its revenues to improve their declining standard of living. The government's replacement of the PDVSA board of directors in the spring of 2002 contributed to efforts to oust Chávez in the failed coup of April 2002. The participation of PDVSA managers and employees in the subsequent work stoppage of December 2002 and January 2003 eventually resulted in the dismissal of thousands of strikers and a loss of benefits. In the past, when the oil workers had struck against the foreign multinationals their efforts had been interpreted as embodying a nationalist sentiment for justice and fairness. Under the present conditions, the PDVSA work stoppage was seen as an effort to preserve special privileges at a time when the government was promising to use oil revenue to aid broad segments of the population. In the aftermath of these events the government gained the initiative and began a complete overhaul of PDVSA, establishing the enterprise as a cornerstone of its economic and social policy. Employing a strategy pursued earlier by the foreign oil companies, the government portrayed PDVSA as the benefactor of the entire nation, and the company dedicated revenues to fund education initiatives, medical services, cultural programs, and a host of so-called missions aimed at the poor. Oil has also become a cornerstone of Venezuelan foreign policy, sold to Caribbean countries under special terms of payment, offered to South American nations in repayment of debts, and provided as heating oil to low-income neighborhoods in the United States.

Under Chávez, PDVSA has also renegotiated the agreements signed during the Apertura Petrolera that granted the state royalties based on the oil law of 1943 transforming these contracts into joint ventures with the state oil company. Heavy crude deposits along the Orinoco River basin presented the government with a similar set of challenges. They were also negotiated by previous governments at very low return to the country and were purposely not considered part of Venezuela's oil deposits. PDVSA has subsequently acquired controlling interest of these heavy crude deposits, bringing to an end the legacy of the "Apertura Petrolera."[179] The inclusion of these heavy crude deposits potentially gives Venezuela the largest crude reserves in the world. High oil prices and new refining methods now permit their extraction, refining, and sale, though costs are higher. PDVSA has also entered into long-term agreements with India and China, no longer depending exclusively on the United States as a market.

Relations between the large foreign oil companies and the Venezuelan government after 1935 reflect a gradual process of change, framed by the concerns of middle-class reformers to gain power and the convergence of corporate geopolitical interests driven first by fears of nationalism and subsequently by the exigencies of the cold war. As political conditions changed in Venezuela, from dictatorship to political openness to democratic governments, the oil companies adapted. They positioned themselves to influence the outcomes, revising their labor and public relations policies and establishing links with labor and middle-class reformers to ensure that they could continue extracting Venezuela's oil. The presence of a fiercely anticommunist reformist leadership in AD, with strong links to the labor movement, assuaged government and corporate concerns in the United States over potential radical social change. The Venezuelan experience demonstrates the common ground of liberal reformist parties and United States policy during the height of the cold war. After their election in 1958, AD party leaders proceeded cautiously with regard to oil policy, seeking to increase revenues but refraining from fundamentally restructuring the relationship that allowed foreign companies to operate freely in the country. This is the fundamental strategic relation that the foreign companies sought to preserve and that the reformers chose not to alter.

Maintaining the oil export economy pushed Venezuela into the political orbit of the United States, forcing political leaders to be attentive to Washington's concerns in matters ranging from foreign policy to economics. With markets firmly in the United States, Venezuelan leaders, apart from a few exceptions, had little reason to be concerned about their Latin American neighbors or about the nations of the so-called Third World. Operating in the United States orbit had other important social and cultural consequences, privileging cultural, social, economic, and even academic exchanges with the United States. The presence of the United States in Venezuela, in all its multiple expressions, became naturalized, the expected outcome of an oil export economy in which the United States was the principal consumer.

Cracks in the arrangements forged by political forces after the events of 1958 became evident throughout the 1980s. Despite having experienced a series of dramatic oil booms, producing tremendous wealth for the nation, serious socioeconomic problems persisted. The expectation of continued and sustained growth generated by the oil economy became a political liability. Public cases of corruption, mismanagement, and political cronyism eroded faith in the political process. The political and class alliances forged during the earlier period could no longer be sustained. As political forces proved incapable or unwilling to address these problems, discontent increased, setting the stage for the election of Hugo Chávez. The election of Chávez's government and the policies it has pursued since 1999 brings to a close a political chapter in Venezuelan history that began, in part, with the dramatic explosion of the Barroso no. 2 well in 1922.

An Enduring Legacy

The oil industry dramatically transformed the Venezuelan economy and social landscape, generating a clash of values and interests that would persist throughout the twentieth century and into the twenty-first. The centrality of oil to the Venezuelan economy inspired a host of debates concerning its role in society. In 1936 one of Venezuela's most revered writers, Arturo Uslar Pietri, optimistically suggested that oil's wealth could be "sowed" to diversify and expand the economy.[1] By 1976, after repeated petrobooms which generated billions of dollars and with inequality still a persistent factor, the former minister of mines Juan Pablo Pérez Alfonzo contended that the country was hopelessly sinking in the "excrement of the devil."[2] The chasm between the idea of "sowing oil riches" and the likening of petroleum to diabolical excrement speaks to the growing disillusionment with oil and the industry as a source of development and its impact on Venezuelan culture and values. By the 1990s even Uslar Pietri viewed dependence on oil as a major calamity not only affecting the economy but also serving irrationally as a symbol of nationality.[3] That oil and nationality could be conflated reflected the extent to which the industry not only dominated the economy but also penetrated the national consciousness since its formation in the 1920s.

The association between oil and nationality is directly linked to the role attributed to the industry in certain quarters. Since its inception, foreign and Venezuelan advocates of the oil industry invariably viewed the enterprise within the context of modernization and its accompanying economic and cultural discourse. This argument accepted, in fact promoted, the notion of Venezuela as an economically poor and culturally backward nation before the discovery of oil. The intersection between economic policy, class aspirations, and a pervasive corporate culture helps to explain the process of change that took place in Venezuela. To only address economic factors associated with this extractive industry was to underestimate the power of oil to influence society, politics, and culture. Beyond monopolizing the economy, oil shaped social values and class aspirations, cemented political alliances, and redefined concepts of citizenship for important segments of the population.

The period after the discovery of oil in the 1920s is depicted as an epic encounter between the supposedly backward forces of tradition and those of modernity struggling to remake the heart and soul of the nation. The Venezuela that existed before oil is stereotypically portrayed as the dominion of unsophisticated dictators, where backward economic practices prevailed and an uneducated population languished, beset by tropical maladies and gripped by superstition. The negative portrayals of the country by both foreigners and Venezuelan élites underscored the racial attitudes underlying the way these groups viewed the Venezuelan population. Undoubtedly, in the 1920s Venezuela lacked the infrastructure, trained personnel, or state apparatus to confront the monumental challenges generated by the industry. However, it is nearly certain that at the beginning of the twentieth century any country in the region would have been similarly overwhelmed by these dramatic occurrences. The argument concerning modernity and tradition masks other objectives—principally the need to legitimate and sanction the operation of the foreign oil companies in Venezuela. In this epic battle the foreign oil companies, as the agents of change, found important allies in the middle classes, their parties, and new élites that also sought to transform the nation in the hope of expanding their social standing and political power. This process was not static; it was not simply the matter of an all-powerful industry imposing its will on the nation. Conditions compelled the foreign oil companies, the state, and various Venezuelan social classes to negotiate the nature of their relationship.

After the death of Gómez, with the rise of new social forces and a changing political landscape, what initially began as an effort to socialize a work force expanded in scope to include a national project aimed at fusing company interests with those of the Venezuelan nation. Controlled by foreign capital and aligned with United States interests, the oil companies nonetheless attempted to portray themselves as allies of the Venezuelan nation. This paternalistic image sought to conflate, if not obscure, potentially conflictive interests including levels of oil production, royalty agreements, and the process of refining in the country. The ability to mask unequal power relations through a strategy of collaboration speaks to the ability of the largest oil companies, Creole and Shell, to astutely adapt to their environment, nurture friendly relations with important political allies, and effectively influence the process of reform before conditions adversely altered their business model. The impact of the foreign oil industry on the economy, coupled with its ability to appropriate a Venezuelan persona, had far-reaching consequences. It skewed traditional class alliances, elevating the role of a relatively small middle class and a labor aristocracy employed by the industry. At the national level company policy and class interests coalesced to form an important bulwark in support of the industry and the expectations that it generated. Moreover, the wealth produced by the industry financed the growth of the state, private development and commerce, and the urban middle class. These interests became stakeholders in the oil export model, perceiving the benefits they received from the industry as an unspoken birthright.

TRACING THE LEGACY

Judging from its meager beginnings, it would have been difficult to predict the lasting impact of the oil industry on Venezuelan society. The first major discoveries, the tar deposits of Guanoco in the east and oil fields of Mene Grande in the west, tantalized but did not fulfill expectations. In 1922, however, the discovery of oil at La Rosa confirmed the country's potential and launched Venezuela into the modern oil age. These boom years proved chaotic and conflictive. Thousands of immigrants from throughout Venezuela flocked to the newly discovered oilfields, overrunning the small rural settlements in the countryside. To accommodate this rapid growth, communities such as Lagunillas and Tía Juana in the state of Zulia expanded almost overnight.

Immigration to the oilfields was not haphazard; most areas that sent labor to the sites had previously interacted with the oil-producing states. The demand for labor produced distinct patterns of migration: an internal *ruta petrolera* took shape, cementing links between sending states such as Lara, Falcón, Trujillo, Sucre, and Nueva Esparta and oil-producing ones such as Anzoátegui, Monagas, and Zulia. The immigrants represented a wide array of occupations and social classes, not just solely the often mentioned illiterate campesino. The repeated description of workers as poor and unsophisticated by some writers and company officials highlighted the purported modernizing role that the oil companies played in Venezuelan society.

Oil production displaced people from their land and initiated an environmental catastrophe, the cost of which has never been fully measured. No government has completely addressed the despoliation of Lake Maracaibo, the incidence of diseases in oil-producing areas, or the long-term damage of oil spills on flora and fauna. As it became an important source of employment, the industry hastened the demise of an already declining agricultural sector throughout Venezuela and contributed to the rise of a prominent merchant élite and a nascent working class.

The development of the oil industry also precipitated important political changes, centralizing authority in the national government, accelerating the political integration of Venezuela, and limiting the power of traditional regional élites. The oil industry severely constrained the ability of traditional regional élites, especially in oil-producing states such as Zulia, to act independently. Oil revenues became a powerful force, permeating politics at all levels and mitigating political differences among regional élites that might have arisen from the process of centralization.

By framing its mission within the context of modernization and development, the oil industry skillfully defused potential opposition. The belief that Venezuela entered a new modern era with the rise of the oil industry was an article of faith for much of the population. The reality proved much more complex. The oil industry and its new social order never completely replaced traditional Venezuelan ways of life. Even at its height, the modern oil industry only employed a small fraction of the population. As the experience of Lagunillas underscores, in the shadow of the new modern oil wells on Lake Maracaibo the great majority of the population still lived as it had for generations. Where possible residents continued to live in homes over the water or on the shore and eked out an existence from the land or the lake. In other cases a floating population gathered at the new oil camps such as Caripito, where people hoped to derive some benefit from living in proximity to this resource. The presence of a relatively impoverished population was a constant reminder that there were two Venezuelas, one benefiting directly from oil and the other surviving largely in the shadow of the industry.

RACE, GENDER, LABOR, AND OIL

The oil industry produced the first major wave of immigration to Venezuela in the twentieth century. For years the national government had attempted to draw white immigrants, mainly Europeans, with meager results. With the oil boom a multiracial labor force, of which some members had experience in the industry and others did not, descended on Venezuela. The United States and European expatriates who arrived assumed mostly skilled or professional jobs in the industry, with other immigrants in service and support positions. The recruitment of an international labor force including significant numbers of black West Indians and Chinese fueled local animosities and laid bare the deeply ingrained racism of Venezuelan society. The myth of Venezuela as a racial democracy, a society likened to café con leche, clashed with a virulent reaction that Afro–West Indians and Chinese confronted upon their arrival in the country. The fear that black immigrants might join forces with Venezuela's own Afro-descended population and alter the country's racial dynamics frightened some, revealing the existence of a distinct socioracial hierarchy in the country.

Labor disputes—fueled by discrimination, a racially stratified wage system, an authoritarian dictatorship, the privileges afforded to foreigners, and the difficult conditions of life—became commonplace. By establishing segregated living arrangements and a racially stratified wage structure, the oil industry reinforced rather than lessened existing racial practices. The dearth of people of color from the United States among the expatriate community further reinforced existing racial attitudes. Within this hierarchy white senior staff from the United States were at the apex, followed usually by lighter-skinned Venezuelan upper- and middle-class professionals, and lastly the larger body of mixed-race laborers. In the oil camps as in society, race was not a fixed criterion defined solely by skin color but a complex socially constructed category informed by family background, education, status, phenotype, and other factors. Exceptions undoubtedly existed; yet racial identity was an important variable in defining a person's position in the oil camps. Through its daily practices and social policies the oil industry confirmed the existing racial hierarchy of Venezuelan society.

The presence of a foreign-controlled industry and a multinational and multiracial labor force compelled Venezuelan governments, starting with Juan Vicente Gómez, to break from their previous isolation and take an active role in international matters. Disputes with Mexico, fueled by political animosities and economic competition as oil producers, forced Gómez's government to fashion how Venezuela was depicted in the United States and throughout Latin America. As a powerful international commodity of strategic importance, oil compelled Venezuela to assume a proactive role in international matters, seeking to defend its position as a major exporter. Diplomatic missions to the United States, Canada, Mexico, and subsequently other oil-producing countries in the Middle East demonstrate the power of oil to recast Venezuela's role in international matters.

OIL CAMPS: SOCIAL LABORATORIES

With the infrastructure of production areas well developed and the majority of those employed in the oil industry living in settled camps, the industry entered a different phase. The residential oil camps stimulated new levels of social interaction between people from diverse regions and of different social status. Working in a national industry and living in residential enclaves composed of people from throughout the country diffused regional identities, creating new opportunities for social and political interaction. The family became a cornerstone of the oil company's broader socialization programs, and particular attention was paid to the role of women as agents of change in creating a new lifestyle. The companies' influence over camp life was pervasive. Even the Catholic Church, whose presence in the camps was typically subsidized by Shell or Creole, feared, as Monsignor Lizardi highlighted, being seen as an appendage of the oil companies.

Broadly speaking, the oil camps constituted a social laboratory, where companies such as Shell and Creole attempted to fashion a model worker, citizen, and by extension family. Thus oil not only remade the Venezuelan economy but also sought to remake the Venezuelans involved in the enterprise. The industry attempted to strip away purported negative characteristics and introduce new patterns of behavior considered more favorable to the operation of the industry. At one level this included introducing western concepts of the work ethic, time management, reconfigured of public and private space, consumer patterns, and leisure. A lifestyle that now included access to schools, social clubs, planned recreation, medical services, subsidized food, and a network of obligations within the camps was a strong incentive in the process of socialization. These new patterns of behavior were not limited to work but designed to influence social practices at home and within society at large. At another level the industry promoted a set of political values deemed important to its operations, including the overarching economic model that permitted foreign companies to operate in Venezuela.

The industry provided a host of services and benefits to its professionals and labor force that remained unattainable to the majority of the population. These benefits were the direct result of early worker militancy and efforts by the large companies to co-opt labor demands before they threatened the companies' prerogatives. Despite the early labor and community disputes evident during the boom period, by the late 1940s camp life had largely become normalized. The industry held out the promise of a middle-class lifestyle, and many of those who lived in these settlements were satisfied with the serenity and cohesion of camp life, in stark contrast to the allegedly disorganized state of Venezuelan society. Those employed in the industry managed to extract significant concessions from it, in the form of Venezolanization, higher wages, and benefits. But precisely because of these arrangements, they increasingly acquired a vested interest in maintaining the system. Thus they failed to challenge the export model that sustained the industry and, by extension, secured their newfound status. The success of the oil sector became a barometer against which the emerging middle class and a relatively well compensated labor force could measure their well-being.

By the 1950s the oil companies' efforts produced palpable results. The skilled and relatively stable workforce exhibited the social conduct and individual responsibility that the foreign companies encouraged. Literacy, time management, and a standardized work ethic were thoroughly incorporated by the workforce and ceased being matters of corporate concern. Both the quality and quantity of work produced by Venezuelans "equaled the standard set by expatriates formerly assigned to such work."[4] The reproduction of corporate values and the pressure for conformity within the labor force were due to the company's selective hiring policies. The companies relied on existing family and personal networks to acquire workers; seldom was anyone hired who lacked some previous contact with the industry. The children of workers who subsequently sought employment in the industry had been raised in the camps and educated in company schools, ensuring the transmission of values. The desire for upward mobility and access to the lifestyle associated with the industry exerted pressure on employees and their families to conform. By the late 1940s and early 1950s the majority of Creole and Shell workers were Venezuelans, and significant numbers occupied positions in the company's professional and administrative hierarchy. Enjoying the highest salaries and benefits of the Venezuelan labor force, these sectors formed strong bonds of solidarity, an esprit de corps that cut across traditional class and racial boundaries.

THE UNITED STATES PRESENCE

The discovery of new Venezuelan oilfields in the 1920s was a magnet, attracting a host of expatriates from the United States with experience in the industry. At first the foreign labor force included an assortment of roughnecks, tool pushers, and drillers, as well as professionals. As the industry settled, and after several economic contractions, the character of the foreign population gradually changed. Efforts to diminish tensions with the local population and remake the image of the companies also influenced decisions about the nature of the expatriate labor force. Gradually a professional and skilled expatriate community began to displace the early foreign oil workers. Unlike previous foreign populations, for instance the Germans, who left no lasting presence on the local cultural and social landscape, the United States left an indelible impression on Venezuelan society.

Depictions of the United States expatriate population in Venezuela range from the classic ignominious "ugly American" to the benevolent foreigner who made a concerted effort to adapt to the local customs. Though both stereotypes could be found among the foreign population, neither fully represents the array of the United States population in Venezuela. As representatives of the foreign oil companies, and by extension of United States society, most foreigners enjoyed a privileged status. Their position was related to the modernizing role that the industry was said to play in society and to their role as purveyors of knowledge and western culture and values. For most members of the expatriate community this status was taken for granted, seldom questioned or challenged.

Most United States expatriates employed by the industry lived in separate and largely protected communities, both rural and urban, where they attempted to recreate the contours of United States culture and society. The decision of the major oil companies to move from a single to a married labor force by the late 1930s had important ramifications for both gender relations and the preservation of United States culture and norms. The presence of women and entire families changed the gender and social dynamics of the expatriate community, recentering the nuclear family and incorporating women into labor dynamics. The ability of expatriate women to organize and structure the life of the residential camps provided a sense of continuity with a United States lifestyle. Women became primarily responsible for recreating the liturgical and political calendars of the United States. Framed by their isolation in Venezuela, these types of activities assumed a special significance and were usually commemorated with an exuberance typically absent in the United States. The ability of women to adapt to local conditions and assume a public role in and out of the camps became an important asset to the expatriate males in the industry trying to ascend the corporate ladder.

An omnipresent oil industry controlled by the United States and a sizable foreign workforce became the stimulus for the dissemination of foreign practices and habits. In line with these relations of power, everyday activities including use of the English language, culinary practices, dress, and sports became part of the normative expectations required to advance in the oil industry and Venezuelan society. Many of those who worked in the industry, especially in the professional sectors, incorporated these new customs, augmenting their cultural repertoire. The ability to straddle the Venezuelan and United States realities and maneuver in each became a valuable asset for middle managers in the industry. On a personal level, Venezuelan staff employees forged long-lasting bonds of friendship with foreigners. Though the company hierarchy gradually included a greater number of Venezuelans in administrative and professional posts, the values and ideals of the United States continued to permeate corporate culture. Not that Venezuelans employed in the industry became "Americanized": rather, certain foreign social practices and values became assimilated and over time considered part of the Venezuelan class attitudes and expectations. At the policy level, foreign control of the industry accentuated the importance of nurturing good relations with the United States. The need to function within the "United States orbit" became an unquestioned outcome of the oil economy. Inversely, the strategic alliance with the United States meant that Venezuela, with few exceptions, had little if any incentive to pursue relations with its Latin American neighbors or the nations of the so-called Third World.

THE INDUSTRY, CIVIL SOCIETY, AND THE STATE

Venezuelan employees of the oil companies, both middle and laboring classes, developed an alternative set of allegiances to the industry that the nation-state found difficult to supplant. Their loyalties did not represent an apparent contradiction with the state or challenge their sense of patriotism, since the companies repeatedly portrayed themselves as partners with the Venezuelan nation, sharing the laudable goal of sowing oil. The skilful manner in which the oil companies projected themselves as allies in the development of the nation and the tacit acceptance of their premise by middle-class political parties mitigated the nationalism seen elsewhere in Latin America. In the latter years, it isolated the left, in particular the communists, whom the companies repeatedly portrayed as a disruptive force.

The presence of the industry was pervasive and could be felt in every aspect of civil society, including in major cities such as Caracas and Maracaibo, which developed clearly defined "petroleum districts." By the end of the Second World War, having perfected their internal public relations apparatus, the companies employed a broad arsenal of institutions, cultural foundations, journals, and publications to deliver their message. These publications, especially *El Farol* and the *Revista Shell*, not only expressed company policy but also went to great lengths to promote a vision of Venezuelan culture that incorporated the views of the nation's leading authors and cultural figures. The role of these prominent Venezuelan intellectuals in civil society and their participation with the industry's public relations endeavors reinforced the image of the foreign companies as national Venezuelan enterprises.

Creole and Shell quickly recognized the power of the media, launching their own radio programs and subsequently television shows. Their programming presence at the inception of the Venezuelan television industry in the early 1950s further validated them as an integral part of local society.

Several United States agencies also provided news feeds to the nascent Venezuelan media. Through these various avenues the oil companies presented a positive image of their contributions to the nation's development. In the process they co-opted the national discourse on sowing oil, and portrayed themselves as the principal means by which Venezuela could achieve this goal.

Creole's identification with Venezuela was strategic; for the company, the nation-state proved the most stable and effective structure through which to organize oil policy. Creole and other companies never intended to supplant the nation-state, despite their vast infrastructure. Instead, faced with little or no infrastructure and a relatively weak state, they simply filled an important void that existed during the first half of the twentieth century. The oil companies fully recognized the advantages of stable relations with a state controlled by middle-class reformists or nationalist governments. The nation-state, after all, remained the best way to preserve the "predictable, social, political and legal order" that the companies needed in order to operate.[5]

As the Venezuelan state expanded and was able to provide basic services, the companies curtailed their activities in these areas. The cost of maintaining their vast residential and support infrastructure also influenced the companies' decision. Where feasible, by the mid- to late 1950s the oil camps were gradually integrated into local communities. Likewise, the companies ended their support for programs aimed at helping the local community, expecting that the government would assume responsibility for services ranging from electricity and water to health services. At another level, after the 1960s the companies expected that United States policy initiatives toward Latin America would allow them to focus their efforts on production. When asked by Venezuelan officials about implementing social programs, one company executive indicated: "That is not our concern; it is a problem for the Alliance for Progress."[6] Despite relinquishing many of these functions, the foreign oil companies' prominence was never threatened. They continued to derive loyalty from employees and others who benefited from their role as the leading force of the Venezuelan economy. The popular expression "Mama Creole," used to describe the Standard Oil subsidiary, typified the quasi-parental role of the all-encompassing company that provided salaries, benefits, and a middle-class lifestyle.

The mutual interests of the foreign companies and the segments of Venezuelan society that had benefited from oil revenues became apparent in the political arena. Early governments extracted concessions from the oil companies but never altered the legal framework under which the foreign enterprises functioned. After Mexico's nationalization, the companies granted concessions in order to avoid fundamental changes, adeptly maneuvering between military and democratic regimes. Through concerted efforts, important concessions were obtained, including the petroleum legislation of 1943, the oil workers' contract of 1946, the process of Venezolanization, and, despite its shortcomings, the 50/50 profit-sharing arrangement. After 1958 a system of "pacted democracy," a power-sharing agreement between the largest parties, helped establish the institutional arrangements that enabled political stability. In the midst of the cold war, the United States government's embrace of the democratic left typified by AD reflected the belief that middle-class "reformists" would help to undermine radical forces. Venezuela became an important model for United States policy in the region, and the State Department described Rómulo Betancourt as being "in the vanguard of the Latin American forces of democratic, evolutionary economic and social reform."[7]

Throughout the 1960s and 1970s continued revenues allowed the state to expand its political apparatus, increasing the size of the bureaucracy. This expansion helped fuel the growth of the middle classes and provided benefits to other sectors. But these resources were not distributed equally throughout the population. Company and government officials nonetheless continued to stress the critical alliance between the oil industry and development. At a meeting of the board of directors of the Venezuelan Journalist Association in 1967, the Shell executive José Giacopini Zárraga continued to promote the well-worn axiom that before oil, Venezuela had been underdeveloped. This assertion appeared hollow in the wake of successive crises, in which decades of continuous oil production had failed to generate sustained growth or significantly diminish levels of inequality. In contrast to previous decades, challenges to the conventional wisdom of oil and development surfaced in multiple arenas. At the same board of directors meeting, Professor Mejia Alarcón publicly criticized the Shell official: "Dr. Giacopini Záraga ... literally said: 50 years ago, Venezuela was an underdeveloped country. Dr. Giacopini Zárraga, 50 years later, it is still an underdeveloped country."[8]

The petroboom of the early 1970s, which generated a new round of expectations, did little to alter the everyday lives of most Venezuelans. Even the much-heralded nationalization of the oil industry in 1976 became mired in political controversy. The oil conglomerate PDVSA, formed after nationalization, retained the independence and operating culture of the foreign multinationals. Nationalization did little to diminish the oil industry's power and influence over the state and society.

On the political front, repeated incidents of public corruption, mismanagement, and lack of accountability generated a recurrent atmosphere of crisis. The imposition of austerity measures in February 1989 produced popular and largely spontaneous rebellions in Caracas and throughout Venezuela. The government's need to rely upon the military to impose order exposed a crisis in leadership, as well as deep fissures within Venezuelan society. The expectations generated from the widely held perception of Venezuela as a wealthy oil nation clashed with the social reality faced by the majority of its citizens; even among the middle classes social discontent increased. In the long run, the social peace and political stability that the oil export model had generated proved unsustainable. As political alliances unraveled, the traditional parties lost legitimacy, as did most institutions identified with the structures of power. Attempted coups in 1992 failed, but they underscored that political discontent had spread to the military. Efforts to reconstitute a new political alliance with the election of the Christian Democrat Rafael Caldera (1994–99) proved ineffective and did little to halt deteriorating political conditions.

The election in 1998 of Hugo Chávez inaugurated a new chapter in Venezuelan politics and witnessed a reformulation of oil policy. During his campaign Chávez blamed Venezuela's ills on the pacted democracy established in 1958 and the use of oil resources to maintain privileges for limited segments of society even as poverty continued to increase throughout the country. Since 1999 Chávez's government has pursued a dual strategy. Internationally he has sought to strengthen OPEC, stabilize world oil prices, and quickly move to assert an independent foreign policy, extricating Venezuela from "the orbit of the United States." Internally he has sought to bring PDVSA under greater state control, passing laws that in essence renationalized the industry and replacing the oil board of directors. Accustomed to their independence, it was not surprising that the oil industry and the oil workers' unions should have become the source of opposition to Chávez. It is also not surprising that the largely middle-class opposition to Chávez should have reacted most vehemently to proposed changes aimed at the PDVSA.

The dramatic lockout and oil strike by industry executives and workers at the end of 2002 marked a turning point for the petroleum industry and the nation. Though the instigators managed to initially paralyze production, in the long run they lost popular support. The government gained control over the enterprise, relaunching a new PDVSA aligned with its political and social objectives. The political and social model that the oil industry had relied upon since its inception failed to mobilize broad support among the Venezuelan population. The ability of Chávez's government to gain the upper hand reflected the extent to which the hegemony that the oil company exercised over Venezuelan culture and politics had eroded. Deprived of its benefits, the majority of the population no longer viewed the industry as the instrument of development and modernization. This outcome brought to an end an important chapter in the history of Venezuela. A new chapter, however, has not fully materialized, and it remains unclear what shape it will take. Though the economy and the government continue to rely exceedingly on the oil industry, the reality is that in contemporary Venezuela oil no longer functions as an irrational symbol of identity.

Notes

To protect their anonymity, some interview subjects are identified only by their initials.

ABBREVIATIONS

AHM	Archivo Histórico de Miraflores
AHZ	Archivo Histórico de Zulia
DDQC	*U.S. Declassified Documents Quarterly Catalog*
FRUS	*Foreign Relations of the United States*
NARA	National Archives and Records Administration
PRO	Public Records Office

PREFACE

1. See for example Salazar Carrillo and West, *Oil Development in Venezuela during the 20th Century.*
2. Schuster, *Petroleros,* and Quintero, *La cultura del petróleo.*
3. Conniff, *Black Labor on a White Canal.*
4. Tinker Salas, *Under the Shadow of the Eagles.*
5. Aviva Chomsky, *West Indian Workers and the United Fruit Company in Costa Rica, 1870–1940* (Baton Rouge: Louisiana State University Press, 1996).
6. Wright, *Café con Leche.*
7. Baptista, *Breve reseña histórica de la industria del petróleo.*
8. Marchand, *Venezuela, travailleurs et villes du pétrole.*
9. Prieto Soto, *Luchas obreras por nuestro petróleo;* Quintero, *La cultura del petróleo;* Croes, *El movimiento obrero venezolano.*
10. Quintero, *La antropología del petróleo.*
11. The most salient exceptions are the works of Nehru Tennassee, *Venezuela;* Bergquist, *Labor in Latin America;* and Ellner, *El sindicalismo en Venezuela.*
12. Gilmore, *Caudillism and Militarism in Venezuela;* Kolb, *Democracy and Dictatorship in Venezuela;* Burggraaff, *The Venezuelan Armed Forces in Politics;* Lombardi, *The Decline and Abolition of Negro Slavery in Venezuela.*

13. Lombardi, "The Invention of Venezuela within the World Systems."

14. Lombardi, *Venezuela*; Ewell, *Venezuela*; Edwin Lieuwen, *Venezuela*; Morón, *A History of Venezuela*.

15. González, *Pueblo en vilo*.

16. Ferry, *The Colonial Elite of Early Caracas*; Roseberry, *Coffee and Capitalism in the Venezuelan Andes*.

17. Rabe, *The Road to* OPEC; Rabe, *Eisenhower and Latin America*; McBeth, *Juan Vicente Gómez and the Oil Companies in Venezuela*.

18. Lieuwen, *Petroleum in Venezuela*.

19. Ellner, *Venezuela's Movimiento al Socialismo*; Bergquist, *Labor in Latin America*.

20. Karl, *The Paradox of Plenty*.

21. Coronil, *The Magical State*.

22. Yarrington, *A Coffee Frontier*; Díaz, *Female Citizen*.

23. Briggs and Mantini-Briggs, *Stories in the Time of Cholera*.

24. Coronil, *The Magical State*, 3.

25. Pérez Schael, *Petróleo, cultura y poder en Venezuela*. Also Coronil, *The Magical State*, 3.

26. See for example Finn, *Tracing the Veins*; Klubock, *Contested Communities*; Chomsky and Lauria Santiago, eds., *Identity and the Struggle at the Margins of the Nation State*; and Putnam, *The Company They Kept*.

27. Coronil, Foreword, xi.

INTRODUCTION: OIL, CULTURE, AND SOCIETY

1. Ellner and Tinker Salas, eds., *Venezuela, Hugo Chávez and the Decline of an "Exceptional Democracy."*

2. Karl, *The Paradox of Plenty*, 54.

3. Alberto Quirós Corradi, "El Petróleo sirvió de excusa para nuestro fracaso, *Nosotros* (Lagoven), June 1984, 27. Quirós Corradi, former Lagoven president, asserts that oil is responsible for the modern Venezuelan state and democracy.

4. Bautista Fuenmayor, *1928–1948*, 9.

5. Rangel, *La moneda ladrona*, 1.

6. Coronil, *The Magical State*, 85.

7. Bautista Fuenmayor, *1928–1948*, 18.

8. Coronil, *The Magical State*, 96.

9. Juan Pablo Pérez Alfonzo, *Memoria del Ministerio de Fomento* (Caracas, 1947), xiii, cited in Mejía Alarcón, *La industria del petróleo en Venezuela*, 115–16.

10. Harwich Vallenilla, *La crisis de 1929 en América Latina*.

11. The third phase appears to have ended with the strike by management and employees of Petróleos de Venezuela against the government of Hugo Chávez Frías in December 2002.

12. Quintero, *La cultura del petróleo*, 68.

13. Crawford, *Building the Workingman's Paradise*, 5.

14. Hoare and Smith, eds., *Selections from the Prison Notebooks of Antonio Gramsci*, 199, 285, 323.

15. See Alberto Quirós Corradi, "El síndrome de la nueva PDVSA," *El Nacional*, 15 July 2007, 7.

16. Uslar Pietri, *Los venezolanos y el petróleo*, 87. Also Arturo Uslar Pietri, "El parasitismo petrolero," *El Nacional*, 3 August 1997.

17. Benet, *Guía general de Venezuela*, 666–67.

18. Rangel, *Venezuela en 3 siglos*, 236.

19. Brown, "Why Foreign Oil Companies Shifted Their Production from Mexico to Venezuela."

20. Crawford, *Building the Workingman's Paradise*, 200.

21. Ibid., 203.

22. Baker, *The Asphalt Lakes of Trinidad and Venezuela*.

23. Sabato, "On Political Citizenship in Nineteenth Century Latin America." Also Dagnino, "Citizenship in Latin America, Latin América," 5–6.

24. See McBeth, *Juan Vicente Gómez and the Oil Companies in Venezuela*, 141.

25. Karl, *The Paradox of Plenty*, 54.

26. Building on their experiences in Venezuela, oil companies based in the United States followed similar policies in their dealings with Saudi Arabia. In fact many officials of Creole from the United States were subsequently transferred to Saudi Arabia. See Vitalis, "Wallace Stegner's Arabian Discovery."

27. Betancourt, *Venezuela, política y petróleo*.

28. Steve Ellner, *Organized Labor in Venezuela, 1958–1991: Behavior and Concerns in a Democratic Setting* (Wilmington: Scholarly Resources, 1993), 144–46. Also Karl, *Paradox of Plenty*, 56.

29. Portes, "Latin American Class Structures," 9.

30. Ibid., 11. Also see Johnson, "Middle Groups in National Politics in Latin America," 321.

31. Ibid., 11. Also see Nun, "A Latin American Phenomenon," 161.

32. Bernardo Mommer, "Subversive Oil," *Politics in the Chávez Era: Class, Polarization and Conflict*, ed. Steve Ellner and Daniel Hellinger (Boulder: Lynne Reiner, 2003), 113–45. Luis Lander, "La insurrección de los gerentes," 13–32.

33. Tinker Salas, "Fueling Concern."

CHAPTER 1: A TROPICAL MEDITERRANEAN

1. *Boletín de la Riqueza Pública de los Estados Unidos de Venezuela*.

2. Okonta and Douglas, *Where Vultures Feast*.

3. "Las dos Venezuela de José Antonio Giacopini Zarraga," *Nosotros*, September 1984, 7.

4. Sáenz de Viteri, *Guía ilustrada del estado de Zulia*, 255.

5. Vila, *Geografía de Venezuela* (Caracas: Ministerio de Educación 1960), 24.

6. Picón Salas, *Los días de Cipriano Castro*, 57.

7. Vila, *Geografía de Venezuela*, 23.

8. Picón Salas, *Los días de Cipriano Castro*, 54.

9. Ibid., 57.

10. Urdaneta de Cardozo, *Autonomía y federalismo en el Zulia*, 65.

11. Germán Cardozo Galué, "Proceso históricos regionales en la formación del estado y nación venezolana," paper presented to the Fourth National Congress of Regional History (1996), cited in Urdaneta de Cardozo, *Autonomía y federalismo en el Zulia*, 69.

12. Rangel, *Los andinos en el poder*, 97.

13. Ibid., 194.

14. Arnold, Macready, and Barrington, *The First Big Oil Hunt*, 59.

15. de Civrieux, "Los cumanagoto y sus vecinos."

16. Ontiveros, *Identidades y post identidad de los andes y oriente venezolanos*, 47.

17. Picón Salas, *Los días de Cipriano Castro*, 10.

18. Roseberry, *Coffee and Capitalism in the Venezuelan Andes*, 14.

19. Rangel, *Los andinos en el poder*, 12.

20. Ibid., 10.

21. Personal communication, Dr. Ramón J. Velásquez, Caracas, summer 1997.

22. Ontiveros, *Identidades y post identidad*, 23.

23. Rode, *Los alemanes en el Táchira*, 151.

24. Ibid., 33.

25. Ibid., 19.

26. Rangel, *Los andinos en el poder*, 15.

27. Archivo Histórico del Estado de Mérida, documento 1847 #1 0030 10 December 1847, "Proyecto que concede privilegio a Rafael Salas y Jesús Uzcategui Rincón para extraer urao."

28. Guevara and Guevara, *Geografía de la región centro occidental*, 2.

29. Ibid., 79.

30. *Venezuela and the Oil Pioneers*, 20.

31. Vila, *Geografía de Venezuela*, 413–15. Also Benet, *Guía general de Venezuela*, vol. 1, 642.

32. Benet, *Guía general de Venezuela*, vol. 1, 646.

33. Redfield and Ketchum, "Report to Creole Petroleum Corporation on the Distribution of Salt in Lake Maracaibo," 9, 14.

34. Arnold, Macready, and Barrington, *The First Big Oil Hunt*, 62; and Cardozo Galué, *Maracaibo y su región histórica*, 143.

35. Spinden, "Travel Notes in Western Venezuela," 408.

36. Carlson, *Geography of Venezuela*, 392.

37. Cardozo Galué, *Maracaibo y su región histórica*, 17–18, 43–44.

38. Marco Aurelio Vila, *Aspectos geográficos del Zulia* (Caracas: Imprenta Nacional, 1952), 167–68.

39. Arnold, Macready, and Barrington, *The First Big Oil Hunt*, 144.

40. Federico Brito Figueroa, *Historia económica y social de Venezuela* (Caracas: Universidad Central de Venezuela, 1966), vol. 1, 154.

41. *XI Censo General de Población de Zulia* (1985), xlv; Bell, *Venezuela*, 186.

42. Jahn, *El estado de Zulia*, 8.

43. Bell, *Venezuela*, 181.

44. Medrano, *Apuntaciones para la crítica sobre el lenguaje maracaibero*, 8.

45. Ferer, *Maracaibo durante el gobierno de los Monagas*, 65. Also Urdaneta de Cardozo, *Autonomía y federalismo en el Zulia*, 35, 101.

46. Arnold, Macready, and Barrington, *The First Big Oil Hunt*, 62; Cardozo Galué, *Maracaibo y su región histórica*, 153.

47. Bell, *Venezuela*, 184. Since the advent of air conditioning it has also been considered the coldest city in Venezuela.

48. Bierstadt, "The Latter Days of a Pirate Stronghold," 17.

49. Cardozo Galué, *Maracaibo y su región histórica*, 220, 237.

50. NARA, RG 59, m 369 roll 12, 15 December 1925, Alexander K. Sloan to secretary of state.

51. Vivanco y Villegas, *Venezuela al día / Venezuela Up to Date*, 918.

52. McBeth, "El impacto de las compañías petroleras en el Zulia," 541.

53. Prieto Soto, *Huellas históricas*, 14.

54. Bermúdez and Ferer, "Unidad y diversidad en torno al lago de Maracaibo," 179.

55. Felix Hurtado, "90 años de progreso," *Nosotros*, September 1984, 15.

56. Bell, *Venezuela*, 188.

57. Hurtado, "90 años de progreso," 15.

58. Vivanco y Villegas, *Venezuela al día / Venezuela Up to Date*, 872.

59. "The Oriental Colony in Venezuela is a Vest Pocket Edition of the Near East," *Literary Digest*, 16 August 1919, 70.

60. Nilda Bermúdez Briñez, *Vivir en Maracaibo en el siglo XIX* (Maracaibo: Biblioteca Temas de Historia del Zulia, 2001), 92–94.

61. F. J. Leggit, "Venezuela Today," *Contemporary Review*, December 1927, 731.

62. Bierstadt, "The Latter Days of a Pirate Stronghold," 17.

63. Bermúdez Briñez, *Vivir en Maracaibo en el siglo XIX*, 43, 87–88.

64. Bierstadt, "The Latter Days of a Pirate Stronghold," 17.

65. Brito Figueroa, *Historia económica y social de Venezuela*, 402.

66. Bell, *Venezuela*, 226.

67. Rode, *Los alemanes en el Táchira*, 23.

68. Benet, *Guía general de Venezuela*, 671.

69. Bolet Paraza, "The Republic of Venezuela," 233.

70. *Venezuela, General Descriptive Data Prepared in June 1909*, 12. Also Leggitt, "Venezuela Today," 733.

71. Cupello, *Salvatore el inmigrante*, 142.

72. *Venezuela: General Descriptive Data Prepared in June 1909*, 13. Also "Venezuela Today," *Bulletin of the Pan American Union*, April 1915, 448.

73. Bermúdez Briñez, *Vivir en Maracaibo en el siglo XIX*, 73.

74. German Cardoso Galué, *Historia zuliana, economía, política y vida intelectual en el siglo XIX* (Maracaibo: Universidad del Zulia, 1998), 17.

75. Karl Appun, "En los trópicos," *La mirada del otro: viajeros extranjeros en la Venezuela del siglo XIX*, ed. Elías Pino Iturrieta and Pedro Enrique Calzadilla (Caracas: Fundación Bigott, 1992), 87.

76. Bell, *Venezuela*, 209.

77. PRO, London, FO 199/222, British vice-consul, Maracaibo, to Foreign Office, "Coffee Production Declined because of Heavy Rains." Also Bell, *Venezuela*, 225.

78. See Bierstadt, "The Gentle Art of Venezuelan Travel," 22. Also Bell, *Venezuela*, 197.

79. Bierstadt, "The Gentle Art of Venezuelan Travel," 23.

80. Paredes Huggins, *Vialidad y comercio en el occidente venezolano*, 129–30.

81. Ibid., 64–65.

82. Bierstadt, "The Gentle Art of Venezuelan Travel," 23.

83. Bell, *Venezuela*, 194.

84. Paredes Huggins, *Vialidad y comercio en el occidente venezolano*, 56; Vivanco y Villegas, *Venezuela al día / Venezuela Up to Date*, 936–37.

85. Bierstadt, "Witchcraft and Murder in the Andes," 13.

86. Rode, *Los alemanes en el Táchira*, 20.

87. See Linder, "Con un pañuelo de seda."

88. Benet, *Guía general de Venezuela*, 678.

89. Ochoa Urdaneta, *Memoria geográfica de la costa oriental del Lago de Maracaibo*, 35.

90. "Environment of the Average Individual," NARA, RG 165, 2656 m-16, 7 November 1922.

91. Arnold, Macready, and Barrington, *The First Big Oil Hunt*, 62.

92. Díaz Sánchez, *Transición, política y realidad en Venezuela*, 21.

93. Prieto Soto, *Huellas históricas*, 43.

94. Ibid., 15; Prieto Soto, *El Chorro:¿ gracia o maldición?*, 16–17.

95. Prieto Soto, *Huellas históricas*, 15.

96. Colina Nava, *Sucesos históricos sobre Cabimas y Lagunillas hasta 1938*, 3.

97. AHZ, 2 May 1914, tomo 1, legajo 1, Gob. Distrito Bolívar (Santa Rita) to Sec. General de Gobierno (Maracaibo), "Sociedades Religiosas."

98. Benet, *Guía general de Venezuela*, 693.

99. Andrade, "Santa Rita y su lago," 115.

100. Vivanco y Villegas, *Venezuela al día / Venezuela Up to Date*, 605.

101. Prieto Soto, *Huellas históricas*, 39.

102. Medina and Camargo, *Aproximación a la historia de Cabimas*, 17, 31.

103. Vila, *Antecedentes coloniales de centros poblados de Venezuela*, 94.

104. Brito Figueroa, *Historia económica y social*, vol. 1, 305.

105. Pedro Emilio Col, ed., *Diccionario de historia de Venezuela*, vol. I (Caracas: Fundación Polar, 1989), 559.

106. Quintero Delgado, "Los campamentos petroleros de la costa oriental del lago de Maracaibo," 51.

107. Prieto Soto, *El Chorro: ¿gracia o maldición?*, 15.

108. Prieto Soto, *Huellas históricas de Cabimas*, 14.

109. Ibid., 46.

110. Ochoa Urdaneta, *Memoria geográfica de la costa oriental*, 19.

111. Spinden, "Travel Notes in Western Venezuela," 408.

112. Vivanco y Villegas, *Venezuela al día / Venezuela Up to Date*, 607.

113. Quintero Delgado, "Los campamentos petroleros de la costa oriental del lago de Maracaibo," 65.

114. Sáenz de Viteri, *Guía Ilustrada del Estado de Zulia*, 271.

115. Briceño Parilli, *Las migraciones internas y los municipios petroleros*, 17–18.

116. Colina Nava, *Sucesos históricos sobre Cabimas y Lagunillas*, 3.

117. See Linder, "Agricultural and Rural Society in Pre-Petroleum Venezuela," 29–30.

118. Ibid., 68.

119. PRO, FO 199/222, 20 January 1911, British vice-consul, Maracaibo, to Foreign Office.

120. Vivanco y Villegas, *Venezuela al día / Venezuela Up to Date*, 613–17.

121. "Vicencio Pérez Soto y Las Compañías Petroleras," *Boletín del Archivo Histórico de Miraflores* 70 (January–February 1972), 319.

122. AHZ, 1926, tomo 4, legajo 34, 8 October 1926, Secretaría, Sección Política y Justicia a Jefe Civil Colón, San Carlos Zulia; also Linder, "Agricultural and Rural Society in Pre-Petroleum Venezuela," 314–65.

123. AHZ, 1928, tomo 5, legajo 8, 18 July 1928, Leonte Olivo, Secretario Gral. del Zulia to Jefe Civil del Distrito Colón, San Carlos del Zulia, Liberación del indígena Ramón Nuñez, de la Hacienda "El Milagro," propiedad del ciudadano José de la Rosa Nuñez, donde trabajaba en forma de esclavitud.

124. Jahn, *El estado de Zulia*, 44.

125. Jahn, *Los aborígenes del occidente de Venezuela*. Also Jahn, *El estado de Zulia*, 34–38.

126. Arnold, Macready, and Barrington, *The First Big Oil Hunt*, 10.

127. "Unspoiled Primitives," *Time*, 5 May 1947, 72–74; and article in the *Tropical Sun* cited in Bernardo Nuñez, *Una ojeada al mapa de Venezuela*, 78.

128. AHZ, 1929, tomo 3, legajo 17, 10 October 1929, T. M. Nava a Presidente del Edo. Zulia, V. Pérez Soto, "Informe sobre la región del Catatumbo."

129. Benet, *Guía general de Venezuela*, 674.

130. NARA, RG 165 2656 M-13, dispatch #624, March 1922, "Origin and Characteristics of the Venezuelan Population."

131. Brito Figueroa, *El problema tierra y esclavos en la historia de Venezuela*, 180.

132. Acosta Saignes, *Vida de los esclavos negros en Venezuela*, 28.

133. See Rodríguez Arrieta, *Manumisión y abolición en la provincia de Maracaibo*, 69, 178. Also Brito Figueroa, *Historia económica y social de Venezuela*, 139–40.

134. Ibid., vol. 1, 244. Also Chancy, *Entre Santa Barbara y Shango*, 117.

135. *Diccionario de historia de Venezuela*, 464.

136. Acosta Saignes, *Vida de los esclavos negros*, 144.

137. Brito Figueroa, *Historia económica y social de Venezuela*, vol. 1, 245.

138. Ibid., 160.

139. Ibid., 257.

140. Acosta Saignes, "Los descendientes de africanos y la formación de la nacionalidad en Venezuela," 40.

141. Perazzo, *La inmigración en Venezuela*, 54. Also Wright, *Café con Leche*, 43.

142. Adriani, *Labor venezolanista*, 84–85. Also Wright, *Café con Leche*, 83–84.

143. Vila, *Geografía de Venezuela*, 23.

144. This is the attitude expressed by Mariano Picón Salas and others. See Picón, ed., *Mariano Picón Salas*.

145. Letter to General Medina Angarita, 23 February 1937, in ibid., 120.

146. Ibid., 121.

147. NARA, RG 165, box 1707, MID stack 370, row 72 (comp 16), shelf 2, #2383–44 dispatch #1516, 30 April 1924, "Population and Social Conditions."

148. NARA, RG 165, G2 E77, folder 2010, report 1710, military attaché, 20 November 1925, "Population."

149. NARA, RG165, box 3255, folder 2400, Venezuelan dispatch #739, 7 June 1922.

150. NARA, RG 165 MID, box 1707, 2556-M-14–2, 22 June 1922, national intelligence.

151. Ibid.

152. NARA, RG 165 MID, box 1707, MID stack 370, row 72 (comp 16), shelf 2, #2656 m-13, March 1922, psychological report.

153. Lee, "Venezuela," vol. 15, p. 16.

154. Burns, *The Poverty of Progress*.

CHAPTER 2: THE SEARCH FOR BLACK GOLD

1. *Creole en acción / Creole in Action* (Caracas: Cromotip, 1965).

2. See Martínez, *Cronología del petróleo venezolano*, 18.

3. McBeth, *Juan Vicente Gómez and the Oil Companies in Venezuela*, 174.

4. Lieuwen, *Petroleum in Venezuela*, 53.

5. Salas, *Petróleo*, 36.

6. Ruptura, *El imperialismo petrolero y la revolución venezolana*, 25; *Venezuela and the Oil Pioneers*, 18.

7. Barberii, *De los pioneros a la empresa nacional*, 29.

8. Harwich Vallenilla, *Asfalto y revolución*; Lavin, *Halo for Gómez*, 286.

9. Harwich Vallenilla, *Asfalto y revolución*, 123.

10. Arnold, Macready, and Barrington, *The First Big Oil Hunt*, 336.

11. Ibid., 29.

12. Harwich Vallenilla, *Asfalto y revolución*, 162.

13. Vila, *Geografía de Venezuela*, 192.

14. Harwich Vallenilla, *Asfalto y revolución*, 501.

15. Martínez, *Cronología del petróleo venezolano*, 38–45.

16. Lieuwen, *Petroleum in Venezuela*, 10. Also *Venezuela and the Oil Pioneers*, 19.

17. Sader Pérez, *The Venezuelan State Oil Company*, 217. See also McBeth, *Juan Vicente Gómez and the Oil Companies in Venezuela*, 10–11. Valladares subsequently became part of Caribbean's legal staff and represented the company on many occasions.

18. See Lieuwen, *Petroleum in Venezuela*, 10.

19. See Betancourt, *Venezuela, política y petróleo*.

20. Lieuwen, *Petroleum in Venezuela*, 11.

21. Arnold, Macready, and Barrington, *The First Big Oil Hunt*, 54.

22. Papers of Ralph Arnold, 1875–1961, Huntington Library, San Marino, California. The Huntington houses the Arnold collection of photographs.

23. Arnold, Macready, and Barrington, *The First Big Oil Hunt*, 24.

24. Ibid., 26.

25. Pedro Emilio Coll, *Memoria y Cuenta del Ministerio de Fomento*, vol. 1 (Caracas: Bolívar, 1914), vii.

26. "Oil Ventures in Venezuela," *Lamp*, April 1922, 20.

27. Arnold, Macready, and Barrington, *The First Big Oil Hunt*, 117.

28. *Venezuela and the Oil Pioneers*, 20.

29. Arnold, Macready, and Barrington, *The First Big Oil Hunt*, 55.

30. Salazar, *Historia de los pueblos de agua*, 63.

31. Ibid., 26–27.

32. *Second Annual Report of the Caribbean Petroleum Corporation* (1915), 56.

33. Ibid., 3.

34. NARA, RG 59, M366, roll 24, Preston McGoodwin to secretary of state, 25 April 1914.

35. Sources differ on when the well began production; the date is given as 15 April by Efrain Barberii and the United States consul, and as 31 July by Anibal Martínez and the anonymous author of *Venezuela's Oil Pioneers*.

36. *Second Annual Report of the Caribbean Petroleum Corporation* (1915), 2.

37. Barberii, *El pozo ilustrado*, 489.

38. Salazar, *Historia de los pueblos de agua*, 101.

39. *Second Annual Report of the Caribbean Petroleum Corporation* (1915), 17–19.

40. Quintero Delgado, "Los campamentos petroleros de la costa oriental del lago de Maracaibo," 60.

41. *Second Annual Report of the Caribbean Petroleum Corporation* (1915), 93.

42. Ibid., 12; and Bell, *Venezuela*, 95.

43. *Seventh Annual Report of the Caribbean Petroleum Corporation* (1920), 14.

44. Arnold, Macready, and Barrington, *The First Big Oil Hunt*, 123.

45. Quintero Delgado, "Los campamentos petroleros de la costa oriental del lago de Maracaibo," 55.

46. Arnold, Macready, and Barrington, *The First Big Oil Hunt*, 118.

47. Crespo, *Mene Grande, la cuna del petróleo venezolano*, 24.

48. Arnold, Macready, and Barrington, *The First Big Oil Hunt*, 118.

49. Crespo, *Mene Grande, la cuna del petróleo venezolano*, 30.

50. Ibid., 33–35.

51. Barberii, *El pozo ilustrado*, 489–90.

52. Vivanco y Villegas, *Venezuela al Día / Venezuela Up to Date*, 1043.

53. *Second Annual Report of the Caribbean Petroleum Corporation* (1915), 105.

54. Crespo, *Mene Grande, la cuna del petróleo venezolano*, 30.

55. *Seventh Annual Report of the Caribbean Petroleum Corporation* (1920), 42.

56. *Second Annual Report of the Caribbean Petroleum Corporation* (1915), 32, 98.

57. Ibid., 32, 98. Also *Tropical Sun* (Maracaibo), 18 February 1928, 11.

58. Bracho Montiel, *Guachimanes*, 8.

59. Arnold, Macready, and Barrington, *The First Big Oil Hunt*, 313.

60. Crespo, *Mene Grande, la cuna del petróleo venezolano*, 31.

61. *Seventh Annual Report of the Caribbean Petroleum Corporation* (1920), 11.

62. *Memoria del Ministerio de Fomento, 1918*, vol. 1 (Caracas: Imprenta Nacional, 1918), 248.

63. NARA, RG 165 MID, 2655-M-74, "Oil Developments in Venezuela during 1922," 8 May 1923, economic dispatch.

64. *Memoria del Ministerio de Fomento, 1918*, 249.

65. *Memoria del Ministerio de Fomento, 1922* (Caracas: Americana, 1922), 106.

66. Ibid.

67. U.S. Bureau of Labor Statistics, *Monthly Labor Review*, September 1922, 13.

68. O'Shaughnessy, *Venezuelan Oil Fields*, 19.

69. *Sixth Annual Report of the Caribbean Petroleum Company* (1919), 49.

70. *Seventh Annual Report of the Caribbean Petroleum Company* (1920), 40.

71. Crespo, *Mene Grande, la cuna del petróleo venezolano*, 44.

72. Prieto Soto, *Huellas históricas*, 67.

73. Aquiles Ferrer, cited in Prieto Soto, *Luchas obreras por nuestro petróleo*, 93.

74. Quintero Delgado, "Los campamentos petroleros de la costa oriental del lago de Maracaibo," 82.

75. Aquiles Ferrer, cited in Prieto Soto, *Luchas obreras por nuestro petróleo*, 93.

76. O'Shaughnessy, *Venezuelan Oil Fields*, 19.

77. Sáenz de Viteri, *Guía ilustrada del estado de Zulia*, 351.

78. *Ministerio de Fomento: Memoria al Congreso* (Caracas: Cosmos, 1923), 126; Crespo, *Mene Grande, la cuna del petróleo venezolano*, 43.

79. Bautista Fuenmayor, *1928–1948*, 16.

80. *Venezuela and the Oil Pioneers*, 28.

81. Martínez, *Cronología del petróleo venezolano*, 56.

82. Carrera Damas, *Una nación llamada Venezuela*, 136.

83. Inman, "Oil Developments in Venezuela," 301–2.

84. "Oil Ventures in Venezuela," *Lamp*, April 1922, 19.

85. Díaz Sánchez, *Mene*, 31.

86. Martínez, *Cronología del petróleo venezolano*, 58.

87. *Venezuela and the Oil Pioneers*, 28.

88. *Memoria del Ministerio de Fomento* (Caracas: Cosmos, 1923), 84.

89. *Memoria del Ministerio de Fomento* (Caracas: Americana, 1922), 109.

90. Ibid., 1008–9.

91. Lee, "The Race for Oil in Venezuela," 157.

92. Vivanco y Villegas, *Venezuela al Día / Venezuela Up to Date*, 1030–31.

93. Manuel Bermúdez, "El Barroso 2: 60 años de un chorro que aun sigue fluyendo," *Nosotros*, December 1982, 34.

94. *Venezuela and the Oil Pioneers*, 28–29.

95. Vivanco y Villegas, *Venezuela al Día / Venezuela Up to Date*, 1030–31.

96. *Venezuela and the Oil Pioneers*, 29.

97. Ministerio de Fomento, *Memoria al Congreso* (Caracas: Cosmos, 1923), 82.

98. Bermúdez, "El Barroso 2," 34.

99. Vivanco y Villegas, *Venezuela al Día / Venezuela Up to Date*, 1030–31; Prieto Soto, *Huellas históricas*, 71. Also Bermúdez, "El Barroso 2," 34.

100. Leonard, *Men of Maracaibo*, 96–97. Leonard offers a similar account for Lagunillas.

101. Paradoxically, during the devastating floods that gripped Venezuela in December 1999, the clergy in Caracas led a procession with the statue of Christ the Nazarene from the San Pablo church, and reportedly the rains stopped the next day.

102. Bermúdez, "El Barroso 2," 34.

103. Lavin, *Halo for Gómez*, 304.

104. de Chene, *La transformación de comunidades petroleras*, 19.

105. NARA, RG 59, m366, roll 24, 22 December 1922, John C. Sanders to secretary of state.

106. "Biggest Oil Well Yet," *New York Times*, 18 March 1923.

107. Imperial and Foreign News Items, *Times* (London), 19 March 1923.

108. "Oil Ventures in Venezuela," *Lamp*, April 1922, 17.

109. Lee, "The Race for Oil in Venezuela," 148.

110. "Trekking South, Curaçao," *Times* (London), 16 June 1927.

111. AHM, 442-C, 28 December 1922, Juan Texier Unda to Juan Vicente Gómez.

112. Lieuwen, *Petroleum in Venezuela*, 19.

113. "Oil Ventures in Venezuela," *Lamp*, April 1922, 17.

114. NARA, RG 165 MID 1917–19–41 2655-M-15, "New American Petroleum Operations in Venezuela," economic attaché, Caracas, 20 November 1919.

115. For a history of Standard Oil of Venezuela see Barberii, *De los pioneros a la empresa nacional*. Also see *Venezuela and the Oil Pioneers*, 26.

116. AHM, # 440-C 1922, Standard Oil Company of Venezuela to Sr. Enrique Urdaneta Maya, 2 December 1922, packages for Gen. Gómez.

117. AHM, 440-C, 13 December 1922, letter to Gómez from Mr. Wall, London.

118. McBeth, *Juan Vicente Gómez and the Oil Companies in Venezuela*, 30, 67.

119. NARA, RG 59, m 366, roll 24, 22 December 1922, United States consul in Maracaibo, John Sanders, to Department of State.

120. *Annual Report 1928, Creole Petroleum Corporation*, E. J. Sadler, January 1929.

121. *Venezuela and the Oil Pioneers*, 31–32.

122. NARA, RG 165 MID 1917–19–41 2655-M-36, Major Gary I. Crockett, census data upon Curaçao, 19 April 1923.

123. AHZ, 1929, tomo 3, legajo 17, fecha: 10 October 1929, T. M. Nava to Presidente del Edo. Zulia, V. Pérez Soto, "Informe Sobre la Región del Catatumbo." And Acervo Histórico del Estado de Zulia, 1929, tomo 3, legajo 17, 8 November 1929, Ministerio de Relaciones Exteriores, Presidente del Edo. Zulia, "Federal Commission to Map Border."

124. Díaz Sánchez, *Mene*, 71.

125. *Tropical Sun* (Maracaibo), 5 May 1928.

126. Leonard, *Men of Maracaibo*, 247.

127. *Venezuela and the Oil Pioneers*, 99–105.

128. Nesbitt, *Desolate Marches*, 17. Nesbitt commented that the majority of the passengers on his ship from the United States were destined for Maracaibo.

129. Leonard, *Men of Maracaibo*, 14.

130. Ibid.

131. McBeth, "El impacto de las compañías petroleras en el Zulia," 538.

132. *Nosotros*, December 1956, 14.

133. *Venezuela and the Oil Pioneers*, 46–47.

134. *Nosotros*, July 1953, 3.

135. McBeth, *Juan Vicente Gómez and the Oil Companies in Venezuela*, 162.

136. Tinker Salas, *In the Shadow of the Eagles*, 169.

137. O'Shaughnessy, *Venezuelan Oil Handbook*, 4.

138. Lee, "The Race for Oil in Venezuela," 154.

139. *Venezuela and the Oil Pioneers*, 29–30.

140. "Trekking South, Curaçao," *Times* (London), 16 June 1927.

141. AHZ, 1924, tomo 3, legajo 13, 25 November 1924; authorities remitted to Caracas 150 questionnaires. No existing record of these could be found in the Zulia state archive.

142. Vivanco y Villegas, *Venezuela al día / Venezuela Up to Date*, 43.

143. Memoria, *Ministerio de Fomento* (Caracas: Sur América, 1928), xxxvii.

144. "Oil Boom in Maracaibo," *New York Times*, 23 May 1926; "Americans in Venezuela," *New York Times*, 5 December 1926.

145. Bell, *Venezuela*, 22.

146. NARA, RG 59, m 366, roll 18, 30 April 1926, report of United States consul Alexander Sloan.

147. Lavin, *Halo for Gómez*, 302.

148. Leonard, *Men of Maracaibo*, 9.

149. Ibid., 10.

150. Ibid., 44–45.

151. Lavin, *Halo for Gómez*, 301.

152. *Venezuela and the Oil Pioneers*, 42.

153. *Tropical Sun*, 4 August 1928.

154. Lee, "The Race for Oil in Venezuela," 151.

155. Ibid.

156. "The Wealth of Venezuela," *Times* (London), 21 June 1929.

157. NARA, RG 59, m 366, roll 18, 30 April 1926, report of United States consul Alexander Sloan.

158. *Venezuela and the Oil Pioneers*, 42.

159. *Tropical Sun* and *Panorama*, Maracaibo, various issues, 1924–31.

160. *Panorama* (Maracaibo) 5 January 1931.

161. *Maracaibo Herald*, 17 February 1945.

162. Sáenz de Viteri, *Guía ilustrada del estado de Zulia*, 286.

163. AHZ, 1926, tomo 4, legajo 35, 18 March, 1926, Bernard Henry Moran to governor, request to publish *Tropical Sun*.

164. *Venezuela and the Oil Pioneers*, 44.

165. *Tropical Sun*, 18 February 1928.

166. *Panorama* (Maracaibo), 12 February 1931.

167. Leonard, *Men of Maracaibo*, 73.

168. "Looking Backward," *Maracaibo Herald*, 24 March 1945 [retrospective issue, recounting events of 28 March 1928].

169. Lieberman, "Maracaibo and Its Neighborhoods, the 1930s." Lieberman, who worked for Creole, published a newsletter in which he wrote about his experiences in Venezuela.

170. *Venezuela and the Oil Pioneers*, 45.

171. AHZ, 1927, tomo 11, legajo 29, Maracaibo, 15 May 1927. Kerold Jensen claimed to have been robbed of 100 bolívares.

172. NARA, RG 59, M366, roll 18, 23 October 1925, legation in Caracas to American minister.

173. Ibid.

174. NARA, RG 59, M366, roll 18, 9 September 1926, Frank B. Kellogg, response from Department of State.

175. Leonard, *Men of Maracaibo*, 40.

176. Calvani, *Nuestro máximo problema*, 54–55; Leonard, *Men of Maracaibo*, 15; Calvany, *Yo fui una de ellas*, 90.

177. *Venezuela and the Oil Pioneers*, 44.

178. Linder, "Con un pañuelo de seda," 14.

179. Lavin, *Halo for Gómez*, 302.

180. Interview, summer 2000, Mérida. José Omar Colmenares, native of the state of Dividive, worked at Mene Grande.

181. Leonard, *Men of Maracaibo*, 85.

182. AHZ, 1930, tomo 5, legajo 27, 17 March 1930, Reglamento del Instituto Profiláctico Anti Venéreo.

183. Calvany, *Yo fui una de ellas*, 86.

184. *Petróleo* (Maracaibo), 21 October 1936.

185. *Panorama* (Maracaibo), 27 August 1936.

186. Ministerio de Sanidad, *Memoria y Cuenta* (Caracas: Imprenta Nacional, 1948), Corresponde al año 1947, 147–49.

187. Lieberman, "Early Impressions of Maracaibo, with Some Attention to the Local Mores," 2.

188. McBeth, *Juan Vicente Gomez and the Oil Companies in Venezuela*, 109.

189. Lavin, *Halo for Gómez*, 303.

190. NARA, RG 59, M366, roll 18, 30 April 1926, report of United States consul Alexander Sloan.

191. Albert Trevilion, manager of Venezuelan Gulf Oil mess hall, in ibid.

192. NARA, RG 59, M366, roll 18, 30 April 1926, report of United States consul Alexander Sloan.

193. "Articulos de primera necesidad," *Excelsior*, 1 March 1926, cited in NARA, RG 59 M366, roll 18, 30 April 1926, report of United States consul Alexander Sloan.

194. PRO, London, F0369/2382, British legation, Caracas, 3 August 1933, to Foreign Office.

195. AHZ, 1924, tomo 3, legajo 15, 15 November 1923, John Sanders, United States consul, to president of Zulia.

196. AHZ, 1924, tomo 3, legajo 15, 24 November 1924, J. A. Weston, Caribbean Petroleum, to British vice-consul.

197. AHZ, 1928, tomo 10, legajo 12, 26 April 1928, Arcaya to Pérez Soto.

198. *Norte*, 8 September 1933.

199. NARA, RG 59, M366, roll 18, 30 April 1926, report of United States consul Alexander Sloan.

200. Rode, *Los alemanes en el Táchira*, 84, 95.

201. NARA, RG 59, M 369, roll 12, 23 November 1925, Alexander K. Sloan, German colony in Maracaibo.

202. Ferer, *Maracaibo durante el gobierno de los Monagas*. Also see Linder, "Con un pañuelo de seda," 6–7.

203. Coronil, *The Magical State*, 85.

204. McBeth, *Juan Vicente Gómez and the Oil Companies in Venezuela*, 129.

CHAPTER 3: LA RUTA PETROLERA

1. *Venezuela and the Oil Pioneers*, 30.

2. Standard Oil Company of Venezuela, *Petroleum Engineering Report* (February 1933), 1.

3. Osorio Álvarez, *Geografía de la población de Venezuela*, 46–47; *Tropical Sun*, 31 March 1928.

4. "Oil Ventures in Venezuela," *Lamp*, April 1922, 19.

5. *Venezuela and the Oil Pioneers*, 49. Also *Paz y Trabajo* (Monagas), 3 November 1923.

6. U.S. Bureau of Labor Statistics, *Monthly Labor Review*, September 1922, 494.

7. Uribe Piedrahita, *Mancha de aceite*; Otero Silva, *Oficina N. 1*; Díaz Sánchez, *Mene*.

8. See McBeth, *Juan Vicente Gómez and the Oil Companies in Venezuela*, 128. McBeth draws this conclusion based on figures provided by Federico Brito Figueroa, *Venezuela Siglo XX* (Havana: Casa de las Americas, 1967).

9. U.S. Bureau of Labor Statistics, *Monthly Labor Review*, September 1922, 493.

10. Briceño Parilli, *Las migraciones internas y los municipios petroleros*, 13.

11. Prieto Soto, *Huellas históricas*, 49, 71.

12. Rangel, *Los andinos en el poder*, 207.

13. Bolívar Chollett, *Población y sociedad, en la Venezuela del siglo XX*, 38.

14. de Chene, *La transformación de comunidades petroleras*, 15; Briceño Parilli, *Las migraciones internas y los municipios petroleros*, 27.

15. Ministerio de Fomento, Dirección General de Estadísticas, *Sexto censo de población, 1936*, vol. 3 (Caracas, Garrido, 1940), 60–61.

16. *Séptimo censo nacional, 1941*, vol. 5 (Caracas: Ministerio de Fomento, 1945), "Presencia de otros estados en Monagas" [unpaged].

17. Briceño Parilli, *Las migraciones internas y los municipios petroleros*, 68.

18. The developing oil camps were not the only poles attracting rural Venezuelans. The development of the oil economy paralleled a process of urbanization that had been gathering steam since the second decade of the twentieth century. Caracas, the capital, became the primary recipient of this migration.

19. See Tinker Salas, *Under the Shadow of the Eagles*.

20. Interview, MRS, Caracas, 2002.

21. "Oil Ventures in Venezuela," *Lamp*, April 1922, 19.

22. de Chene, *La transformación de comunidades petroleras*, 27.

23. Ibid., 38.

24. Ibid., 39.

25. Ibid., 21.

26. Arguments concerning the "rural or backward" origins of workers and the purported burden of oil companies and educated classes to uplift this sector of the population resonate with similar experiences throughout Latin America. First-generation immigrants to mining centers in Mexico were also portrayed in much the same manner. Likewise immigrants to urban centers, such as those arriving in Buenos Aires in the 1930s, were viewed as "backward," especially when they became politically involved.

27. "Labor Situation in Maracaibo District," NARA, RG 59, m366, roll 18, 20 July 1925, 30 July 1925, Alexander Sloan.

28. Ministro de Fomento, *Memoria y Cuenta, 1947* (Caracas: Grafolit, 1948).

29. McBeth, *Juan Vicente Gómez and the Oil Companies in Venezuela*, 109.

30. NARA, RG 59, m366, roll 18, 6 April 1926, Alexander K. Sloan.

31. Interview, Edgar Campos, Maracaibo, October 1997.

32. Interview, MRS, Caracas, June 2002.

33. Interview, Antonio José Sarache, Mérida, July 1998.

34. Interview, José Omar Colmenares, Mérida, 1998 and 2003.

35. Prieto Soto, *Conformación ideológica petrolera venezolana*, 67.

36. *El Farol*, 1949.

37. Briceño Parilli, *Las migraciones internas y los municipios petroleros*, 28.

38. *Concurso de la hacienda, Primer congreso de agricultores, ganaderos, industriales y comerciantes de Venezuela*, 53.

39. Ibid.

40. Roseberry, *Coffee and Capitalism in the Venezuelan Andes*, 128; Yarrington, *A Coffee Frontier*, 156.

41. Parra, *El petróleo y su influencia en la transformaciones culturales de la región zuliana, caso Cabimas y Lagunillas*, 15.

42. Linder, "Agricultural and Rural Society in Pre-Petroleum Venezuela," 473.

43. Coronil, *The Magical State*, 87.

44. McBeth, *Juan Vicente Gómez and the Oil Companies in Venezuela*, 120. Parra, *El petróleo y su influencia en la transformaciones culturales de la región zuliana*, 8.

45. Bolívar Chollett, *Población y sociedad en la Venezuela del siglo XX*, 54.

46. *Venezuela and the Oil Pioneers*, 48.

47. Medina and Camargo, *Aproximaciones a la historia de Cabimas*, 183.

48. Lieuwen, *Petroleum in Venezuela*, 53.

49. Briceño Parilli, *Las migraciones internas y los municipios petroleros*, 34.

50. Marchand, *Venezuela*, 23. This work was selected for publication by the Creole Foundation.

51. AHZ, 1926, tomo 4, legajo 30, 6 February 1926, Jefatura Civil Distrito Bolívar.

52. Prieto Soto, *El Chorro: ¿gracia o maldición?*, 105.

53. Lavin, *Halo for Gómez*, 304.

54. AHZ, 1925, tomo 3, legajo 18, 1 May 1925, Venta de terrenos. Also Rómulo Betancourt, *Problemas venezolanos*, 82–87.

55. AHZ, 1929, tomo 7, legajo 18, 5 March 1929, Jefe Civil, Encontrados.

56. Ibid., Encontrados a Gobierno del Estado, Petición de habitantes.

57. AHZ, 1927, tomo 4, legajo 28, 31 March 1927, Judson Wood, Venezuelan Gulf, to Pérez Soto; AHZ, 1927, tomo 4, legajo 28, 20 September 1927, Howland Bancroft, Lago Petroleum, to Pérez Soto.

58. AHZ, 1927, tomo 4, legajo 28, 20 September 1927, William Purves Taylor, Mara Oil Fields, to Pérez Soto.

59. Eudomario Castillo, "Memorias, confesiones y reflexiones de un cabimero" (unpublished MS, 1987), cited in Medina and Camargo, *Aproximaciones a la historia de Cabimas*, 168.

60. AHZ, 1928, tomo 3, legajo 21, 28 July 1928, Jefe Civil, Sucre, to Sec. General Gobierno; Caribbean, 15 August 1928.

61. AHZ, 1926, tomo 4, legajo 32, 13 October 1926, Carlos Dupuy to VOC.

62. Ibid., 18 December 1926, VOC and municipio de Lagunillas, Terreno en Tasajeras del Sur.

63. AHZ, 1928, tomo 3, legajo 21, 15 June 1928, Jefe Civil Cabimas to Sec. de Gobierno VOC taladro dentro del pueblo de Cabimas; Pérez Soto to Ministro del Interior, 9 August 1928, ordeno suspender taladro.

64. AHZ, 1926, tomo 4, legajo 32, 20 October 1926, Chester Crebbs, Venezuelan Gulf Oil.

65. Lavin, *Halo for Gómez*, 306.

66. AHZ, 1929, tomo 8, legajo 22, 22 March 1929, Jefe Civil Distrito Bolívar to Secretario Gobierno, Zulia.

67. *Venezuela and the Oil Pioneers*, 38.

68. Alexander Sloan, United States consul in Maracaibo, to secretary of state, 14 June 1926, cited in Lieuwen, *Petroleum in Venezuela*, 52.

69. AHZ, 1929, tomo 8, legajo 22, 20 February 1929, Manuel Borjas Hernández, Elías Borjas P., Carlos Parra, Guillermina Suárez, Abrahán Perozo, and Antonio Fernández to Juan Vicente Gómez.

70. AHZ, 1929, tomo 8, legajo 22, 22 March 1929, V. Pérez Soto to J. V. Gómez.

71. AHZ, 1929, tomo 8, legajo 22, 8 March 1929, Manuel Borjas Hernández to V. Pérez Soto.

72. McBeth, *Juan Vicente Gómez and the Oil Companies in Venezuela*, 109–39; Prieto Soto, *Huellas históricas*, 76.

73. PRO, London, FO 199/222, 24 November 1925, British consul in Maracaibo to Foreign Office.

74. Bermúdez Romero, *Cabimas: Reventón de ilusiones idas*, 28.

75. Colina Nava, *Sucesos históricos sobre Cabimas y Lagunillas hasta 1938*, 12; Prieto Soto, *El Chorro:¿ gracia o malidición?*, 105.

76. Prieto Soto, *Huellas históricas*, 104.

77. AHM, 1-1-3, 16 November 1942, Secretario Pro Mejoras Cabimas—Ambrosio, Rafael Atuñez, Jesús Piña, "Necesitamos Agua, a causa de estar las aguas del Lago contaminadas de petróleo y otras impurezas."

78. Standard Oil Company of New Jersey, "Agenda for Spring Conference," Seaview Country Club, Absecon, New Jersey, 10 May 1937, 1.

79. AHZ, 1929, tomo 8, legajo 22, 20 February 1929, petition, residents of Cabimas to J. Vicente Gómez.

80. *Nosotros* (1950), 23.

81. Medina and Camargo, *Aproximaciones a la historia de Cabimas*, 200.

82. Quintero, *La cultura del petróleo*, 59–68.

83. "Corito," *El Taladro*, 9 June 1934.

84. Uribe Piedrahita, *Mancha de aceite*, 23.

85. Prieto Soto, *Luchas obreras por nuestro petróleo*, 63.

86. AHM, caja 1, Margariteños, 1-1-3, Cabimas, 15 November 1942, Bernardo Velásquez, Sociedad Pro La Guardia.

87. Prieto Soto, *Luchas obreras por nuestro petróleo*, 63.

88. AHZ, 1927, tomo 4, legajo 28, 5 May 1927, Queja de obreros to Pres. Edo. Zulia.

89. Aquiles Ferrer Vale, interview in Prieto Soto, *Luchas obreras por nuestro petróleo*, 94–95.

90. AHZ, 1928, tomo 10, legajo 16, 26 April 1928, Jefe Civil de Cabimas to Secretario General del Gobierno.

91. Colina Nava, *Sucesos históricos sobre Cabimas y Lagunillas hasta 1938*, 12.

92. AHZ, 1928, tomo 10, legajo 16, 26 April 1928, Jefe Civil de Cabimas to Secretario General del Gobierno.

93. AHZ, 1928, tomo 10, legajo 12, 7 May 1928, telegram from V. Pérez Soto to J. V. Gómez.

94. "Ojeda se asoma al futuro," *Nosotros*, December 1979, 9.

95. Leonard, *Men of Maracaibo*, 70.
96. Aquiles Ferrer Vale, interviewed in Prieto Soto, *Luchas obreras por nuestro petróleo*, 93.
97. Leonard, *Men of Maracaibo*, 70.
98. AHM, 568-C, 9 July 1926, Ana Cleotilde Sánchez to J. Vicente Gómez.
99. Briceño Parilli, *Las migraciones internas y los municipios petroleros*, 27.
100. AHZ, 1928, tomo 4, legajo 4, 8 July 1928, unknown correspondent to J. Vicente Gómez.
101. *Tropical Sun*, 6 June 1928.
102. AHZ, 1928, tomo 3, legajo 18, 4 July 1928, telegram, V. Pérez Soto to Ministro del Interior.
103. AHZ, 1928, tomo 9, legajo 1, n.d., Junta distribuidora de Fondos de Socorros entre los damnificados del Incendio de Lagunillas.
104. AHZ, 1928, tomo 9, legajo 1, 2 August 1928, Presidente de la Sociedad Venezolana de la Cruz Roja, Obispo del Zulia, Presidente de la Junta Recolectora de Fondos a favor de los Damnificados de Lagunillas.
105. AHZ, 1928, tomo 9, legajo 1, 15 June 1928, Lista de 958 personas que recibieron ayuda con el incendio de Lagunillas.
106. AHZ, 1928, tomo 3, legajo 18, 4 July 1928, telegram, V. Pérez Soto a Ministro del Interior.
107. *Tropical Sun*, 3 March 1928.
108. AHZ, 1928, tomo 4, legajo 4, 19 July 1928, Faria Hermanos y Arandia Alvarez to Vicencio Pérez Soto, Disputa entre los comerciantes de Lagunillas y las compañías petroleras; AHZ, 1928, tomo 4, legajo 4, 12 July 1928, Pobladores de Lagunillas, Faría Hermanos, Francisco Castellano, Antonio M. Portillo, Genero Salvatierra, Luis Hurtado, Octavio Mendez, Rafael Vezga, Carlos Luis Martines, P. V. Asprina, Simón Paris, Domingo Tebet, Cleofe Mata, Alfonzo Pretersz, Luis López, Cesar Fuenmayor, Arquimedes Flores, and others to J. V. Gómez.
109. AHZ, 1928, tomo 4, legajo 4, 8 July 1928, unknown correspondent to Juan Vicente Gómez.
110. Ibid.
111. McBeth, *Juan Vicente Gómez and the Oil Companies in Venezuela*, 149–50.
112. *La Esfera* (Caracas), 17 November 1939.
113. AHM, 570-c, telegram, 13/14 November 1939, Lagunillas, Jesús Farias to Gen. E. López Contreras.
114. AHM, 570-c, 20 November 1939, summary of radio conversation between Sres. Thompson, Caribbean, Maracaibo, and Taylor in Caracas.
115. AHM, 570-c, Maracaibo, 23 November 1939, Maldonado to Gral. E. L. C.
116. Eleazar López Conteras, Decreto Ejecutivo, 19 January 1937, Ministerio de Relaciones, *Memoria Ministro de Relaciones Interiores* (Caracas: Imprenta Nacional, 1938 [Año Civil 1937]), 3.

117. Lorenzo González Casas and Orlando Marín Castañeda, "El transcurrir tras el cercado: ámbito residencial y vida cotidiana, en los campamentos petroleros de Venezuela (1940–1975)," paper presented at X Jornada Nacional sobre Investigación y Docencia de la Historia, Fundación Buria, Barquisimeto, Lara, Venezuela, July 2003. Problems persisted between residents and the oil companies; see Archivo Histórico de Miraflores, 1-1-3, 16 November 1942, Pliego de Campesinos de Lagunillas, Dotación de Agua, Protección ante las pretensions de desalojo por parte de la VOC.

118. "Ojeda se asoma al futuro," *Nosotros*, December 1979, 7.

119. "VOC reglamento de trabajo Maracaibo May 15, 1915," cited in Medina and Camargo, *Aproximaciones a la historia de Cabimas*, 156–57.

120. Ibid.

121. PRO, FO 371/21554, interview with C. W. Jenks, 25 June 1938, International Labor Bureau, Geneva.

122. *Concurso de la hacienda: Primer congreso de agricultores, ganaderos, industriales y comerciantes de Venezuela*, 123.

123. Harold Lieberman, interview, Creole annuitants meeting, Little Rock, May 1999.

124. "VOC reglamento de trabajo Maracaibo May 15, 1915," cited in Medina and Camargo, *Aproximaciones a la historia de Cabimas*, 156–57.

125. Ministerio de Fomento, *Memoria al Congreso* (Caracas: Cosmos, 1923), 82–88.

126. Bolívar Coastal Oil Fields, Lago Petroleum Corporation, Monthly General Report, December 1932.

127. *Anuario petrolero de Venezuela* (Caracas: Ministerio de Fomento, 1950), 88.

128. *Venezuela and the Oil Pioneers*, 48; also Aquiles Ferrer Vale, cited in Prieto Soto, *Luchas obreras por nuestro petróleo*, 93–94.

129. *Venezuela and the Oil Pioneers*, 48.

130. Ibid.

131. Lee, "The Race for Oil in Venezuela," 155.

132. McBeth, "El impacto de las compañías petroleras en el Zulia," 539.

133. Prieto Soto, *Huellas históricas*, 76.

134. Harold Lieberman, interview, Creole annuitants meeting, Little Rock, May 1999.

135. *Venezuela and the Oil Pioneers*, 48.

136. Aquiles Ferrer Vale, interviewed in Prieto Soto, *Luchas obreras por nuestro petróleo*, 93–94.

137. Ochoa Urdaneta, *Estampas de Cabimas*, 45.

138. Aquiles Ferrer Vale, interviewed in Prieto Soto, *Luchas obreras por nuestro petróleo*, 93–94.

139. Commissioner Jonas González Miranda, 3 October 1930, cited in McBeth, *Juan Vicente Gómez and the Oil Companies in Venezuela*, 156.

140. Cited in Matos Romero, *El problema petrolero en Venezuela*, 88.

141. Ibid., 90.

142. AHM, serie 3–1-6, # 2 SPOTP, Jusepín, 17 March 1945, Pliegos de trabajadores. Workers referred to conditions in effect for over six years.

143. Briceño Parilli, *Las migraciones internas y los municipios pretroleros*, 13.

144. de Chene, *La transformación de comunidades petroleras*, 43. Before 1936 the oil companies could also deduct building expenses from the taxes they paid the Venezuelan government.

145. Prieto Soto, *Luchas obreras por nuestro petróleo*, 95; Briceño Parilli, *Las migraciones internas y los municipios petroleros*, 33.

146. Lavin, *Halo for Gómez*, 305.

147. "En Cabimas," *Petróleo*, 6 May 1936.

148. *Venezuela and the Oil Pioneers*, 48.

149. Ibid.

150. Prieto Soto, *Huellas históricas*, 114.

151. Colina Nava, *Sucesos históricos sobre Cabimas y Lagunillas hasta 1938*, 12.

152. AHZ, 1925, tomo 3, legajo 19, 28 May 1925, Distrito Mara y Páez, Fuertes cantidades de licor, mas que lo normal, Alambiques ilegales.

153. Santos Matute to Gómez, 9 June 1923, in *Boletín del Archivo Histórico de Miraflores* 19 (July–December 1977), 4.

154. Nehru Tennassee, *Venezuela*, 136–37. Also Pérez Schael, *Petróleo, cultura y poder en Venezuela*, 86.

155. Prieto Soto, *Luchas obreras por nuestro petróleo*, 95.

156. AHZ, 1925, tomo 3, legajo 21, 23 May 1925, Mensaje del Presidents de Zulia a la Asamblea, May 1925. The governor complained about the proliferation of illegal gambling activity.

157. AHZ, 1927, tomo 11, legajo 30, 11 November 1927, Chester Marvin Crebbs, Venezuelan Gulf Oil, to governor.

158. Calvani, *Nuestro máximo problema*, 54–55.

159. Ibid, 54.

160. *El Bronce* (Lagunillas), 20 August 1932.

161. Ibid.

162. McBeth, *Juan Vicente Gómez and the Oil Companies in Venezuela*, 150.

163. "Primer Venezolano que pasa de Caporal a jefe de Guardia," *Petroleo*, 30 May 1936. Tranquilino Chávez assumed charge of the guard unit at the Mene Grande gas facility.

164. *El Farol*, March 1943, 10.

165. AHM, 566-c, Cabimas, 26 June 1926, Rufo Antonio Mora to J. V. Gómez.

166. Bracho Montiel, *Guachimanes*, 17.

167. Interview, Alí López, Mérida, 12 July 2004.

168. Ochoa Urdaneta, *Estampas de Cabimas*, 47.

169. Interview, Alí López, Mérida, 12 July 2004.
170. Colina Nava, *Sucesos históricos sobre Cabimas y Lagunillas hasta 1938*, 16.
171. *Petróleo*, 21 October 1936.
172. Bracho Montiel, *Guachimanes*, 17.
173. Ibid.

CHAPTER 4: OIL, RACE, LABOR, AND NATIONALISM

1. McClintock, "'No Longer in a Future Heaven.'"
2. Graham, ed., *The Idea of Race in Latin America*.
3. Chomsky and Lauria Santiago, eds., *Identity and the Struggle at the Margins of the Nation State*; Putman, *The Company They Kept*.
4. For scholars who are addressing this issue see Euraque, "The Threat of Blackness to the Mestizo Nation," 229–49.
5. NARA, MID RG 165, 2655-M-95, military attaché, Venezuela, 30 January 1924, interpretation of immigration laws.
6. González Ripoll Navarro, *Trinidad la otra llave de América*.
7. *Concurso de la hacienda*, 109; José Alberto Figueroa, "Historia pre petrolera de Caripito: Una contribución a su estudio" (master's thesis, Universidad Santa Maria, 1988), 79.
8. PRO, FO 371/2157, Annual Report, British Consul, Caracas, 13 April 1914, 4.
9. *Concurso de la hacienda*, 109.
10. PRO, FO 371/2157, Annual Report, British Consul, Caracas, 13 April 1914, 4.
11. PRO, FO 371/11202, 16 June 1926, Col. Medlicott to Foreign Office concerning plans by Gen. Alcantara in Trinidad to recruit forces for an invasion of the mainland. Also Archivo Histórico de Miraflores, 566-c, 29 June 1926, Diogenes Escalante (Londres) a J. V. Gómez, Cónsul Noruega en Trinidad. Mr. Lindblad presentó ante directiva de British Controlled Oilfields Alcántara proyectaba invasión desde Trinidad.
12. McBeth, *Juan Vicente Gómez and the Oil Companies in Venezuela*, 152.
13. *Memoria Ministro de Relaciones Interiores 1937* (Caracas: Imprenta Nacional, 1937), 419. José Pascual González's parents had sent him to Trinidad at the age of six but forgotten to register his birth in Venezuela; he was therefore forced to request his citizenship from the minister of the interior.
14. Pollak-Eltz, *La negritud en Venezuela*, 85.
15. PRO, FO 371 7325, Annual Report, British Consul, Caracas, 11 January 1922.
16. PRO, FO 371/2157, Annual Report, British Consul, Caracas, 13 April 1914, 4.
17. Ibid.
18. Gordon, "Effects of Underdevelopment on Migration from Trinidad and Tobago to the U.S.," 17–18. Also Lewis, *The Growth of the Modern West Indies*, 201; Williams, *From Columbus to Castro*, 348.

19. Arthur Shipley, "Trekking South, *Times* (London), 16 June 1927."

20. Oster R. A. Bayne, "My Recollections of Venezuela, 1925–1953" (unpublished MS, Port of Spain, 1972), 8.

21. *Sunday Guardian*, 5 February 1933.

22. AHZ, 1929, tomo 13, legajo 27, 19 May 1929, Jefatura Civil de Municipio Cabimas Distrito Bolívar del Edo. Zulia, Carta emitida para el interesado Joseph H. Allis.

23. Leonard, *Men of Maracaibo*, 215.

24. Standard Oil Company of New Jersey, Seaview Golf Club, Absecon, 19 May 1937, agenda for spring conference, "Training of Native Employees for Skilled and Semi Skilled Positions."

25. Ibid.

26. Ibid.

27. Ewell, *Venezuela and the United States*, 135.

28. NARA, RG 59, m366, roll 21, 28 November 1925, Alexander K. Sloan, preparations for census.

29. *Nosotros*, October 1956, 23.

30. *Petróleo*, 29 April 1936, letter signed by directors of Caribbean, Lago, and Gulf; *Petróleo*, 30 May 1936.

31. *Amuay: 25 años en la historia de una refinería* (Caracas: Creole Petroleum Corporation, 1975), 25; *Nosotros*, September 1955, 11.

32. *Nosotros*, October 1957, 11–12.

33. *Nosotros*, April 1954, 10.

34. *Nosotros*, March 1949, 31.

35. *Nosotros*, October 1957, 11–12.

36. Ibid.

37. Frank Laurie, Lago Petroleum Corporation, *Report of Operations, Month of May 1930*, submitted 7 June 1930. The category of "house boy" appears repeatedly throughout the 1930s.

38. NARA, RG 59, m366, roll 21, 7 August 1926, Walter S. Keineck, Martinique, French West Indies.

39. AHZ, 1929, tomo 1, legajo 1, 12 February 1929, Pedro Arcaya to Pres. of Zulia.

40. NARA, RG 59, m366, roll 21, 8 October 1927, immigration, Willis Cook to American minister.

41. NARA, RG 238, roll 352, Maracaibo Post report, June 1949, "Domestic Servants."

42. George, *A Is for Abrazo*, 44.

43. AHM, caja E39:15.2, Comisión de la Oficina Central de Coordinación y Planificación, 7 October 1959.

44. AHZ, 1929, tomo 6, legajo 16 and 18, 5 June 1929 and 12 July 1929, letters of recommendation.

45. AHZ, 1929, tomo 13, legajo 27, 20 May 1929, L. Walker, vice-consul.

46. Anne Rainey Langley, "I Kept House in a Jungle," *National Geographic*, January 1939, 97.

47. Standard Oil Company of Venezuela, manager's review (H. E. Linam, acting manager), January 1932, 28.

48. *Caracas Journal*, 10 January 1949.

49. George, *A Is for Abrazo*.

50. Allen, *Venezuela*, 245.

51. AHZ, 1929, tomo 13, legajo 27, 2 April 1929, H. Bryan Jones, Caribbean, to Presidente de Zulia.

52. AHZ, 1929, tomo 13, legajo 27, 8 May 1929, Gordon Short, the Caribbean Petroleum Company, letter for Leonore Harley.

53. AHZ, 1929, tomo 13, legajo 27, 10 April 1929, Jefe de Garaje de la VOC al interesado, Egerton Goddard.

54. AHZ, 1929, tomo 13, legajo 27, 5 March 1929, Caribbean Petroleum Company: a quien le concierna.

55. AHZ, 1929, tomo 13, legajo 27, 25 May 1929, Jefe del Departamento, VOC, Carta de aval para Alfred Small que desea traer su esposa; AHZ, 1929, tomo 14, legajo 1, 22 March 1929, Lago, W. H. Rinehart, superintendente de campo (Lagunillas), Recomendación, el Sr. J. G. Briggs propone traer su novia la Señorita Julia Ballet residenciada en Puerto España, Trinidad, y piensa casarse con ella tan pronto llegue a Maracaibo.

56. AHZ, 1929, tomo 13, legajo 27, 20 May 1929, Caribbean Petroleum Company, Carta de aval para Srta. Doris Arthur.

57. Laurie, *Report of Operations*, January 1930 (prepared 7 February 1930) and May 1930 (prepared 7 June 1930), Terminal Laundry.

58. AHZ, 1929, tomo 14, legajo 1, 11 March 1929, Jorge Ford al residente del Edo. Zulia, Carta de Aval para Sta. Florencia Marcial de 29 años de edad.

59. AHZ, 1929, tomo 14, legajo 1, 17 March 1929, Washington Hotel Bar-Restaurant, Plaza Sucre (Maracaibo), E. Jensen re: Sra. Daisy Assang to Presidente de Edo Zulia.

60. *Diario de Occidente* (Maracaibo), 2 August 1951; Díaz Sánchez, *Mene*, 96.

61. *Tropical Sun*, 28 April 1928.

62. PRO, FO 924/441, British legation, Caracas to Foreign Office, 19 December 1945.

63. PRO, FO 924/441, Foreign Office comments to a report sent from Venezuela on 8 April 1946.

64. AHZ, 1929, tomo 13, legajo 27, 27 May 1929, VOC, Sid Roberts, Supt. Lake Transportation: A quien corresponda Egbert Searly.

65. Hallacas resemble tamales but are prepared differently and are wrapped in banana leaves.

66. *El Diario de Caracas,* 30 December 1992.

67. *Nosotros,* October 1956, 23.

68. Ibid.

69. *Nosotros,* January 1961, 13.

70. *Nosotros,* December 1954, 19.

71. *Nosotros,* October 1957, 11–12.

72. *Memoria Ministro Relaciones Interiores 1938* (Caracas: Imprenta Nacional, 1939), 457, documento 369.

73. *Petróleo,* 7 October 1936.

74. Mireya Tabuas, "¿Porque no hay chinos en los cementerios de Venezuela?," *Nacional,* 3 August 1994, Sección especial, Venezuela Camino de sueños, 10.

75. Interview, Angel Kingland, Mérida, 21 June 1997.

76. AHZ, 1929, tomo 14, legajo 1, n.d., Henry Ching Fong to Presidente del Edo Zulia.

77. AHZ, 1929, tomo 16, legajo 16–18, Cabimas, Jefe Civil, 11 June 1929 and 13 June 1929 (Chinese names are reproduced the way they appear in the original Venezuelan documents).

78. NARA, RG 59, m366, roll 21, 15 October 1920, Frederick Job, Chicago, to Dudley Dwyre, United States consul in Maracaibo.

79. *Tropical Sun,* 18 February 1928.

80. *Tropical Sun,* 7 April 1928.

81. AHZ, 1929, tomo 11, legajo 30, 9 September 1929, Caribbean to Secretario de Estado; AHZ, 1929, tomo 11, legajo 30, 17 September 1929, Cartas de recomendación Caribbean, San Lorenzo.

82. AHZ, 1929, tomo 14, legajo 1, 21 July 1929, Caribbean Petroleum Company, Jefe de Campo Kenneth Afoon de nacionalidad China.

83. AHZ, 1929, tomo 14, legajo 1, n.d., Bien Sang Long to Presidente del Edo Zulia.

84. Interview, I.S., camp resident, November 1997.

85. AHZ, 1929, tomo 14, legajo 1, 19 February 1929, Rafael París de "Juan París & Co." (Maracaibo), constancia para Vicente Ching.

86. *El Condor* (Lagunillas), 10 December 1933; *El Escudo* (Lagunillas), 5 July 1929; *Suplemento de la Guía Industrial y Comercial 1943* (Caracas: Vargas, 1944), 57.

87. *Guía Industrial y Comercial de Venezuela, 1943 (Monagas y Anzoátegui)* (Caracas: Vargas, 1944), 253.

88. NARA, RG 59, m366, roll 21, 8 October 1927, immigration, Willis Cook to American minister.

89. AHM, caja E39:15.2, Comisión de la Oficina Central de Coordinación y Planificación, 7 October 1959.

90. *Guía Industrial y Comercial de Monagas, 1943,* 253.

91. Laurie, *Report of Operations,* May 1930, submitted 7 June 1930.

92. Lago Petroleum Corporation, Reports of Operations, and Standard Oil Company, Reports of Operations, 1930–1940s.

93. NARA, RG 59, m 366, roll 18, Alexander Sloan, United States consul, Maracaibo, to Department of State, 30 July 1925, 10.

94. Interview, Edgar Campos, Maracaibo, October 1997.

95. Ibid.

96. NARA, RG 59, m366, roll 18, Alexander K. Sloan, 6 April 1926.

97. Nehru Tennassee, *Venezuela*, 59, 136.

98. Alexander Sloan, United States consul in Maracaibo, to secretary of state, 1 October 1926, cited in Donnelly, "Juan Vicente Gómez and the Venezuelan Worker," 149.

99. Godio, *El movimiento obrero venezolano*, 62.

100. See *New York Times*, 6 December 1928, cited in Victoria Chia, "Twentieth Century Colombia, the United Fruit Company and the Magical Realism of Gabriel García Marquez" (unpublished MS, April 2006), 7.

101. *Tropical Sun*, 11 February 1928, 3.

102. Ibid., 16.

103. *Maracaibo Herald*, 29 November 1947.

104. McBeth, *Juan Vicente Gómez and the Oil Companies in Venezuela*, 141.

105. See Rómulo Betancourt, Plan de Barranquilla, 22 March 1931, in which he also refers to Gómez as the Díaz of Venezuela. See Hallgren, "Oil in Venezuela," 496–98.

106. NARA, MID RG 165, box 1707, MII, 2657-M-32, Mexican attack on Gómez, 22 November 1920.

107. Prieto Soto, *Luchas obreras por nuestro petróleo*, 22–23.

108. Prieto Soto, *Conformación ideológica petrolera venezolana*, 6; Bautista Fuenmayor, *1928–1948*, 58.

109. "Vuelven los del Superior," *El Universal* (México), 9 January 1932 and 20 January 1932.

110. José Vasconcelos, cited by Felícitas López Portillo, "Mexico y Venezuela: Un recuento de sus relaciones diplomaticas, 1910–1958,"256.

111. PRO, FO 371 7325, Annual Report 1921, Mr. Beaumont to Marques Curzon of Kedleston, Caracas, 11 January 1922.

112. AHZ, 1928, tomo 3, legajo 21, 13 December 1928, V. Pérez Soto to Pan American Petroleum Company. Also to Jefes Civiles of Zulia.

113. Thomas Rourke, *Gómez, Tyrant of the Andes* (New York: William Morrow, 1941), 239.

114. López Portillo, "Mexico y Venezuela," 258.

115. For the shift from Mexico and Venezuela see Brown, "Why Foreign Oil Companies Shifted their Production from Mexico to Venezuela," 380.

116. AHM, #442-C, 27 December 1922, Pedro Arcaya to Gómez.

117. Rangel, *Los andinos en el poder*, 227–28.

118. "La Ruptura de Mexico," *Paz y Trabajo*, 3 November 1923.

119. López Portillo, "Mexico y Venezuela," 259.

120. NARA, RG 165, box 1701, MII, 30 June 1924, "Estimate of the Political Situation."

121. Cited in López Portillo, "Mexico y Venezuela," 260.

122. NARA, RG 165, box 1701, MII, 30 June 1924, "Estimate of the Political Situation," 3.

123. *New York Times*, 6 October 1923; *Washington Post*, 20 November 1923.

124. NARA, RG 165, box 1707, MII, #2327-M-4, Mexico and Venezuela, 4 December 1923 and 20 December 1923.

125. NARA, RG 165, box 1707, MII, #2327-M-4, 20 December 1925, dispatch no. 1415.

126. Arcaya, *New Notes on Political History*, 10–11. Also see Pedro Manuel Arcaya, *The Gómez Regime in Venezuela and its Background* (Washington, 1936).

127. For new interpretations of Gómez see Segnini, *Las luces del gomecismo*, 187.

128. Vivanco y Villegas, *Venezuela al día / Venezuela Up to Date*, 1033.

129. AHZ, 1928, tomo 3, legajo 2, 13 December 1928, Prohibición a la entrada de Mexicanos a Venezuela por ser nacionales de un país enemigo a Venezuela.

130. Interview, Edgar Campos, Maracaibo, October 1997.

131. Interview, José Antonio Sarache, Mérida, July 1998, and José Omar Colmenares, Mérida, October 1997. Sarache worked at Cabimas and Colmenares at Mene Grande; NARA, Consular Trade Reports, 1943–50, M238, reel 137, 14 July 1943, Caracas Venezuelan Motion Picture Report, Maurice Bernbaum.

132. Quintero, *La cultura del petróleo*, 36.

133. United States consul Alexander K. Sloan to secretary of state, Marcaibo, 16 December 1926, N. 149 831.00/1218, RDS Internal Affairs microcopy m366, reel 7, cited in Linder, "Agricultural and Rural Society in Pre-Petroleum Venezuela."

134. NARA, RG 59, m366, roll 18, 20 July 1925, "Labor Situation in Maracaibo District," 30 July 1925, Alexander Sloan.

135. Ewell, *Venezuela and the United States*, 135.

136. AHZ, 1927, tomo 11, legajo 30, 7 January 1927, V. Pérez Soto to manager of British-controlled oil fields.

137. Díaz Sánchez, *Mene*, 95; Quintero, *La cultura del petróleo*, 38.

138. AHZ, 1929, tomo 14, legajo 2, 11 September 1929, Jefe Civil del Municipio Lagunillas, Entradas y Salidas de Arrestados de la Policía y sus sanciones durante el día de 10 de Septiembre de 1929.

139. Ibid.

140. PRO, FO 369/2340, British Legation, Caracas to Foreign Office, 3 August 1933.

141. Vitalis, "Wallace Stegner's Arabian Discovery."

142. Calvani, *Nuestro máximo problema*, 24.

143. *Venezuela and the Oil Pioneers*, 50.

144. Ibid.

145. Daniel Bendahán, *Petrolerias, cuentos petroleros* (Caracas: Corpoven, 1984), 12.

146. Bracho Montiel, *Guachimanes*, 15.

147. Drechsel, *From Venezuela with Love*, 72.

148. Uribe Piedrahita, *Mancha de aceite*, 6.

149. Ibid., 5.

150. "Otro Mister indeseable," *Petróleo*, 27 February 1937.

151. "En el infierno Petrolero," *Petróleo*, 25 April 1936, 2.

152. Prieto Soto, *Conformación ideológica petrolera venezolana*, 68.

153. *Seventh Annual Report of the Caribbean Petroleum Company*, 1 January to 31 December 1920.

154. Otero Silva, *Oficina N.1*; George, *A Is for Abrazo*, 33.

155. *Petróleo*, 29 April 1936.

156. Lago Petroleum Corporation, Reports of Operations, and Standard Oil Company, Reports of Operations, 1930–40.

157. Standard Oil Company of Venezuela, *Petroleum Engineering Report*, prepared by H. E. Linam, January–April 1938. This classification appears in the Standard records for several years.

158. Standard Oil Company of Venezuela, Statement of Payrolls, February 1933, in *Petroleum Engineering Report*, January–June 1933. Also see Standard Oil Company of Venezuela, *Petroleum Engineering Report*, January 1941, 4.

159. Otero Silva, *Oficina N. 1*.

160. Uribe Piedrahita, *Mancha de aceite*.

161. Díaz Sánchez, *Mene*, 98–104.

162. *El Taladro* (Cabimas), 2 June 1934.

163. *Memoria*, Ministerio de Fomento (Caracas: Cosmos, 1923), 19 April 1923.

164. Lago Petroleum Corporation, *Monthly Operating Report*, January 1939.

165. Calvani, *Nuestro máximo problema*, 27.

166. NARA, RG 59, m366, roll 18, H. M. Walcott, United States consul, 14 February 1928.

167. Standard Oil Company of Venezuela, *Monthly Operating Report*, January–June 1933 and February 1940.

168. *Petróleo*, 7 October 1936.

169. AHZ, 1927, tomo 4, legajo 28, 2 May 1927, Lago to V.P. Soto.

170. AHZ, 1927, tomo 4, legajo 28, 3 May 1927, VOC G. Witteven to Secretario de Gobierno.

171. *Petróleo*, 14 October 1936.

172. Ibid.

173. AHZ, 1927, tomo 4, legajo 28, 5 May 1927, Carta de Obreros despedidos to J. V. Gómez.

174. Nehru Tennassee, *Venezuela*, 153.

175. Rodolfo Quintero, "Prologo," in Prieto Soto, *Luchas obreras por nuestro petróleo*, xiii.

176. Pedro Arcaya, *Memoria Ministro de Relaciones Interiores* (Caracas: Lito del Comercio, 1930), xv.

177. Ibid., xv, xvi.

178. Berglund, "Las bases sociales y económicas de las leyes de inmigración venezolanas," 954.

179. Wright, *Café con Leche*; Lewis, *Ethnicity and Identity in Contemporary Afro Venezuelan Literature*.

180. Veracoechea, *El proceso de la inmigración en Venezuela*, 217.

181. AHM, nos. 16–1:7–2, 23 April 1926, Ing. Civil Pedro José Rojas to Gómez.

182. Rivas Aguilar, *La Revolución de Octubre*, xviii–xix.

183. Arturo Uslar Pietri in *El Universal*, July 1937, cited ibid.

184. Letter to General Isaías Medina Angarita, 23 February 1937, in Picón, ed., *Mariano Picón Salas*, 120.

185. Blanco Fombona, *Bolívar y la guerra a muerte*, 44–45.

186. AHZ, 1929, tomo 1, legajo 1, 5 September 1930, Pres. Zulia to MRI.

187. Letter to General Isaías Medina Angarita, 23 February 1937, in Picón, ed., *Mariano Picón Salas*, 120.

188. Droit, *Visas pour l'Amérique du Sud*, 53.

189. *Panorama*, 13 January 1931.

190. *Petróleo*, 2 September 1936.

191. NARA, MID RG 165, 2655-M-95, military attaché, Venezuela, 30 January 1924, interpretation of immigration laws.

192. *Times* (London), 2 November 1929.

193. *New York Times*, 2 November 1929.

194. *Tropical Sun*, 31 March 1928.

195. AHZ, 1927, tomo 4, legajo 28, 5 May 1927, Carta de Obreros despedidos a J. V. Gómez.

196. AHZ, 1929, tomo 8, legajo 21, 9 April 1929, Presidente del Edo. Zulia Pérez Soto al Administrador de la Aduana de Maracaibo. The category of "undesirable alien" also included political enemies of the state. Also Lago Petroleum, *Report of Operations*, Land and Legal Department, January 1930.

197. *Tropical Sun*, 7 April 1928. The paper reported that in March 1928, 1,035 ships had crossed the San Carlos Bar at the entrance to Lake Maracaibo. It estimated that 15,000 ships would arrive in Maracaibo by the end of 1928.

198. Blanco-Fombona, *Bolívar y la guerra a muerte*, 45.

199. AHZ, tomo 16, legajo 16 and 18, Jefe Civil, Lagunillas, 10 July 1929.

200. AHZ, 1929, tomo 11, legajo 30, 9 September 1929, Caribbean to Secretarío de Estado.

201. AHZ, 1929, tomo 16, legajo 16 and 18, 28 March 1929, Caribbean Petroleum.

202. AHZ, 1930, tomo 1, legajo 4, 17 November 1930, Caribbean Petroleum.

203. AHZ, 1929, tomo 14, legajo 1, 5 March 1929. Venezuela Gulf Oil Company, Cabimas, certificado para Jeremiah Julian (Negro).

204. AHZ, 1929, tomo 14, legajo 1, 15 March 1929, Martín Peréz to Secretario Gral. del Edo Zulia: Constancia La Señora Hellen Daniel de color Negro.

205. AHZ, 1929, tomo 14, legajo 1, 18 February 1929, George Henry to Secretario Gral. del Gobierno.

206. AHZ, 1929, tomo 16, legajo 16 and 18, 12 June 1929, Luis Lampp a Pérez Soto.

207. Public Records Office, FO A2202, Mister Gainer to Viscount Halifax, 26 March 1940, review of politics 1939.

208. *Panorama*, 27 August 1936.

209. *Petróleo*, 29 August 1936.

210. *Petróleo*, 16 May 1936.

211. *Petróleo*, 10 June 1936.

212. *Maracaibo Herald*, 18 January 1947.

213. *Petróleo*, 16 May 1936.

214. AHZ, 1928, tomo 3, legajo 18, 23 July 1928, Min del Interior to J. Vicente Gómez. Report on purported Soviet agent provocateurs preparing to arrive in Venezuela.

CHAPTER 5: OUR TROPICAL OUTPOST

1. *Second Annual Report of the Caribbean Petroleum Company* (1915), 106.

2. *Caracas Journal*, 6 January 1955.

3. Interview, 3 March 2000, Morse and Govea Travers. He worked for the Otis Elevator Company and regularly socialized with those in the oil industry.

4. Anne Rainey Langley, "I Kept House in a Jungle," *National Geographic*, January 1939, 97.

5. *Maracaibo Herald*, 8 November 1947, 9.

6. *Second Annual Report of the Caribbean Petroleum Company* (1915), 106.

7. NARA, RG 59, m366, roll 18, 9 September 1926, Frank B. Kellogg, response from Department of State.

8. Standard Oil Company of New Jersey, agenda for spring 1936 conference, Seaview Golf Club, Absecon, New Jersey, 20 April 1936.

9. Ibid.

10. Drechsel, *From Venezuela with Love*, 15. Drechsel lived in the Caripito camp during the 1940s (16). And Schuster, *Petroleros*, 77.

11. Creole Petroleum Corporation, *Working with Creole in Venezuela*, 20–31.

12. Drechsel, *From Venezuela with Love*, 15.

13. NARA, RG 238, roll 137, 15 March 1941, U.S. Embassy, General Commercial Information.

14. *Caracas Journal*, 13 August 1948. Also *El Nacional*, 1 January 1954.

15. Creole Public Relations, *An Oil Well with an Interest in You* (Caracas: Cromotip, 1955).

16. Interview, AMS, Creole annuitants meeting, Little Rock, 1999.

17. Interview, Jim Barnett, Creole annuitants meeting, Las Vegas, 2000.

18. Creole Petroleum Corporation, *Working with Creole in Venezuela*, 15; Standard Oil Company of New Jersey, agenda of the Coordination Committee Group Meeting, Miami, 8–13 February 1946.

19. Ibid.

20. *El Farol*, April 1946.

21. Interview, Harold Lieberman, Creole annuitants meeting, Las Vegas, 2000. Also Creole Petroleum Corporation, "Supplementary Data Regarding Employment in Venezuela" (November 1948), 3.

22. NARA, RG 238, roll 352, 4 December 1943, Frank Corrigan to secretary of state.

23. Interview, Harold Lieberman, Creole annuitants meeting, Little Rock, 1999.

24. *Diario de Occidente*, 27 January 1958.

25. Interview, S.J., Creole annuitants meeting, Little Rock, May 1999.

26. *Caracas Journal*, 10 September 1948.

27. Schuster, *Petroleros*, 95.

28. Standard Oil Company of New Jersey, "Minutes of the Seaview Conference," Seaview Golf Club, 15–19 May 1939, 103.

29. Schuster, *Petroleros*, 120.

30. "Creole in Cabimas" (Creole: Cabimas, 1951) [orientation manual].

31. George, *A Is for Abrazo*.

32. Ewell, *Venezuela and the United States*, 186.

33. *Caracas Journal*, 18 January 1946.

34. Kamen-Kayes, *Caracas Everyday*; Kamen-Kayes, *Speaking of Venezuela*.

35. *Caracas Journal*, 23 February 1945.

36. Drechsel, *From Venezuela with Love*, 47, 71.

37. Interview, Harold Lieberman, Creole annuitants meeting, Las Vegas, 2000.

38. Schuster, *Petroleros*, 94–95.

39. Ibid., 16, 81; interview, B.D., Creole annuitants meeting, Little Rock, May 1999; interview, A.T., Creole annuitants meeting, Las Vegas, May 2000.

40. Ewell, *Venezuela and the United States*, 186.

41. Interview, I. S., C.C., Caracas, November 1997.

42. Several interviews, I.S., L.A.T, and C.C., November 1997.

43. Prieto Soto, *Huellas históricas*, 522.

44. *El Farol*, no. 134 (1951), 26 (during this period *El Farol* did not indicate the month of publication).

45. Interview, Harold Lieberman, Creole annuitants meeting, Las Vegas, 2000.

46. Interview, Jim Barnett, Creole annuitants meeting, Las Vegas, 2000.

47. Interview, Morse Travers, 3 March 2000; Fergusson, *Venezuela*; Y. T. Ybarra, *Young Man of Caracas* (New York: Ives Washburn, 1941).

48. Anonymous interview, Creole annuitants meeting, Little Rock, May 1999.

49. Langley, "I Kept House in a Jungle," 97; Burchfiel, "Our Tropical Outpost in Venezuela."

50. Allen, *Venezuela*, 245.

51. *Creole en acción / Creole in Action* (Caracas: Cromotip, 1957).

52. Drechsel, *From Venezuela with Love*, 61.

53. *Tropical Sun*, 21 April 1928.

54. *Tropical Sun*, 28 April 1928.

55. *Caracas Journal*, 4 June 1955.

56. *Diario de Occidente*, 17 January 1952.

57. Drechsel, *From Venezuela with Love*, 15.

58. Langley, "I Kept House in a Jungle," 97.

59. *Caracas Journal*, 3 January 1949.

60. "Todo en Domingo," *El Nacional*, 1 May 2007, 31.

61. Report from Bella Vista Camp, *Tropical Sun*, 10 March 1928.

62. *El Farol*, no. 85 (June 1946).

63. Frank G. Laurie, Lago Petroleum Corporation, *Report of Operations*, May 1930, 8.

64. Ibid.

65. Interview, Myriane Marret Woolen, Creole annuitants meeting, Little Rock, 28 May 1999.

66. Ibid.

67. Lawrence, *Cuba for Christ*, 100.

68. *Venezuela and the Oil Pioneers*, 46.

69. Lieberman, "Early Impressions of Maracaibo, with Some Attention to the Local Mores," 2.

70. *Edificio Creole* (Caracas: Cromotip, 1955).

71. Vicente, "La arquitectura urbana de las corporaciones petroleras," 395.

72. Ibid. Vicente and others point out the existence of an earlier district in central Caracas.

73. Interview, Myriane Marret Woolen, Creole annuitants meeting, Little Rock, 28 May 1999.

74. *Caracas Journal*, 7 January 1952.

75. *Caracas Journal*, 16 March 1945.

76. *Caracas Journal*, 25 July 1949.

77. Drechsel, *From Venezuela with Love*, 16.

78. Arnold, Macready, and Barrington, *The First Big Oil Hunt*, 24.

79. *Caracas Journal*, 12 October 1955.

80. Interview, Myriane Marret Woolen, Creole annuitants meeting, Little Rock, 28 May 1999.

81. *Caracas Journal*, 27 August 1948.

82. Schuster, *Petroleros*, 94–95.

83. Ibid., 33.

84. Ibid. Among women salty dogs (a drink prepared from vodka, gin, and canned grapefruit juice) and bloody marys proved to be the drinks of choice.

85. Ibid., 79.

86. *Caracas Journal*, 3 May 1946.

87. Schuster, *Petroleros*, 95.

88. Langley, "I Kept House in a Jungle," 98.

89. Ibid., 99.

90. Interview, Myriane Marret Woolen, Creole annuitants meeting, Little Rock, 28 May 1999.

91. Schuster, *Petroleros*, 95.

92. Ewell, *Venezuela and the United States*, 186.

93. *Buen Provecho*.

94. *Amuay Cooking Capers, Recipes along Venezuela's B.C.F.*, and Pamela Singletary Soligo, *Pruebalo*.

95. Drechsel, *From Venezuela with Love*, 19–20.

96. *Caracas Journal*, 28 June 1946.

97. Schuster, *Petroleros*, 173.

98. Interview, Myriane Marret Woolen, Creole annuitants meeting, Little Rock, 28 May 1999.

99. *Caracas Journal*, 15 June 1945.

100. *Caracas Journal*, 23 February 1945.

101. *Maracaibo Herald*, 25 February 1950.

102. *Caracas Journal*, 9 May 1947.

103. *Maracaibo Herald*, 8 November 1947.

104. *Caracas Journal*, 5 December 1946.

105. *Maracaibo Herald*, 30 December 1950.

106. *Caracas Journal*, 7 January 1952.

107. *Caracas Journal*, 10 January 1949.

108. *Caracas Journal*, 28 June 1946.

109. *Nosotros*, May 1956.

110. *El Farol*, August 1941; Drechsel, *From Venezuela with Love*, 40.

111. *Caracas Journal*, 13 October 1952.

112. *El Farol*, May 1940.

113. *Nosotros*, October 1955.

114. *Caracas Journal*, 24 March 1954.

115. *Caracas Journal*, 7 September 1945.

116. Otero Silva, *Oficina N. 1*; and Schuster, *Petroleros*.

117. Schuster, *Petroleros*, 194.

118. "Everybody Is Crazy in Caracas," *Cosmopolitan*, April 1948, 21.

119. *Caracas Journal*, 7 May 1948.

120. The Cuban singer Beny More also recorded a composition entitled "Maracaibo" that many have assumed, mistakenly, to refer to the Venezuelan city. In fact, in the Cuban context maracaibo is a musical genre also known as *chanquí* and has nothing to do with Venezuela.

121. Burl Ives, "Venezuela," *Poor Wayfaring Stranger* (Decca Records, 1950).

122. Harry Belafonte, "Venezuela" (Colonet Records, 1950).

123. Guy Lombardo, "Venezuela," *Lombardo Goes Latin* (Capitol Records, 1958).

124. Sterling Silliphant, *Maracaibo* (New York: Farrar Straus, 1955).

CHAPTER 6: THE OIL INDUSTRY AND CIVIL SOCIETY

1. Karl, *Paradox of Plenty*, 54.

2. Coronil, *The Magical State*, 68.

3. Ministro de Fomento, *Memoria y Cuenta*, 1947, 11.

4. NARA, RG 59, reel 238, #143, U.S. Department of State, Thomas C. Mann, attachment to Petroleum Venezuela annual report, 1948; Briceño Parilli, *Las migraciones internas y los municipios petroleros*, 120.

5. Walter Dupouy, "Consideraciones sobre algunos efectos económicos y sociales de la industria del petróleo en Venezuela," *El Farol*, July 1949, 8.

6. *El Farol*, no. 129 (1950) (during this period *El Farol* did not indicate the month of publication); *Nosotros*, November 1947.

7. *El Farol*, February 1945.

8. *Tropical Sun*, 10 March 1928.

9. Burchfiel, "Our Tropical Outpost in Venezuela," 196.

10. *Octavo Censo General de Población, XII Resumen General de la República*, part A, *Población (26 November 1950)* (Caracas: Ministerio de Fomento, Dirección General de Estadística y Censos Nacionales, 1957), 35.

11. Siro Vázquez, "Study Home Purchase Aid Plan as a Basis for Community Development, La Salina District" (Caracas: Creole Petroleum Corporation, Production Department, 1953), 4–6.

12. Vázquez, "Study Home Purchase Aid Plan as a Basis for Community Development, La Salina District," 3.

13. Ibid.

14. *Viviendas y servicios públicos, campo de Jusepín* (Creole Petroleum Corporation, May 1960).

15. AHM, serie 3–1-6, # 2 SPOTP, Jusepín, 17 March 1945, Pliegos de trabajadores.

16. Interview, José Omar Colmenares, Mérida, July 2003.

17. Similar conditions prevailed in Iran. See Kaveh Ehsani, "Social Engineering and the Contradictions of Modernization in Khuzestan's Company Towns: A Look at Abadan and Masjed-Soleyman," *International Review of Social History* 48 (2003), 361–99.

18. *Study of Operations, Temblador District* (Petroleum Engineer Department, Standard Oil Company of Venezuela, October–November 1942).

19. Vázquez, "Study Home Purchase Aid Plan," 3.

20. Ibid., 12; Moreno was interviewed in 1953 by Creole officials to determine the viability of a home loan program.

21. Interview, Alí López, Mérida, July 2004. López attended school in the camp although his parents were not employed by the company.

22. *El Farol, Suplemento de Occidente*, May 1943.

23. *El Farol*, November 1944.

24. E. A. Bauman, "Creole Relations with Churches, Clubs and Charitable Organizations," Creole Petroleum Corporation, *Human Relations Conference*, 222.

25. Siro Vázquez, Untitled comments from a conference, Creole Petroleum Corporation, *Human Relations Conference, June 1, 16, 17, 1953*, 230.

26. Ibid., 12.

27. Standard Oil Company of New Jersey, agenda for spring 1936 conference, Seaview Golf Club, Absecon, New Jersey, 20 April 1936.

28. *Second Annual Report of the Caribbean Petroleum Company* (1915), 106.

29. *El Farol, Suplemento de Oriente*, February 1945.

30. *El Farol*, 1949 (no month given).

31. *Diario de Occidente*, 2 October 1951, 1. Also interviews of women who lived in the oil camps.

32. Interview, C.C., Caracas, 29 June 1997.

33. *El Farol*, January 1942.

34. *El Farol*, March 1949.

35. Interview, Creole annuitants meeting, Little Rock, 1999.

36. "A Significant Pan American Conference," *Bulletin of the Pan American Union*, July 1922, 34; "Pan American Commission of Women," *Bulletin of the Pan American Union*, September 1928, 875–79; "Inter American Commission of Women," *Inter Americana Monthly*, December 1942, 29.

37. Friedman, *Unfinished Transitions*, 53.

38. *Conferencia Preparatoria del Primer Congreso Venezolano de Mujeres* (Caracas: Bolívar, 1941).

39. *El Farol*, November 1945.

40. Ibid.

41. *El Farol*, March 1949.

42. For further discussion see Dore, ed., *Gender Politics in Latin America*, 25.

43. Interview, Harold Lieberman, Creole annuitants meeting, Las Vegas, 2000.

44. Quintero, *La cultura del petróleo*, 51.

45. "El Músculo," cited in *El Farol*, January 1940.

46. *El béisbol en Venezuela: un siglo de pasión* (Caracas: Biblioteca Nacional, 1996), 9; Also Ewell, *Venezuela and the United States*, 189.

47. *El Farol*, June 1942.

48. *El Farol*, February 1940.

49. *El Farol*, no. 136 (1951) (no month given).

50. *El Farol*, no. 134 (1951) (no month given).

51. *El Farol*, no. 125 (1949) (no month given); *El Farol*, no. 133 (1951); *Nosotros*, August 1955.

52. Interview, Harold Lieberman, Creole annuitants meeting, Little Rock, 1999.

53. Petroleum Engineer Department, Standard Oil Company of Venezuela, *Study of Operations, Temblador District*, October–November 1942, 4.

54. *El Farol*, February 1949.

55. *Diario de Occidente* (Maracaibo), 2 October 1951.

56. Rabe, *The Road to* OPEC, 74; Coronil, *The Magical State*, 68.

57. L. Duggan, "Legislation and the Latin American Oil Industry," agenda of the Coordination Committee, Group Meeting, Standard Oil Company of New Jersey, Miami, 8–13 February 1946, 11.

58. "Corporate Citizen No. 1," *Time*, 22 May 1964.

59. For a development of this perspective see Carlos Luis Villalobos, "Las representaciones sociales de la tecnocracia petrolera y las transformaciones de la política petrolera," paper presented at "La Visión de Venezuela," Sección venezolana of LASA, Maracaibo, 13–14 June 2002.

60. Daniel Bendahán, *Petrolerias, cuentos petroleros* (Caracas: Corpoven, 1984), 12–30.

61. Interview, I.S., Caracas, November 1997.

62. *El Farol*, July 1942.

63. *Nosotros*, August 1946.

64. *Nosotros*, May 1947.

65. Ibid.

66. Interview, José Omar Colmenares, 10 July 2003, Mérida, Venezuela. Mr. Colmenares worked as an office boy in Mene Grande during the 1930s.

67. Ibid. Also interview, I.S., Caracas, November 1997.

68. *El Farol*, 1949 (no month given).

69. *Collective Contract Entered into between the Syndical Federation of Petroleum Workers of Venezuela and the Creole Petroleum Corporation*; and AHM, F4:2–1, May 1950, Informe Comisión que Estudia Organización y Funcionamiento de los Economatos.

70. AHM, serie 3–1-6 #2 SPOTP Jusepín, Pliego, 17 March 1945, 10.

71. *El Farol*, 1950 (no month given).

72. Ewell, *Venezuela and the United States*, 188; Rivas, *Missionary Capitalism*, 126–27.

73. *Creole en acción/ Creole in Action* (Caracas: Cromotip, 1965).

74. Ewell, *Venezuela and the United States*, 188.

75. Uslar Pietri, *Los venezolanos y el petróleo*, 23–25. The statement captured the sentiment of a generation of Venezuelan intellectuals, and the idea of sowing oil may in fact have been expressed by others as well.

76. Betancourt, *Venezuela, política y petróleo*, 343.

77. "Address of his Excellency, the Minister of Mines and Hydrocarbons, Dr. Santiago Vera Izquierdo, Coordinating Group Meeting, Creole Petroleum Corporation, February 19–21, 1951."

78. Carrera Damas, *Una nación llamada Venezuela*, 137.

79. LaCueva Teurel, *Historia del petróleo en Venezuela*, 7.

80. *El Farol*, July 1949.

81. *El Farol*, April–June 1964.

82. "Creole Petroleum: Business Embassy," *Fortune*, February 1949, 92.

83. R. T. Haslam, "Public Relations, Requirements and Activities," Standard Oil Company of New Jersey, Seaview Conference, Abescon, New Jersey, 16 May 1944, 36: 2–3.

84. Ibid.

85. Interview, Harold Lieberman, Creole annuitants meeting, Las Vegas, 2000.

86. Rabe, *The Road to OPEC*, 47.

87. Duggan, "Legislation and the Latin American Oil Industry," 5.

88. Pérez Alfonzo, *La dinámica del petróleo en el progreso de Venezuela*, 63.

89. Haslam, "Public Relations, Requirements and Activities," 36:6.

90. Pérez Alfonzo, *La dinámica del petróleo en el progreso de Venezuela*, 63.

91. Sader Pérez, *The Venezuelan State Oil Company: Reports to the People*, 20.

92. Chester F. Smith, Opening Remarks, Coordination Committee Group Meeting, Standard Oil Company of New Jersey, Miami, 8–13 February 1946.

93. "Our Legacy in Public Relations," agenda for Seaview Conference, Standard Oil Company of New Jersey, Seaview Country Club, Abescon, New Jersey, 16 May 1944, 36–1 to 36–13.

94. "Marketing Developments and Trends: Section 1, Venezuela," Coordination Committee Group Meeting, Standard Oil Company of New Jersey, Miami, 8–13 February 1946, 7.

95. K. E. Cook, "Creole's Public Relations Job," Creole Petroleum Corporation, Coordination Committee Meeting, Caracas, 19–21 February 1951, 14.

96. Duggan, "Legislation and the Latin American Oil Industry," 9.

97. The program continued, known simply known as "El Observador."

98. Albornoz, "Valores sociales en la educación venezolana," 150.

99. Compañia Shell de Venezuela, *Resumen de Actividades 1959* (Caracas: Litografía, 1959), 57.

100. DDQC, 1992, #2987, "Operations Coordinating Board," Analysis of Internal Security Situation in Venezuela and recommended action, NSC, 13 June 1956, 10.

101. Fundación Shell, "Servicio Shell para el agricultor," *Noticias Agrícolas* (January 1965).

102. *Compañia Shell de Venezuela, Resumen de Actividades en 1959* (Caracas: Miangolarra, 1959), Prologue.

103. "Corporate Citizen No. 1"; *El Periodista* (Maturin), 24 October 1956, 16. Also Rivas, *Missionary Capitalism*, 164.

104. *Fundación Creole: Los Primeros Diez Años* (Caracas: Cromotip, 1967).

105. "Inter American Notes," *Americas* 15, no. 2 (October 1958), 183.

106. "Corporate Citizen No. 1."

107. *El Farol*, February 1944.

108. José Omar Colmenares, interview, summer 2004.

109. *El Farol*, August 1942.

110. *El Farol*, February 1946; *Nosotros*, February 1947.

111. *El Farol*, April 1953.

112. This practice continues today, as the Bigott Foundation, owner of a major cigarette brand, casts itself as one of the most important promoters of Venezuelan "traditional" culture.

113. *El Farol*, April–June 1964.

114. Interview, Mauricio Pérez Badell, June 2002, Maracaibo.

115. *El Farol*, April–June 1965.

116. *El Farol*, March–April 1959; *El Farol*, September–Octuber 1958; *El Farol*, June 1946.

117. *Creole en acción / Creole in Action* (Caracas: Cromotip, 1965).

118. *El Farol*, May 1942; *El Farol*, January 1942.

119. Coronil, *The Magical State*, 109.

120. Ali Primera, *Que mi canto no se pierda, cancionera* (Caracas: Fundarte, 2006), 11.

121. "Venezuela, June 30, 1950," FRUS, 1950, vol. 2, 1025.

122. H. A. Grimes, "Creole's Efforts to Develop Independent Communities in the Work Areas: A New Creole Doctrine," Creole Coordination Group Meeting, Caracas, 19–21 February 1951, 3.

123. Harry Jarvis, "Speech before the Venezuelan Chamber of Commerce," *Caracas Journal*, 4 May 1955.

124. *El Nacional*, 28 February 1954.

125. *El Farol*, September 1952, 18–21. Judibana was unique at many levels. Because it was situated on an isolated peninsula, the National Guard could easily guard access to the area.

126. Jarvis, "Speech before the Venezuelan Chamber of Commerce."

127. Creole Petroleum Corporation, "Proyecto de urbanización del poblado de Judibana, Amuay, Venezuela" (September 1952).

128. Jarvis, "Speech before the Venezuelan Chamber of Commerce."

129. Vázquez, "Study Home Purchase Aid Plan as a Basis for Community Development, La Salina District."

130. Ibid.

131. *El Nacional*, 8 October 1954.

132. *El Nacional*, 3 February 1954; at Jusepín production had declined from 75,000 barrels a day to 27,000.

133. Lieberman, "A Revolution and Some Minor Aftermaths."

134. Jarvis, "Speech before the Venezuelan Chamber of Commerce."

CHAPTER 7: OIL AND POLITICS

1. DDQC, 1978, vol. 4, 60A, Report to the National Security Council, 6 January 1953, 5.

2. "It's Hot in Venezuela," *Fortune*, May 1949, 101.

3. Karl, *Paradox of Plenty*, 55.

4. Rabe, *The Road to* OPEC, 11–37.

5. F. Mieres cited in Mejía Alarcón, *La industria del petróleo en Venezuela*, 100.

6. Burggraaff, *The Venezuelan Armed Forces in Politics*, 41.

7. "Venezuela: Too Much Money," *United Nations World* 2 (May 1948), 27. Also FRUS, 1946, vol. 11, 1359.

8. See Manuel Egaña, personal archive. Manuel Egaña to Cristóbal L. Mendoza, 24 November 1937. Dispatched to Washington in 1937 to confer with the companies based in the United States, Manuel Egaña was outraged to learn how López Contreras, through indirect channels, had already assured Shell and Standard that "he had no problem with them and would pursue no policy that might endanger their position in the country." Egaña insisted that the general's actions undermined his mission, gave the appearance of a divided government, and strengthened the position of hard-liners in the foreign companies. Also see Lieuwen, *Petroleum in Venezuela*, 33.

9. DDQC, 1981, vol. 8 (81), 231A, research memorandum, Department of State, "The Armed Forces and Police in Venezuela," 15 September 1967, 3. Also see *New York Times*, 20 October 1945; Jorge Valero, *¿Como llego Acción Democrática al poder en 1945?*

10. See Rabe, *The Road to* OPEC, 61–65.

11. Standard Oil Company of New Jersey, agenda for Seaview Conference, Absecon, New Jersey, 10 May 1937.

12. Standard Oil Company of New Jersey, topics for Seaview Conference, Absecon, New Jersey, May 1940.

13. Duggan, "Legislation and the Latin American Oil Industry," 8.

14. *FRUS*, 1945, vol. 9, 1405–6.

15. Philip, *Oil and Politics in Latin America*, 64.

16. Standard Oil Company of New Jersey, "Relations with Labor Organizations, Venezuela," agenda of Coordination Committee Group, Miami, 8–13 February 1946, 6.

17. Report of Technical Meeting, Creole Petroleum Corporation, 2–7 February 1948, Caracas (stamped "confidential").

18. Duggan, "Legislation and the Latin American Oil Industry," 8.

19. Also see John J. Johnson, *Political Change in Latin America: The Emergence of the Middle Sector* (Stanford: Stanford University Press, 1958). For an opposing view see José Nun, "The Military Middle Class Coup," *Politics of Conformity in Latin America*, ed. Claudio Veliz (London: Oxford University Press, 1967).

20. "Public Relations Development," Coordination Committee Group Meeting, Standard Oil Company of New Jersey, Miami, 8–13 February 1946, 3.

21. Duggan, "Legislation and the Latin American Oil Industry," 8.

22. Creole Petroleum Corporation, "Labor Developments in Venezuela," Report of the Technical Meeting, Caracas, 2–7 February 1948.

23. "New Venezuelan Government to Respect Oil Laws," *Oil and Gas Journal*, 3 November 1945, 63.

24. See Uslar Pietri, *Los venezolanos y el petróleo*; and Picón, ed., *Mariano Picón Salas*.

25. Dhahran to State, 11 August 1958, conversation with an official of ARAMCO, RG 59, 886A.2553/8–1158, 55, cited in Robert Vitalis, "America's Kingdom: Saudi Arabia and the World Oil Frontier, 1945–1970" (unpublished MS), 12.

26. K. E. Cook, "Creole's Public Relations Job," Creole Petroleum Corporation, Coordination Committee Meeting, Caracas, 19–21 February 1951, 12.

27. *FRUS*, 1945, vol. 9, 1417.

28. Pérez Alfonzo, *Petróleo y dependencia*, 9, and A. T. Proudfit, Opening Address, Creole Coordination Committee Meeting, Caracas, 19–21 February 1951.

29. Pérez Alfonzo, *Petróleo y dependencia*, 9–10.

30. *Oil and Gas Journal*, 3 November 1945, 63.

31. de la Plaza, *Petróleo y soberanía nacional*, 99.

32. "Economic Development in Venezuela since the 1950's," *Economic Bulletin for Latin America* 5 (1960), 1; also see Vallenilla, *Oil*, 62.

33. DDQC, 1978, vol. 4, (78)59C, A Report to the National Security Council, 8 December 1952.

34. Wayne C. Taylor and John Lindeman, *Venezuela Sows Its Petroleum* (Washington: National Planning Association, 1955), 62.

35. Standard Oil Company of New Jersey, "Trends of World Demand and Supply over the Next 10 Years and Influence of Venezuelan Crude Outlet," agenda for the Seaview Conference, Absecon, New Jersey, 12 May 1941, 2.

36. Valero, *¿Como llego Acción Democrática al poder en 1945?*, 51.

37. *FRUS*, 1948, vol. 9, 757.

38. Ibid. During the war years steel products were under export control.

39. "Creole Petroleum, Business Embassy," *Fortune*, February 1949, 178.

40. "It's Hot in Venezuela," *Fortune*, May 1949, 161.

41. Steve Ellner, "The Venezuelan Petroleum Corporation and the Debate over Government Policy in Basic Industry, 1960–1976," University of Glasgow, Latin American Studies, Occasional Paper 47 (1987), 13; Philip, *Oil and Politics in Latin America*, 57–58.

42. Duggan, "Legislation and the Latin American Oil Industry."

43. *FRUS*, 1945, vol. 9, 1415.

44. Pérez Alfonzo, *La dinámica del petróleo en el progreso de Venezuela*, 56.

45. Coronil, *The Magical State*, 137.

46. Ibid.

47. Pérez Alfonzo, *Petróleo y dependencia*, 57; *FRUS*, 1948, vol. 9, 756.

48. López Maya, *EE.UU. en Venezuela*, 76.

49. "It's Hot in Venezuela," *Fortune*, May 1949, 102; *FRUS*, 1948, vol. 9, 759.

50. Taylor, Lindeman, and López, *The Creole Petroleum Corporation in Venezuela*, 2; also see "Creole in Operation," *Fortune*, February 1949, 180.

51. *DDQC*, 1978, vol. 4 (78)59c, "A Report to the NSC on National Security Problems Concerning Free World Petroleum Demands and Potential Supplies, December 8, 1952," 34.

52. Thomas Mann cited in *FRUS*, 1951, vol. 2, 1448; "Looking Ahead," *World Oil*, March 1948, 34; also "New Horizons in Foreign Oil," *Lamp*, summer 1956, 2–5; "50/50," *Lamp*, winter 1957–58, 24–25.

53. *Venezuelan Newsletter*, 15 May 1947.

54. Aranda, *La economía venezolana*, 27.

55. *Memoria Ministro de Relaciones Interiores (Año Civil 1937)* (Caracas: Imprenta Nacional, 1938), xxvi, Formación de Cuerpo de Seguridad Nacional, Guardia Nacional Interna.

56. Standard Oil Company of Venezuela, Petroleum Engineering Department, Caripito, *Study of Operations, Temblador District* (1942), 6.

57. *Memoria de Guerra y Marina, (Año Civil 1944)* (Caracas: Talleres Patria, 1945), xxi.

58. DDQC, 1981, vol. 7 (81) 231A, "Armed Forces and Police in Venezuela," research memorandum, U.S. Department of State, 15 September 1967. See Kelvin. Singh, "Oil Politics during the López Contreras Administration," *Journal of Latin American Studies* 21 (February 1994), 94. Also Blanco Muñoz, *Pedro Estrada Hablo*, 56–57.

59. DDQC, 1992, #2987, National Security Council, Operations Coordinating Board, "Analysis of the Internal Security Situation in Venezuela and Recommended Action" (13 June 1956), 5, 11.

60. Personal papers of Clinton C. Leiffers, employee of Creole, in author's possession.

61. Lieffers Papers, Creole Petroleum Corporation, job description for industrial services administrator, 21 October 1968.

62. Ibid.

63. Interview, NRT, Mérida, July 1985.

64. Letter from Clinton Lieffers to H. J. Gillespie, 26 October 1972, requesting police background checks on several employees.

65. Rabe, *The Road to* OPEC, 121, 222.

66. DDQC, 1992, #2987, National Security Council, Operations Coordination Board, "Analysis of the Internal Security Situation in Venezuela and Recommended Action" (13 June 1956), 7.

67. See for example ibid., 7.

68. NARA, RG 165m regional file, box 3264, 1922–44, U.S. Naval Attaché, Caracas, 25 September 1945, Caripito.

69. DDQC, 1992, #2987, National Security Council, Operations Coordination Board, "Analysis of the Internal Security Situation in Venezuela and Recommended Action" (13 June 1956), 5, 11.

70. Central Intelligence Agency, declassified documents, Information Report, "Fight for control of STP in Caripito," 25 July 1950.

71. Lieffers Papers, Creole Petroleum Corporation, job description for industrial services administrator, 21 October 1968.

72. Lieffers Papers.

73. Daniel Bendahán, *Petrolerias, cuentos petroleros* (Caracas: Corpoven, 1984), 27.

74. Lieffers Papers, Letter from Manuel Pérez to Lagunillas Security office, 15 June 1961.

75. "Venezuelan Denies Communism Charges," *New York Times*, 14 August 1946, 8; "Venezuela, Teapot Storm," *Inter American*, October 1946, 9–10.

76. Cited in Consalvi, *Auge y caida de Rómulo Gallegos*, 94; communiqué, 14 April 1947, Corrigan to Mr. Hall and Mr. Wells.

77. "Venezuela, Teapot Storm," 9; also "Venezuela, Heady Freedom," *Inter-American*, April 1946, 12.

78. DDQC (6) R38B, "Vulnerability to Sabotage of Petroleum Installations in Venezuela, Aruba and Curaçao," Central Intelligence Agency, 14 May 1948.

79. PRO, FO 371/22851, British legation, Caracas, to Foreign Office, 27 June 1939. The British in fact complained about the press coverage that United States missions to Venezuela obtained in the local press.

80. Sánchez, *The Development of Education in Venezuela*.

81. Howard Penniman, ed., *Venezuela at the Polls* (Washington: American Enterprise Institute, 1980), 4.

82. Wolfgang Hein, "Oil and the Venezuelan State," *Oil and Class Struggle*, ed. Teresa Turner (London: Zed, 1980), 236.

83. Ellner, "Venezuela," 149.

84. *FRUS*, 1948, vol. 9, 765, 767.

85. DDQC (6)R38B, "Vulnerability to Sabotage of Petroleum Installations in Venezuela, Aruba and Curaçao," Central Intelligence Agency, 14 May 1948, 2–3.

86. Blanco Muñoz, *Pedro Estrada Hablo*, 97.

87. "Gun Theft Case," *Venezuela Newsletter*, 15 June 1947, 6. Also *FRUS*, 1947, vol. 8, 1062.

88. Interview with Marcos Pérez Jiménez, *Oil and Gas Journal*, 2 December 1948, 43.

89. *Department of State Bulletin*, 19 December 1948, 777.

90. "Creole Petroleum, Business Embassy," *Fortune*, February 1949, 179.

91. "It's Hot in Venezuela," *Fortune*, May 1949, 101.

92. *FRUS*, 1952–54, vol. 4, 1621. Also see DDQC 1982, #002367, vol. 7, "Probable Development in Venezuela," 24 July 1952, 2.

93. *New York Times*, 25 November 1948, 11.

94. Ewell, *Venezuela*, 110.

95. Standard Oil Company of New Jersey, agenda of the Seaview Conference, Absecon New Jersey, 12 May 1941.

96. "Venezuela: Too Much Money," *United Nations World* 2, no. 4 (May 1948), 30.

97. *Lamp*, summer 1956, 2–5.

98. Joseph E. Pogue, "Oil in Venezuela," part 2, *Petroleum Engineer*, November 1949, A-53.

99. PRO, London Foreign Office FO 371/75117, British legation, Teheran to Foreign Office, 3 October 1949.

100. PRO, FO 371/75117, British Embassy, Caracas, to Foreign Office, London, 8 September 1949.

101. PRO, FO 371/75117, British Embassy, Baghdad, to Foreign Office, London, 3 November 1949.

102. "Economic Development in Venezuela in the 1950's," *Economic Commission on Latin America*, 1960, 25.

103. *FRUS*, 1952–54, vol. 4, 1593. Rockefeller, according to the United States ambassador in Venezuela, agreed to lobby John R. Steelman, assistant to President Eisenhower, on this matter.

104. Ibid., 1592–93, 1618–19, 1631. Also see *Department of State Bulletin*, 21 January 1952, 92.

105. "The New Regimes in Latin America," *Magazine of Wall Street and the Business Analyst*, 15 March 1958, 742. By comparison, imports from the United States in 1954 totaled only $360.9 million; "Economic Development in Venezuela in the 1950's," 21.

106. *FRUS*, 1952–54, vol. 4, 1593.

107. K. E. Cook, "Creole's Public Relations Job," Creole Petroleum Corporation, Coordination Committee Meeting, Caracas, 19–21 February 1951.

108. "Peru Enacting Favorable Law," *Oil and Gas Journal*, 16 December 1948, 61.

109. Proudfit, Opening Address, Creole Coordination Group Meeting, 19–21 February 1951.

110. "Venezuela," *World Oil*, 15 August 1956, 247.

111. Ibid. Also Taylor, Lindeman, and López, *The Creole Petroleum Corporation*, 2.

112. "Looking at Venezuela for Opportunities," *Oil and Gas Journal*, 3 February 1958, 76. Also "An Independent Looks at Venezuelan Oil," *Petroleum Engineer*, January 1958, 26.

113. *Economic Commission on Latin America*, 1960, 23. The exchange rate was 3.335 bolívares to the dollar.

114. "Wise Use of Oil Income Gives Venezuela Bright Outlook," *World Oil*, July 1957, 177.

115. Mayhall, "Modernist, but Not Exceptional."

116. Chase Manhattan Bank, *Latin American Highlights, Quarterly Reports*, 1954, 11, and 1958, 23. Expenditures for previous years were similar; in fiscal 1956–57 they totaled $627 million.

117. Ibid., March 1957, 22.

118. *Oil and Gas Journal*, 5 February 1957, 97.

119. Ibid., 77. Also "Too Much Oil Supply," *Barron's*, 20 January 1958, 5.

120. "Middle East," *Lamp*, fall 1958, 1.

121. *FRUS*, 1950, vol. 2, 1027.

122. "A Letter from the President," *Lamp*, summer 1959, 1.

123. "Gusher in Trouble: U.S. Import Curbs, Dwindling Demand Hit Venezuelan Oil Producers," *Barron's*, 30 December 1957, 3.

124. Rabe, *The Road to OPEC*, 158.

125. "Restricción Voluntaria," *El Universal*, 27 December 1957, 1.

126. *El Farol*, May–June 1960, 17. The figures in *El Farol* reflect all oil producers. For Creole see Taylor, Lindeman, and López, *The Creole Petroleum Corporation*, 20. According to the report, 37 percent of Creole production was shipped to the United States.

127. "Se estudian repercusiones," *El Universal*, 27 December 1957, 1; "Venezuela revisaría su política económica exterior si se erigen como principio las restricciones," *El Universal*, 29 December 1957, 1.

128. DDQC, 1983, vol, 9 (2) 001244, 21 November 1958, memo from Acting Secretary Christian Herter to Lewis Straus, Secretary of Commerce.

129. "Ha llegado el momento de revisar el tratado comercial con EEUU," *El Universal*, 27 December 1957, I.

130. "Telegram Ambassador (Warren) to State Department," 30 March 1955, in FRUS, 1955–57, vol. 7, 1120–21.

131. DDQC, 1987, vol. 12, 235, I, "Venezuelan Oil Refinery," White House Staff Notes #82, 11 March 1957.

132. DDQC, 1981, vol. 7, 81(231A), "Armed Forces and Police in Venezuela," 16 September 1967, 29; *Foreign Relations of the United States*, 1952–54, vol. 4, 63, 238.

133. DDQC, 1992, #2987, National Security Council, "Operations Coordinating Board, "Analysis of the Internal Security Situation in Venezuela and Recommended Action" (13 June 1956). This was not the first time that Pérez Jiménez had acted unpredictably. In 1952, when news of monopoly practices of the big oil companies surfaced, Pérez Jiménez threatened action against the foreign concerns. See DDQC, 1978, vol. 4 (78)59C, National Security Council Report, 8 December, 1952, 42.

134. "Junta Patriótica," *El Universal* (Caracas), 28 January 1958, 8.

135. Burggraaff, *The Venezuelan Armed Forces*, 151.

136. "Caracas Exiles set Joint Front," *New York Times*, 24 January 1958, 3.

137. Valmo Acevedo, *Bohemia*, 23 January 1978, 30.

138. See L.G. Matheus, *El Tiempo* (Valera), 15 November 1958.

139. *Oil and Gas Journal*, 27 January 1958, 142.

140. *El Farol*, January–February 1958, I.

141. FRUS, 1958–60, vol. 5, microfiche supplement, Caracas, 12 February 1958, Telegram Charge in Venezuela (Burrows) to Department of State.

142. *Wall Street Journal and Analyst*, 15 March 1958.

143. *World Petroleum*, July 1958, 4.

144. "Rebels Boast of Refinery Fire," *Oil and Gas Journal*, 10 February 1958, 85.

145. *El Universal*, 11 February 1958 and 15 February 1958; *El Nacional*, 25 January 1959.

146. *El Farol*, January–February 1958, I; *El Universal*, 12 February 1959, 7.

147. Barberii, *De los pioneros a la empresa nacional*, 267.

148. DDQC, 1983, vol. 9:2 001499 Confidential, 4 March 1959.

149. "50/50," *Lamp*, winter 1958, 24–25.

150. DDQC, 1987, vol. 13, 001127, 19 August 1958, "White House Memo," Brigadier General A. J. Goodpaster to president.

151. DDQC, 1984, vol. 10, 000794, 19 December 1958, Allen Dulles, "Profit Sharing Practices of the U.S. Firms Operating in Venezuela," CIA memorandum for the president; also "Foster Dulles," *El Universal*, 12 June 1958, 10.

152. DDQC, 1984, vol. 10, 00794, 19 December 1958, CIA memorandum, Dulles to president; also Pogue, "Oil in Venezuela," A-53. Pogue maintains that as early as 1949

Venezuela was deriving a much higher profit ratio than the ostensible 50/50 split. Also see interview with Pérez Jiménez, *U.S. News & World Report*, 26 June 1953, 82. Pérez Jiménez boasted that the country was deriving "58% of the total profits of the oil industry."

153. *Economic Commission on Latin America*, 1960, 32.

154. Gardner Withrow, *Congressional Record*, House, 14 May 1958, 8717; for biographies of other Venezuelan leaders see DDQC, 1983, vol. 9 000807, Central Intelligence Agency, Office of Central Reference, Biographic Register, December 1961.

155. FRUS, 1952–54, vol. 4, 1668–69, 1672–73. After the Trienio, Betancourt applied for a visa to enter the United States as a "Communist defector."

156. AHM, 1848C, 1846C, and 1849C, 1952–57, letters to and from Betancourt, intercepted in the United States and delivered to the Pérez Jiménez government. Also see "Numerosas personalidades extranjeras invitadas por el Presidente Betancourt," *El Universal*, 11 February 1959, 1–9. Among those present at Betancourt's inauguration were George Meany of the AFL-CIO, Congressman Charles O. Porter, and Professor Robert Alexander.

157. AHM, #1843-c, letter from Lieuwen to Betancourt at Stanford, 15 July 1957.

158. *World Petroleum*, July 1958, 46.

159. *El Universal*, 4 December 1958, 13.

160. For a discussion of views in the United States on nationalist governments see DDQC, 1981, 2982 vol. 7 (335A), "NSC Report on Latin America," 21 May 1958, 30.

161. *El Universal*, 14 March 1958, 1.

162. *El Universal*, 9–10 November 1958, 1.

163. *El Universal*, 12 June 1959, 10.

164. DDQC, 1983, vol. 9 (2), 001244, 21 November 1958, Christian A. Herter, acting secretary, to Lewis L. Straus, secretary of commerce.

165. Eisenhower to Betancourt, document #1444, 28 April 1959, www.eisenhower memorial.org/presidential-papers/second-term/documents/1144.cfm.

166. Ibid.

167. Sader Pérez, *The Venezuelan State Oil Company*, 252.

168. Pérez Alfonzo cited in Porras, *Juan Pablo Pérez Alfonzo*, 148.

169. See Ellner and Tinker Salas, eds., *Venezuela, Hugo Chávez and the Decline of an "Exceptional Democracy."*

170. Karl, *Paradox of Plenty*, 3.

171. Ibid., 153–54.

172. *Petróleos de Venezuela, 1976–1985*.

173. Parker, "Chávez and the Search for an Alternative to Neo-liberalism," 41.

174. "South America's Most Stable Democracy Explodes," *Newsweek*, 13 March 1989.

175. "Venezuela's Two Faced Boom: Riches and Riots," *New York Times*, 21 January 1993.

176. "Esta semana Caracas es la capital petrolera del mundo con la licitación de 20 campos," *El Nacional*, 2 June 1997.

177. "Opening the Door to Foreign Investment: The Venezuelan Oil Opening," *Time* (Latin American edition), 21 July 1997.

178. Arturo Uslar Pietri, "El paratismo petrolero," *El Nacional*, 3 August 1997, § A, 4.

179. "Venezuela pone punto final a la Apertura Petrolera, *Panorama*, 1 July 2007, 1–5.

CONCLUSION: AN ENDURING LEGACY

1. The origins of this term are still contentious. Several other authors coined similar phrases: see Adríani, *Labor venezolanista*. Uslar Pietri, however, is credited with popularizing the term.

2. Pérez Alfonzo, *Hundiéndonos en el excremento del diablo*.

3. Arturo Uslar Pietri, "Sembrar el Petroleo," *Ahora*, 14 July 1936, cited in Uslar Pietri, *Los venezolanos y el petróleo*.

4. Standard Oil Company of New Jersey, Topics for Seaview Conference, Absecon, New Jersey, May 1940, 3.

5. Meiksins Wood, *Empire of Capital*, xi.

6. Sader Pérez, *The Venezuelan State Oil Company*, 269.

7. DDQC, 1979, #323A, position paper on President Eisenhower's visit, Mr. Moskowitz, 6 December 1961.

8. Comments of Professor Mejia Alarcón, meeting of board of directors of Venezuelan Newspapermen Association, 19 July 1967, in Sader Pérez, *The Venezuelan State Oil Company*, 186.

Bibliography

PRIMARY SOURCES

Archives

Archivo Histórico del Estado de Zulia
Archivo de Petróleos de Venezuela, Lagoven
Archivo General de la Nación
Archivo Histórico del Estado de Mérida
Archivo Histórico de Miraflores
Biblioteca Nacional, Febres Cordero, Mérida
Biblioteca Nacional de Venezuela
Biblioteca Salvador de la Plaza, Universidad de los Andes
Biblioteca y Hemeroteca de Humanidades, Universidad de los Andes
Public Records Office, London
U.S. National Archives and Records Administration (NARA)

Newspapers and Magazines

La Balanza, Cabimas
Boletín de la Camara de Comercio de Caracas
Boletín de la Camara de la Industria del Petróleo
El Bronce, Lagunillas
Caracas Journal, subsequently *Daily Journal*
El Cóndor, Lagunillas
El Diario de Occidente, Maracaibo
El Escudo, Lagunillas
El Escudo, Santa Barbara de Zulia
La Esfera, Caracas
El Nacional, Caracas
El Obrero, Jusepín
El País, Caracas

El Taladro, Cabimas
El Universal, Caracas
Excélsior, México
Fantoches, Caracas
Granito, Santa Rita, Zulia
Maracaibo Herald
National Geographic
New York Times
Norte, Maracaibo
Panorama, Maracaibo
Petróleo, Maracaibo
Revista del Colegio de Ingenieros
Revista Misionera
Saber, Caracas, Servicio Informativo y Cultural de la Embajada de los Estados
Unidos
Times (London)
Tropical Sun
Washington Post
Washington Star

Business and Industry Publications

Annual Reports of the Caribbean Petroleum Corporation
Barron's
Boletín de Actividades Culturales (later *Boletín Cultural*), Creole Petroleum Corporation
Business Week
El Circulo Anaranjado, Gulf, later Mene Grande
Collective Contract Entered into between the Syndical Federation of Petroleum Workers of Venezuela and the Creole Petroleum Corporation. Caracas: Grafolit, 1948.
Creole Petroleum Corporation. *Human Relations Conference, June 1, 16, 17, 1953*. Caracas: Creole Petroleum Corporation, 1953.
————. *Working with Creole in Venezuela*. Caracas: Cromotip, 1956.
Defendiendo lo Nuestro, Creole
Deussen, Alexander, and Louise Huntely. *Creole Petroleum Corporation and Lago Petroleum Corporation: Evaluation of Properties as of April 30, 1943*. Houston: J. L. Block and Company Public Accountants, 1944.
El Farol, Creole Petroleum Corporation
Fortune
Inter-American
Lamp, Standard Oil Company of New Jersey
Nosotros, Creole Petroleum Corporation
Nuestro, Lagoven

Oil and Gas Journal
Petroleum Engineer
Petro Oriente, Standard Oil Company de Venezuela
Resumen de Actividades de la Shell en Venezuela
Revista Shell, 1950–75
Temas Petroleros (Caracas: Creole Petroleum Corporation, 1966)
Tópicos de Shell de Venezuela
United States Congressional Record
Venezuela and the Oil Pioneers. Caracas: Lagoven, 1989 [1958].
Voz del Lago, Lago Petroleum Corporation
Wall Street Journal and Analyst
World Oil
World Petroleum

Other Published and Unpublished Sources

Allen, Henry J. *Venezuela: A Democracy*. New York: Doubleday, 1941.
Amuay, Moderna Refinería. Caracas: Cromotip, 1955.
Arcaya, Pedro Manuel. *New Notes on Political History*. Washington, 1924.
Arnold, George, Ralph A. Macready, and Thomas W. Barrington. *The First Big Oil Hunt: Venezuela, 1911–1916*. New York: Vantage, 1960.
Aspects of Venezuela. Caracas: Ministry of the Interior, 1964.
Baker, Henry D. *The Asphalt Lakes of Trinidad and Venezuela*. American Consular Bulletin, 1924. Philadelphia: General Asphalt Company, 1930.
Baptista, Federico G. *Breve reseña histórica de la industria del petróleo*. Caracas: Creole Petroleum Corporation, 1955.
Bell, P. L. *Venezuela: A Commercial and Industrial Handbook*. Washington: Government Printing Office, 1922.
Benet, Fernando. *Guía general de Venezuela*. Caracas, 1929.
Bennett, H. H., D. S. Hubbell, W. X. Hull, and J. E. Caudle. *Land Conditions in Venezuela and Their Relation to Agriculture and Human Welfare*. Washington: U.S. Department of Agriculture, 1942.
Bernardo Nuñez, Enrique. *Una ojeada al mapa de Venezuela*. Caracas: Ávila, 1949.
Betancourt, Rómulo. *Problemas venezolanos*. Santiago: Futuro, 1940.
———. *Venezuela, política y petróleo*. Bogota: Senderos, 1969.
———. *Venezuela's Oil*. London: George Allen and Unwin, 1978.
Bierstadt, Edward Hale. "The Latter Days of a Pirate Stronghold." *Travel Magazine*, August 1924.
———. "The Gentle Art of Venezuelan Travel." *Travel Magazine*, September 1924.
———. "Witchcraft and Murder in the Andes." *Travel Magazine*, January 1927.
Blanco-Fombona, Rufino. *Bolívar y la guerra a muerte, epoca de Boves, 1813–1814*. Caracas: Ministerio de Educación, 1969.

Blanco Muñoz, Agustín. *Habla el General, Marcos Pérez Jiménez.* Caracas: Universidad Central de Venezuela, 1983.

———. *Pedro Estrada Hablo.* Caracas: Universidad Central de Venezuela, 1983.

Boletín de la Riqueza Pública de los Estados Unidos de Venezuela. Caracas: Ministerio de Fomento, 1891.

Bolet Paraza, Nicanor. "The Republic of Venezuela." *New England Magazine,* October 1892, 220–34.

Bracho Montiel, G. *Guachimanes: Doce aguafuertes para ilustrar la novela el petróleo.* Santiago: Francisco Javier, 1954.

Burchfiel, William. "Our Tropical Outpost in Venezuela." *Journal of Geography* 45 (May 1945), 196.

Calvani, Luis. *Nuestro máximo problema.* Caracas: Grafolit, 1947.

Cardón. Caracas: Shell de Venezuela, 1960.

Cardón: Una descripción de la refinería Shell de Cardón Estado Falcón. Caracas: Shell de Venezuela, n.d.

Carlson, Fred. *Geography of Venezuela.* New York: Prentice-Hall, 1936.

Colina Nava, J. A. *Sucesos históricos sobre Cabimas y Lagunillas hasta 1938.* Maracaibo: Cervantes, 1965.

Compañía de Inversiones Creole. Caracas: Cromotip, 1962.

Concurso de la hacienda: Primer congreso de agricultores, ganaderos, industriales y comerciantes de Venezuela. Caracas, 1921.

Contrato Colectivo de Trabajo. *Creole Petroleum Corporation y la Federación Sindical de Trabajadores Petroleros de Venezuela,* 1948.

———. *Shell Caribbean Petroleum Corporation y Organización Sindical de Marinos Petroleros.* Caracas: Equipo Comercial, 1952.

Croes, Hemmy. *El movimiento obrero venezolano.* Caracas: Movimiento Obrero, 1972.

Cuadernos de Información Económica. Caracas: Corporación Venezolana de Fomento, 1950–55.

Díaz Sánchez, Ramón. *Mene.* Buenos Aires: Universitaria de Buenos Aires, 1966.

———. *Transición, política y realidad en Venezuela.* Caracas: Monte Ávila, 1973.

Dickey, Herbert Spencer. *The Misadventures of a Tropical Medico.* New York: Dodd, Mead, 1929.

———. *1976-1985: diez años de la industria petrolera nacional.* Caracas: Petróleos de Venezuela, 1986.

Donnelly, Vernon C. "Juan Vicente Gómez and the Venezuelan Worker, 1919–1929." Ph.D. diss., University of Maryland, 1975.

Drake, Darcy, and Stewart Schackne. *Petróleo en el mundo.* Caracas: Creole, 1955, 1962.

Droit, Michel. *Visas pour l'Amérique du Sud.* Paris: Gallimard, 1956.

La economía venezolana en los últimos veinticinco años, hechos y cifras relevantes. Caracas: Banco Central de Venezuela, 1966.

Federación de Trabajadores Petroleros de Venezuela Contrato Colectivo. *Federación de Trabajadores Petroleros de Venezuela y Creole Petroleum Coporation*. Caracas, 1963.

Foreign Relations of the United States (FRUS), 1945–60.

George, Mary. *A Is for Abrazo*. Caracas: Venezuelan American Association of University Women, 1961.

González, Godofredo. *La revolución de los barrosos*. Caracas, 1987.

Gordon, Charles. "Effects of Underdevelopment on Migration from Trinidad and Tobago to the U.S." Ph.D. diss., Howard University, 1984.

Inman, Samuel Guy. "Oil Developments in Venezuela." *Pan American Magazine*, October 1919, 301–2.

Jahn, Alfredo. *Los aborígenes del occidente de Venezuela: Su historia, etnografía y afinidad lingüística*. Caracas: Lit y Tip. del Comercio, 1927.

———. *El estado de Zulia: Esbozo histórico geográfico*. Caracas: Vargas, 1927.

Jarvis, Harry A. *Optimismo ante el futuro*. Caracas: Creole, 1955.

Kamen-Kayes, Dorothy. *Caracas Everyday*. Caracas: Caracas Journal, 1947.

———. *Speaking of Venezuela*. Caracas: Caracas Journal, 1947.

Lavin, John. *Halo for Gómez*. New York: Pageant, 1954.

Lawrence, Una. *Cuba for Christ*. Atlanta: Southern Baptist Convention, 1926.

León, David. *De agro-pecuario a petrolero*. Caracas: Garrido, 1944.

Leonard, Jonathan Norton. *Men of Maracaibo*. New York: G. P. Putnam, 1933.

Lieberman, Harold. "Maracaibo and Its Neighborhoods, the 1930s." Newsletter, April 1988.

———. "A Revolution and Some Minor Aftermaths." Newsletter, May 1992.

———. "Early Impressions of Maracaibo, with Some Attention to the Local Mores." Newsletter, September 1996.

Machado, Eduardo. *Petróleo en Venezuela*. Caracas: Magrija, 1958.

Matos Romero, Manuel. *El problema petrolero en Venezuela*. Caracas: Bolívar, 1938.

McDermond, C. C. *Quien es quien en Venezuela / Who Is Who in Venezuela?* Maracaibo, 1932.

Medrano, José Domingo. *Apuntaciones para la crítica sobre el lenguaje maracaibero*. Caracas: Centauro, 1990 [1883].

Ministerio de Educación. *Memoria y Cuenta (1940–1960)*. Caracas: Americana, 1960.

Ministerio de Fomento. *Revista de Fomento*. Caracas: Ministerio de Fomento, 1939–50.

———. *Estado de Falcón: Censo industrial y comercial y empresas que prestan servicio*. Caracas: América, 1941.

———. *Estado de Monagas: Censo industrial y comercial y empresas que prestan servicio*. Caracas: América, 1941.

———. *Introducción a la Memoria del Ministerio de Fomento*. Caracas: Cooperativa de Artes Graficas, 1941.

———. *División político territorial de la República*. Caracas: Vargas, 1944, 1948.

———. *Boletín Mensual de Estadística*. Caracas: Americana, 1945–50.

———. *Memoria y Cuenta, 1918–1970*. Caracas: Ministerio de Fomento, 1970.

Ministerio de Guerra y Marina. *Memoria y Cuenta, 1918–1970*. Caracas, 1970.

Ministerio de Minas e Hidrocarburos. *Convención nacional de petróleo*. Tulsa: Banknote Printing Company, 1951.

Ministerio de Trabajo. *Memoria y Cuenta*. Caracas: Servicio de Publicaciones, 1918–70.

———. *Revista del Trabajo*. Caracas: Servicio de Publicaciones, 1950–60.

Moll, Roberto. *Lecciones de economía venezolana*. Caracas: Ministerio de Fomento, 1956.

Octavo Censo General de Población. *XII Resumen General de la República (26 noviembre de 1950)*. Caracas: Ministerio de Fomento, Dirección General de Estadística y Censos Nacionales, 1957.

O'Shaughnessy, Michael. *Venezuelan Oil Fields*. New York: Potter, 1924.

———. *Venezuelan Oil Handbook*. New York: Potter, 1924.

Otero Silva, Miguel. *Oficina N. 1*. Buenos Aires: Losada, 1961.

Panorama 1969: Una mirada al futuro. Caracas: Creole, 1970.

El petróleo, su origen, historia general y desarrollo de la industria en Venezuela. Caracas: Litografía y Tipografía del Comercio, 1940.

Petróleo y otros datos estadísticos, 1973. Caracas: Ministerio de Minas y Hidrocarburos, 1973.

The Petroleum Handbook. London: Shell International Petroleum, 1959.

Pino Iturrieta, Elias, and Pedro Enrique Calzadilla, eds. *La mirada del otro: Viajeros extranjeros en la Venezuela del siglo XIX*. Caracas: Fundación Bigott, 1992.

Quintero Delgado, Julio Ramón. "Los campamentos petroleros de la costa oriental del lago de Maracaibo: el sindicato como factor de integración comunitaria, caso Maraven." Master's thesis, Universidad del Zulia, 1991.

Redfield, Alfred C., and Bostwick H. Ketchum. "Report to Creole Petroleum Corporation on the Distribution of Salt in Lake Maracaibo." Unpublished MS, Woods Hole Oceanographic Institution, 15 October 1953.

Rota, Mario. *El sueño del petróleo, "Miro Guagua."* Caracas: Paulinas, 1980.

Sáenz de Viteri, Ernesto. *Guía ilustrada del estado de Zulia: Venezuela a la vista*. Caracas: Elite, 1933.

Sánchez, George I. *The Development of Education in Venezuela*. Washington: U.S. Department of Health, Education and Welfare, 1963.

Servicio Shell Para el Agricultor. Caracas: Fundación Shell, 1964.

Sindicato de Trabajadores Petroleros de Puerto La Cruz. *Los Trabajadores Petroleros y el Contrato Colectivo de Trabajo*. Puerto La Cruz: Sindicato de Trabajadores Petroleros, 1951.

Smith, Fred, ed. *Venezuela Sows Its Petroleum: Case Study of the Creole Petroleum Corporation of Venezuela*. Washington: National Planning Association, n.d. [1956].

Spinden, Herbert J. "Travel Notes in Western Venezuela." *Scientific American*, 30 June 1917.

Taylor, Wayne C., John Lindeman, and Victor López. *The Creole Petroleum Corporation in Venezuela*. Washington: National Planning Association, 1955.

U.S. Declassified Documents Quarterly Catalog (DDQC)

U.S. Department of Labor, *Monthly Labor Review*

U.S. Department of State Bulletin (DSB)

Uribe Piedrahita, Cesar. *Mancha de aceite*. Bogotá: Renacimiento, 1935.

Venezuela: General Descriptive Data Prepared in June 1909. Washington: Government Printing Office, 1909.

Venezuela, bajo el nuevo ideal nacional. Caracas: Servicio Informativo Venezolano, 1954.

Venezuela Newsletter, 1947–48. Washington: Venezuelan Embassy.

Venezuela Up to Date. Caracas: United States Embassy, 1955.

Vila, Marco Aurelio, and J. Juan Pericchi. *Zonificación geoeconómica de Venezuela*. Caracas: Corporación Venezolana de Fomento, 1968.

Vivanco y Villegas, Aurelio de. *Venezuela al día / Venezuela Up to Date*. Caracas: Bolivar, 1928.

Zuloaga, Guillermo. *Influencia de la industria petrolera en la economía venezolana*. Caracas: Cromotip, 1952.

SECONDARY SOURCES

Acosta Saignes, Miguel. "Los descendientes de africanos y la formación de la nacionalidad en Venezuela." *Anuario* 3 (1956).

———. *Vida de los esclavos negros en Venezuela*. Caracas: Hesperides, 1967.

Adríani, Alberto. *Labor venezolanista*. Caracas: La Nación, 1937.

Albornoz, Orlando. "Valores sociales en la educación venezolana." *Boletín Bibliográfico: Memoria escuela de sociología y antropología*, 143–61. Caracas: Facultad de Economía, Universidad Central de Venezuela, 1964.

Andrade, Adaulfo. "Santa Rita y su lago." *Cronistas del Lago de Maracaibo*. Maracaibo: Biblioteca de Temas de Historia del Zulia, 2001.

Aranda, Sergio. *La economía venezolana*. Bogotá: Siglo XXI, 1977.

———. *Las clases sociales y el estado en Venezuela*. Caracas: Pomaire, 1983.

Armas Chitty, J. A. *Historia de la tierra Monagas*. Maturín: 1956.

Balestrini, Cesar C. *La industria petrolera en América Latina*. Caracas: Universidad Central de Venezuela, 1971.

Baloyra, Enrique. "Oil Policies and Budgets in Venezuela, 1938–1968." *Latin American Research Review* 9, no. 2 (summer 1974), 28–72.

Barberii, Efraín. *De los pioneros a la empresa nacional, 1921–1975: La Standard Oil of New Jersey en Venezuela*. Caracas: Lagoven, 1997.

———. *El pozo ilustrado*. Caracas: PDVSA, 1998.

Barbozo, Isilio, and José Alí Lobo. *Estudio económico sobre turismo en Venezuela, Sección Occidental.* Caracas: Corporación Nacional de Fomento, 1966.

Bautista Fuenmayor, Juan. *1928–1948: Veinte años de política.* Madrid: Mediterráneo, 1968.

———. *Historia de la Venezuela política contemporánea.* Caracas, 1981.

Berglund, Susan. "Las bases sociales y económicas de las leyes de inmigración venezolanas, 1831–1935." *Boletín de la Academia Nacional de la Historia,* October–December 1982.

Bergquist, Charles. *Labor in Latin America: Comparative Essays on Chile, Argentina, Venezuela, and Colombia.* Stanford: Stanford University Press, 1986.

Bermúdez, Nilda, and Dilian Ferer. "Unidad y diversidad en torno al lago de Maracaibo." *Cronistas del Lago de Maracaibo.* Maracaibo: Biblioteca de Temas de Historia del Zulia, 2001.

Bermúdez Romero, Manuel Cabimas. *Reventón de ilusiones idas.* Maracaibo: Futuro, 2001.

Besson, Juan. *Historia del Estado de Zulia.* Maracaibo: Banco Hipotecario de Zulia, 1973.

Bethel, Leslie, and Ian Roxborough, eds. *Latin America between the Second World War and the Cold War, 1944–1948.* London: Cambridge University Press, 1992.

Bolívar Chollett, Miguel. *Población y sociedad en la Venezuela del siglo xx.* Caracas: Tropykos, 1994.

Briceño de Alfaro, Olga. *Bajo esos techos rojos.* Caracas: Monte Ávila, 1993.

Briceño Parilli, A. J. *Las migraciones internas y los municipios petroleros.* Caracas: ABC, 1947.

Briggs, Charles, and Clara Mantini-Briggs. *Stories in the Time of Cholera: Racial Profiling during a Medical Nightmare.* Berkeley: University of California Press, 2003.

Brito Figueroa, Federico. *Ensayos de historia social venezolana.* Caracas: Universidad Central de Venezuela, 1960.

———. *Venezuela contemporánea, país colonial.* Caracas: Universidad Central de Venezuela, 1972.

———. "La contribución de Laureano Vallenilla Lanz a la comprensión histórica de Venezuela." *Revista Universitaria de Historia,* September–December 1982, 62–94.

———. *El problema tierra y esclavos en la historia de Venezuela.* Caracas: Universidad Central de Venezuela, 1985.

Brown, Jonathan C. "Why Foreign Oil Companies Shifted Their Production from Mexico to Venezuela." *American Historical Review* 90, no. 2 (April 1985), 362–85.

Burggraaff, Winfield. *The Venezuelan Armed Forces in Politics, 1935–1959.* Columbia: University of Missouri Press, 1972.

Burns, E. Bradford. *The Poverty of Progress: Latin America in the Nineteenth Century.* Berkeley: University of California Press, 1980.

Calvany, Condesa. *Yo fui una de ellas: El tenebroso mundo de la prostitución en América Latina*. Barcelona: Plaza and James, 1978.

Cardozo Galué, German. *Maracaibo y su región histórica: El circuito agro exportador, 1830–1860*. Maracaibo: Universidad del Zulia, 1991.

———. *Maracaibo en el siglo XIX*. Caracas: Historiadores, 1992.

Carlson, Fred. *Geography of Venezuela*. New York: Prentice Hall, 1936.

Carrera, Gustavo Luis. *La novela del petróleo en Venezuela*. Caracas, 1971.

Carrera Damas, Germán, ed. *Formación histórico social de Venezuela*. Caracas: Universidad Central de Venezuela, 1981.

———. *Una nación llamada Venezuela*. Caracas: Monte Ávila, 1983.

Castillo D'Imperio, Ocarina. *Los años del buldózer*. Caracas: Tropykos, 1990.

Castro Leyva, Luis. *El dilema Octubrista, 1945–1948*. Caracas: Lagoven, 1988.

Chancy, Michaelle Ascencio. *Entre Santa Barbara y Shango: La herencia de la plantación*. Caracas: Universidad Central de Venezuela, 2001.

Chomsky, Aviva, and Aldo Lauria Santiago, eds. *Identity and the Struggle at the Margins of the Nation State: The Laboring People of Central America and the Hispanic Caribbean*. Durham: Duke University Press, 1998.

Conniff, Michael. *Black Labor on a White Canal: Panama, 1904–1981*. Pittsburgh: University of Pittsburgh Press, 1985.

Consalvi, Simon Alberto. *Auge y caida de Rómulo Gallegos*. Caracas: Monte Ávila, 1991.

Coronil, Fernando. *The Magical State: Nature, Money and Modernity in Venezuela*. Chicago: University of Chicago Press, 1997.

———. Foreword. *Close Encounters of Empire: Writing the Cultural History of U.S. Latin American Relations*, ed. Gilbert M. Joseph, Catherine C. Legrand, and Ricardo D. Salvatore. Durham: Duke University Press, 1998.

Crawford, Margaret. *Building the Workingman's Paradise: The Design of American Company Towns*. London: Verso, 1995.

Crespo, Eddy Rafael. *Mene Grande, la cuna del petróleo venezolano*. Maracaibo, 1984.

Crist, Raymond E., and Edward P. Leahy. *Venezuela: Search for a Middle Ground*. New York: Van Nostrand Reinhold, 1969.

Cunil Grau, Pedro. "La geografía histórica en la conceptualización regional venezolana." *La Región Histórica*, 38–51. Caracas: Tropykos, 1994.

Cupello, Myriam. *Salvatore el inmigrante*. Caracas: Franco, 1987.

Dagnino, Evelina. "Citizenship in Latin America, Latin América." *Latin American Perspectives* 30, no. 2 (March 2003), 3–17.

de Chene, Andrés D. *La transformación de comunidades petroleras*. Caracas: Andrés de Chene, 1969.

de Civrieux, Marc. "Los cumanogoto y sus vecinos." *Los aborígenes de Venezuela*. Monografia no. 26. Caracas: Fundación La Salle/Instituto Caribe de Antropología y Sociología, 1980.

de la Plaza, Salvador. *Estructuras de integración nacional.* Caracas: Pensamiento Vivo, 1959.

———. *La economía minera y petrolera de Venezuela.* Caracas: Universidad Central de Venezuela, 1973.

———. *El petróleo en la vida venezolana.* Caracas: Fondo Editorial Salvador de la Plaza, 1976.

———. *Petróleo y soberanía nacional.* Mérida: Universidad de los Andes, 1996.

de León, Juan Francisco. *Enfoque clasista del problema petrolero venezolano.* Caracas: Fondo Editorial Salvador de la Plaza, 1972.

Díaz, Arlene. *Female Citizen, Patriarch and the Law in Venezuela, 1786–1904.* Lincoln: University of Nebraska Press, 2004.

Diccionario de Historia de Venezuela. Caracas: Fundación Polar, 1988.

Dore, Elizabeth, ed. *Gender Politics in Latin America: Debates in Theory and Practice.* New York: Monthly Review Press, 1997.

Drechsel, Edwin J. *From Venezuela with Love.* Berkeley: Creative Arts, 2002.

Ehsani, Kaveh. "Social Engineering and the Contradictions of Modernization in Khuzestan's Company Towns: A Look at Abadan and Masjed-Soleyman." *International Review of Social History* 48 (2003), 361–99.

Ellner, Steve. "The Venezuelan Left in the Era of the Popular Front, 1936–45." *Journal of Latin American Studies* 2, no. 1 (1979), 170–84.

———. "Venezuelans Reflect on the Meaning of the 23 de Enero." *LARR* 20, no. 1 (1985), 244–56.

———. *Venezuela's Movimiento al Socialismo: From Guerrilla Defeat to Innovative Politics.* Durham: Duke University Press, 1988.

———. "Venezuela." *Latin America between the Second World War and the Cold War, 1944–1948,* ed. Leslie Bethel and Ian Roxborough, 147–69. London: Cambridge University Press, 1992.

———. *El sindicalismo en Venezuela, en el contexto democrático.* Caracas: Fondo Editorial Tropykos, 1995.

Ellner, Steve, and Miguel Tinker Salas, eds. *Venezuela, Hugo Chávez and the Decline of an "Exceptional Democracy."* Boulder: Rowman and Littlefield, 2007.

Escobar, Marcos F. *Compilación histórica de temas estadísticos.* Caracas: Sociedad Venezolana de Estadística, 1962.

Euraque, Darío A. "The Threat of Blackness to the Mestizo Nation: Race and Ethnicity in the Honduran Banana Economy, 1920s and 1930s." *Banana Wars,* ed. Steve Striffler and Mark Moberg. Durham: Duke University Press, 2003.

Ewell, Judith. *Venezuela: A Century of Change.* Stanford: Stanford University Press, 1984.

———. *Venezuela and the United States: From Monroe's Hemisphere to Petroleum Empire.* Athens: University of Georgia Press, 1996.

Ferer, Dilian. *Maracaibo durante el gobierno de los Monagas: Relaciones de poder y autonomía, 1848–1858.* Maracaibo: Bibliotecas Temas de Historia del Zulia, 2000.

Fergusson, Erna. *Venezuela.* New York: Alfred A. Knopf, 1939.

Ferry, William J. *The Colonial Elite of Early Caracas: Formation and Crisis, 1567–1767.* Berkeley: University of California Press, 1989.

Finn, Janet. *Tracing the Veins: Of Copper, Culture, and Community from Butte to Chuquicamata.* Berkeley: University of California Press, 1988.

Friedman, Elisabeth J. *Unfinished Transitions: Women and the Gendered Development of Democracy in Venezuela, 1936–1996.* University Park: Pennsylvania State University Press, 2000.

Gallegos, Romulo. *Doña Barbara.* New York: Peter Smith, 1948 [orig. pubd in Spanish, 1931].

Gilbert, Joseph M., Catherine C. Legrand, and Ricardo D. Salvatore, eds. *Close Encounters of Empire: Writing the Cultural History of U.S. Latin American Relations.* Durham: Duke University Press, 1998.

Gil Fortoul, José. *El béisbol en Venezuela: Un siglo de pasión.* Caracas: Biblioteca Nacional, 1996.

Gilmore, Robert. *Caudillism and Militarism in Venezuela.* Columbus: Ohio State University Press, 1964.

Godio, Julio. *El movimiento obrero venezolano, 1850–1944.* Caracas: Nueva Sociedad, 1985.

González, Luis. *Pueblo en vilo: Micro historia de San José de Gracia.* Mexico City: Colegio de México, 1972.

González Batista, Carlos. *Historia de Paraguaná.* Mérida: Venezuela, 1984.

González Ripoll Navarro, María. *Trinidad la otra llave de América.* Caracas: Lagoven, 1992.

Graham, Richard, ed. *The Idea of Race in Latin America, 1870–1940.* Austin: University of Texas Press, 1990.

Grayson, George W. "Oil and Latin American Politics." *Latin American Research Review* 24, no. 3 (1989), 200–210.

Guevara, Cesar A., and Catherine De R. de Guevara. *Geografía de la región centro occidental.* Caracas: Ariel-Seix Barral, 1983.

Hallgren, Mauritz A. "Oil in Venezuela." *Nation,* 25 April 1928, 496–98.

Harwich Vallenilla, Nikita. *La crisis de 1929 en América Latina: El caso de Venezuela.* Caracas: Universidad de Santa Maria, 1984.

———. *Asfalto y revolución: La New York and Bermúdez Company.* Caracas: Monte Ávila, 1992.

Hoare, Quintin, and Geoffrey Nowel Smith, eds. *Selections from the Prison Notebooks of Antonio Gramsci.* New York: International, 1981.

Howard, Harrison Sabin. *Rómulo Gallegos y la revolución burguesa en Venezuela*. Caracas: Monte Ávila, 1976.

Johnson, John. "Middle Groups in National Politics in Latin America." *Hispanic American Historical Review* 37, no. 3 (August 1957), 313–29.

Karl, Terry Lynn. "Petroleum and Political Pacts: The Transition to Democracy in Venezuela." *Latin American Research Review* 22, no. 1 (1987), 63–94.

———. *The Paradox of Plenty: Oil Booms and Petro-states*. Berkeley: University of California Press, 1997.

Klubock, Thomas Miller. *Contested Communities, Class, Gender and Politics in Chile's El Teniente Copper Mine*. Durham: Duke University Press, 1998.

Kolb, Glen. *Democracy and Dictatorship in Venezuela, 1945–1958*. New London: Connecticut College Press, 1974.

LaCueva Teurel, Aurora. *Historia del petróleo en Venezuela*. Caracas: Tinta Papel y Vida, 1991.

Lander, Luis E. "La insurrección de los gerentes: PDVSA y el gobierno de Chávez." *Revista venezolana de economía y ciencias sociales* 10, no. 2 (May–August 2004), 13–32.

———, ed. *Poder y petróleo en Venezuela*. Caracas: UCV FACES, PDVSA, 2003.

Lee, Thomas F. "Venezuela: Impressions of a Country and Its People Gathered during Recent Months of Travel and Observation." *Mentor*, November 1925, 1–20.

———. "The Race for Oil in Venezuela." *World's Work*, December 1925, 148–61.

Lewis, Gordon K. *The Growth of the Modern West Indies*. New York: Modern Reader, 1968.

Lewis, Marvin A. *Ethnicity and Identity in Contemporary Afro-Venezuelan Literature: A Culturist Approach*. Columbia: University of Missouri Press, 1992.

Licha, Isabel. *Tecno-burocracia y democracia en Venezuela, 1936–1948*. Caracas: Tropykos, 1990.

Lieuwen, Edwin. *Petroleum in Venezuela*. New York: Russell and Russell, 1954.

———. *Venezuela*. London: Oxford University Press, 1961.

Linder, Peter S. "Agricultural and Rural Society in Pre-Petroleum Venezuela: The Sur del Lago Zuliano 1880–1920." Ph.D. diss., University of Texas, 1992.

———. "Con un pañuelo de seda: Vicencio Pérez Soto and Political Centralization in Zulia, 1926–1935." Paper delivered at the meeting of the Latin American Studies Association (LASA), Washington, September 2001.

Llovera, LL. B. *El exodo rural en Venezuela*. Caracas: Cuatricentenario, 1966.

Lombardi, John. *The Decline and Abolition of Negro Slavery in Venezuela, 1820–1854*. Westport: Greenwood, 1971.

———. *Venezuela: The Search for Order*. New York: Oxford University Press, 1982.

———. "The Invention of Venezuela within the World Systems: The Century of Transition, 1750–1850." Academia Nacional de la Historia Conferencia "José Gil Fortoul," Caracas, 26 October 2000.

López, José Eliseo. *La expansión demográfica de Venezuela*. Mérida: Universidad de los Andes, 1963.

López Maya, Margarita. *EE.UU. en Venezuela: 1945–1948*. Caracas: Universidad Central de Venezuela, 1996.

López Portillo, Felícitas. *El Perezjimenismo: Génesis de las dictaduras desarrollistas*. Mexico City: Universidad Autónoma Nacional de México, 1986.

———. "Mexico y Venezuela: Un recuento de sus relaciones diplomáticas, 1910–1958." *Montalban* 35 (2002), 253–80.

Malave Mata, Hector. *Petróleo y desarrollo económico en Venezuela*. Caracas: Pensamiento Vivo, 1962.

Marchand, Bernard. *Venezuela, travailleurs et villes du pétrole*. Paris: Institut des hautes études de l'Amérique latine, 1971.

Martínez, Aníbal R. *Cronología del petróleo venezolano*. Caracas: Librería Historia, 1970.

———. *Petróleo, seis ensayos*. Caracas: Edreca, 1971.

———. *Venezuelan Oil, Development and Chronology*. London: Elsevier Applied Science, 1989.

Mayhall, Marguerite. "Modernist, but Not Exceptional: The Debate over Modern Art and National Identity in 1950s Venezuela." *Venezuelan Exceptionalism Revisited: The Unraveling of Venezuela's Model Democracy*. Latin American Perspectives, ed. Steve Ellner and Miguel Tinker Salas, issue 141, vol. 32, no. 2 (March 2005), 124–46.

McBeth, Brian S. *Juan Vicente Gómez and the Oil Companies in Venezuela*. London: Cambridge University Press, 1984.

———. "El impacto de las compañías petroleras en el Zulia, 1922–1935." *Tierra Firme*, October–December 1985, 537–50.

McClintock, Anne. "'No Longer in a Future Heaven': Gender, Race and Nationalism." *Dangerous Liaisons: Gender, Nation, and Postcolonial Perspectives*, ed. Anne McClintock, Aamir Mufti, and Ella Shohat. Minneapolis: University of Minnesota Press, 1997.

Medina, Carlos, and Magda de Camargo. *Aproximación a la historia de Cabimas*. Maracaibo: Universidad del Zulia, 1995.

Medina Rubio, Arístides. "Coloquios y congresos de historia regional y local en Venezuela, 1981–1994." *Tierra Firme*, January–March 1995, 7–20.

Meiksins Wood, Ellen. *Empire of Capital*. London: Verso, 2005.

Mejía Alarcón, Pedro Esteban. *La industria del petróleo en Venezuela*. Caracas: Universidad Central de Venezuela, 1972.

Melcher, Dorothea. *Estado y movimiento obrero, represión e integración hasta 1948*. Caracas: Academia Nacional de Historia, 1992.

Morillo, Alejandro F. "La Comunidades petroleras, su significación social." *El Farol*, July–September 1970, 14–19.

Morón, Guillermo. *A History of Venezuela*. London: George Allen and Unwin, 1964.

Nehru Tennassee, Paul. *Venezuela: Los obreros petroleros y la lucha por la democracia.* Caracas: Popular, 1979.

Nesbitt, L. M. *Desolate Marches: Travel in the Orinoco Llanos of Venezuela*. New York: Harcourt, Brace, 1936.

Novoa Montero, Dimas, Carlos Piñerua, and Raúl Henriquez. *Contratación colectiva petrolera venezolana, 1946–1973*. Caracas: Litocromo, 1974.

Nun, José. "A Latin American Phenomenon: The Middle-Class Military Coup." *Latin American Reform or Revolution?*, ed. James Petras and Maurice Zeitlin, 145–85. Greenwich: Fawcett, 1965.

Nuñez-Tenorio, J. R. *Venezuela, modelo neocolonial*. Caracas: Universidad Central de Venezuela, 1969.

Ochoa Urdaneta, Humberto. *Estampas de Cabimas*. Maracaibo: Centro Histórico de Cabimas, 1993.

———. *Memoria geográfica de la costa oriental del Lago de Maracaibo*. Maracaibo: Centro Histórico de Cabimas, 1994.

Ojer, Pablo. *La formación del oriente venezolano*. Caracas: Universidad Central de Venezuela, 1966.

Okonta, Ike, and Oronto Douglas. *Where Vultures Feast: Shell, Human Rights and Oil in the Niger Delta*. San Francisco: Sierra Club Books, 2001.

Ontiveros, Benigno. *Identidades y post identidad de los andes y oriente venezolanos*. Caracas: Universidad Pedagógica Experimental Libertador, 1997.

Osorio Álvarez, Emilio A. *Geografía de la población de Venezuela*. Caracas: Ariel-Seix Barral, 1985.

Paredes Huggins, Nelson. *Vialidad y comercio en el occidente venezolano: Principios del siglo XX*. Caracas: Tropykos, 1984.

Parker, Dick. "Chavez and the Search for an Alternative to Neo-liberalism." *Venezuelan Exceptionalism Revisited: The Unraveling of Venezuela's Model Democracy*. Latin American Perspectives, ed. Steve Ellner and Miguel Tinker Salas, issue 141, vol. 32, no. 2 (March 2005), 39–50.

Parra, Fabiola. *El petróleo y su influencia en la transformaciones culturales de la región zuliana, caso Cabimas y Lagunillas*. Maracaibo: Universidad del Zulia, 1985.

Perazzo, Nicolas. *La inmigración en Venezuela, 1830–1850*. Caracas: Archivo General de la Nación, 1973.

Pérez Alfonzo, Juan Pablo. *Petróleo, jugo de la tierra*. Caracas: Arte, 1961.

———. *La dinámica del petróleo en el progreso de Venezuela*. Caracas: Universidad Central de Venezuela, 1965.

———. *Petróleo y dependencia*. Caracas: Síntesis Dos Mil, 1974.

———. *Hundiéndonos en el excremento del diablo*. Caracas: Lisbona, 1976.

Pérez Schael, María Sol. *Petróleo, cultura y poder en Venezuela*. Caracas: Monte Ávila, 1993.

Philip, George. *Oil and Politics in Latin America*. Cambridge: Cambridge University Press, 1982.

Picón, Delia, ed. *Mariano Picón Salas, Embajador de Venezuela*. Caracas: Ministerio de Relaciones Exteriores, 1987.

Picon Rivas, Ulises. *Indice constitucional de Venezuela*. Caracas: Elite, 1944.

Picón Salas, Mariano. *Los días de Cipriano Castro*. Lima: Editorial Latinoamericana, 1958.

———. *Venezuela independiente, 1810–1960*. Caracas: Fundación Eugenio Mendoza, 1962.

Pollak-Eltz, Angelina. *La negritud en Venezuela*. Caracas: Lagoven, 1991.

Porras, Eloy. *Juan Pablo Pérez Alfonzo, el hombre que sacudió al mundo*. Caracas: Ateneo Caracas, 1979.

Portes, Alejandro. "Latin American Class Structures: Their Composition and Change during the Last Decades." *Latin American Research Review* 20, no. 3 (1985), 7–39.

Prieto Soto, Jesús. *El Chorro: ¿Gracia o Maldición?* Maracaibo: Universidad de Zulia, 1962.

———. *Luchas obreras por nuestro petróleo*. Maracaibo: Lorenzo, 1970.

———. *Conformación ideológica petrolera venezolana*. Barranquilla: Mejoras, 1975.

———. *Del chorro a la reversión*. Caracas: INCE, 1977.

———. *Huellas históricas*. Bogotá: García e hijos, 1980.

Putnam, Lara. *The Company They Kept: Migrants and the Politics of Gender in Caribbean Costa Rica, 1870–1960*. Chapel Hill: University of North Carolina Press, 2002.

Quintero, Rodolfo. *La cultura del petróleo*. Caracas: Universidad Central de Venezuela, 1968.

———. *El petróleo y nuestra sociedad*. Caracas: Universidad Central de Venezuela, 1970.

———. *La antropología del petróleo*. Caracas: Fuentes, 1972.

Rabe, Stephen G. *The Road to OPEC: The United States and Venezuela, 1917–1976*. Austin: University of Texas Press, 1982.

———. *Eisenhower and Latin America: The Foreign Policy of Anticommunism*. Chapel Hill: University of North Carolina Press, 1988.

Rangel, Domingo Alberto. *Los andinos en el poder*. Mérida: Universidad de los Andes, 1964.

———. *La moneda ladrona, la devaluación en el banquillo*. Caracas: Pensamiento Vivo, 1964.

———. *Capital y desarrollo, el rey petróleo*. Caracas: Universidad Central de Venezuela, 1970.

———. *Venezuela en 3 siglos*. Caracas: Vadell Hermanos, 1998.

Rivas, Darlene. *Missionary Capitalism: Nelson Rockefeller in Venezuela*. Chapel Hill: University of North Carolina Press, 2002.

Rode, Heinrich. *Los alemanes en el Táchira*. Caracas: Bibliotecas de Autores y Temas Tachirenses, 1993.

Rodríguez Arrieta, Marisol. *Manumisión y abolición en la provincia de Maracaibo, 1810–1864*. Maracaibo: Bibliotecas de Temas de Historia del Zulia, 2001.

Rodríguez Campos, Manuel. *Venezuela, 1948–1958: Proceso económico y social*. Caracas: Tropykos, 1991.

Roseberry, William. *Coffee and Capitalism in the Venezuelan Andes*. Austin: University of Texas Press, 1983.

Ruptura (Comisión Ideológica). *El imperialismo petrolero y la revolución venezolana: Las ganancias extraordinarias y la soberanía nacional*. Caracas: Ruptura, 1977.

Sabato, Hilda. "On Political Citizenship in Nineteenth Century Latin America." *American Historical Review* 106, no. 4 (October 2001), 1290–1315.

Sader Pérez, Rubén. *The Venezuelan State Oil Company: Reports to the People*. Caracas: Corporación Venezolana del Petróleo, 1969.

Salas, Guillermo J. *Petróleo*. Caracas: Monte Ávila, 1982.

Salazar, Ivan. *Historia de los pueblos de agua: San Timoteo y San Lorenzo*. Maracaibo: Universidad de Zulia, 1996.

Salazar Carrillo, Jorge. *Oil in the Economic Development of Venezuela*. New York: Praeger, 1976.

Salazar Carrillo, Jorge, and Bernadette West. *Oil Development in Venezuela during the 20th Century*. Westport: Praeger, 2004.

Sarabia, Vicente. *El petróleo en la economía venezolana*. Caracas: San José, 1962.

Schuster, Joan. *Petroleros: A Novel*. Lake Park, Fla.: GoodeNough, 1992.

Segnini, Yolanda. *Las luces del gomecismo*. Caracas: Alfadil, 1997.

Slatter, J. E. "Problems and Results of a U.S. Investment in a Foreign Country: A Review of the Creole Petroleum Corporation." Unpublished MS, University of Vermont, 25 July 1955.

Sullivan, William. *Cipriano Castro en la Caricatura Mundial*. Caracas: Biblioteca Nacional, 1980.

Sullivan, William M., Brian S. McBeth, and Brian Stuart. *Petroleum in Venezuela: A Bibliography*. Boston: G. K. Hall, 1985.

Tinker Salas, Miguel. *Under the Shadow of the Eagles: Sonora and the Transformation of the Border during the Porfiriato*. Berkeley: University of California Press, 1997.

———. "Fueling Concern: The Role of Oil in Venezuela." *Harvard International Review* 26, no. 4 (winter 2005), 54–60.

Tugwell, Franklin. *The Politics of Oil in Venezuela*. Stanford: Stanford University Press, 1972.

Turner, Terisa, and Peter Nore. *Oil and Class Struggle*. London: Zed, 1980.

Urdaneta de Cardozo, Arlene. *Autonomía y federalismo en el Zulia*. Maracaibo: Biblioteca de Temas de Historia del Zulia, 1998.

Uslar Pietri, Arturo. *Sumario de la economía venezolana*. Caracas: Centro de Estudiantes de Derecho, 1945.

———. *Tierra venezolana*. Caracas: Edime, 1965.

———. *Los venezolanos y el petróleo*. Caracas: Banco Central, 1990.

Valero, Jorge. *¿Como llego Acción Democrática al poder en 1945?* Caracas: Tropykos, 1993.

Vallenilla, Luis. *Oil: The Making of a New Economic Order, Venezuelan Oil and OPEC*. New York: McGraw-Hill, 1975.

———. *Petróleo venezolano, auge, declinación y porvenir*. Caracas: Monte Ávila, 1975.

Velasquez, Ramón. *Venezuela moderna, medio siglo de historia, 1926–1976*. Madrid: Ariel, 1976.

Veracochea, Ermila Tronconis de. *El proceso de la inmigración en Venezuela*. Caracas: Academia Nacional de Historia, 1986.

Vicente, Henry. "La arquitectura urbana de las corporaciones petroleras: Conformación de Distritos petroleros en Caracas durante las décadas de 1940 y 1950." *Espacio Abierto*, July–September 2003.

Vila, Marco Aurelio. *Las regiones naturales de Venezuela*. Caracas: Imprenta Nacional, 1952.

———. *Antecedentes coloniales de centros poblados en Venezuela*. Caracas: Universidad Central de Venezuela, 1978.

Vila, Pablo. *Geografía de Venezuela*. Caracas: Ministerio de Educación, 1960.

Vitalis, Robert. "Black Gold, White Crude: An Essay on American Exceptionalism, Hierarchy, and Hegemony in the Gulf." *Diplomatic History* 26, no. 2 (spring 2002), 185–213.

———. "Wallace Stegner's Arabian Discovery: The Imperial Entailments of a Continental Vision." Paper delivered at the conference of the American Historical Association, 2002.

Williams, Eric. *From Columbus to Castro*. New York: Vintage, 1970.

Wright, Winthrop. *Café con Leche: Race, Class and National Image in Venezuela*. Austin: University of Texas Press, 1990.

Yarrington, Douglas. *A Coffee Frontier: Land, Society and Politics in Duaca, Venezuela, 1830–1936*. Pittsburgh: University of Pittsburgh Press 1997.

Cookbooks

Amuay Cooking Capers. Amuay: Women's Auxiliary of the Amuay Bay Square and Compass Club, 1952.

Buen Provecho. Caracas: British War Charities, 1943.

Recipes along Venezuela's B.C.F. Tía Juana: Women's Guild, Lago United Church, 1965.

Singletary Soligo, Pamela. *Pruebalo*. Maracaibo: Maracaibo Ladies Club, 1982.

Index

Bolívar, Simón, 29, 134

Bordellos, 40, 66–67, 100–101, 105

Boyd, Oswald, 60

Brack, Fred, 56

British Controlled Oilfields, 53

British Equatorial, 74

Brito Figueroa, Federico, 33

Buckley, William F., Sr., 60–61

Burchfiel, William, 173–74

Burns, E. Bradford, 36

Cabimas, 81–82, 87–90, 174

Café con leche, 34, 133–36, 241

Caldera, Raphael, 230

Caldwell, Mona, 151

Campesinos, 17

Campos obreros. See Residential camps

Campos petroleros. See Residential camps

Caracas: élites in, 16, 148, 220; petroleum district of, 159–60, 246; transformation of, 220

Cardozo Galue, Germán, 17, 21

Cardozo, Joaquín, 48

Caribbean Petroleum Company, 39, 42, 45, 50, 68. *See also* Mene Grande

Caripito (oil camp), 155, 174; Asians in, 120–21; bar and bordello in, 115; CIA views of, 214–15; daily rhythm of, 175; expatriate activities in, 161; floating population of, 240–41; foreign-Venezuelan contact in, 152; malaria and tropical diseases in, 157; migration and, 77; senior staff residence of, 201; social activities in, 156, 166–67; structure of, 200; trade and, 17, 109

Carrera Damas, German, 53

Castro, Cipriano, 17, 42, 43

Catholic Church, 177–78

Celebrations, 165–66

Central Intelligence Agency (CIA), 214–16

Central Venezuelan Sugar Company, 30

Chávez Frías, Hugo, 1–2, 13, 43, 184, 206, 230–35, 249–50

Chene, Andrés de, 78

Chinese, 107, 118–21, 127–28, 132, 135–38, 241

Citizenship, 9, 171

Civil society, 4–5, 193–99, 246–48

Class: in early oil industry, 8; emerging structures of, 36; merchant class, 37–38; restructuring, 1, 2–3, 11; working class, 9, 105–6. *See also* Élites; Middle class

Club de Comercio, 69–70

Coffee production, 16, 69, 74

Coll, Pedro Emilio, 44

Colón (district), 27, 30, 32, 77

Colón Development Company, 42, 53–54, 59, 97, 99

Comité de Organización Política Electoral Independiente (COPEI), 216

Commissaries, 8

Communists, 3, 208, 213–16

Compañía de Utilidades Públicas, 174

Compañía Petrolea del Táchira, 40–41

Company towns, 81–86; emerging, 6–8

Concubines, 174

Conservatives, 16

Consumerism, 188–89

Cook, Willis, 65

COPEI (Comité de Organización Política Electoral Independiente), 216

Coronil, Fernando, 3, 172

Cost of living, 40, 67–72, 105, 188

Creole Petroleum Corporation, 3; camp integration viewed by, 200–201; as industry leader, 220; Lake Maracaibo study and, 20–21; nation-state and, 247; parental role of, 247; public relations work of, 191, 193, 195–96; security and, 214–15

Crocket, Gary, 59

Guardia Nacional (GN), 213, 215
Guards, 102–5
Güiria, 109–10, 134
Gulf Oil, 59
Guzmán Blanco, Antonio, 109
Guzmán, Salvador, 124

Haight, H. W., 224
Hein, Wolfgang, 216
Herrera Campins, Luis, 232
Homeownership, 201
Hospitals, 158

Immigration: encouragement of, 139;
    policies on, 108, 133; racial identity and,
    108; regionalism and, 88–89. *See also*
    Migration
Industrialism, 2, 12
Inman, Samuel Guy, 53
Integration, of residential camps, 199–202
Ives, Burl, 168
Izquierdo, Santiago Vera, 190

Japanese, 136
Jarvis, Harry, 191, 199–200, 202
Johnston, George, 60
Judibana camp, 200–201
Junta Patriótica, 208–9, 212, 222–23
Jusepín (oil camp): CIA views of, 214–15;
    commissaries in, 188; expatriate
    activities in, 161; social activities in, 167;
    worker criticism of, 99–100

Karl, Terry Lynn, 172, 228
Kaymen-Kaye, Dorothy, 151

Labor force, 5, 186, 243; aristocracy and, 11;
    bolívar labor squad, 97, 184; collective
    bargaining and, 96, 201; Communists
    and, 213–16; contracts and, 209;
    demands of, 3, 241; employment

statistics and, 173; integrating, 171;
    Junta and, 208–9; leisure activities of,
    100–102; married employees in, 143–44,
    146–48, 245; militancy of, 2, 97, 122, 140;
    model worker in, 10, 183–85, 203, 242–
    43; new patterns of, 73, 94–96; political
    divisions in, 3; securing of, 7, 47; wage
    structures in, 46, 96–98; women in,
    179; work rules and, 95. *See also* Strikes;
    Unions
Lago Petroleum Company, 59, 85
Lagunillas (oil camp), 83–84, 90–94, 120,
    239
Lake Maracaibo, 16–19, 21–22, 28–30, 38–
    46, 240; agriculture and, 53, 68; coffee
    production and, 15, 69; commerce and,
    86–87; eastern shore of, 27–31, 47, 58,
    74, 81, 87, 130; housing and, 89; lake
    basin of, 20–27; politics and, 27; racial
    mix and, 31–37; social practices and, 15;
    transportation and, 20, 23–24, 25–27.
    See also Maracaibo (city)
Landed élites, 9
Language acquisition, 61, 129, 148
Lara, 76
Larrazábal, Wolfgang, 224, 226–27
Lavin, Jack, 57
Leisure activities, 100–102
Leonard, Jonathan, 62
Liberals, 16
Lieuwen, Edwin, 43, 57, 226
Lizardi, Ramón, 178, 242
Lockouts, 1, 13
Lola, Doña (Laura Fullerton), 115
Lombardo, Guy, 169
López, Ali, 103
López Contreras, Eleázar, 93, 207, 213, 222
López Portillo, Felícitas, 125

Mack, John, 44
Mack, Panchita, 151